M000283456

The Palestine Nakba

About the Author

NUR MASALHA is Professor of Religion and Politics and director of the Centre for Religion and History at St Mary's University College, UK. He is also editor of *Holy Land Studies: A Multidisciplinary Journal* (Edinburgh University Press).

The Palestine Nakba

Decolonising History,
Narrating the Subaltern,
Reclaiming Memory

NUR MASALHA

ZED BOOKS
London & New York

The Palestine Nakba: Decolonising History, Narrating the Subaltern, Reclaiming Memory was first published in 2012 by Zed Books Ltd, 7 Cynthia Street, London N1 9JF, UK and Room 400, 175 Fifth Avenue, New York, NY 10010, USA

www.zedbooks.co.uk

Copyright © Nur Masalha 2012

The right of Nur Masalha to be identified as the author of this work has been asserted by him in accordance with the Copyright, Designs and Patents Act, 1988

Designed and typeset by illuminati, Grosmont in ITC Bodoni Twelve
Index by John Barker
Cover designed by www.alice-marwick.co.uk

Distributed in the USA exclusively by Palgrave Macmillan, a division of St Martin's Press, LLC, 175 Fifth Avenue, New York, NY 10010, USA

All rights reserved. No part of this publication may be reproduced, stored in a retrieval system or transmitted in any form or by any means, electronic, mechanical, photocopying or otherwise, without the prior permission of Zed Books Ltd.

A catalogue record for this book is available from the British Library
Library of Congress Cataloging in Publication Data available

ISBN 978 1 84813 971 8 hb
ISBN 978 1 84813 970 1 pb

Contents

Acknowledgements

This book could not have been written without the intellectual and emotional support of my family and friends. First, I would like to thank the many friends and colleagues who have encouraged me over the years and help me, directly and indirectly, with ideas, conversations, criticism, material, logistics and moral support, including Ahmad Sa'di, Sherna Berger Gluck, Ilan Pappé, Isabelle Humphries, Oren Ben-Dor, Mary Grey, John Docker, Duncan Macpherson, Claire Norton, Mark Donnelly, Ghada Karmi, Isma'el Abu-Sa'ad, Seif D'ana, David Evans, Sari Hanafi, Saad Chedid, Keith Hammond, As'ad Ghanem, Abbas Shiblak, Ronit Lentin, Haim Bresheeth, Rahela Mizrahi, Bernard Regan, Colin South and Sam Kuruvilla. At Zed Books I am particularly indebted to editors Jakob Horstmann and Tamsine O'Riordan for their comments and practical help. Last but not least, I owe enormous gratitude to my wife Dr Stephanie Cronin, a highly original historian of the modern Middle East, and my daughter Maryam Masalha for their tremendous enthusiasm and emotional support. Stephanie, in particular, helped me with brilliant ideas and sharp comments without which this volume would not have been completed. Any credit for this book should be shared with Stephanie and the people above, but all shortcomings are mine alone.

Introduction

1948 was the year of the Palestine Nakba (Catastrophe), the uprooting of the Palestinians and the dismemberment and de-Arabisation of historic Palestine. In the course of the 1948 war and immediate post-Nakba period the name 'Palestine' was wiped off the map. In 2012 Palestinians commemorate the 64th anniversary of the Nakba, which is a key date in Palestinian collective memory and the most traumatic event in the history of the Palestinian people. The rupture of 1948 and the ethnic cleansing of Palestine are central to both the Palestinian society of today and Palestinian social history and collective identity. Resisting ethnic cleansing and politicide has been a key feature of the modern history of the Palestinians as a people. In *Politicide: Sharon's War against the Palestinians* (2003), Israeli sociologist Baruch Kimmerling (1939–2007) defines the 'politicide' of the Palestinian people as the gradual but systematic attempt to cause their annihilation: 'the dissolution of the Palestinian people's existence as a legitimate social, political and economic entity'. Politicide, Kimmerling asserts, has been present throughout Zionism's struggle with the Palestinians before, during and after the 1948 Nakba. Politicide also epitomised the settler-colonial policies and actions of General Ariel Sharon against the Palestinians. Kimmerling writes:

The Israeli state, like many other immigrant-settler societies, was born in sin, on the ruins of another culture, one which suffered politicide and a partial ethnic cleansing, even though the new state did not succeed in annihilating the rival aboriginal culture as many other immigrant-settler societies have done. (2003: 214-15)

As Chapter 1 will show, for decades Zionists themselves used terms such as 'colonisation' (*hityashvut*) to describe their project in Palestine – a project which resulted in the creation of a state in 1948 by the destruction of a country. 1948 saw not only the establishment of a settler-colonialist state on nearly 80 per cent of Mandatory Palestine, but also the destruction of historic Palestine and the ethnic cleansing of the Palestinians. The dismantling of Palestinian society was carried out as an integral part of the infamous Plan Dalet, a prime objective of which was the destruction of Palestinian towns and villages (Masalha 1992; Pappé 2006: 128; see also Khalidi 1988: 3-37). This plan was accompanied by a series of atrocities, of which the massacre of Dayr Yasin in April 1948 is the most notorious. From the territory occupied by Israel in 1948-49, about 90 per cent of the Palestinians were driven out – many by psychological warfare and/or military pressure and a large number at gunpoint. The 1948 war simply provided the opportunity for the creation of an enlarged Jewish state on most of historic Palestine. It concentrated Zionist minds and provided the security, military-strategic and immigrant-settler-demographic explanations and justifications for 'purging' the Jewish state.

The standard Zionist solution for the indigenous inhabitants of the land was predicated on the claim for monopolised Jewish ownership of and Zionist sovereignty over the 'land of the Bible' (Masalha 1997). As Chapters 1, 2 and 3 will show, much of the Palestinian material culture, landscape, toponymy and geography, which had survived the Latin Crusades, were obliterated by the Israeli state – a state created in the name of the Hebrew Bible by a New Hebrew Man and his European settler-colonial community (the Yishuv) that emigrated to Palestine in the period between 1882 and 1948. The Israeli state first took over the land of the 750,000 refugees, who were barred from returning; Jewish immigrants were settled in homes and neighbourhoods belonging

to Palestinian refugees. In order to present European colonialism
as a continuation of an ancient Jewish ownership of the land,
the historic Arabic names of geographical sites were replaced by
newly coined modern Hebrew names, some of which resembled
biblical names. The invention and mobilisation of the ethnocentric
paradigm of 'promised land-chosen people' – and the myth that
the Hebrew Bible provides for the Zionists sacrosanct 'title deed'
to the land of Palestine signed by God – became a key tool in
Zionist settler-colonial and ethnic cleansing policies in Palestine.
The myth of Jewish 'return' after two thousand years of exile and
the deep-seated inclination among Zionists to see Palestine as a
country without its indigenous inhabitants (the infamous Zionist
slogan 'a land without a people for a people without a land') were
always potent rallying calls for Zionist colonisation of Palestine
(Masalha 2007).

The Nakba is the turning point in the modern history of Palestine
– that year over 500 villages[1] and towns and a whole country and
its people disappeared from international maps and dictionaries.
This sudden shattering of Palestinian society (Falah 1996: 256–85;
Abu-Lughod 1971: 139–63; Hadawi 1967; Khalidi 1992a; Kamen
1987: 453–95; Masalha 1992, 2003, 2005) is what made the Nakba
a key date for the Palestinian people – a year of traumatic rupture
in the continuity of historical space and time in Palestinian history
(Masalha 2005; Sa'di and Abu-Lughod 2007; Matar 2011: 12).

> A society that had existed as far as human memory can go back disap-
> peared during a few months; the homeland, the place of residence,
> the land – a major source of wealth, dignity and influence – and the
> physical and cultural environment, the validity and endurance of which
> Palestinians had never questioned, turned out to be most insecure.
> (Sa'di 2005: 7–26)

The Nakba, in the words of French theorist of memory Pierra
Nora (1996), has become the key Palestinian 'site of memory' (*lieux*

1. In *All that Remains* (1992: xvii–xx), Walid Khalidi, relying on the *Palestine Index
Gazetteer* (1945) and the *Village Statistics* (1945), both compiled by the British Mandatory
authorities, listed 418 depopulated and destroyed villages. However, Salman Abu-Sitta's
figure of 531 includes 77 destroyed Bedouin villages in the south (2004: 71). See also
Pappé 2006: xiii.

de mémoire) – a site of trauma, dispossession and anger. The two anniversaries of the Nakba Day on 15 May and (since 1976) the Land Day on 30 March are the most important days on the Palestinian popular calendar of commemorations, of strikes, demonstrations, defiance and resistance.

In the words of Israeli revisionist historian Avi Shlaim, the dismantling of Palestinian society in 1948 was a form of war crime, catastrophe and politicide: 'to deny the Palestinian people any independent political existence in Palestine'.[2] Walid Khalidi (born in 1925 into one of the leading families of Jerusalem)[3] likens the Nakba to the 'ineluctible climax of the preceding Zionist colonisation and the great watershed in the history of the Palestinian people, marking the beginning of their Exodus and Diaspora' (Khalidi 1992a: xxxi). Commenting on the post-1948 processes of de-Palestinisation, Palestinian scholar and author of *Palestine 1948: L'Expulsion* (1984) Elias Sanbar observes:

> That year, a country and its people disappeared from maps and dictionaries ... 'The Palestinian people does not exist', said the new masters, and henceforth the Palestinians would be referred to by general, conveniently vague terms, as either 'refugees', or in the case of a small minority that had managed to escape the generalized expulsion, 'Israeli Arabs'. A long absence was beginning.[4]

Elias Sanbar is referring to the infamous statement made by Israeli prime minister Golda Meir in 1969 (Meir, who was brought up in the USA and herself migrated to Palestine in 1921, was born in the Ukraine as Golda Mabovitch and was known as Golda Myerson from 1917 to 1956), who denied the existence of the Palestinian people:

> There was no such thing as a Palestinian people ... It was not as though there was a Palestinian people considering itself as a Palestinian people

---

2. Avi Shlaim, 'This Time in Washington, Honest Brokerage is Not Going To Be Enough', *Guardian*, 7 September 2010, www.guardian.co.uk/commentisfree/2010/sep/07/peace-talks-washington-israel-palestinians.
3. The Khalidis trace their family to Khalid ibn al-Walid, a companion of Prophet Muhammad and one of the most successful commanders in early Islamic history.
4. Sanbar 2001a: 87–94; Sa'di and Abu-Lughod 2007: 4; Sanbar 1984. Sanbar's work is situated at the crossroads of personal and collective history. See Sanbar 1994, 1996, 2001b, 2004.

and we came and threw them out and took their country away from them. They did not exist.[5]

Meir's statement to the *Sunday Times* is a classic case of Nakba denial. Sanbar is articulating the exclusion of the Nakba after 1948 not only from Israeli and Western discourses but from some official Arab discourses on Palestine. Upholding the Israeli narrative of denial is still seen in the West as neutral, while anything more critical is seen as biased. Zionism was (and remains) not just about the colonisation of Palestinian land, but also about colonising minds – Jewish, Arab, European, American.

The clearing out and displacement of the Palestinians did not end with the 1948 war; the Israeli authorities continued to 'transfer' (a euphemism for the removal of Palestinians from the land), dispossess and colonise Palestinians during the 1950s (Masalha 1997; Boqa'i 2005: 73). As a result of the Nakba only a small minority of 160,000 out of 900,000 Palestinians remained in the part of Palestine upon which Israel was established. After 1948 the Palestinians inside Israel had to endure eighteen years of military administration, which restricted their movements, controlled almost every aspect of their life and acted as an instrument for the expropriation of the bulk of their lands (Sa'di 2005: 7-26; Jiryis 1976; Lustick 1982; Kamen 1987: 484-9, 1988: 68-109; Falah 1996: 256-85; Benziman and Mansour 1992; Kretzmer 1987). The military government (1948-66) declared Palestinian villages 'closed military zones' to prevent displaced Palestinians from returning. The Israeli army and the Jewish National Fund (JNF; in Hebrew Keren Kayemet L'Yisrael, literally the 'Perpetual Fund for Israel'), Zionism's main executive arms, became the two institutions key to ensuring that the Palestinian refugees were unable to return to their lands, through complicity in the destruction of Palestinian villages and homes and their transformation into Jewish settlements, historical and archaeological theme parks, forests and even car parks. The first director of the JNF's Land Settlement Department, Yosef Weitz, a quintessential labour Zionist

5. *Sunday Times*, 15 June 1969; *Washington Post*, 16 June 1969; also Khalidi 1992a: 17.

colonial functionary (and a prolific diarist), who helped conceive and orchestrate the 'transfer' of the Palestinians, wrote in a now widely known and notorious entry to his diary in 1940:

> It must be clear that there is no room in the country for both peoples ... If the Arabs leave it, the country will become wide and spacious for us ... The only solution is a Land of Israel ... without Arabs ... There is no way but to transfer the Arabs from here to the neighbouring countries, to transfer all of them, perhaps with the exception of Bethlehem, Nazareth and the old Jerusalem. Not one village must be left, not one tribe. (Weitz 1940)

The JNF played a key role in the mass expulsion of 1948 and the state-organised memoricide of the Nakba (see Chapters 2 and 3). After 1948 it planted forests in the depopulated villages to 'conceal' Palestinian existence (Boqa'i 2005: 73). In the post-1948 period the minority of Palestinians – those who remained behind, many of them internally displaced – became second-class citizens, subject to a system of military administration by a government that confiscated the bulk of their lands. Today almost a quarter of the 1.3 million Palestinian citizens of Israel (known as 'Israeli Arabs' in Israeli Zionist discourse, but 'Palestinians of 1948' in Palestinian parlance) are 'internal refugees'.[6]

Israel and the Hashemite Kingdom of Jordan were the two immediate beneficiaries of the dismemberment of Palestine, its erasure from the political lexicon, the 'redistribution' of the Palestinians (Jordan formally annexed the West Bank in April 1950) and the elimination of their leadership; both countries refused to recognise the existence of the Palestinian people or a separate Palestinian identity; both granted citizenship to Palestinians under their jurisdiction, while seeking to eliminate Palestinian identity through Israelisation/Hebrewisation and Jordanisation/annexationism; both took measures to prevent the Palestinians from commemorating Israeli and Zionist massacres (Sayigh 1979: 111; Cohen 2010: 144); the two countries occupied the two halves

---

6. For a historical overview of 'Palestinian Internally Displaced Persons inside Israel', see release by BADIL Resource Center, 6 November 2002, www.badil.org/Publications/Press/2002/press277-02.htm (accessed 25 March 2008); also Kamen 1987: 484-9, 1988: 68-109; Cohen 2000.

of Jerusalem; both regimes produced a hegemonic political culture and relied on a combination of coercion and persuasion designed to subordinate Palestinians; both imposed a tight system of control and surveillance on their Palestinian communities – and a system of patronage through which notables (*nikhbadim* in Hebrew), village mukhtars, hamula (clan) leaders and tribal sheikhs were co-opted and integrated into their system of control; both countries used walls of fear and their internal security services (the Shin Bet[7] in Israel and the Mukhabarat in Jordan) to suppress Palestinian identity and popular discontent (Cohen 2010; Sayigh 1979: 110). In each country Palestinians both collaborated in and resisted their de-Palestinisation; in each the 'politics of notables' and dignitaries remains a key obstacle to the narration of Palestinian history and the recent reassertion of Palestinian popular identity. In both Israel and Jordan the dominant political elites, in government and society, continue to question the allegiance of the Palestinians (Massad 2001; Cohen 2010).

In 1948 the ancient and prosperous coastal cities of Palestine – Jaffa, Haifa and Acre – were largely depopulated. The small groups of Palestinian residents who remained were concentrated in poor neighbourhoods. Jaffa, more than any other place in Palestine, epitomises the destruction of Palestinian society in 1948; it was transformed from a leading nationalist, cultural and commercial centre, and a major and cosmopolitan export–import port, into a slum (Sa'di 2005: 7–26). In *Good Arabs: The Israeli Security Agencies and the Israeli Arabs, 1948–1967*, Hillel Cohen (of the Hebrew University of Jerusalem) shows how the Israeli state tried to change the consciousness of the Palestinian minority that survived the Nakba with the aim of eliminating Palestinian identity and creating a 'new Israeli Arab identity'. This was carried out through a whole range of collaborators and informers, including Arab school-teachers and headmasters, village mukhtars, tribal chiefs, church leaders, 'dignitaries', local imams and sheikhs (Cohen 2010).[8]

---

7. Sherut Habitahon Haklali (General Security Service), also known by the acronym Shabak.
8. On the politics of collaboration of Arab mukhtars and 'dignitaries', see Sa'di 2005: 7–26; Cohen 2010.

On Israel's Independence Day (15 May), the Israeli state actively
encouraged the so-called 'Israeli Arabs' to celebrate the Zionist
colonisation and destruction of historic Palestine; this strategy
scored some successes in the first two decades of the state (Cohen
2010). In Jordan the main priority of the Hashemite rulers was to
keep the Palestinian refugee camps under close surveillance and
prevent Nakba commemoration. A Palestinian refugee attending
a camp school between 1958 and 1967 recalls:

> The camps are always more supervised on certain dates, for instance
> May 15 (the establishment of Israel). When we were children in school,
> before 1967, tanks would surround the camps so that no demonstration
> could take place against the Uprooting [Nakba]. On those days they
> would make the school children walk in single file, three or four metres
> apart, and we were forbidden to talk together. When we reached our
> street each one of us had to go straight to his home and stay there. We
> weren't allowed to listen to the Voice of the Arabs [radio] from Cairo
> or to Damascus (Saudi Arabia, Amman and Israel were permitted).
> Soldiers filled the camp all the time and used to listen at the windows
> to hear which [radio] station we were listening to. People used to put
> blankets over their windows to stop the sound going out. (quoted in
> Sayigh 1979: 111)

Although Israel's strategy of control, through the combination of
repression, fear, segmentation and patronage, was fairly effective,
today it looks as though the efforts at encouraging Palestinian
citizens to embrace the Zionist ideological discourse have ended
largely in failure (Cohen 2010).

Denied the right to self-determination, independence and statehood, the Palestinians were treated after 1948 as 'Arab refugees'
(*lajiin* in Arabic) – either as a 'humanitarian problem', deserving
the support of international aid agencies, more specifically the
United Nations Relief and Works Agency (UNRWA) (Sa'di and
Abu-Lughod 2007; Sanbar 2001a: 87–94), or as an 'economic problem' requiring 'dissolution' through resettlement and employment
schemes (Masalha 2003). 'To some extent, dispossession erased
gaps between urban and rural, well-to-do and poor, literate and
illiterate, Palestinians in many countries facing myriad restric-
tions on their political and economic opportunities, irrespective

of their previous station or lot in life in Palestine' (Dajani 2005: 42-3).

The account that follows combines reference to a wide range of historical sources with the study of knowledge and power; historiography and popular memory accounts; oral, subaltern and resistance narratives; indigenous, counter-hegemonic, postcolonial and decolonising methodologies (Foucault 1972, 1980; Young 2003; Prakash 1994: 1475-90, 1476; Guha 1997; Guha and Spivak 1988; hooks 1990: 241-3; Abu-Sa'ad 2005: 113-41, 2008: 17-43; Smith 1999). The word 'narrative' derives from the Indo-European root 'gno', 'to know', and from the Latin verb *narrare*, 'to recount', 'to narrate'. Historical-critical methodologies, narratives and discourses are all critical to our 'knowledge from the past' and the study of the Palestine-Israel struggle. Cultural and Subaltern Studies and decolonising approaches are particularly relevant to the popular experience, resistance and uprisings of the Palestinians. The term 'subaltern' was famously coined by the imprisoned Italian Marxist theorist Antonio Gramsci, as a codeword for the proletariat/the economically dispossessed/subordinate peoples and in order to evade Fascist censorship of his *Prison Notebooks*. Today cultural theorists give the term a variety of connotations and usages, but here the term refers not only to non-elite groups in Palestine-Israel but more specifically to the marginalised, oppressed, colonised and dispossessed and ethnically cleansed indigenous people of Palestine. This includes the Palestinian minority inside Israel, the Palestinians in the West Bank and Gaza Strip, and the millions of Palestinian refugees in neighbouring Arab countries. All three constituencies have been engaged in efforts to produce counter-hegemonic narratives.

The second part of this work, in particular, focuses on the decolonising indigenous, popular, cultural and subaltern histories and methodologies of Palestine. It challenges hegemonic, top-down, elite, masculinist and nationalist discourses on Palestine-Israel. It emphasises the importance of using decolonising methodologies and a critical language and terminology to reflect the reality of the situation on the ground in Palestine-Israel. It frames the history of Palestine 'from the ground up' and employs terms such as 'ethnic cleansing', 'settler-colonisation', 'Apartheid/Separation Wall', 'de-Arabisation', 'ethnocracy', 'memoricide', 'politicide' and 'toponymicide' (see Chapter 2) to reflect accurately the historical and contemporary realities of Palestine-Israel. It contrasts 'top-down' Israeli, 'old and new histories' with 'bottom up' Palestinian popular and gendered narrative histories. The work also, crucially, argues that the Palestine Nakba is an example of both 'politicide' and 'cultural genocide' (see below). The ethnic cleansing and politicide of 1948 were immediately followed by Nakba memoricide: the systematic erasure of the expelled Palestinians and their mini-holocaust from Israeli collective memory and the excision of their history and deeply rooted heritage in the land, and their destroyed villages and towns from Israeli official and popular history. One of the key tools of the de-Arabisation of the land has been 'toponymicide': the erasure of ancient Palestinian place names and their replacement by newly coined Zionist Hebrew toponymy.

Collective memory, remembering and narrating of the conflict have constituted a key site of the ongoing struggle in Palestine-Israel. In the midst of the war and during the last phases of the Palestinian refugee exodus, the prominent Arab historian Constantine Zurayk wrote a book entitled *Ma'na al-Nakba* (The Meaning of the Catastrophe), later translated into English as *The Meaning of the Disaster* (1956). The book deals with the terrifying shock, humiliation and trauma surrounding the sudden destruction of Palestine. But it was also written as a critique of the catastrophic Arab defeat in 1948 and as a reawakening call. Zurayk's title struck a resounding chord among ordinary Palestinians and Arabs, and the 'Nakba' became the term Palestinians have since used for the traumatic cataclysm that befell them that year. Elias Khoury is a Lebanese novelist and the author of *Gate of the Sun* (*Bab al-Shams*, 1998, 2006), a fictionalised attempt to render an account of the Palestinian Nakba and the continuity of the trauma. The novel is based on the experience of Palestinian refugees in Lebanon; it focuses on the lives of those refugees whose ancestral villages in Galilee, now in northern Israel, were wiped out of existence, forcing them into desperate exile. According to Khoury, Constantine Zurayk coined the term 'Nakba' 'deliberately to convey the impossibility of blocking the project for the Jewish state [in Palestine] after the Holocaust'.[9] Beyond its strategic-geographic location and immense military power, Israel has had enormous significance for post-Second World War Western politics. The 'Jewish state' has been seen as an opportunity to redeem Europe (and the West) from the genocidal crimes of the Nazi Holocaust and, at the same time, to serve as a vehicle for Western projects in the oil-rich Middle East.

Since 1948 the Nakba has been central to Palestinian public memory and national identity. Memories of trauma, memory construction and reinvention, remembrance and forgetfulness have also been critical to the struggle in Palestine–Israel. The memories and histories of the European Jewish Holocaust and Palestinian Nakba are distinct; yet, as Australian Jewish scholar John Docker argues, these histories illuminate each other. To begin with, the meaning of the Hebrew term for the Holocaust, *Shoah*, literally 'catastrophe', is identical to the Arabic term for the Nakba. Moreover, the term 'cultural genocide' is particularly relevant to illuminating the history of the Palestinian Nakba. The term was coined by Polish Jewish scholar Raphael Lemkin (1900–1959), the founding father of Genocide Studies in the West. For Lemkin, it meant the destruction and elimination of the cultural pattern of a group, including language, local traditions, shrines, monuments, place names, landscape, historical records, archives, libraries, churches – in brief, the shrines of the soul of a nation.[10] As we shall see in Chapters 2 and 3, this is exactly what happened to the Palestinian people in and after 1948. Furthermore, in *The Ethnic Cleansing of Palestine*, Israeli historian Ilan Pappé argues that the term 'Nakba' was adopted 'as an attempt to counter the moral weight of the Jewish Holocaust (Shoa)' (2006: xvi). However, unlike the rise of Holocaust Studies in the West, which paved the way for the emergence of Trauma Studies – an academic discourse which

---

9. Elias Khoury, 'For Israelis, an Anniversary. For Palestinians, a Nakba', *New York Times*, 18 May 2008, www.nytimes.com/2008/05/18/opinion/18khoury.html.

10. Cited in John Docker, 'Raphael Lemkin, Creator of the Concept of Genocide: A World History Perspective', *Humanities Research* 16, no. 2, 2010, http://epress.anu.edu.au/apps/bookworm/view/Humanities+Research+Vol+XVI.+No.+2.+2010/1331/docker.xhtml.

deals with the psychological consequences of mass trauma – the Palestinian Nakba is rarely acknowledged in Western academic discourses and never mentioned within the context of Trauma Studies or Genocide Studies.

The Nakba as a continuing trauma occupies a central place in the Palestinian psyche. Memory accounts of the traumatic events of 1948 are central to the Palestinian society of today. The Nakba is the demarcation line between two contrasting periods, before and after 1948. It changed the lives of the Palestinians at both individual and national levels drastically and irreversibly; it continues to structure Palestinians' lives and inform Palestinian culture (Sa'di and Abu-Lughod 2007; Nabulsi 2006: 16).

The trauma of the Nakba affected Palestinian national identity in two contradictory ways. On the one hand the Nakba led to the destruction of much of Palestinian society and the dispersal and fragmentation of the Palestinian people. But, on the other hand, following the encounter with and rejection by neighbouring Arab states, the Nakba also led to the crystallisation of a distinct and resistant Palestinian identity (Litvak 2009: 103-11). While the formation of Palestinian *national* identity had taken root long before 1948, there is no doubt that the Nakba was a key event in the consolidation and reconstruction of a strong and clearly defined contemporary Palestinian identity (Sayigh 1977: 3-22, 1977a: 17-40). Commenting on the centrality of the Nakba to Palestinian history and national identity formation, Palestinian scholar Omar Dajani writes:

> The *nakba* is the experience that has perhaps most defined Palestinian history. For the Palestinian, it is not merely a political event – the establishment of the state of Israel on 78 percent of the territory of the Palestine Mandate, or even, primarily a humanitarian one – the creation of the modern world's most enduring refugee problem. The *nakba* is of existential significance to Palestinians, representing both the shattering of the Palestinian community in Palestine and the consolidation of a shared national consciousness. In the words of Baruch Kimmerling and Joel Migdal, 'Between the last month of 1947 and the four and a half months of 1948, the Palestinian Arab community would *cease to exist* as a social and political entity.' Hundreds of villages would be destroyed, urban life in Palestine's most populous Arab communities

would disappear, and almost a million Palestinians would be rendered homeless and/or stateless.

> At the same time, 'the shared events of 1948 ... brought the Palestinians closer together in terms of their collective consciousness, even as they were physically dispersed all over the Middle East and beyond ... Although it bears emphasising that Palestinian political consciousness predated the *nakba* by several decades and many Palestinians' sense of connection to their towns and lands extends back many generations further, it seem clear that nothing forged Palestinian identity so surely as the loss of Palestine. (Dajani 2005: 42-3)

The Nakba led to the dispersal, disintegration and fragmentation of the Palestinian people and to a major division between the minority of Palestinians who remained inside Israel and the Palestinian refugees forced outside its borders; today these are numbered in millions. During the June 1967 war, hundreds of thousands of Palestinian refugees were also driven out from the West Bank and East Jerusalem into Jordan. Since 1967 Israel has fostered further Palestinian splits: between East Jerusalem and the West Bank; between the West Bank and Gaza; and more recently between the main rival political movements, Fatah and Hamas; and since the Oslo Accords of 1993 between the leadership of the Palestinian Authority and refugee and diaspora communities. Yet the traumatic rupture of the Nakba remains rooted in Palestinian collective consciousness; memory of pre-1948 life and the shock, devastation, humiliation and suffering wrought by the mass displacements of 1948 and 1967 continue to shape Palestinian politics and remain central to the Palestinian society of today. With millions still living under Israeli colonialism, occupation or in exile, the Nakba remains at the heart of both Palestinian national identity and political resistance (Nabulsi 2006: 16).

Palestinians, hardly surprisingly, perceive their catastrophe as something unique; after all, the Nakba brought about a dramatic rupture in modern Palestinian history. Many Palestinians perceive the ocean of suffering by the refugees as unique. Palestinian author Dr Salman Abu Sitta, a refugee from the Bir al-Saba' (Beersheba) district in British Mandatory Palestine, has spent years producing maps and atlases which catalogue the impact and consequences of the Nakba (2004, 2010). His description of the catastrophe is a case in point:

> The Palestinian Nakba is unsurpassed in history. For a country to be occupied by a foreign minority, emptied almost entirely of its people, its physical and cultural landmarks obliterated, its destruction hailed as a miraculous act of God and a victory for freedom and civilised values, all done according to a premeditated plan, meticulously executed, financially and politically supported from abroad, and still maintained today, is no doubt unique. (Abu Sitta 1998: 5)

The Holocaust has a central place in Jewish history. But while the Holocaust is an event in the past, the Nakba and ethnic cleansing of Palestinians from Jerusalem and other parts of the West Bank are continuing. Writing on the 62nd anniversary of the Nakba – and shortly after the Israeli attack on the international aid flotilla attempting to break the siege of Gaza – Palestinian scholar Dr Adel Samara observed in June 2010:

> ethnic cleansing takes place against a nation mainly once and for a certain period of time, but in the case of Palestinian ethnic cleansing it has been carried out till the present time. What they did and still do against us is different. They have never been satisfied with the 1948 occupation and they have been committing ethnic cleansing since then: on a daily basis in Jerusalem, confiscating land in the WB [West Bank], and making Gaza the largest jail in history. What they did and still do is a total destruction of our geography, social fabric, class structure, demography, economy, and even their culture they did not hesitate to steal.[11]

Today some two-thirds of the 11 million Palestinians are refugees or internally displaced persons; there are nearly 6 million Palestinian refugees in the Middle East and many more worldwide. Although Palestinian refugee suffering is bound to be perceived as 'unique' by the Palestinian people, it is, however, resonant with all extreme human suffering, including historic Jewish persecution and suffering in Europe. Surely the Nakba and ongoing Palestinian suffering are a reminder of the reality of the suffering of Jews in Europe. Some observers have rightly observed that it is precisely

---

11. *Kana'an*, the e-Bulletin, X, no. 2273, 22 June 2010, http://kanaanonline.org/ebulletin-en/.

because of the Jewish Holocaust that the truth about the Nakba and the continuing horrific suffering of the Palestinian people have remained invisible to enlightened public opinion in the West (Davis 2003: 18). Of course acknowledging the truth of what took place in Europe can never morally justify the uprooting of another people outside of Europe and the destruction of historic Palestine. However, as we shall see below, there are more than historical and semantic links between the Nakba and Shoah, the two key events which illuminate each other and are central to both Jewish and Palestinian histories.

Structure and Themes

This book addresses an urgent crisis in Palestine–Israel and the imperilled future of the Palestinians as a society and people. The immigrant-settler nation-state of Israel is a blatantly racist state, regarding its indigenous people – once by far the overwhelming majority population of historic Palestine – as less than human, as disposable, expendable and 'transferable'. How can the Palestinians survive, and how can an increasingly horrified world understand this crisis? Critical scholarship over the last three decades in various related and converging fields – revisionist historiography, post-colonial theory, oral history and 'history from below', memory as people's archive of past struggles and hopes for the future, critical biblical studies and critical archaeology, the new historiography of ethnic cleansing[12] and trauma studies, the historiography of settler-colonial projects, new research in indigenous studies and theories of memory – can illuminate how this crisis came to be and how reconciliation in Palestine–Israel can be achieved.

The work begins by looking at some of the enduring themes of the Zionist colonisation of Palestine and provides historical explorations and a comparative contextualisation of long-standing Zionist ideas of 'population transfer' and ethnic cleansing. The book is constructed around several interrelated themes: (i) the

---

12. For further discussion of the general history of ethnic cleansing, see Bell-Fialkoff 1993: 110–21, 1999.

Nakba as a key site of Palestinian popular memory; (ii) official
Zionist narratives and the memoricide of the Nakba; (iii) Palestinian oral history, subaltern narratives, popular and gendered
memories; (iv) the historian's methodology, 'history from below'
and rewriting the history of Palestine; (v) 'post-Zionism' and the
Israeli 'new history' of 1948; (vi) Nakba commemoration and empowerment among Palestinians inside Israel; (vii) indigenous and
decolonising methodologies and the reclaiming of memory; (viii)
memory production and Palestinian hopes of return.

Structurally and thematically the book is organised around
seven chapters. Chapter 1 focuses on the colonisation paradigm,
looks at the Nakba and politicide, and examines the 1948 massacres
within the context of Trauma Studies. Chapters 2, 3 and 4 discuss
the memoricide of the Nakba, the looting and destruction of the
Palestinian records, and the elimination of the cultural heterogeneity of Palestine before 1948 and cultural memory. Chapter 3
focuses on the afforestation policies of the Jewish National Fund
(JNF) and the consequential memoricide, and the Fund's efforts to
'green-wash' the Nakba and make the ancient landscape of Palestine appear Jewish-European. Chapter 4 discusses the destruction
of Palestinian documentation centres and the appropriation of
Palestinian documents since 1948. The process of eliminating the
cultural heritage and heterogeneity of Palestine by a settler-colonial
state continues today. Chapters 2 and 3 describe the erasure of
Palestinian villages and deletion of the reality of historic Palestine;
the invention of a New Hebrew identity and consciousness; and
the historicisation of the Bible as an invented collective national
enterprise, biblical naming and the Hebrewisation of Palestine's
landscape and geographical sites since 1948. The destruction of
Palestinian villages, which continued well into the 1960s, and
the deletion of the demographic and political realities of historic
Palestine and the erasure of Palestinians from history centred on
key issues, the most important of which is the contest between a
'denial' and an 'affirmation'. The deletion of historic Palestine was
designed not only to strengthen the newly created state but also
to consolidate the myth of the 'unbroken link' between the days
of Joshua and the Israeli state.

All history is contemporary history, argued Italian philosopher and humanist Benedetto Croce (1866–1952); that is, history writing comes out of concerns of the present (Docker 2010: 148; Curthoys and Docker 2005: 92). The past shapes the present and the formation of historical consciousness and collective memory. The past is also shaped by present perceptions. Chapter 5 explores the emergence of an Israeli revisionist historiography in the late 1980s which challenged the official Zionist narrative of 1948. Exploring the theme of knowledge, history rewriting and power, the chapter assesses the impact of the 'new historians' on history writing in Israel and situates this 'new' discourse within both the multiple crises of Zionism and the repeated cycles of critical liberal Zionist narratives. It further argues that, although the terms of the academic discourse in Western academia have been transformed under the impact of this development, both the 'new history' and 'post-Zionism' have remained confined to the margins of an immigrant-settler society. The 'new historians' have always been loosely defined and have now become bitterly divided. Also, crucially, rather than developing a post-colonial discipline or a decolonising methodology, the 'new historians' have simply reflected contradictory and unresolved currents within Israeli society. Today the 'new historians' range from the passionate Zionist nationalist and the liberal coloniser to the 'post-Zionist' critic. More ominously, their most influential protagonist, Benny Morris, has become an advocate of ethnic cleansing. In an interview in *Haaretz* Morris had this to say:

> Ben-Gurion was right ... Without the uprooting of the Palestinians, a Jewish state would not have arisen here ... There are circumstances in history that justify ethnic cleansing. I know that this term is completely negative in the discourse of the 21st century, but when the choice is between ethnic cleansing and genocide ... I prefer ethnic cleansing.[13]

Advocating old and new Zionist colonial methods, Morris (echoing demands by Israeli politicians and ministers) threatens the Palestinians with another Nakba.

---

13. Ari Shavit, 'Survival of the Fittest? An Interview with Benny Morris', *Haaretz* magazine, 9 January 2004.

Barbara Allen and William Lynwood Montell, in their work
*From Memory to History: Using Oral Sources in Local Historical
Research* (1981), write: 'The term *oral history* ... can refer to the
method by which oral information about the past is collected and
recorded, and it can also mean a body of knowledge that exists only
in people's memories and will be lost at their deaths' (1981: 23).
Clearly the Palestinian generation of the 1948 Nakba is now disappearing. Chapters 6 and 7 deal with Nakba memory, remembering
and commemorating within the context of Palestinian oral history,
'social history from below', subaltern studies and the formation of
popular and gendered memories. The chapters focus on Palestinian
oral history, cultural resistance, collective memory of the Nakba
and the historian's methodology. The chapters explore not only
Palestinian elite representations of the past in public commemorations and memorialisation but, more crucially, also the role of oral
history and personal narratives and the influence of the new media
in shaping Palestinian historical consciousness. The two chapters
explore the emergence of new methods of remembering and commemorating the Nakba by grassroots Palestinian communities in
the last two decades. These new ways of commemoration and the
production of memory keep alive Palestinian hopes of return.

In recent decades Nakba commemoration by Palestinians inside
Israel articulated new forms of cultural resistance to Zionism and
promoted collective rights and Palestinian reunification. With the
Palestinian refugees being excluded from recent Middle East peacemaking efforts, and with the failure of both the Israeli state and
the international community to acknowledge the ethnic cleansing
of 1948, memories of the Nakba continue to underpin the Palestine–Israel conflict. This book argues that to write more truthfully
about the Nakba is not just to practise a professional historiography;
it is also a moral imperative of acknowledgement and liberation.
The struggles of the millions of Palestinian refugees to publicise
the truth about the Nakba is a vital way of protecting Palestinian
rights and keeping alive the hope for peace and justice.

I

Zionism and European Settler-Colonialism

Blood, Soil, Race and Land Conquest

The modern invention of the nation was a typical secular European practice of using collective memory highly selectively by manipulating certain elements of the religious past, suppressing some and elevating and mobilising others in an entirely functional way and for political purposes; thus mobilised memory is not necessarily authentic but rather useful politically (Said 1999: 6–7). Competing modes of modern nation-building and nationalist myth-making, with its invented national memory and its rewriting of history, have received extensive critical reappraisal in the works of Benedict Anderson (1991: 6, 11–12), Eric Hobsbawm (1990, 1996), Anthony Smith (1986, 1989: 340–67), Ernest Gellner (1983) and Elie Kedourie (1960). Hobsbawm's most comprehensive analysis of nation-building and myth-making in Europe is found in *Nations and Nationalism since 1780*; published in 1990 with the subtitle 'Programme, Myth, Reality', this work is about the 'invention of tradition', the creation of national culture, and the construction of national identities from a mixture of folk history and historical myths. In *The Invention of Tradition* (1996) Hobsbawm and Terence Ranger explore the way social and political authorities in the Europe of the mid-nineteenth century set about creating supposedly age-old traditions by providing invented memories of the past as a way of creating a new sense of identity for ruler and ruled (1996: 1–14, 263–83).

Inspired by German romantic nationalists such as Johann Gottfried Herder (1744–1803), the ideologue of the eighteenth-century German cultural renaissance, members of the nationalist elites of central and eastern Europe sought to create and transmit the new national ideology to their children. Their aim was to create a literature in the national idiom, in order to create a 'common descent' and a 'national spirit', indispensable for the nation-state to come into being (Rabkin 2010: 131). Inspired by post-Herder German völkisch nationalism of the nineteenth century, political Zionism was an anachronistic form of European romantic nationalism and a project of myth-making; it adopted a German version of European Enlightenment thought (Massad 2004: 61). German nationalist principles such as biology, racial purity, historical roots, and blood and soil (*Blut und Boden*), and a mystical attitude to the land, all became key features of, and guided, secular Zionist secular nationalism and its invention of Jews as a nation with its own land, the land of the forefathers (*nahalat avot*) (Massad 2004: 61). This is a form of tribal, 'organic nationalism' which espoused common descent and racialism. This intolerant organic (integral) nationalism celebrated the relationship of the *Volk* to the land they occupied and cultivated, and it placed a high value on the mystical virtues of cultivating a national soil and rural living.

Political Zionism originated in the conditions of late-nineteenth-century eastern and central Europe and European primordialist nationalist ideologies. This 'new' Zionist tradition of historical writing and its obsession with the rewriting of the history of the 'Jewish people' were further developed by Israeli historians and authors dedicated to 'writing the homeland' through what Laor has dubbed *Narratives With No Natives* (1995). According to Kimmerling, the invention of the Zionist nationalist project should be credited to two outstanding Jewish historians: German Jewish biblical critic Heinrich Graetz (1817–1891) and Russian Simon Dubnow (1860–1941), both of whom used Jewish (especially religious) and non-Jewish sources and texts to reconstruct a collective national consciousness of Judaism as an 'ancient nationality' existing from time immemorial. Dubnow thought that the Jews had been transformed into a 'European nation' and that it was up to them to demand the status of a national minority within the European and American nation-states. Among other writers, Lithuanian novelist Abraham Mapu sought, in his novel *Love of Zion* (1845) – in the French romantic tradition – to create a sense of Jewish collectivity within the framework of the biblical Jewish kingdom in ancient Palestine (Kimmerling 1999: 339–63). Although Zionism was a latecomer to the European romantic national tradition, the invention of the Jewish people and construction of a new collective consciousness in the nineteenth century – a tradition recast with 'historical depth' and ancient roots – was in line with other eastern and central European national projects of the age. These Zionist historians reinvented a new Jewish historiography which was not only divorced from Jewish collective memory but also at odds with it.

A new vernacular, land and soil 'redemption' (*geolat adama and geolat karka'a*), 'land conquest' (*kibbush adama*), immigrant settler-colonisation and demographic transformation of the land and the 're-establishment' of Jewish statehood in Palestine, an obsessive search for ancient Hebrew roots, the historicisation of the Bible as a collective national enterprise and the creation of a new hegemonic Jewish consciousness, the Judaisation of Palestine and the Hebrewisation of its landscape and geographical sites have all been permanent themes of modern, dynamic and creative Zionism. The reinvention of both the Jewish past and modern Jewish nationhood in Zionist historiography and the creation of a modern Hebrew consciousness have received some scholarly attention (Myers 1995; Ram 1995; 91–124; Piterberg 2001: 31–46; Raz-Krakotzkin 1993: 23–56, 1994: 113–32). Commenting on the invention of a nationalist Jewish tradition and transformation of Jewish religion into nationalist ideology, Kedourie observes in *Nationalism*: 'Nationalist historiography operates ... a subtle but unmistakable change in traditional conceptions. In Zionism, Judaism ceases to be the *raison d'être* of the Jew, and becomes, instead, a product of Jewish national consciousness' (1960: 71).

Political Zionism was in fact a radical break from two thousand years of Jewish tradition and rabbinical Judaism; Zionist nationalism, a latecomer among the national movements of eastern and central Europe, looked for 'historical roots' and sought to reinterpret distant pasts in the light of newly invented European nationalist ideologies. According to American Jewish historian and theoretician of nationalism Hans Kohn, Zionist nationalism 'had nothing to do with Jewish traditions; it was in many ways opposed to them' (quoted in Khalidi 2005: 812–13). Zionist nationalism adopted German völkisch theory: people of common descent should seek separation and form one common state. But such ideas of racial nationalism ran counter to those held by liberal nationalism in Western Europe, whereby equal citizenship regardless of religion or ethnicity – not 'common descent' – determined the national character of the state.

Secular Zionist nationalism was a classic case of the invention of a people in late-nineteenth-century Europe and the synthesising of a national project. This invented tradition considered the Jews as a race and a biological group, and borrowed heavily from romantic nationalisms in central and eastern Europe. Political Zionism mobilised an imagined biblical narrative, which was reworked in the late nineteenth century for the political purposes of a modern European movement intent on colonising the land of Palestine. As an invented late-modern (European) tradition, Zionism was bound to be a synthesising project. As Israeli scholar Ronit Lentin has powerfully argued in *Israel and the Daughters of the Shoah: Reoccupying the Territories of Silence* (2000), Israeli masculinised and militarised nationalism has been constructed in opposition to a 'feminised' Other. The founding fathers of Zionism re-imagined the New Hebrew collectivity in total opposition to the despised Jewish Diaspora unable to resist the European anti-Semitism which led to the Holocaust. Zionism's contempt for Diaspora Jews and rejection of a 'feminised' Diaspora and its obsession with synthesising a nation are reflected by the fact that its symbols were an amalgam, chosen not only from the Jewish religion and the militant parts of the Hebrew Bible but also from diverse modern traditions and sources, symbols subsequently appropriated as 'Jewish nationalist',

Zionist or 'Israeli': the music of Israel's national anthem, ha-Tikva, came from the father of Czech music, the nationalist composer Bedřich Smetana; much of the music used in nationalist Israeli songs originated in Russian folk songs; even the term for an Israeli-born Jew free of all the 'maladies and abnormalities of exile' is in fact the Arabic word for *sabar*, Hebrewised as (masculine and tough) *tzabar* or *sabra* (Bresheeth 1989: 131), the prickly pear growing in and around the hundreds of Palestinian villages destroyed by Israel in 1948. Even the 'national anthem of the Six Day War', No'ami Shemer's song 'Jerusalem of Gold', was a plagiarised copy of a Basque lullaby song (Masalha 2007: 20, 39).

Creating a Zionist Language

Zionist ideology emerged in late-nineteenth-century Europe at the height of the popularity of social-scientific racism and social Darwinist ideologies, not only in Victorian Britain but also in France, Germany and other parts of central and eastern Europe. Language construction (and the so-called 'Aryan languages'), the myth of common descent, the search for historical roots, ethno-linguistic 'organic' nationalism and superior-versus-inferior 'civilisations' were all central to the European reinvention of 'race' and racism in this period (Beasley 2010). In the European pseudo-sciences of the period, 'language' became a property of 'ethnicity', and the speakers of the Indo-European languages ('Aryan languages') were racialised and reinvented as the 'Aryan races', in contradistinction to the 'Semitic races'. Language and the resurrection of dead languages became one of the key ingredients of newly imagined 'ethnic nationalisms' – located mainly but not exclusively in central and eastern Europe – of which Zionism is but one example (Rabkin 2010: 129, 2006: 54–7). The Aryanisation/racialisation of the New German Man, for instance, and Semitisation of the New Hebrew Man (and European Jewry in general) were an integral part of the same social Darwinist racist projects.

In time Zionism was accorded paramount importance, likened to the 'resurrection of a dead language'. Yet, as a Zionist language, modern secular Hebrew, which took hold in the decade

before the First World War, is about as distant from the Hebrew
Bible's idiom as new Israeli *sabras* is from the ancient Israelites.[1]
In modern Zionism's efforts to construct a common past with a
common vernacular for its culturally, linguistically and ethnically
diverse Jewish settlers from many different parts of the world, the
reconstruction of Palestine's heritage as uniquely centred in an
ethno-linguistic understanding of Judaism has played a central
political role in efforts to de-Arabise Palestine and disinherit and
displace the indigenous Palestinian population (Thompson 2011:
97–108; also 2008, 2009).

With the rise of secular Jewish Zionism in the late nineteeth
century, modern secular Hebrew was invented and designed to
play a major role in the educational and political efforts to create
a New Hebrew Man, the mythological *sabra*[2] who, an antithesis
of the Diaspora and European Jew, was to live 'as a free man'
in his own land (Rabkin 2010: 129–45, 2006: 54–7). The lexical
'modernisation' of Hebrew was the result of the literary work of the
European Zionist Jewish intellectuals in the nineteenth century.
New words and expressions were coined and adapted as neologisms
from a large number of languages and from the Hebrew Bible. Only
partly based on biblical Hebrew, it was in particular influenced by,
borrowed from or coined after Slavic languages, German, Yiddish,
Russian, English, French, Italian, modern Arabic and ancient
Aramaic. Yiddish (*idish*, literally 'Jewish') itself was a middle-high
German language of Ashkenazi Jewish origin which developed
around the tenth century as a fusion of German dialects with
Slavonic languages and biblical Hebrew. It was called *mame-loshn*
(literally 'mother tongue') to distinguish it from biblical Hebrew,
which was collectively termed *loshn-koydesh* ('holy tongue').

Eliezer Ben-Yehuda (1858–1922), universally considered to be
the instigator of the Hebrew revival and the creator of a modern
Zionist vernacular, was originally 'Lazar Perlman', graduate of
a Talmudic school in Belarus in the Russian Empire (Rabkin
2010: 132, 2006: 54–7). A linguistic utopian and secular 'organic-

---

1. Benjamin Balint, 'Confessions of a Polyglot', *Haaretz*, 23 November 2008, www.
haaretz.com/news/confessions-of-a-polyglot-1.258033.
2. For further discussion of the 'mythological sabra', see Zerubavel 2002: 115–44.

linguistic nationalist', the most influential lexicographer of the Zionist vernacular also borrowed many words from colloquial Arabic. A newspaper editor, Ben-Yehuda, who emigrated to Palestine in 1881, became the driving spirit behind this Zionist vernacular revolution (Stavans 2008). He set out to resurrect and develop a new language that could replace Yiddish and other languages spoken by the European Zionist colonists in Palestine. As a child he was schooled in traditional subjects such as the Torah, Mishnah and Talmud; later he learned French, German and Russian. He also studied history and politics of the Middle East at the Sorbonne University in Paris and learned Palestinian colloquial Arabic. In the four years he spent at the Sorbonne he took Hebrew classes. It was this experience in Paris, and his exposure to the rise of French linguistic nationalism at the end of the nineteenth century, that inspired Ben-Yehuda to attempt the 'resurrection' of Hebrew as a practical and vital nationalist project.

After arriving in Palestine in 1881, Ben-Yehuda became the first to use modern Hebrew as a vernacular. He subsequently raised his son, Ben-Zion Ben-Yehuda (the first name meaning 'son of Zion'), entirely through the speaking medium of 'Modern Hebrew'. Ben-Yehuda served as editor of a number of Hebrew-language newspapers, including *Ha-Tzvi*. The latter was closed down by the Ottoman authorities for a year following fierce opposition from Jerusalem's Jewish Orthodox community, which objected to the use of Hebrew, the 'holy tongue', for everyday conversation. In Jerusalem Ben-Yehuda became a central figure in the establishment of the Committee of the Hebrew Language (Vaʻad HaLashon), later named the Israeli Academy of Hebrew Language; he also compiled the first Modern Hebrew dictionary. Many of the new words coined by him have become part of the Hebrew language of today, but some never caught on. For instance, his word for 'tomato' was *badura*, from the Palestinian colloquial Arabic *bandura*; today Israeli Hebrew speakers use the word *agvania*[3] – a word that reflects the European (and vulgar) term 'love apple' (French *pomi d'amore*, Italian *pomodoro*) for the fruit which originated in Latin America.

---

3. Balint, 'Confessions of a Polyglot'.

Zionist efforts were crowned with success when the British colonial authorities in Palestine decided, after World War I, to recognise Modern Hebrew as one of the three official languages of Mandatory Palestine, alongside Arabic and English. This achievement came in the wake of a series of important victories for the new language, such as the adoption of Hebrew as the medium in Zionist schools and Jewish settlements and the publication of several Hebrew-language periodicals and newspapers (Rabkin 2010: 132).

But the first Zionist novel written in Hebrew retraced the biblical story in a format reminiscent of other eastern European romantic nationalist literatures. It was written within the confines of the Russian Empire, in Lithuania, where two 'ethnic nationalisms' – Polish and Lithuanian – were locked in conflict, each glorifying its mythical past in modern literary forms, and in its own national language. Sometimes they had to share the same literary heroes, for example Adam Mickiewicz for the Poles, Adomas Mickevicius for the Lithuanians (Rabkin 2010: 132).

Zionist romantic resurrectionism and restorationism, the invention of modern secular Hebrew, and construction of the modern themes of Zionist colonisation of Palestine also incorporated some of the land and conquest traditions of the Hebrew Bible. These were singled out by the founding fathers of Zionism as the origins of the birth of the nation. The same masculinised traditions provided nineteenth-century Zionism with a romantic form of ethnic and racial nationalism. In *The Founding Myths of Israel* (1998) the Israeli historian Zeev Sternhell argues that what was presented to the world as an Israeli 'social democracy' was in fact a 'nationalist socialist' ideology designed to create a new community of blood and common descent, to redeem the biblical 'soil' by conquest, and to submit the Jewish individual to an ethnic collectivity driven by messianic fervour. Focusing on the 'nationalist socialist' ideology of Labour Zionism, which dominated the heavily militarised Jewish Yishuv[4] in Palestine and then the State of Israel from the 1930s

---

4. In modern Hebrew, *yishuv* means literally 'settlement'. The term is used to refer to the collective European Jewish settler community from the late nineteenth century onwards.

into the 1970s, Sternhell illustrates ideological parallels between it and the early-twentieth-century tribal and völkisch nationalism of eastern and central Europe, which condemned liberalism – along with individual and civic rights – and universalism on moral intellectual and political grounds (Sternhell 1998: 10-11, 16, 27). Instead Labour Zionists gave precedence to the realisation of their nationalist project: the establishment in Palestine of a sovereign Jewish state. In this project collectivism was deployed as a useful mobilising myth. Sternhell argues that Zionism as a whole was a romantic form of nationalism of 'blood and soil' emphasising religion and ethnicity, promoting the cult and myths of ancient history, revival of a seemingly dead language, the advocacy of the supremacy of the Hebrew language over Yiddish in Zionist colonies in Palestine,[5] a desperate drive for cultural renewal and a bitter struggle for political independence and territorial expansionism.

The analogies between central and eastern European populist nationalisms and Labour Zionism go further; Labour Zionists repudiated liberal individualism and were suspicious of bourgeois liberal democracy. In this illiberal legacy of Labour Zionism, Sternhell finds the seeds of current Israeli problems – the lack of a constitution, an inadequate concept of universal human rights, the failure to separate religion and state, and so on. Deflating the socialist pretensions of Labour Zionism, Sternhell implies that Labour Zionists and the right-wing Revisionist movement of Betar, founded by a Russian Jew, Vladimir Yevgenyevich Zhabotinsky (later partially Hebrewised to 'Zeev Jabotinsky') (1880-1940), through Menahem Begin (born in Poland 'Mieczysław Biegun') (1913-1992) and Yitzhak Shamir (born in Belarus 'Icchak Jeziernicky') to Binyamin Netanyahu, were all integral nationalists. He argues that Labour Zionism ran its course with the founding of the state and there were no social perspectives or ideological directions beyond a nationalism based on 'historical rights to the whole land of Israel'. This legacy of Labour Zionism, with its

---

5. For Eliezer Ben-Yehuda, the colonisation of Palestine and the replacement of Yiddish and other European languages by Hebrew as the language of instruction in Zionist colonies in Palestine went hand in hand.

obsession with land settlement, ethnic and demographic separation (*hafrada*), continued after the founding of the Israeli state in
1948. With no social perspectives or ideological directions beyond
a racialised nationalism and mystical attitudes towards the soil,
based on abstract 'historical rights to the whole land of Israel',
the mould set in the pre-state period did not change. After 1967,
unable to come to terms with Palestinian nationalism, Labour
Zionism inevitably pursued its settler-colonial expansionism in
the occupied territories and continued to press ahead with its
decades-long methods of 'creating facts on the ground' (Sternhell
1998). Six decades after the Nakba the Israeli settler expansion in
Palestine is persistent, blatant and relentless.

The New Hebrew Man was invented as a 'man of iron', as many
Zionists dreamt of converting the Jews, whom they imagined as
effeminate, diasporic, meek and pliable, into a fighting nation of
iron, surrounded by an 'Iron Wall':

> Iron, from which everything that the national machine requires should
> be made. Does it require a wheel? Here I am. A nail, a screw, a girder?
> Here I am. Police? Doctors? Actors? Water carriers? Here I am. I have
> no features, no feelings, no psychology, no name of my own. I am a
> servant of Zion, prepared for everything, bound to nothing, having one
> imperative: Build! (Schechtman 1961: 410; Rabkin 2010: 133-4)

In the 1930s and 1940s the Zionist leadership found it expedi-
ent to euphemise, using the term 'transfer' or *ha'avarah* – the
Hebrew euphemism for ethnic cleansing – one of the most enduring
themes of Zionist colonisation of Palestine. Other themes included
demographic transformation of the land and physical separation
between the immigrant-settlers and the indigenous inhabitants
of Palestine. All these colonising themes were central to Zionist
muscular nationalism, with its rejection of both liberal forms of
universalism and Marxism, along with individual rights and class
struggle. Instead, Zionism gave precedence to the realisation of
its ethnocratic völkisch project: the establishment of a biblically
sanctioned Jewish state in Palestine. Although largely secular,
Labour Zionism instrumentally emphasised Jewish religion and
Jewish 'ethnicity', promoted the cult and mythologies of ancient

history and biblical battles, revived a seemingly dead language, built up a powerful army, surrounded its 'ethnically' exclusive, 'pure' Yishuv with an 'Iron Wall' (Shlaim 2000; Masalha 2000) and waged a bitter struggle for political independence and territorial expansion throughout the land.

For David Ben-Gurion and the other founding fathers of Zionism the invention of a tradition and the synthesising of a nation meant that the Hebrew Bible was not a religious document or a repository of a theological claim to Palestine; it was reinvented as a nationalised and racialised sacred text central to the modern foundational myths of secular Zionism. As a leader of a primordialist movement of secular nationalism, asserting the antiquity of Jewish nationalism (Smith 1986, 1989: 340–67), inspired by Eurocentric völkisch and racial ideologies, Ben-Gurion viewed the Bible in an entirely functional way: the biblical narrative functioned as a mobilising myth and as a 'historical account' of Jews' 'title to the land' – a claim not necessarily borne out by recent archaeological findings. For Ben-Gurion it was not important whether the biblical narrative was an objective and true record of actual historical events. It is not entirely clear whether he assumed that the ancient events Israel was re-enacting had actually occurred. But as he explains:

> It is not important whether the [biblical] story is a true record of an event or not. What is of importance is that this is what the Jews believed as far back as the period of the First Temple. (Pearlman 1965: 227; also Rose 2004: 9)

Ben-Gurion represented a radical secular Zionist revolution against Jewish traditionalism. His ambivalence towards both Jewish traditionalism and the religious city of Jerusalem in particular was expressed by the fact that when, in 1906 at age 20, he emigrated to Palestine, he did not bother to visit the city for three years (Wasserstein 2002: 5). His nationalism was a form of secular (east European) nationalism and he sought to redefine the Hebrew Bible and traditional Judaism along similar lines. For him the Hebrew Bible was central to Jewish myth-making and Israel's civic religion. Ben-Gurion tried to give political Zionism – and all Zionist politics and policies – a 'historical character' linked to the Hebrew Bible. As a deeply secular man, he used the Bible instrumentally as a nationalist tool to further Zionist objectives. Like Ben-Gurion, many secular Labour Zionists displayed from the outset a deeply ambivalent attitude towards Jerusalem. Although the movement's name is derived from the word 'Zion' – which was originally the name of a fortress in Jerusalem – Zionism reinvented the 'religious yearnings' of generations of Jews for Jerusalem, which were expressed in the prayers and customs mourning Jerusalem's destruction, and translated them into political action. Furthermore, Zionism had ambitions to create a new Jewish society that would be different from Jewish life in the Diaspora and did not see multi-religious and pluralistic Jerusalem as the appropriate place for the founding of such a New Society. Not only was it full of aliens (native Arabs), but it was also inhabited by the peaceful 'old Jewish Yishuv', whose members were part of the anti-Zionist ultra-Orthodox community. It is no wonder, therefore, that the Zionists preferred to build the new (and pure) Jewish city of Tel Aviv on the Mediterranean coast, just outside the Palestinian city of Jaffa. Tel Aviv was founded in 1910 in a region which, according to the Bible, was ruled by the Philistines (not the Israelites) from the twelfth century BCE onwards. It was named after a Babylonian city mentioned in Ezekiel (3:15) and chosen by Zionist leader Nahum Sokolow as the title of his Hebrew translation of Theodor Herzl's futuristic utopian novel *Altneuland* ('Old-New Land') (1902; see also below). But the ethno-religious 'purity' of the European Jewish Yishuv was best illustrated by the fact that during the Mandatory period its Zionist leaders preferred to live in the ethnically exclusive Tel Aviv rather than in multi-religious Jerusalem.

Those Zionist immigrants who chose to live in Jerusalem settled outside the historic city and built new Jewish neighbourhoods and the first Jewish university – the Hebrew University. Tel Aviv remained home to the Histadrut and all the Hebrew daily papers, and while Zionist leaders of the Yishuv continued to swear by the name of Jerusalem, they did not live there and most of the Jewish immigrants to Palestine, about 80 per cent, settled along the Mediterranean coast, a region that (according to Professor Avishai

Margalit of the Hebrew University) had never been the historic homeland of the Jewish people.[6]

Shortly after 1967 Israel's leading novelist, Amos Oz (born in Mandatory Palestine in 1939 as 'Amos Klausner', to a family of Zionist immigrants from eastern Europe), wrote in an article in the Hebrew daily *Davar*:

> Some of our first arrivals thought that, by right, the Arabs should return to the desert and give the land back to its owners, and, if not, that they (the Zionists) should 'arise and inherit', like those who conquered Canaan in storm: 'A melody of blood and fire ... Climb the mountain, crush the plain. All you see – inherit ... and conquer the land by the strength of your arm.' (Tchernichovsky, 'I Have a Tune').
> (Oz 1988: 21)

Shaul Tchernichovsky (1875-1943), a Russian Jew and one of the most influential Hebrew poets, was greatly influenced by the muscular culture of Ancient Greece. In his Hebrew poems he contributed to the development of militant muscular Zionism by calling upon Jewish youth to remember the heroic battles of the biblical zealots. He celebrated 'blood and soil' and the virility and primitive heroism of the Israelite tribes, emerging (according to the Bible) from the desert under Joshua's leadership, overrunning and conquering Canaan. Not surprisingly Tchernichovsky also had a major influence on Jabotinsky's 'Iron Wall' doctrine of military might which would protect Greater Israel.[7] Jabotinsky, the forerunner of the present-day Likud, developed his concept of militant Zionism in his historical novel *Samson* (1930) – titled after the legendary biblical figure who is said to have lived during the period when the Israelites were oppressed by the power of the Philistines. In the novel the final message masculine Samson sends to the Israelites consists of two words: 'Iron' and 'King', the two themes the Israelites were told to strive for so that they would become the lords of Canaan (cited in Bresheeth 1989: 123).

---

6. Avishai Margalit, 'The Myth of Jerusalem', *New York Review of Books* 38, no. 21, 19 December 1991.

7. Kohn in Khalidi 2005: 818-19. See also Masalha 2000; Shlaim 2000.

Earlier, in the 1920s, Vladimir Jabotinsky developed his 'Iron Wall' doctrine to highlight the separateness, purity and militarism of the Zionist Yishuv and explain that the Zionist colonisation of Palestine can only be carried out against the wishes of the indigenous Arab majority. In an article entitled 'The Iron Wall: We and the Arabs' (1923), Jabotinsky cites both the conquest methods of the Spanish colonists in Mexico and Peru and Joshua to justify Zionist policies towards the indigenous Palestinians and the transformation of Palestine into the 'Land of Israel':

> Every reader has some idea of the early history of other countries which have been settled. I suggest that he recall all known instances. If he should attempt to seek but one instance of a country settled with the consent of those born there he will not succeed. The inhabitants (no matter whether they are civilized or savages) have always put up a stubborn fight. Furthermore, how the settler acted had no effect whatsoever. The Spaniards who conquered Mexico and Peru, or our own ancestors in the days of Joshua ben Nun behaved, one might say, like plunderers ... Zionist colonization, even the most restricted, must either be terminated or carried out in defiance of the will of the native population. This colonization can, therefore, continue and develop only under the protection of a force independent of the local population – an iron wall which the native population cannot break through. This is, in toto, our policy towards the Arabs. To formulate it any other way would only be hypocrisy.[8]

The invention of a new masculine collective memory based on hegemonic state power, 'New Hebrew' language, 'New Hebrew Man', new and militarised society and an exclusively Jewish 'Hebrew City' (Tel Aviv), 'New Yishuv' was also reflected in the new and armed Hebrew workers of the 'Histadrut', the 'General Federation of Hebrew Workers in the Land of Israel. Established in 1920, the militarised Histadrut and military service were central to the Zionist conquest project. They represented that newly constructed muscular and militant national identity. The Histadrut,

---

8. Vladimir Jabotinsky, 'The Iron Wall: We and the Arabs', first published in Russian under the title 'O Zheleznoi Stene in *Rasswyet*, 4 November 1923; published in English in *Jewish Herald* (South Africa), 26 November 1937; quoted in Brenner 1984: 74–5, and in Masalha 1992: 28–9, 2000: 56; the article is available at www.marxists.de/middleast/ironwall/ironwall.htm; accessed 2 June 2006.

in particular, both dominated the economic military-security infrastructure of the Zionist Yishuv and played a major role in immigration, land settlement and colonisation, economic activities, labour employment, and military organisation and defence (the 'Haganah') – with trade-union work as only one of its activities.[9] Palestinian citizens of Israel were not admitted as members until 1959. The Histadrut became central to this drive designed to create a 'New Settlement' of blood and common descent and redeem the 'biblical soil' by conquest. Thus in 1929, Ben-Gurion wrote of the need for an 'Iron Wall of [Zionist] workers' settlements surrounding every Hebrew city and town, land and human bridge that would link isolated points' and that would be capable of enforcing the doctrine of exclusive 'Hebrew labour' (*'avoda 'ivrit*) and 'Hebrew soil' (*adama 'ivrit*) (Masalha 1992: 24–5).

European Zionist Narratives and Colonial Reality

Zionism, as a European settler-colonial ideology and movement, would not have been able to achieve its goals without the overall support of the Western imperialist powers. The Israeli state was, and still is, central to the West's project in the 'East'. The Israeli state owes its very existence to the British colonial power in Palestine, despite the tensions that existed in the last decade of the British Mandate between the colonial power and the leadership of the European Yishuv. Under the Ottomans the European Zionist colonists were not given a free hand in Palestine; had the Ottomans been left in control of Palestine after the First World War, it is very unlikely that a Jewish state would have come into being. The situation changed radically with the occupation of Palestine by the British in 1918; already on 2 November 1917, Zionism was granted title to Palestine in the Balfour Declaration, a letter sent by Foreign Secretary Arthur James Balfour to the Zionist Federation, via Baron Walter Rothschild, wherein the British government declared its commitment to the establishment of a 'Jewish national

---

9. Uri Davis, 'The Histadrut: Continuity and Change', www.passia.org/seminars/2000/israel/part9.html.

home' in Palestine. Over the next thirty years, the colonial power allowed the Zionist movement to settle hundreds of thousands of European Jews in Palestine, to establish hundreds of settlements, including several cities, and to lay the political, economic, industrial, military and cultural foundations of the State of Israel.[10] The term 'Zionism' originated in Europe in the late nineteenth century. Political Zionism was in part the product of the religious and racial intolerance of the Europeans. Zionism also emerged in the age of European empires and at the height of European colonisation. This reflected the fact that political Zionism was the product of east and central European nationalist ideas and colonialist movements of the period. The nationalism of the father of modern political Zionism, Theodor Herzl (1860–1904), an Austro-Hungarian Jewish journalist, was taken from German sources (Kohn 1958, in Khalidi 2005: 813. Herzl was a deeply secular man. He set out the Zionist programme in his 1896 book *Der Judenstaat: Versuch einer modernen Lösung der Judenfrage* (*The State of the Jews: Proposal of a Modern Solution for the Jewish Question*). He called for a Jewish state to be set up in an 'undeveloped' country outside Europe. From the outset it was clear to Herzl that the Jewish state would be part of the system of Western colonial domination of Asia, Africa and Latin America. In *Der Judenstaat* Herzl mooted the possibility of a Jewish state in Argentina. Other potential territories for Zionist colonisation were considered, including Uganda, North Sinai and Madagascar. But with the decisive influence of Russian Zionists, Palestine was chosen by the Zionist movement as the biblical 'promised land'.

One of the most enduring themes of the Zionist project in Palestine was the notion of European Jews as carriers and transmitters of European *mission civilisatrice* to the backward Orient: the spread of Western modernity, enlightenment, reason, modern sciences and technology to an underdeveloped and semi-deserted Asiatic geography (Massad 2004: 61). Hannah Arendt has shown that the founder of political Zionism '[Theodor] Herzl thought in terms of

---

10. Tom Segev, 'The Makings of History: An Intriguing "What If"', *Haaretz*, 6 August 2010, www.haaretz.com/magazine/week-s-end/the-makings-of-history-an-intriguing-what-if-1.306388.

nationalism inspired from German sources' (quoted by Kohn 1958, in Khalidi 2005: 813. The 'New Society'/New Jew theme was at the centre of *Altneuland* (*'Old-New Land'*), the futuristic novel written by Herzl in 1902 and devoted to the love of the 'Old-New Land' and the colonising-cum-civilising mission of Zionism. The World Zionist Organization (WZO) was founded in 1897. Its first president was Theodor Herzl. The 'Jewish Colonial Trust' was the first financial institution of the WZO set up at Herzl's initiative. It was approved by the Second Zionist Congress in 1898 and established a year later (in 1899) and registered as a limited colonial company in London. Its objectives were to encourage Jewish migration from Europe and the economic development of Jewish colonies in Palestine. Earlier, in 1882, B'nai B'rith (Sons of the Covenant) was one of the earliest modern Zionist organisations founded in the West. It was established by German Zionist Jews[11] to foster European Jewish colonisation in Palestine. B'nai B'rith provided financial support to early Zionist colonies in Palestine and published a weekly newspaper proudly titled *Der Kolonist*.

Following Herzl, political Zionism went on to construct a whole discourse of European (Jewish) colonisation-cum-modernisation versus Oriental (Arab) backwardness, based on the 'New Society'/'New Yishuv' versus the 'Old Yishuv' – a pre-1882 backward space inhabited by non-Zionist religious Jews living in the mixed Arab–Jewish cities of Jerusalem, Tiberias, Safad and al-Khalil (Hebron). The European colony of the New Yishuv, by contrast, was composed of secular, modern, scientifically minded, urbane, rational and civilised people. One of the main characters in *Altneuland* is a Palestinian Arab called 'Reschid Bey', an engineer who welcomes with open arms the Zionist *mission civilisatrice* and Jewish colonisation of Palestine; the dispossessed indigenous Palestinian is extremely grateful to his European Zionist-Jewish neighbours for 'making the Asiatic desert boom' and transforming the economic conditions of the country through 'the scientific measures of the 'New Hebrew Man' (Herzl 2000 [1997]: 121–3). As Mizrahi scholar Ella Shohat puts it:

---

11. An original Jewish organisation was founded in New York in 1843.

Herzl's 1902 futuristic novel *Altneuland*, which deals with the two-decades metamorphosis of a miserable turn of the century Palestine into a wonderfully civilized oasis of scientific progress and humanist tolerance, already relied on the 'good Arab' (Raschid Bey and his wife Fatma) to witness the advantages of Zionism's Manifest Destiny. The fragile project of occupying an Eastern site to implant Zionism's Western utopia perhaps even required the expressed approval of the vanishing Arab. (Shohat 2010: 264)

Almost from the beginning the Herzlian utopia had its own Jewish critics. Asher Ginsberg (1856–1927) – better known by his pen name Ahad Ha'am, the Russian founder of cultural Zionism and promoter of the vision of a Jewish 'spiritual centre' in Palestine – criticised Herzl's political Zionism. In his critique of *Old-New Land*, Ahad Ha'am pointed out that there was no sign of new Jewish cultural activity or creativity in Herzl's New Society. Its culture was European and German; the language of the educated classes was German, not Hebrew. Jews were not depicted as producers or creators of culture, but simply transmitters, carrying the (imperialist) culture and civilisation of the West to the Orient.[12]

Also, from the start it became clear that the Jewish 'restorationist' project could only be achieved with the backing and active support of the European powers. From Herzl to Chaim Weizmann and David Ben-Gurion, the Zionist leadership was fully aware that its programme could not be secured without the support of the imperialist powers. When Herzl published *Der Judenstaat* in 1896, he was explicit that the 'state of the Jews' could only be established with the support of one or more major European powers, at a time when the imperial powers were carving up the non-European world between them. The establishment of a Jewish state would have to be secured and guaranteed in public law – *volkerrechtig* – with the backing of the great powers. Once such official backing had been secured, the Zionist movement would conduct itself like other colonising ventures. Thus the history of the early Zionist movement in the years between 1896 and the British Balfour Declaration of 1917 is characterised by relentless Zionist efforts to secure imperialist backing. Aware of the growing German influences

12. Cited in Jacques Kornberg's 'Preface', in Herzl 2000: xxviii.

on the Ottoman state, Herzl initially strove in favour of German imperialist backing. In *Der Judenstaat*, Herzl wrote frankly about the (non-European) Asiatic land 'reclaimed' by Zionism and the setting up of a quasi-European state in Palestine:

> If His Majesty the Sultan were to give us Palestine, we could in return undertake to regulate the whole finances of Turkey. We should form there part of a wall of defence for Europe in Asia, an outpost of civilisation against Barbarism.[13]

In October 1898 Herzl travelled to Ottoman Palestine to meet with Kaiser Wilhelm II of Germany. However, the meeting with the Kaiser turned out to be only ceremonial, and the Kaiser refused to commit himself. When these efforts became unsuccessful, Herzl and his successors turned to the British Empire (Polkehn 1975: 76-90). In his diaries, Herzl explicitly drew parallels between himself and Cecil Rhodes (1853-1902), an English-born businessman, the founder of the diamond company De Beers, ardent believer in colonialism and British imperialism in South Africa, and the founder of Rhodesia: 'Naturally there are big differences between Cecil Rhodes and my humble self, the personal ones very much in my disfavor, but the objective ones greatly in favor of our [Zionist] movement' (cited in Davis 1987: 3-4).

While the Hebrew Bible was not the only 'justification', it certainly was the most powerful one, without which political Zionism was only another conquering European colonial ideology. Read at face value, in a literalist fashion, and without recourse to doctrines of universal human rights and international law, the Hebrew Bible indeed appears to propose that the taking possession of ancient Palestine and the forcible expulsion of the indigenous population (the Canaanites) was the fulfilment of a divine mandate. From scrutiny of the language used in the Hebrew Bible and the language of political Zionism from the late nineteenth century onwards it is possible to see the way in which a secular European conquering ideology and movement mobilised the figurative language of the Jewish religion into a sacrosanct 'title deed' to the land of Palestine

---

13. Theodor Herzl, *Der Judenstaat* (1914 edn, Cologne): 30, cited in Polkehn 1975: 76. Also Herzl 1972: 30; and cited in Rodinson 1973: 14.

signed by God (Wetherell 2005: 69-70). Very little is said about
the actual genealogy and provenance of Zionism, especially the
European settler-colonial context of the late nineteenth-century
from which Zionism drew its force; and almost nothing is said
about what the creation of the State of Israel entailed for the
indigenous inhabitants of the land (Said 1980: 57). Despite its
distinct features and its nationalist ideology ('return' to the land
of the Bible) political Zionism followed the general trajectory of
colonialist projects in Africa, Asia and Latin America: European
colonising of another people's land while seeking to remove or
subjugate the indigenous inhabitants (Ruether 1998: 113).

Zionist colonisation of Palestine has taken place in four distinct
phases: the first, 1882-1918, began on a small scale under Ottoman
rule; the second (important) phase, 1918-48, took place under
British imperial protection; the third, 1948-67, was characterised
by 'internal colonisation' and Judaisation within the Green Line;
the fourth began in 1967 and is still going on today. At the time
of the first Zionist congress in Basle, Switzerland, in 1897, 95 per
cent of the population of Palestine was Arab and 99 per cent of
the land was Arab-owned (Khalidi 1992b: 17). Today over 90 per
cent of the land in historic Palestine is controlled by Israel and
designated for Jewish use only. From the late nineteenth century
and throughout the Mandatory period the demographic and land
policies of the Zionist Yishuv in Palestine continued to evolve. But
its demographic and land battles with the indigenous inhabitants
of Palestine were always a battle for 'maximum land and minimum
Arabs' (Masalha 1992, 1997, 2000).

Throughout much of the nineteenth and the first half of the
twentieth centuries the terms Zionist 'colonisation' and Jewish
'colonies' in Palestine were proudly proclaimed and universally
used by Zionist leaders and writers. Benjamin Lee Gordon's *New
Judea: Jewish Life in Modern Palestine and Egypt*, published in
Philadelphia in 1919, a typical Zionist publication of the period,
uses terms such as 'Jewish colonies' and 'Jewish colonists' in
Palestine dozens of times throughout the book, systematically and
as a term of endearment. The same colonialist methodology and
terminology are found in the 1950s in the publications of Israeli

diplomat Yaakov Morris – the father of Israeli historian Benny Morris – including his 1953 book *Pioneers from the West: History of Colonization in Israel by Settlers from the English-speaking Countries*,[14] is just one example of this proudly colonialist Zionist tradition. In Zionist writings the Hebrew words for Moshava and (plural) Moshavot were synonymous with Jewish 'colony'/'colonies' and Jewish colonists. Indeed 'Moshava' and 'Moshavot' were coined as a literal translation of the English terms 'colony' and 'colonies'. This proudly trumpeted colonial legacy of early Zionist colonists and pioneers has been suppressed or deleted from memory in recent Zionist historiography, including the writings of the Israeli revisionist historians (see Chapter 5).

In the Zionist colony (Moshava), as opposed to the subsequent communal settlements like the Kibbutz and the Moshav, all the land and property are privately owned. The first Zionist colonies ('Moshavot') such as Rishon LeZion ('First in Zion'), Rosh Pinna ('Cornerstone'), Zichron Yaakov ('Memory of Jacob'), Yesud Hama'alei and Petah Tikva ('Opening of Hope') were universally described as 'colonies' in both Zionist and professional literature of the time. Their economy was based on agriculture, and, like all European colonies, they exploited cheap indigenous labour. Illustrative of the extent of their dependence on cheap Arab labour was Zichron Yaakov, founded in 1882 by French coloniser, financier and patron of early Zionist colonies Baron Edmond-James de Rothschild, (in 'memory' of his father Jacob) and 200 Jewish colonists from Romania employing 1,200 Arab labourers; similarly Rishon LeZion, with 41 Jewish families and 300 families of Arab labourers (Lehn with Davis 1988: 39).

Also, crucially, these early Jewish colonies were preceded by and modelled on the German Christian Templer colonies established in Palestine in the middle to late nineteenth century – with farmhouses of one or two storeys and with slanting tiled roofs and shuttered windows. Interestingly even today the 'German Colony' south-west of the Old City of Jerusalem, established in 1878 by members of the German Templer Society (*Tempelgesellschaft*),

14. Published by the Youth and ha-Halutz Department of the World Zionist Organisation (London: Greenwood Press, 1953; new edn 1972).

is known in Hebrew as *Hamoshava Hagermanit*. Earlier in 1868 the 'German Colony' in Haifa was set up by the Templers. This was followed by another six German colonies: Jaffa (1869); Sarona (1878), now next to where the Israeli army Kirya military complex sits in Tel Aviv (1878); Jerusalem (1881); Wilhelma, near Lydda (1902); Galilean Bethlehem (1906); and Waldheim (1907). For the Templers colonising Palestine was part of their faith: the Holy Land had to be prepared for the Second Coming of Christ. Secular Zionist historiography depicts mid-nineteenth-century German colonists as forerunners of the Zionist movement, and early Zionists themselves adopted them as a 'model to be emulated' (Yazbak 1999: 40–54). In Zionist writings the Templers were considered to be responsible for bringing technology to Palestine, in architecture, agriculture and industry, and as a symbol of progress and modernity. In *Yehuda ve-Yerushalayim*, the newspaper of Yoel Moshe Salomon, he himself wrote about the Templer colonies:

> We have also noticed the colonies established over the past few years by the Germans from Wittenburg (not of our people) and their homes are built in good order, as in all the cities of Europe, with wide streets and magnificent buildings, so that anyone who walks along their streets will forget that he is walking in the country of the soul, and will feel as though he is in one of the populated cities of Europe.[15]

Zionist writer Zev Smilansky, the father of Israeli writer S. Yizhar (see below), described in 1905 the Valhalla Colony and compared it to the Jewish neighbourhoods in Jaffa:

> When we passed the small neighborhood of Germans built opposite Neve Tzedek, we enjoyed seeing pretty houses built in good taste ... as compared to our arrival in the Jewish neighborhoods in Jaffa, we felt sorrow. How poor are your tents, O Jacob, and how goodly are the dwellings of the Germans.[16]

Bordering the 'German Colony' in Jerusalem is the 'Greek Colony', known in Hebrew as *Hamoshava Hayevanit*. Following

---

15. Quoted in Adi Schwartz, 'The Nine Lives of the Lorenz Café', *Haaretz*, 20 January 2009, www.haaretz.com/print-edition/features/the-nine-lives-of-the-lorenz-cafe-1.237605.
16. Quoted in ibid.

in the footsteps of the German Templer colonists, the 'American Colony' was established in Jerusalem in 1881 by members of a Christian messianic society. A neighbourhood and a famous hotel in East Jerusalem are still known by that name. Today the side streets of the former 'German Colony' are named by Israel after Christian Zionists and European imperialists, including South African prime minister Jan Smuts, British prime minister David Lloyd George, British Labour Party leader Josiah Wedgewood, and Sir Wyndham Henry Deedes, a Christian Zionist British general, who was also the chief secretary to British High Commissioner of Palestine Sir Herbert Samuel from 1920 to 1922. Deedes represented a British Christian Zionism which was deeply entwined with Western Christian imperialism in the Middle East. This Christian Zionism, represented then by the British Empire and now by the American empire, is deeply rooted in the politics of uniqueness and exceptionalism and the supremacist biblical theology of the people of God, 'elect nations' and 'chosen peoples', nations which are the heirs of God's election of the biblical Israelites. This Christian Zionist imperialist mission includes a duty to patronise the 'Jewish people' by 'restoring' them to their 'ancestral homeland' in Palestine, backed by a global Christian empire, then British and now American (Masalha 2007).

In Zionist and pro-Zionist imperialist writing, the 'backwardness' of the indigenous inhabitants of 'undeveloped' Palestine was used to justify Jewish 'restorationism' and the displacement of the Palestinians (Sayigh 1979: 188). In *T.E. Lawrence*, Desmond Stewart cites the typically racist comments made in 1909 by the future 'Lawrence of Arabia'. Lawrence was then a student at Oxford University on a three-month walking tour through the Galilee and Syria studying Crusader castles. Later, in 1911–14, posing as an amateur archaeologist, he went on a British expedition and a spying mission in Syria. Lawrence had this to say about Zionist colonists in the Galilee 'making the desert bloom': 'The sooner the Jews farm it all, the better; their colonies are bright spots in the desert' (quoted in Stewart 1977: 48).[17] What Lawrence neglected

17. Lawrence continued his colonial-biblical archaeological expeditions in the Middle East until the outbreak of the First World War. In January 1914 he was used by British

to mention, however, was that there were no deserts in the Galilee and no Jewish colonies in the Naqab/Negev desert.

The officially named 'Palestine Jewish Colonisation Association (PICA) was established in 1924 and played a major role in supporting the European 'Yishuv' in Palestine. It was disbanded only in 1957. Earlier in 1891 the 'Jewish Colonisation Association' (ICA) was founded as an English company by the German Jewish banker Baron Maurice de Hirsch in 1891 to support Jews from Russia and Romania to migrate and settle in agricultural colonies in Argentina and Palestine. After de Hirsch died in 1896 the ICA began to support Jewish colonies in Palestine. In 1899 Edmond-James de Rothschild (1845-1934), a French member of the Rothschild banking family, a strong supporter of Zionism and a major donor to the Yishuv, transferred title to his colonies in Palestine plus 15 million francs to the ICA, which was reorganised as the 'Palestine Jewish Colonisation Association' in 1924, under the direction of Edmond's son James Armand de Rothschild. After 1948 James de Rothschild instructed PICA to transfer most of its land in Israel to the Jewish National Fund (Fischbach 2003: 162-4).

Edmond-James de Rothschild also supported the removal of Palestinians to Iraq. Following a meeting with de Rothschild in Paris, Vladimir Jabotinsky wrote in a letter to a friend that the Baron 'is willing to give money to the Arabs in order to enable them to purchase others lands, but on condition that they leave Palestine'. Referring to de Rothschild's plan, Mapai leader Shabtai Levi, of Haifa, who had been a land purchasing agent of PICA, wrote in his memoirs:

> He advised me to carry on in similar activities, but it is better, he said, not to transfer the Arabs to Syria and Transjordan, as these are part of the Land of Israel, but to Mesopotamia (Iraq). He added that in these cases, he would be ready to send the Arabs, at his expense, new agricultural machines, and agricultural advisors. (quoted in Masalha 1992: 22)

---

intelligence as an archaeological smokescreen for a British military survey of the Naqab desert – an expedition funded by the Palestine Exploration Fund (PEF) to search for an area described in the Bible as the 'Wilderness of Zin'. The PEF had mounted colonial-geographical map-making expeditions in Palestine in the late nineteenth century and its expeditions and activities had a major impact on the emergence of a colonial typonomy in Palestine.

In *All That Remains: The Palestinian Villages Occupied and Depopulated by Israel in 1948*, Walid Khalidi observed in 1992: 'There is no denying that the Zionist colonisation of Palestine, which began in the early 1880s and continues to this day, represents one of the most remarkable colonizing ventures of all time' (1992a). Six decades after the 1948 Nakba, Zionist colonisation processes in Palestine continue unchecked. Writing on the 60th anniversary of the Nakba, Palestinian scholar Joseph Massad wrote:

> I will suggest to you that there is much at stake in all of this [accepting the Nakba as a fact of history], in rendering the Nakba an event of the past, a fact on the ground that one cannot but accept, admit, and finally transcend; indeed that in order to move forward, one must leave the Nakba behind. Some have even suggested that if Israel acknowledges and apologises for the Nakba, the Palestinians would forgive and forget, and the effects of the Nakba would be relegated to historical commemorations, not unlike the one we are having this year.
>
> In my view, the Nakba is none of these things, and the attempt to make this year the 60th anniversary of the Nakba's life and death is a grave error. The Nakba is in fact much older than 60 years and it is still with us, pulsating with life and coursing through history by piling up more calamities upon the Palestinian people. I hold that the Nakba is a historical epoch that is 127 years old and is ongoing. The year 1881 is the date when Jewish colonisation of Palestine started and, as everyone knows, it has never ended. Much as the world would like to present Palestinians as living in a post-Nakba period, I insist that we live thoroughly in Nakba times. What we are doing this year is not an act of commemorating but an act of witnessing the ongoing Nakba that continues to destroy Palestine and the Palestinians. I submit, therefore, that this year is not the 60th anniversary of the Nakba at all, but rather one more year of enduring its brutality; that the history of the Nakba has never been a history of the past but decidedly a history of the present. (Massad 2008)

Framing the Conflict: Settler-colonialism, *Herrenvolk* Democracy, Ashkenazi Ethnocracy

Central to the debate on Palestine–Israel are questions of power asymmetry, European hegemonic narratives and discourses, indigenous memory and counter-hegemony, and how to conceptualise and frame the ongoing conflict between the immigrant-settler and the indigenous. This work contextualises the 1948 Palestinian Nakba against the backdrop of the enduring themes of Zionist colonisation of Palestine from the late 1880s to the present. It argues that both the 1948 Nakba and the current Palestinian struggle to resist the continuing Nakba are at the heart of the struggle between the settler-colonialist State of Israel and the indigenous inhabitants of Palestine. I also argue that Zionist 'resettlement' of Palestine, the establishment of a settler state in historic Palestine and Zionist Israel as an intensely racialised society, in relation both to the indigenous inhabitants of Palestine and to the Arab Jews, the Mizrahim, have to be challenged and deconstructed first and foremost by rewriting history through the experience of indigenous inhabitants of Palestine and the continuing Nakba as a story telling of huge devastation, trauma, painful struggle, survival and resistance. The tragedy of the Israel–Palestine conflict lies in the fact that the very state established by Jews in the aftermath of the Jewish Holocaust, a key event in Jewish history, has been a settler state where racial and religious discrimination, militarism and injustice prevail. But while the Holocaust is an event in the past, the colonisation of Palestine and the ethnic cleansing of Palestinians continue.

The mega-narrative of the State of Israel conflates Judaism with Zionism and frames the conflict with the Palestinians within its Zionist ideological moorings: Zionism is a product of a 'national liberation movement' of the Jewish people; the 'biblical Israelites' returning (from the late nineteenth century onwards) to 'redeem the ancient homeland' and 'restore Jewish statehood' after two millennia of absence and exile.

Israel is an 'outpost' of Western culture and European civilisation in the Middle East, surrounded by an Islamic 'Orient'. The mega-narrative of Zionism, repeated *ad nauseam* in the Western media, describes Israel as a 'liberal democracy' and the 'only democracy in the Middle East'. With the rise of Israeli critical scholarship in the 1980s, this concept of 'liberal democracy', however, was critiqued by a 'new generation' of Israeli social scientists who introduced the concept of Israel as an 'ethnic democracy', a

kind of second-class democracy. Sociologist Sammy Smooha, of
Haifa University, who led this public discourse, highlighted the
second-class nature of Palestinian citizenship in Israel, the tight
control of the dominant Jewish group over the state apparatus, and
the systemic discrimination against Palestinian citizens (Smooha
1997: 198–224). This conception, however, still views Zionism as a
'national liberation movement' of the Jewish people, but bemoans
its practices inside the Green Line and in the 1967 occupied territories. The 'ethnic democracy' model was enthusiastically embraced by many Israeli social scientists, including some Palestinian
academics inside Israel.[18]

However, in effect in the post-1948 era Israeli social scientists
and biblical scholars have conveniently substituted a fictional
'Jewish ethnicity' for the mythical 'Jewish race' – a nineteenth-
century European racist construct which had become politically
unacceptable and completely discredited after the horrors of the
Jewish Holocaust. (In a similar vein the self-describing term Jewish
'colonies' of the Mandatory period was expediently substituted by
the term Jewish 'settlements' in the post-1948 period.) However,
as Philip Spencer and Howard Wollman have powerfully argued,
in the twentieth century 'ethnicity' (as common descent) was a
convenient replacement for 'race' (biology and blood) as the key
ingredient of European social scientific racism and organic nationalist ideologies – race, 'racial categorization and racist discourses'
were central 'to the development of nationalism, particularly in
the European context' of the nineteenth century (2002: 64).

> By contrast with race, the concept of ethnicity is relatively new, emerg-
> ing in social science discourse only in the twentieth century ... the
> concept itself, even or particularly in its culturalist form, was only
> developed when overt racist ideology became first theoretically unten-
> able (since scientific evidence of the existence of races was impossible
> to produce) and politically unacceptable (certainly after the experience
> of Nazism). (Spencer and Wollman 2002: 65)

More recently political theorists have referred to Israel as *herrenvolk* or ethnocratic or Ashkenazi 'elite democracy'. In particular

18. Rouhana and Ghanem 1993: 163–88, 1999: 223–46; Yiftachel 1992: 125–36, 1993:
51–9.

the myth of 'ethnic democracy' has been challenged by As'ad
Ghanem, Nadim Rouhana and Oren Yiftachel (1998: 253-67). The
three Israel-based scholars have highlighted the inherent contradiction between the inclusive nature of democracy and the overt
exclusivity of ethnicity, and the fact that Jewish identity is central
to the self-definition of the Israeli state (Rouhana 2006: 64-74).
Subsequently Yiftachel, of Ben-Gurion University in the Negev,
became a leading exponent of the concept of 'Israeli ethnocracy'
(in *Ethnocracy: Land and Identity Politics in Israel/Palestine*,
2006): Israel, like Sri Lanka, Turkey, Latvia, Lithuania and Es-
tonia, functions as an exclusionist ethnocratic state; ethnicity
(with religion) and not citizenship regulates the distribution of
resources and power in the country; the political system and basic
laws enshrine the permanent domination of one ethno-religious
group (Jews) over the native Palestinians.

Strictly speaking the term 'ethnocracy' is misleading. The Jews
in Israel (as well as worldwide) belong to a wide range of 'ethnicities'. However, the overt racist manifestations of Israeli ideological
'ethnocracy' are widely documented. The 'democratic' aspects
of the Israeli regime are skin-deep; the ideological objective of
the Israeli 'ethnocracy' is to maintain Jewish domination over
the indigenous Palestinians. Although over the years Israeli Jews
became more realistic in their attitudes towards the existence
of a Palestinian minority in Israel, the creation of Israel did not
alter Zionism's premises and fundamentals with regard to the
Palestinian minority remaining under Israeli control.[19] After 1948,
European Zionist (völkisch) 'ethnonationalism' created in Israel
what Meron Benvenisti, the former deputy mayor of Jerusalem,
has described (1987) as a *herrenvolk* democracy, with first-class
citizenship for Jews, second-class citizenship for the Palestinian

---

19. The Israeli State Archives in Jerusalem contain many official files with extensive
information pertaining to Israel's policies towards the Arab minority, including what
usually is described in Israel as 'population transfers'. Although a substantial proportion
of these files are open to researchers and have been used in the writing of this book,
many official files remain classified. However, some idea about the contents of these
closed files may be gathered from the Archives' index listing of those files of the Ministry
of Minorities: 'Expulsion of Inhabitants', 'Transfer of Inhabitants', 'Concentration of
Arab Residents', 'Complaints about Police Treatment', 'Demolition of Arab Houses',
and 'Acts against Civilians'.

citizens inside Israel, and completely disenfranchised Palestinians in the occupied territories. The term '*herrenvolk* democracy' was coined by Belgian sociologist Pierre L. van den Berghe in *The Ethnic Phenomenon* (1981) *and Race and Racism: A Comparative Perspective* (1967; also 1978: 401-11) to describe ethnocentrism and a political system based on an imagined biological ethnic-racial nationalism, in which full citizen rights are only granted to the dominant ethnic-racial group in society; apartheid South Africa and Zionist Israel are the best illustrative cases. The pre-1948 obsession of the founding fathers of Zionism with 'transfer' was linked in post-1948 Zionist thinking with the European nationalist (romantic) idea of the völkisch/ethno-racial state and the construction of the Israeli state as an ethnocracy (Yiftachel 2006) and an imagined form of '*herrenvolk* republic'.

Systematic discrimination and Jewish control and privileges are legislated into the structure of citizenship in all basic aspects of life: access to land and water, the economy, education, the civil service and political institutions.[20] Adalah ('Justice'), 'the Legal Centre for Arab Minority Rights in Israel', has documented Israel's systematic discrimination against its 1.3 million Palestinian citizens, counting thirty-five Israeli laws which explicitly privilege Jews over non-Jews.[21] In fact Israel is a heavily militarised 'democracy for Jews' and an apartheid state for the indigenous inhabitants of Palestine. The Israeli state operates a subtle form of apartheid within the Green Line but a fully fledged Bantustan system in the 1967 occupied territories.

Colonialism, Anti-colonialism and Post-colonialism

By contrast to the Israeli-Zionist narratives, the Palestinian national narrative, as set out in the Palestinian National Charter of 1964, for instance, makes a clear distinction between Judaism as

---

20. See also Jonathan Cook, 'My Oath to Israel's "Jewish Democracy"': Why My Fingers Will Be Crossed', 16 October 2010, www.redress.cc/palestine/jcook20101016.
21. Cited in George Bisharat and Nimer Sultany, 'Second-class Citizens', *Miami Herald*, 15 August 2010, www.miamiherald.com/2010/08/15/1776256/second-class-citizens.html.

a 'divine religion' (Article 18) and Zionism as a political ideology
and a colonisation movement. Article 19 states:

> Zionism is a colonialist movement in its inception, aggressive and
> expansionist in its goal, racist in its configurations, and fascist in
> its means and aims. Israel, in its capacity as the spearhead of this
> destructive movement and as the pillar of colonialism, is a permanent
> source of tension and turmoil in the Middle East, in particular, and to
> the international community in general.

Palestinian authors, in contrast with Israeli or pro-Zionist Western rewriters, have tended to highlight the 'facts on the ground' and the practical settlement and ethnic cleansing dimensions of Zionism. But conceptualisation of the conflict is often derived from political positions and reflects desirable political solutions. The advocacy of the 'two-state' concept as a 'historical compromise' in Palestine–Israel, for instance, has led some Palestinian historians to reframe the conflict as basically a struggle between 'two national movements', while at the same time highlighting the colonialist dimensions of Zionism. Walid Khalidi, for instance, described Zionism in 1991 as a 'national movement' of the Jewish people:

> The crux and kernel of the Palestine Problem is the struggle between
> two national movements: on the one hand, the Zionist movement (and,
> since 1948, its embodiment, Israel) and on the other, the Palestinian
> national movement. The crux and kernel of this struggle has been, and
> continues to this day to be, the issue of the control or sharing of the
> land of Palestine. (Khalidi 1991: 5-6)

Like Walid Khalidi, Palestinian historian Rashid Khalidi has also combined the two conceptions of Zionism: the struggle between 'two national movements' and indigenous struggle against a European settler-colonialist project. In *The Iron Cage* (2006), Rashid Khalidi is critical of the 'reductionist view of Zionism as no more than a colonial enterprise'. He nonetheless argues that

> This enterprise was and is colonial in terms of its relationship to the
> indigenous Arab population of Palestine. Palestinians fail to under-
> stand, or refuse to recognize, however, that Zionism *also* served as
> the national movement of nascent Israeli polity being constructed at
> their expense. There is no reason why both positions cannot be true:

there are multiple examples of national movements, indeed nations, that were colonial in their origins, not least of them the United States. (Khalidi 2006: xxxiv)

Israeli and Jewish critics of Zionism (as in the case of Uri Davis) have described Israel as an 'apartheid state', sharing many features with apartheid South Africa (Davis 1987). In 1979 Palestinian-Canadian sociologist Elia Zureik, in *The Palestinians in Israel: A Study in Internal Colonialism*, presented a model of Israel's relations to Palestinian citizens within the Green Line as 'internal colonialism'. Far from creating a democratic state, Zionism, as a settler movement, by nature subordinates, excludes and marginalises the native Palestinian community (Zureik 1979: 8–30).

More recently, Israeli author and activist Jeff Halper combined creatively a range of ideas to describe Israel, including settler-colonialism, ethnic cleansing, de-Arabisation, apartheid, separation walls and ethnocracy to describe the 'creation of the Land of Israel'. He writes:

A hard-hearted approach to the natives is intrinsic to colonialism and ethnocracy. The land must be taken and a relationship of domination established. Everything truly human, let alone personal, must be eliminated lest the native 'raise his head' (Judges 8:28) ... we cannot escape strong colonial elements of Zionism. Unlike the case of other ethnocracies – the Serbs or the Russians, for example – but as in Kenya, Jewish settlers arrived from abroad. And as in Kenya they had to pacify the natives by force, since the latter would never accept dispossession voluntarily. De-humanization was necessary and inevitable. My cause, whether 'bringing civilizations to the benighted' or 'reclaim our ancient homeland,' must, as Jabotinsky astutely noted, stand on its own merits, for if the claims and rights of the indigenous are seriously entertained, our whole colonial enterprise will be called morally into question. In order to preserve my humanity while carrying out objectively immoral acts, then, I must make my victims unworthy of a human response; indeed, I must justify my actions as mere responses, forced upon me by the savage natives. ... Thus were the Palestinians – the 'Arabs' – doubly removed from their land. Physically, of course, but also existentially. In what was to become Israel, their very claim to peoplehood, to having any legitimate collective existence whatsoever, would be negated. The process of de-Arabizing Palestine, a component

of *nishul* [dispossession], steadily and thoroughly became the mirror
process of 'Judaizing' the landscape and creating the Land of Israel.
(2008: 135–6)

From the late 1970s to the early 1990s the great Palestinian
secular-humanist writer Edward Said attempted to frame the
Palestine struggle in terms of 'post-colonial theory' (Said 1978;
1994). Said was greatly influenced by the anti-colonial literature
of the 1950s and early 1960s. In the midst of French colonial wars
and the struggle for independence in North Africa four extraordinary books on the dehumanising aspects of colonialism, cultural
hegemony and anti-colonial resistance were published: Frantz
Fanon's *Black Skin, White Masks* (1952, 1967), Aimé Césaire's
Discourse on Colonialism (1955), Albert Memmi's *The Colonizer
and the Colonized* (1957, 1991), and Fanon's *The Wretched of the
Earth* (*Les Damnés de la terre*, 1961, 1967), this last volume written
during the Algerian struggle for independence.

Fanon (1925–1961) was a psychiatrist and revolutionary from
Martinique, who became an Algerian during that country's national
liberation struggle. In particular, Fanon explored the psychological
effect of colonisation on the psyche of the colonised and coloniser
alike, and assessed the broader implications for building a movement of cultural resistance and liberation. Colonised people, Fanon
argues, are not just those whose labour has been appropriated but
also, especially, those 'in whose soul an inferiority complex has
been created by the death and burial of its local cultural original-
ity' (Fanon 1967: 18).

Memmi's *The Colonizer and the Colonized* also explores the
psychological, social and cultural effects of colonialism: racism
is ingrained in every colonial institution which establishes the
'subhumanity' of the colonised; through cultural domination,
the coloniser creates a group of Francophiles who can attain a
slightly higher status; the coloniser's rewriting of history to his
glorification removes the colonised from history; the colonised
child is not taught his own history, but rather the unknown set-
tings of his coloniser's history; the colonised become 'divorced
from reality' (Memmi 1991).

Césaire was also a scholar and revolutionary from Martinique, while Memmi was a radical Tunisian Jew who moved to France. These francophone authors, who explored the injustice and oppressive daily humiliations of the colonised and paved the way for post-colonial studies, influenced a whole generation of scholars and activists involved in the anti-colonial liberationist struggle in Africa and Latin America, the Middle East and the Civil Rights Movement in the USA (Galbo 2007). In *Culture and Imperialism* (1994) Edward Said describes Memmi as one of the few intellectuals during the colonial era who managed to bridge the gap between the 'colonised and the coloniser'. Ned Curthoys, who discusses the 'leftist coloniser' in Albert Memmi's *The Colonizer and the Colonized*, suggests that the 'leftist coloniser' desires a future nation characterised by a fraternity of all peoples, while hopes for inter-communal dialogue are continuously disrupted by the structural violence of colonialism (Curthoys 2007: 115).

Zionism and the Israeli state, following the example of all European settler projects, continue to colonise, subjugate, dehumanise and dispossess the indigenous people of Palestine. Palestinians are still being depicted in Israeli textbooks as 'conniving', 'dishonest', 'lazy', 'treacherous', 'liars', 'murderous' and 'Nazis'. Zionist historiography provides ample evidence suggesting that from the very beginning of the Yishuv in Palestine the attitude of most Zionist groups towards the native Arab population ranged from a mixture of indifference and patronising racial superiority to outright denial of its national rights, the goal being to uproot and 'transfer' it to neighbouring countries. Leading figures such as Israel Zangwill, a prominent Anglo-Jewish writer, close lieutenant of Theodor Herzl and advocate of the 'transfer' solution, worked relentlessly to propagate the slogan that Palestine was 'a land without a people for a people without a land'.

In recent years, however, Memmi has declared his disillusionment with left-wing anti-colonial struggles and has moved closer to a right-wing position which on cultural matters can be viewed as deeply anti-Arab and anti-Muslim neoconservative (Galbo 2007: 1-7). Memmi's *Decolonisation and the Decolonized* (2006), which reflects this neoconservative orientation, became closely associated with a resurgent neo-colonial lobby in France. His recent historical revisionism also struck a chord among a section of the French public and, especially, a group of thinkers known as 'French-Jewish intellectuals', which includes Bernard Kouchner, Bernard–Henri Lévi, Alain Finkielkraut and André Glucksmann, all of whom at one point or another have either supported the 2003 invasion of Iraq or expressed anti-Muslim sentiments (Galbo 2007: 1–7). This resurgence of 'Orientalism' would not have surprised Edward Said (Said 1978, 1981, 1997), who had systematically challenged the linguistic imagery in Orientalist literature and Western media – imagery embedded in anti-Arab and anti-Muslim racist representation (Galbo 2007: 1–7).

In the 1990s Israeli revisionist historian Ilan Pappé, inspired by Edward Said's 'post-colonial theory', attempted, in two articles in *Journal of Palestine Studies* (1997: 37–43, 1998: 99–105; see also Nimni 2003) to reframe the Palestine–Israel question in 'post-Zionist' terms. But how, it might be asked, could the conflict be framed in post-colonial and post-Zionist terms when the Zionist colonisation of Palestine is still in full swing and with no sign of decolonisation in or liberation for Palestine?

In recent years Pappé's fellow revisionist historian Benny Morris has been rewriting and reframing his own 'new history' of the late 1980s and early 1990s by reconceiving the Israel-Palestine struggle in social Darwinist terms ('survival of the fittest') and as 'a clash of civilisations' (see Chapter 5). Rather than challenging the enduring themes of Zionist colonisation of Palestine, Morris provides moral justification for the dispossession of the (mostly Muslim) Palestinians, within a wider global context of neo-colonialist resurgence. The 'clash of civilisations' discourse, which encapsulates this neo-colonial resurgence, was itself first constructed by veteran British (and US-based) Jewish Orientalist historian Bernard Lewis in an article in the September 1990 issue of the *Atlantic Monthly* entitled 'The Roots of Muslim Rage'.[22] But it was Samuel Huntington (1927–2008), an American Jewish political scientist, who developed the thesis further in a 1992 lecture at the

---

22. 'The Roots of Muslim Rage', *Atlantic Monthly*, www.cis.org.au/Policy/summer01-02/polsummo1-3.pdf.

Washington DC-based American Enterprise Institute for Public Policy Research,[23] a neoconservative think-tank closely associated with the influential American pro-Israel lobby. Huntington then developed his argument in a 1993 *Foreign Affairs* article titled 'The Clash of Civilizations?' Huntington's work complemented that of rivals in the policymaking ranks, such as the theorist Francis Fukuyama, whose 'End of History' thesis celebrated the fall of the Soviet Union and Eastern Bloc, the end of the Cold War, the rise of 'unipolar US imperialism', and the triumph of Western neoliberalism as the 'final form of human government'.[24] Of course the USA itself was built on the bones and wiped out civilisations of its own indigenous inhabitants. US-based academics such as Fukuyama, Huntington, Lewis, Fuad Ajami and Niall Ferguson represent the other side of the public historian, who writes in the service of empire and Western imperialism. For them, Israel is an outpost of 'Western civilisation' and enlightenment, surrounded by a backward Arabo-Islamic civilisation. Huntington went on to expand his ideas in a 1996 book *The Clash of Civilizations and the Remaking of World Order*. His thesis, which attracted a great deal of media attention, proposed that 'cultural and religious identities' (not ideologies or economics) will be the primary source of conflict in the post-Cold War 'new political order'. Huntington, Lewis and other policy experts have contributed to the 'Israelisation' of American Middle East policy discourse.[25]

How Unique is the Zionist Settler-Colonial Project?

In 1919, when indigenous Palestinian Arabs constituted nine-tenths of the population of the country, Chaim Weizmann (1874–1952), president of the Zionist Organisation and later first president of

---

23. www.aei.org/issue/29196.
24. Dabashi 2001: 10–11; Fukuyama 1989, 1992; Edward W. Said, 'The Clash of Ignorance', *The Nation*, 22 October 2001, www.thenation.com/article/clash-ignorance; John J. Mearsheimer, 'Imperial by Design', *The National Interest*, 16 December 2010, http://nationalinterest.org/article/imperial-by-design-4576.
25. For further discussion of the Israelisation of American discourse, see Beinin 2003: 125–39.

Israel, viewed the Palestinian Arabs as a 'backwards race' (cited in Flapan 1979: 71), declaring in an address to the English Zionist Federation on 21 September 1919:

> By a Jewish National Home I mean the creation of such conditions that as the country is developed we can pour in a considerable number of immigrants, and finally establish such a society in Palestine that Palestine shall be as Jewish as England is English, or America American. (cited in Masalha 1992: 41 n24; also Weizmann 1949, 1952)

Born in Belarus and educated in Germany, Weizmann had become a British citizen in 1910 and taught chemistry at Manchester University. During the First World War he was director of the British Admiralty laboratories (1916–19), and in 1917 he worked very closely with the Christian Zionist foreign secretary Arthur Balfour to obtain the British Balfour Declaration. For Weizmann the natives of Palestine were akin to 'the rocks of Judea, as obstacles that had to be cleared on a difficult path' (cited in Masalha 1992: 17). As the British Mandate progressed and the Palestinians began to resist this Zionist colonisation-cum-*mission civilisatrice*, the Zionists resolved (in the 1930s) to crush Palestinian resistance, dismantle much of Palestinian society and 'transfer'/expel the majority of the indigenous population (Masalha 1992; Massad 2004: 57–70).

Conceived and constructed as a settler state, Zionist colonisation of Palestine was, in theory and practice, both intrinsically ethnic cleansing and politicidal (Kimmerling 2003: 214–15). In *Israel: A Colonial-Settler State?* (1973) – originally based on an article in French in June 1967, under the title 'Israel, fait colonial' ('Israel, a colonial fact'), published in Jean-Paul Sartre's *Les Temps Modernes* – the great French Jewish scholar of the Middle East Maxime Rodinson (1915–2004) explored the question why Israel should be considered a settler-colonial society. In France the book was considered scandalous at the time; indeed Jean-Paul Sartre – who had written the Introduction to Albert Memmi's *The Colonizer and the Colonized* (1957, 1991) – suggested that Rodinson should be psychoanalysed in order to cure his mind of such odd notions about Zionism and the State of Israel (reported by Rodinson in the introduction to *Cult, Ghetto, and State: The Persistence of the Jewish Question*, 2001). Rodinson's pioneering work on settler-colonialism in Palestine and his critique of Zionism were based on two main reproaches: the attempt to impose upon world Jewry an extraterritorial nationalist ideology, and the Judaising of Palestine at the cost of expulsion and domination of the Palestinians. He wrote:

> the creation of the State of Israel on Palestinian soil is the culmination of a process that fits perfectly into the great European-American movement of expansion in the nineteenth and twentieth centuries whose aim was to settle new inhabitants among other peoples or to dominate them economically and politically. (Rodinson 1973a: 91)

Rodinson's pioneering work documented the colonialist and racist attitudes towards the indigenous Palestinians that permeated the Zionist movement, especially its Labour groupings. He showed how early Zionist leaders constantly appealed to European powers, emphasising the advantages of having a modern outpost of Europe in the Middle East and highlighting the advantages of the 'white man's' colonisation of the Holy Land. British Zionist leader Chaim Weizmann – a close friend of General Jan Smuts, an advocate of racial segregation and prime minister of South Africa (1919–24 and 1939–48) – argued, 'A Jewish Palestine would be a safeguard to England, in particular in respect to the Suez Canal' (cited in Weinstock 1989: 96). When east European Jewish settlers moved to Palestine, their attitudes to the indigenous population were typical of colonial attitudes towards 'inferior' and 'uncivilised' peoples. But the Zionist settlements remained very small until the British occupied Palestine in 1918. After that the colonisation processes accelerated rapidly under the protection of the colonial power. The settlers made no effort to integrate their struggles with those of the Palestinians fighting against British colonialism. On the contrary, they proceeded from the conviction that the indigenous population would have to be subjugated or removed, with the help of the British. Rodinson also critiques several Zionist myths, including 'exile and return' and the argument that the Jewish people had lived there some two thousand years earlier.

Using such reasoning, Rodinson points out, the Muslims should lay claim to Spain. Nor was Palestine underpopulated, semi-deserted or 'empty' and waiting for European Jewish settlers to develop it (Rodinson 1973).

How unique is the Zionist model in the history of European settler-colonisation? Inevitably, due to political and ideological considerations, Israeli historians and social scientists have always shunned any attempt to compare European Zionism with European colonialism. Zionist settler-colonialism is particular but it is not unique. In line with common colonial practices the Israeli state was founded on the ruin, ethnic cleansing, displacement and re-placement of the indigenous people of Palestine. Nearly every European settler-colonisation project has used the Bible to redeem colonialism and the dispossession of indigenous peoples. European immigrant settler-colonial societies developed different strategies towards indigenous peoples. In North America, Australia and New Zealand, the local peoples were treated as part of the hostile natural environment, an 'attitude that ended with their genocide' (Kimmerling 2003: 21). In Afrikaner and apartheid South Africa and Rhodesia, the indigenous peoples were used as cheap labour and severely segregated from the white race. In Catholic Latin America, the Spanish and Portuguese conquerors pursued an-nihilationist strategies towards the local culture and indigenous civilizations (Aztec and Inca) combined with mass conversion of the bulk of the surviving indigenous populations. In Palestine, the European Zionist Yishuv was 'partially dependent on [cheap] Arab labour and completely dependent on [mostly absentee] Arab land owners from whom they purchased property'. But the European Yishuv was built as a 'pure Zionist Jewish colony' (Yiftachel 2006: 54; Shafir 1999).

> [It] institutionally, cognitively, and emotionally built within an ex-clusionary Jewish 'bubble.' The plans for the new Jewish state were similarly exclusive. The Jewish state was supposed to be purely Jewish and no political and bureaucratic tools were prepared for the possibility, mentioned in all partition proposals, that large Arab minorities would remain within the boundaries of the Jewish state. (Kimmerling 2003: 22)

In the late 1980s and 1990s, three Israeli sociologists, Baruch Kimmerling (2003), Uri Ram (1993: 327-50, 1999: 55-80) and Gershon Shafir (1996a, 1999: 81-96), attempted to break away from the Zionist tradition and apply a critical approach to historical writing on the Israel–Palestine question, by choosing to highlight certain 'colonial' features of the evolving Zionist Yishuv in Palestine. More recently, Israeli revisionist historian Ilan Pappé, in an article entitled 'Zionism as Colonialism', argued that the 'comparative approach validates the need to further examine Zionism as a settler-colonialist phenomenon, despite its unique origins and chronological timing' (2008: 611-33). In a 1999 collection edited by Pappé, entitled *The Israel/Palestine Question: Rewriting Histories* (1999), both Pappé and Uri Ram hugely overstate the impact of the 'colonialist perspective on Zionism' and as a tool of historical writing within Israeli academia, citing Shafir's *Land, Labor and the Origins of the Israeli–Palestinian Conflict, 1882–1914* (1996a) as an example of this new development (Ram 1999: 55-80).

However, far from breaking with earlier presentations of Zionism as a modernising project, Shafir's analysis is a continuation of traditional Zionist historiography rather than a distinct new model. In a 1996 article 'Zionism and Colonialism: A Comparative Approach', Shafir (regurgitating the official line) argues that Zionism and the State of Israel lack many of the core features of European colonialism (Shafir 1996b: 227-44).[26] Shafir's *Land, Labor and the Origins of the Israeli–Palestinian Conflict, 1882–1914* is in fact written in defence of the unique Zionist model of colonisation and the Yishuv as an enlightened and progressive colony. Originally published in 1989, the book is highly critical of the 'orthodox pro-Palestinian theoretical perspective [which] views Palestine as a "typical European colony with a typical European settler minority"' (Shafir 1996a: 211). Dismissing 'pro-Palestinian perspectives' on Zionist settle-colonialism put forward by Maxime Rodinson and Edward Said (in *The Question of Palestine*, 1980) as completely

---

26. Zionist author Jonathan Adelman, who relies on Shafir's thesis to argue that Zionism lacks key aspects of European colonialism, writes: 'To the extent that Israel had colonial-like aspects as a settler colony of people coming to Israel from other lands, it mainly resembled the British settler colonies which gave birth to the United States, Canada, Australia and New Zealand' (2008: 17).

'ahistorical' (1996a: 211–13), Shafir (following traditionalist Zionist historian Anita Shapira) rehashes many Israeli myths (many of which were demolished by the Israeli revisionist historians; see Chapter 7). He argues that the creation of a 'self-contained' and 'pure' Zionist Yishuv in Palestine and the insistence on '*exclusive* Jewish employment' led to a Yishuv '*modest* in its demand for territorial expansion' and to 'the success of the Jewish side in establishing its state and winning its military victory against the Arab world in 1948'; due to the pragmatism, 'moderate territorial ambitions' and progressive features of the Zionist project in Palestine, the country was in effect 'partitioned' between the Arabs and Jews in 1948 (1996a: 211–14).

Failing to recognise the enduring themes and patterns of Zionist colonisation of Palestine, Shafir's work ultimately fits into the dominant approach in Israeli historical writing. As Joel Beinin argues, the preoccupation with what the Zionist Jews intended to do rather than the actual consequences of the Zionist project for the indigenous Palestinians is the hallmark of mainstream Israeli historical writing on the history of Zionism and the Arab–Zionist conflict.[27] As late as 1947, after half a century of Zionist colonisation and tireless land-purchasing efforts, the land holdings of the Yishuv amounted to a mere 6.6 per cent of the land area of Palestine. In 1948 the establishment of a Jewish state on this territory, comprising widely scattered areas of land in Palestine, was completely unviable. As Israeli revisionist historian Benny Morris has pointed out,

> large sections of Israeli [Yishuv] society – including the Ahdut Ha'avodah party, Herut, and Mapai leaders such as Ben-Gurion – were opposed to or extremely unhappy with partition and from early on viewed the war as an ideal opportunity to expand the new state's borders beyond the UN-earmarked partition boundaries and at the expense of the Palestinians. Like Jordan's King Abdullah, they too were opposed to the emergence of a Palestinian Arab state and moved to prevent it.[28]

27. Joel Beinin, 'No More Tears: Benny Morris and the Road Back from Liberal Zionism', *Middle East Report* 230, Spring 2004, www.merip.org/mer/mer230/230_beinin.html.

28. Benny Morris, 'Looking Back: A Personal Assessment of the Zionist Experience', *Tikkun* 13, no. 1, March–April 1998, www.tikkun.org/9803/9803morris.html.

The Yishuv's leadership was fully aware of the South African model of colonisation with its exploitation of cheap indigenous black labour by the European white settlers. Evidently its determination not to replicate the South African model, and its policy of employing exclusively Jewish 'labour' and excluding the indigenous inhabitants from the Jewish economy and land purchased by the Jewish National Fund, were linked in the minds of David Ben-Gurion and other Mapai leaders with the concept of 'transfer' as a key component of Zionist ideology and strategy (Masalha 1992: 22-3). Therefore it is precisely these distinct features of the Zionist colonisation of Palestine, the 'exclusive' nature of the European Yishuv and creation of a pure Zionist colony, which led to the destruction of Palestine and the Nakba; as we will see below, Zionist 'ethnic cleansing' and the premisses of 'maximum land and minimum Arab', and Arab 'transfer', led to the massive Zionist 'territorial expansion' in and conquest of Palestine (from 6.6 per cent in 1947 to 78 per cent by early 1949).

From the beginning the drive for ethnic, racial and demographic exclusivity was central to the Zionist colonial project in Palestine. In 1948 'ethnic cleansing' was at the heart of the military campaign to eliminate the indigenous population from the 'Jewish homeland' in order to create a more secure, ethnically homogeneous 'Jewish state'. In fact a *pattern* can be detected in the use of Hebrew terms in the military orders and operations which the Haganah/IDF High Command passed down to the army units on the ground: *tihur* or *le-taher* ('cleansing' and 'purging'), *nikkuy* ('clearing'), *hisul* ('liquidation'), *gerush* ('expulsion'), *'le-hashmid* ('to destroy' or 'to exterminate'), *le-fanot* ('to evacuate'), *le-hatrid* ('to harass'), *siluk* ('removal'), *ha'vara* ('transfer'), *pinuy* ('evacuation'), *Mivtza Matate* ('Operation Broom'), *Mivtza Bi'ur Hametz* ('Operation Passover Cleaning'), *Pe'ulat Misparayim* ('Operation Scissors'), Jaffa as 'a "cancer" in the Jewish body-politic' – while individual Palestinian villages were ordered to be 'cleaned', 'cleansed', 'destroyed', 'removed'/*siluk*, 'transferred', 'nudged'.[29]

---

29. Pappé 2006: 72, 108, 110, 128, 138, 147, 155; Morris 1987: 64, 75, 95, 121, 122, 134-8, 235.

For over half a century, in the period between 1882 and 1948, terms such as Zionist 'colonies' and Zionist 'colonisation' were universally and unashamedly used by senior Zionist leaders. In June 1932 Vitaly (Haim) Arlozoroff (1899–1933), a Russian-born influential leader of Mapai, the most important Zionist party in the Yishuv, writing to Chaim Weizmann, observed: 'I am forced to the conclusion that with present day methods and under the present regimes there exists virtually no opportunity for solving the problem of large-scale immigration and colonization' (quoted in Khalidi 2005: 246). Arlozoroff's pessimistic outlook came in the aftermath of the Sir John Hope Simpson report of 1 October 1930, a British official report which was commissioned to look into the roots of Palestinian unrest and grievances under the British Mandate and following the widespread Arab–Jewish clashes of 1929. The report concluded that Palestinian fears of the devastating impact of the Zionist Yishuv and its land-purchase policies were well founded. It also recommended limiting Jewish immigration to Palestine due to the lack of agricultural land to support it:

> Actually the result of the purchase of land in Palestine by the Jewish National Fund has been that land became extra territorial. It ceases to be land from which the Arab can gain any advantage either now or at any time in the future. Not only can he never hope to lease or cultivate it, but, by the stringent provisions of the lease of the Jewish National Fund, he is deprived forever from employment on the land ...[30]
>
> It is impossible to view with equanimity the extension of an enclave in Palestine from which the Arabs are excluded. The Arab population already regards the transfer of lands to Zionist hands with dismay and alarm. These cannot be dismissed as baseless in light of the Zionist policy described above...[31]

The report refers throughout to the destructive impact of the 'colonisation policies' of the Yishuv: 'Zionist policy in regards to Arabs in their colonies'; 'the effect of the Zionist colonisation policy on the Arab'; 'Reasons for the exclusion of the Arab' in

---

30. Sir John Hope Simpson, *Palestine: Report on Immigration, Land Settlement, and Development*, London: His Majesty's Stationary Office, 1930, Cmd. 3686, p. 56
31. Ibid., p. 135.

Zionist colonies; 'The principle of the persistent and deliberate boycott of Arab labour in the Zionist colonies';

> the General Federation of Jewish Labour [Histadrut] ... is using every effort to ensure that it [boycott of Arab labour] shall be extended to the colonies of P.I.C.A ... Great pressure is being brought to bear on the old P.I.C.A. colonies in the Maritime Plain ... that pressure may be cited the construction of a Labour Kvutzoth (communal colony) ... It is certain that the employers of that village will not be able to resist the arguments of the General Federation [Histadrut], reinforced by the appeals of the vigorous labour colony at its gate.[32]

The report showed that Palestinian Arab 'unemployment is serious and general', partly due to the Histadrut labour policy extending to all Zionist enterprises. The displaced Palestinian Arab farmer could not find non-agricultural employment: 'There can be no doubt that there is at the present time serious unemployment among Arab craftsmen and among Arab laborers.' The Histadrut claim that the Palestinian Arab worker benefited from Zionist colonisation was rejected by the report:

> The policy of the Jewish Labour Federation is successful in impeding the employment of Arabs in Jewish colonies and in Jewish enterprises of every kind. There is therefore no relief to be anticipated from an extension of Jewish enterprise unless some departure from existing practice is effected.[33]

Settler-colonialism and the Yishuv's 'Transfer Committees' and Schemes, 1937–48

European settler colonies uprooted and almost completely destroyed indigenous peoples in North America and Australia. Land-grab was the driving force behind these European settler-colonial societies. In Palestine land, demography and water were (and still are) at the heart of the struggle between the European Zionist settlers and the indigenous Palestinians. For the European Zionist coloniser, who is 'returning' after 2000 years 'to redeem the 'land of the Bible', the

---

32. Sections of the report are reproduced in Khalidi 2005: 303–7.
33. Hope Simpson, *Palestine: Report on Immigration, Land Settlement, and Development*, p. 133.

indigenous inhabitants of Palestine earmarked for dispossession were usually invisible. They are simultaneously divested of their human reality and national existence and classed as a non-people. As I demonstrate in *Expulsion of the Palestinians: The Concept of 'Transfer' in Zionist Political Thought 1882–1948* (1992) and *A Land Without a People* (1997), both of which are in part based on Hebrew and Israeli archival sources, the Zionist quest for land and demography underpinned the Zionist concept of 'transfer' in the pre-1948 period. In a sense, Zionism's long-lasting battle against the native Palestinians was a battle for 'more land and fewer Arabs'. This battle essentially was dictated by Zionism's colonial premisses and fundamental principles: the 'ingathering' of the world's Jews in Palestine, the acquisition and conquest of land (*kibbush haadama*), and the establishment of a 'state for the Jews' – who mostly had yet to arrive in Palestine – at the expense of the would-be displaced and 'transferred' Palestinians. The above-cited works show that the idea of 'transferring' the Palestinians – a euphemism denoting the organised removal of the Palestinians to neighbouring or distant countries – was held widely in mainstream Zionism.

The concept – delicately described by its proponents as population exchange, Arab return to Arabia, emigration, resettlement and rehabilitation of the Palestinians in Arab countries, and so on – is deeply rooted in Zionism. The transfer notion was embedded in the Zionist perception that the Land of Israel or Palestine is a Jewish birthright and belongs exclusively to the Jewish people as a whole, and consequently Palestinian Arabs are 'strangers' who either should accept Jewish sovereignty over the land or depart. The two cited works also show that the concept had occupied a central position in the strategic thinking of the Zionist movement and the Jewish Yishuv as a solution to the Zionist land and 'Arab demographic' and political problems. Although the desire among the Zionist leaders to 'solve' the 'Arab question' through transfer remained constant until 1948, the envisaged modalities of transfer changed over the years according to circumstances. From the mid-1930s onwards a series of specific plans, generally involving Transjordan, Syria and Iraq, were produced by the Yishuv's transfer committees and senior officials. I also show that the idea was advocated by the most important founding fathers of Zionism – including David Ben-Gurion, Theodor Herzl, Zeev Jabotinsky, Berl Katznelson, Moshe Sharett, Nahman Syrkin, Menahem Ussishkin, Yosef Weitz and Chaim Weizmann.

We have mountains of evidence to show how deeply rooted in Zionist thinking the Yishuv leadership was. From the mid-1930s the Yishuv leadership was obsessed with the 'transfer solution'. Advocates of 'transfer' in the pre-1948 period asserted, often privately, that there was nothing 'immoral' about these proposals; that the earlier twentieth-century transfer of Greeks and Turks, Indians and Pakistanis, Germans and other Europeans provided a 'precedent' for similar measures vis-à-vis the Palestinian Arabs; that the uprooting and transfer of the Palestinians to Arab countries would constitute a mere relocation from one district to another; that the Palestinians would have no difficulties in accepting Jordan, Syria or Iraq as their homeland; that the Palestinian Arabs had little emotional attachment and few real ties to the particular soil in Palestine and would be just as content outside the 'Land of Israel'; that the Palestinian Arabs were marginal to the Arab nation and their problems might be facilitated by a 'benevolent' and 'humanitarian' policy of 'helping people to leave'. Such assertions were crucial to legitimise Zionism's denial of the Palestinian Arabs' right to self-determination in Palestine before 1948. Supporters of transfer asserted that the Palestinians were not a distinct people but merely 'Arabs', an 'Arab population' that happened to reside in the Land of Israel. Closely linked to this idea of the non-existence of the Palestinians as a nation and their non-attachment to the particular soil of Palestine was the idea of their belonging to an Arab nation with vast territories and many countries. As Ben-Gurion put it in 1929, 'Jerusalem is not the same thing to the Arabs as it is to the Jews. The Arab people inhabit many great lands' (Teveth 1985: 39). After all, if the Palestinians did not constitute a distinct separate nation and were not an integral part of the country and were without historical ties to it, then they could be transferred to other Arab countries without undue prejudice. Similarly, if the Palestinians were merely a marginal local part of a larger population of Arabs, then they were not a major party to the conflicts with Israel; therefore Israeli efforts to deal over their heads were justified. It is thus that Israeli pronouncements were full of references to the vast Arab territories and to the notion that the Palestinians were bound to other centres in Syria, Iraq and the Arabian Peninsula, the homeland of the Arab people.

Abundant references to the Palestinian population in early Zionist texts show clearly that from the beginning of the Zionist settlement in Palestine, the Palestinian Arabs were far from being an unseen or hidden presence. Despite their propaganda of a backward, underpopulated land; of Palestine's cultural and civilisational 'barrenness'; and of making 'the desert bloom' – slogans designed for external consumption – the Zionists from the outset were well aware that not only were there people on the land, but that they were there in large numbers. Zangwill, who had visited Palestine in 1897 and come face to face with the demographic reality of the country, himself acknowledged in a 1905 speech to a Zionist group in Manchester that

> Palestine proper had already its inhabitants. The pashalik [district] of Jerusalem is already twice as thickly populated as the United States, having fifty-two souls to the square mile, and not 25 percent of them Jews. (Zangwill 1937: 210)

Thus Yitzhak Epstein, an early settler leader who arrived in Palestine from Russia in 1886, warned not only of the moral implications of the Zionist colonisation but also of the political dangers inherent in the enterprise. In 1907, at a time when Zionist land purchases in the Galilee were stirring opposition among Palestinian peasants forced off land sold by absentee landlords, Epstein wrote an article entitled 'The Hidden Question' in which he strongly criticised the methods by which Zionists had purchased Arab land. In his view, these methods entailing dispossession of Arab farmers were bound to cause political confrontation in the future. Reflected in the Zionist establishment's angry response to Epstein's article are two principal features of mainstream Zionist thought: the belief that Jewish acquisition of land took precedence over moral considerations, and the advocacy of a physically separate, exclusionist and literally 'pure' Jewish Yishuv. 'If we want

Hebrew redemption 100 percent, then we must have a 100 percent Hebrew settlement, a 100 percent Hebrew farm, and a 100 percent Hebrew port', declared Ben-Gurion at a meeting of the Va'ad Leumi, the Yishuv's National Council, on 5 May 1936 (Ben-Gurion 1971–72: 163).

There is a great deal of evidence showing that in the pre-1948 period, 'transfer'/ethnic cleansing was embraced by the highest levels of Zionist settler-colonialist leadership, representing almost the entire political spectrum. Nearly all the founding fathers of the Israeli state advocated transfer in one form or another, including Theodor Herzl, Leon Motzkin, Nahman Syrkin, Menahem Ussishkin, Chaim Weizmann, David Ben-Gurion, Yitzhak Tabenkin, Avraham Granovsky, Israel Zangwill, Yitzhak Ben-Tzvi, Pinhas Rutenberg, Aaron Aaronson, Vladimir Jabotinsky and Berl Katznelson (Masalha 1992). Supporters of 'voluntary' transfer included Arthur Ruppin, a co-founder of Brit Shalom, a movement advocating bi-nationalism and equal rights for Arabs and Jews; moderate leaders of Mapai (later the Labour Party) such as Moshe Shertok and Eli'ezer Kaplan, Israel's first finance minister; and leaders of the Histadrut (Hebrew Labour Federation) such as Golda Meyerson (later Meir) and David Remez (Masalha 1992).

From the 1930s onwards a series of specific plans, generally involving Transjordan, Syria and Iraq, were produced by the Yishuv's 'transfer committees' and senior officials. In 1930, against the background of the 1929 disturbances in Palestine, Weizmann, then president of both the World Zionist Organisation and the Jewish Agency Executive, began actively promoting ideas of Arab 'transfer' in private discussions with British officials and ministers. He presented the colonial secretary, Lord Passfield, with an official, albeit secret, proposal for the transfer of Palestinian peasants to Transjordan whereby a loan of 1 million Palestinian pounds would be raised from Jewish financial sources for the resettlement operation. Lord Passfield rejected the proposal. However, the justification Weizmann used in its defence formed the basis of subsequent Zionist transfer arguments. Weizmann asserted that there was nothing immoral about the concept of transfer; that the transfer of Greek and Turkish populations in the early 1920s provided a precedent for a similar measure regarding the Palestinians; and that the uprooting and transportation of Palestinians to Transjordan, Iraq, Syria or any other part of the vast Arab world would merely constitute a relocation from one Arab district to another. Above all, for Weizmann and other Jewish Agency leaders, transfer was a systematic procedure, requiring preparation, money and a great deal of organisation, which needed to be planned by strategic thinkers and technical experts.

While the desire among the Zionist leadership to be rid of the 'Arab demographic problem' remained constant until 1948, the extent of the preoccupation with, and the envisaged modalities of, transfer changed over the years according to circumstances. Thus the wishful and rather naive belief in Zionism's early years that the Palestinians could be 'spirited across the border', in Herzl's words, or that they would simply 'fold their tents and slip away', to use Zangwill's formulation, soon gave way to more realistic assessments. Between 1937 and 1948 extensive secret discussions of transfer were held in the Zionist movement's highest bodies, including the Zionist Agency Executive, the Twentieth Zionist Congress, the World Convention of Ihud Po'alei Tzion (the top forum of the dominant Zionist world labour movement), and various official and semi-official transfer committees.

Many leading figures justified Arab removal politically and morally as the natural and logical continuation of Zionist colonisation in Palestine. There was a general endorsement of the ethical legitimacy of transfer; the differences centred on the question of compulsory transfer and whether such a course would be practicable (in the late 1930s/early 1940s) without the support of the colonial power, Britain.

From the mid-1930s onwards the 'transfer' solution became central to the assessments of the Jewish Agency (then effectively the government of the Yishuv). The Jewish Agency produced a series of specific plans, generally involving Transjordan, Syria or Iraq. Some of these plans were drafted by three 'transfer committees'. The first two committees, set up by the Yishuv leadership, operated between 1937 and 1944; the third was officially appointed by the Israeli cabinet in August 1948.

As of the late 1930s, some of these transfer plans included proposals for agrarian legislation, citizenship restriction and various taxes designed to encourage Palestinians to transfer 'voluntarily'. However, in the 1930s and early 1940s, Zionist transfer proposals and plans remained largely confined to private and secret talks with British (and occasionally American) senior officials. The Zionist leadership generally refrained from airing the highly sensitive proposals in public. (On one occasion, Weizmann, in a secret meeting with the Soviet ambassador to London, Ivan Mikhailovich Maisky, in February 1941, proposed transferring 1 million Palestinians to Iraq in order to settle Polish Jews in their place.) More importantly, however, during the Mandate period, for reasons of political expediency, the Zionists calculated that such proposals could not be effected without Britain's active support and even actual British implementation. Moreover, the Zionist leadership was tireless in trying to shape the proposals of the Royal (Peel) Commission of 1937, which proposed a 'partition' of Palestine between Jews and Arabs as well as the 'transfer' of the Palestinians from the proposed Jewish state. In the case of Palestine 'transfer' and ethnic cleansing were an integral part of the 1937 proposed 'partition solution'. It has generally escaped the attention of historians that the most significant 'transfer' proposal submitted to the Commission – the one destined to shape the outcome of its findings – was put forward by the Jewish Agency in a secret memorandum containing a specific paragraph on Arab 'transfer' to Transjordan.

In the middle of the war, in May, the Zionist leadership issued the 'Declaration of Independence', which stated: 'the Land of Israel was the birthplace of the Jewish people. Here their spiritual, religious and national identity was formed. Here they ... created a culture of national and universal significance. Here they wrote and gave the Bible to the world.' While the State of Israel itself, according to the Declaration, was founded on the basis of 'natural and historical rights' and on the basis of the November 1947 partition resolution of the UN, it was also supposed to be based 'on the precepts of liberty, justice and peace', as 'taught by the Hebrew prophets'. The Declaration added that the state 'will uphold the full social and political equality of all its citizens, without distinction of race, creed or sex' – but not nationality (Kimmerling 1999: 339-63).

The 'War of Liberation', which led to the creation of the State of Israel on 78 per cent of historic Palestine (not the 55 per cent according to the UN partition resolution), resulted not in 'equality for all citizens' 'as taught by the Hebrew prophets' but in the destruction of much of Palestinian society, and much of the Arab landscape, in the name of the Bible, by the Zionist Yishuv, a European settler community that emigrated to Palestine in the period between 1882 and 1948. The 1948 war was presented by the Zionist leadership in messianic terms as a 'miraculous clearing of the land' and as another 'war of liberation' modelled on the Book of Joshua. The question is, from whom was the land 'liberated'? From the British, whose colonial administration in Palestine after 1918 had alone made it possible for the growth of the European Jewish settlement against the will of the overwhelming majority of Palestinians? Or from its indigenous inhabitants, who had tilled the land and owned the soil for many centuries (Kohn 1958, in Khalidi 2005: 836) and for whom the Bible had become an instrument mandating expulsion (Prior 2002: 44-5, 1997, 1999, 2001).

From the territory occupied by the Israelis in 1948, about 90 per cent of the Palestinians were driven out – many by psychological warfare and/or military pressure and a very large number at gunpoint. The war simply provided the opportunity and the necessary background for the creation of a Jewish state largely free of Arabs. It concentrated Jewish-Zionist minds, and provided the security, military and strategic explanations and justifications for purging the Jewish state and dispossessing the Palestinian people (Masalha 1992, 1997, 2003). Today some 70 per cent of Palestinians are refugees; there are millions of refugees in the Middle East and many more worldwide. In 1948 the minority of Palestinians – 160,000 – who remained behind, many of them internally displaced, became second-class citizens of the State of Israel, subject to a system of military administration by a government that confiscated the bulk of their lands.

The conquest narrative of the Hebrew Bible contains the legend of the Israelites, under the leadership of Joshua, sacking the city of Jericho and killing its inhabitants, after the city's (legendary) walls came tumbling down 'miraculously'. Central to the conquest narrative of the Zionist leadership was the 'miraculous clearing of the land' in 1948. Following the 1948 conquest Ben-Gurion and other leaders invented several foundational myths, including the myth of 'no expulsions', the myth of 'self defence' and the Haganah slogan/myth of 'purity of arms' (see below). The myth of 'no expulsion' was echoed by the first United States ambassador to Israel, James McDonald, who told of a conversation he had with the president of Israel, Chaim Weizmann, during which Weizmann spoke in 'messianic' terms about the 1948 Palestinian exodus as a 'miraculous simplification of Israel's tasks'. McDonald said that not one of Israel's 'big three' – President Weizmann, Prime Minister David Ben-Gurion and Foreign Minister Moshe Sharett – and no responsible Zionist leader had anticipated such a 'miraculous clearing of the land' (MacDonald 1951: 160–61). The available evidence (based on Israeli archival documents), however, shows that the big three had all enthusiastically endorsed the concept of 'transferring' the Palestinians in the 1937–48 period and had anticipated the mass exodus of Palestinians in 1948 and the Nakba.

In the official Zionist rendition of the 1948 war the events are presented as a battle between a Jewish David and an Arab Goliath. As we shall see below, the Israeli 'new historians', including Avi Shlaim, Ilan Pappé and Simha Flapan, reject the myth of David and Goliath. Benny Morris concluded in 1988: 'The stronger side won' (Morris 1988: 21; also Morris 1987: 20–21). Central to key narratives in Israeli culture is the myth that depicts the Israel-Palestine conflict as a 'war of the few against the many'. Since the early twentieth century Zionist historiography has based this narrative of the 'few against-the-many' on the biblical account of Joshua's conquest of ancient Palestine, while mainstream Israeli historians continue to portray the 1948 war as an unequal struggle between a Jewish David against an Arab Goliath, and as a desperate, heroic and ultimately successful Jewish struggle against overwhelming odds.[34] The European Zionist settlers brought with them to Palestine

34. Avi Shlaim, 'The New History of 1948 and the Palestinian Nakba', first published by www.miftah.org,18 March 2004, www.miftah.org/PrinterF.cfm?DocId=3336.

the 'few-against-the-many' narrative – a widespread European
cultural myth which has appeared in many variations, including the
American western cowboy variation of the early twentieth century
(Gertz 2000: 5). Turning the Jewish faith into secular ideology,
Israeli historians and authors have adopted and reinterpreted biblical sources and myths and mobilised them in support of post-1948
Israeli objectives (Gertz 2000: 5). The few, who overcame the many
by virtue of their courage and absolute conviction, were those
European Zionist settlers who emulated the fighters of ancient
Israel, while the many were those Palestinians and Arabs who
were the embodiment of various ancient oppressors. The Zionist
struggle against the indigenous Palestinians was thus portrayed
as a modern re-enactment of ancient biblical battles and wars,
including David's slaying of Goliath, the Hasmonean (Maccabean)
uprising against ancient Greece, and the Jewish wars against the
Romans, with the zealots' last stand at Masada in 73 CE and the
Bar-Kohkva revolt sixty-seven years later (Gertz 2000: 5).

While the David-and-Goliath version of the Israel–Palestine
conflict consolidates its hegemony in the Western media, since
the late 1980s many of the myths that have come to surround the
birth of Israel have nevertheless been challenged by revisionist
Israeli historians, including Flapan (1987), Morris (1987), Pappé
(1992), Shlaim (1988, 2000; Rogan and Shlaim 2001). Furthermore, recent historiography of Palestine–Israel has shown that
the 1948 Palestinian catastrophe was the culmination of over
half a century of often secret Zionist plans and, ultimately, brute
force. The extensive evidence shows a strong correlation between
'transfer' discussions, their practical application in 1948 and the
Palestinian Nakba. The primary responsibility for the displacement and dispossession of three-quarters of a million Palestinian refugees in 1948 lies with the Zionist-Jewish leadership, not
least David Ben-Gurion. The work of revisionist Israeli historians
has contributed to demolishing some of the long-held Israeli and
Western misconceptions surrounding Israel's birth. Containing
remarkable revelations based on Hebrew archival material, their
studies throw new light on the conduct of the Labour Zionist
founding fathers of the Israeli state.

Israeli revisionist historiography (see Chapter 5) shows that in reality throughout the 1948 war the Israeli army outnumbered all the Arab forces, regular and irregular, operating in the Palestine theatre. Estimates vary, but the best suggest that on 15 May 1948 Israel fielded 35,000 troops whereas the Arabs fielded 20–25,000.[35] Moreover, during the war arms imported from the Eastern Bloc – artillery, tanks, aircraft – decisively tipped the military balance in favour of Israel. During the second half of 1948 the Israelis not only outnumbered but also outgunned their opponents. While 'the Arab coalition facing Israel in 1948 was one of the most deeply divided, disorganised and ramshackle coalitions in the history of warfare', the 'final outcome of the war was not a miracle but a reflection of the underlying Arab–Israeli military balance'.[36] Furthermore, since 1948 the Arab–Israeli military imbalance has been illustrated by the fact that Israel (with US backing) has developed the fourth most powerful army in the world and has become the only nuclear power in the region.

Ben-Gurion's 1948 war against the Palestinians was a form of politicide.[37] Ben-Gurion entered the 1948 war with a mindset and premeditation to expel Palestinians. On 19 December 1947, he advised that the Haganah, the Jewish pre-state army, 'adopt the method of aggressive defence; with every [Arab] attack we must be prepared to respond with a decisive blow: the destruction of the [Arab] place or the expulsion of the residents along with the seizure of the place' (Ben-Gurion 1982: 58). There is also plenty of evidence to suggest that as early as the beginning of 1948 his advisers counselled him to wage a total war against the Palestinians, and that he entered the 1948 war with the intention of expelling Palestinians.

First, there was Plan Dalet. This Haganah plan, a straightforward document, of early March 1948, was in many ways a blueprint for the expulsion of as many Palestinians as possible. It constituted an ideological-strategic anchor and basis for the destruction of

---

35. Ibid.
36. Ibid.
37. The term 'politicide' is used by Kimmerling in connection with Ariel Sharon's war against the Palestinians (2003).

Arab localities and expulsion of their inhabitants by Jewish commanders. In conformity with Plan Dalet, the Haganah cleared various areas completely of Arab villages.

Second, the general endorsement of transfer schemes and the attempt to promote them secretly by mainstream Labour leaders, some of whom played a decisive role in the 1948 war, highlights the ideological intent that made the 1948 refugee exodus possible. Ben-Gurion in particular emerges as both a persistent advocate of compulsory transfer in the late 1930s and the great expeller of the Palestinians in 1948 (Masalha 1992; Morris 1987; Flapan 1987; Segev 1986; Pappé 1992; Shlaim 1996; Rogan and Shlaim 2001). In 1948 there was no need for any cabinet decision to drive the Palestinians out. Ben-Gurion and senior Zionist military commanders, such as Yigal Allon, Moshe Carmel, Yigael Yadin, Moshe Dayan, Moshe Kalman and Yitzhak Rabin, played a key role in the expulsions. Everyone, at every level of military and political decision-making, understood that the objective was a Jewish state without a large Arab minority.

Ben-Gurion, who was personally responsible for many of the myths surrounding 1948, had this to say in the Israeli Knesset debate of 11 October 1961:

> The Arabs' exit from Palestine ... began immediately after the UN resolution, from the areas earmarked for the Jewish state. And we have explicit documents testifying that they left Palestine following instructions by the Arab leaders, with the *Mufti* at their head, under the assumption that the invasion of the Arab armies at the expiration of the Mandate will destroy the Jewish state and push all the Jews into the sea, dead or alive.[38]

Ben-Gurion was propagating two myths: (a) there were orders from the neighbouring Arab states and the Haj Amin Al-Husseini, the Mufti of Jerusalem, for the Palestinians to evacuate their homes and lands on the promise that the Arab armies would destroy the nascent Jewish state; (b) that those armies intended to 'push all the Jews into the sea, dead or alive'. Ben-Gurion gave no attribution for

---

38. Quoted in William Martin, 'Who is Pushing Whom into the Sea?', 11 March 2005, www.counterpunch.org/martin03112005.html; accessed 14 March 2005.

this phrase; nor did he claim that it was a quotation from an Arab source. Since the Second World War the Jewish Holocaust/Shoah had been used as a legitimiser of Zionism. However, the phrase 'push all the Jews into the sea' – a highly emotive phrase invoking images of the Holocaust, though adapted to a Mediterranean setting – has since acquired extraordinary mythical dimensions as it is constantly invoked by Israelis and Zionists to justify Israel's policies towards the Palestinians as well as the continuing colonisation of the West Bank and East Jerusalem.[39]

Although Ben-Gurion and his commanders did not drive the Palestinians into the sea, they did drive them from their homes, villages and ancestral lands, and from Palestine into squalid refugee camps. The irony of Ben-Gurion's 'chilling phrase' should not escape us. He demanded deference to a fictitious intention on the part of the Palestinians and Arabs[40] while denying his own direct and personal involvement in the very real expulsion of the Palestinians.

In 1948 more than half of the Palestinians were driven from their towns and villages, mainly by a deliberate Israeli policy of 'transfer' and ethnic cleansing. The name 'Palestine' disappeared from the map. To complete this transformation of the country, in August 1948 a de facto 'Transfer Committee' was officially (though secretly) appointed by the Israeli cabinet to plan the Palestinian refugees' organised resettlement in the Arab states. The three-member committee was composed of 'Ezra Danin, a former senior Haganah intelligence officer and a senior Foreign Ministry adviser on Arab affairs since July 1948; Zalman Lifschitz, the prime minister's adviser on land matters; and Yosef Weitz (born in Russia in 1890, emigrated to Palestine in 1908), head of the Jewish National Fund's land settlement department, as head of the Committee. The main Israeli propaganda lines regarding the Palestinian refugees and some of the myths of 1948 were cooked up by members of this official Transfer Committee. Besides doing everything possible to reduce the Palestinian population in Israel,

39. Ibid.
40. Ibid.

Weitz and his colleagues sought in October 1948 to amplify and
consolidate the demographic transformation of Palestine by:

• preventing Palestinian refugees from returning to their homes
  and villages;
• destroying Arab villages;
• settling Jews in Arab villages and towns and distributing Arab
  lands among Jewish settlements;
• extricating Jews from Iraq and Syria;
• seeking ways to ensure the absorption of Palestinian refugees
  in Arab countries and launching a propaganda campaign to
  discourage Arab return.

Apparently, Prime Minister Ben-Gurion approved of these proposals, although he recommended that all the Palestinian refugees
be resettled in one Arab country, preferably Iraq, rather than
dispersed among the neighbouring states. Ben-Gurion was also
set against refugee resettlement in neighbouring Transjordan
(Morris 1986b: 549-50).

An abundance of archival documents show a strong correlation
between the Zionist 'transfer'/ethnic cleansing solution and the
1948 Palestinian Nakba. By the end of the 1948 war, hundreds of
villages had been completely depopulated and their houses blown
up or bulldozed. The main objective was to prevent the return
of refugees to their homes, but the destruction also helped to
perpetuate the Zionist myth that Palestine was virtually empty
territory before the Jews entered. An exhaustive study by a team
of Palestinian field researchers and academics under the direction
of Walid Khalidi details the destruction of 418 villages falling
inside the 1949 armistice lines. The study gives the circumstances
of each village's occupation and depopulation, and a description
of what remains. Khalidi's team visited all except fourteen sites,
made comprehensive reports and took photographs. The result is
both a monumental study and a kind of memorial. It is an acknowledgement of the enormous suffering of hundreds of thousands of
Palestinian refugees (Khalidi 1992a).

1948: A Pattern of Repeated Atrocities

Thirty minutes by car from Tel Aviv is the Israeli-Palestinian village of Kafr Qasim, where on 29 October 1956 Israeli border guards murdered in cold blood forty-nine villagers (mostly women and children) returning from their fields. In *Good Arabs*, Hillel Cohen writes: 'In addition to preventing the [Israeli] Arabs from commemorating the massacre of Kafr Qasim, Israel manipulated the inhabitants to participate in a formal *sulha* (forgiveness ceremony) with state officials [in] 1957' (2010: 144).

But the trauma continued after the establishment of Israel. The pattern of Israeli massacres of Palestinian civilians established in 1948 has been maintained: for example, the massacres at Qibya in October 1953;[41] the al-Azazme tribes in March 1955;[42] Kafr Qasim on 29 October 1956;[43] Samo'a in the 1960s; the villages of the Galilee during Land Day on 30 March 1976; Sabra and Shatila on 16–18 September 1982;[44] al-Khalil (Hebron) on 25 February 1994;[45] Kfar Qana in 1999, Wadi Ara in 2000; the Jenin refugee camp on 13 April 2002;[46] the mass killing during the popular Palestinian uprisings (intifadas) against Israeli occupation in the West Bank and Gaza (1987–1993 and 2000–2002);[47] Gaza (December 2008–January 2009);[48] the Gaza flotilla raid on 31 May 2010.[49] As

---

41. Israeli troops of the notorious Unit 101 of the Israeli army, under the command of Ariel Sharon, attacked the West Bank village of Qibya, killing 69 Palestinians, many while hiding in houses blown up over their heads; 45 houses, a school, and a mosque were also destroyed (Shlaim 2000: 90–93; Morris 1997: 257–76; Chomsky 1983: 383–5).

42. Members of the Azazmeh tribe, including women and children, suffered a massacre at the hands of Unit 101.

43. The Israeli Border Guard massacred 48 Arab citizens, including 6 women and 23 children aged 8–17.

44. The large-scale massacre of Palestinian civilians by the Israeli-allied Kataib Lebanese militia; estimates of those killed are between 800 and 3,500.

45. The massacre of 29 Muslim worshippers in Hebron by a fundamentalist Jewish settler Dr Baruch Goldstein.

46. The Israeli army attacked the camp using bulldozers, tanks and Apache helicopters; estimates of the dead included hundreds of children, women and men, although the exact toll is not known as many bodies were buried under the rubble.

47. Tens of thousands of Palestinians have been killed and injured by the Israeli army since the first intifada of 1987.

48. Palestinian human rights organisations reported that 1,417 people were killed, including more than 900 civilians.

49. Nine of the international activists board the flotilla's largest ship, the MV *Mavi Marmara* were killed by Israeli commandos; dozens were wounded and hundreds were arrested.

Ilan Pappé shows in the *The Ethnic Cleansing of Palestine*, 'in addition there are the numerous killings Betselem, Israel's leading human rights organisation, keeps track of. There has never been an end to Israel's killing of Palestinians' (2006: 258).

Raphael Lemkin, a Polish Jewish lawyer and scholar, was best known for his work on genocide. He first used the word in print in *Axis Rule in Occupied Europe: Laws of Occupation – Analysis of Government – Proposals for Redress* (1944). In his unpublished history of genocide, Lemkin points to recurring features of historical genocides: deportations under harsh conditions often involving forced marches; attacks on family life; mass mutilations involving the separation of men and women and denial of the right to procreate; removal and transfer of children; destruction of political leadership; death from illness, hunger and disease through overcrowding on reserves and in concentration camps (Curthoys and Docker 2008: 12).

Characterised by politicide, the ethnic cleansing of 1948 included the destruction of much of Palestinian society and mass killing, with scores of massacres carried out in 1948, including mutilation (in Dayr Yasin); hundreds of Palestinians died from illness, thirst and exhaustion during the 'death march' – the mass deportation of the inhabitants of the twin towns of Lydda and Ramle (a former capital of Palestine, founded *c.* 705–715 by the Muslim Umayyad Caliph Suleiman ibn Abd al-Malik) during the hot summer of 1948:[50]

> Quite a few refugees died – from exhaustion, dehydration and disease – along the roads eastwards, from Lydda and Ramleh, before reaching temporary rest near and in Ramallah. Nimr Khatib put the death toll among the Lydda refugees during the trek eastward at 335; Arab Legion commander John Glubb Pasha more carefully wrote that 'nobody will ever know how many children died'.[51]

---

50. See also below; also Audeh G. Rantisi and Charles Amash, 'The Lydda Death March', *Americans for Middle East Understanding* 33, no. 3, July–August 2000, www.ameu.org/summary1.asp?iid=64.

51. Donald Neff, 'Expulsion of the Palestinians – Lydda and Ramleh in 1948', *Washington Report on Middle East Affairs*, July–August 1994, www.washington-report.org/backissues/0794/9407072.htm.

The 1948 war proved that engineering mass evacuation was not possible without perpetrating a large number of massacres.

The pattern of massacres and ethnic cleansing and the traumatic memory of the Nakba are at the heart of the contrast between indigenous Palestinian and Israeli settler collective memories of 1948. Zionism's self-perception is based on a morally and ethically superior European (white) immigrant/community (armed with the Hebrew Bible and superior claims of 'divine rights' and 'promised lands') whose basic war ethics were based on the so-called 'purity of arms' (*tohar haneshek*) – a slogan initially coined by the Jewish forces of the Haganah and Palmah during the 1948 war. Although this myth was fundamentally questioned by the Israeli revisionist historians in the face of the evidence (see Chapter 7), it has never been abandoned by Israeli official spokespersons and has in fact remained central to Israeli official *hasbara*/propaganda industry in the West (Prior 1999: 208–10).

In the period between the mid-1930s and 1948, the Yishuv Labour leadership had embraced the concept of 'transfer' while quietly pondering the question of whether there was a 'more humane way' of expelling the indigenous Palestinians. In *Land and Power: The Zionist Resort to Power*, Anita Shapira shows that already during the Great Palestinian Rebellion of 1936–39 the Zionist leadership abandoned the slogan of *havlaga* – a restrained and proportionate response – and legitimised the use of terror against Palestinian civilians: the Zionist nationalist end justified the means (Shapira 1992: 247–9, 350).

The massacre of Dayr Yasin (9 April) and other Zionist atrocities in 1948 have 'left an indelible mark of horror in Palestinian memory' (Ateek: 1989: 31). Benny Morris admits, in a 2004 article in *Haaretz* entitled 'Survival of the Fittest', that the 1948 events constitute ethnic cleansing.[52] He also suggests that 'twenty four' Israeli massacres were perpetrated in 1948[53] – although the 'atrocities were limited in size, scope and time' (Morris 2004: 482).

---

52. Ari Shavit, 'Survival of the Fittest? An Interview with Benny Morris', *Haaretz*, 9 January 2004.
53. Ibid.

Dr Saleh Abdel Jawad, director (1994-97) of Birzeit University's Centre for Research and Documentation, who has compiled a list of sixty-eight massacres in the period 1947-49 – a list largely based on Palestinian oral history (Abdel Jawad 2007: 59-127) – however, has shown that the size and significance of the 1948 atrocities were far beyond the scope previously recorded by historians. According to Israeli military historian Arieh Yitzhaki (a former director of the Israeli army's archives) about ten major massacres (of more than fifty victims each) and about a hundred smaller massacres were committed by Jewish forces in 1948-49. Yitzhaki argues that these massacres, large and small, had a devastating impact on the Palestinian population by inducing and precipitating the Palestinian exodus. Yitzhaki suggests that in almost every village there were murders (Masalha 2003: 32). Another Israeli historian, Uri Milstein, corroborates Yitzhaki's assessment and goes even further to suggest that each battle in 1948 ended with a massacre: 'In all Israel's wars, massacres were committed but I have no doubt that the War of Independence was the dirtiest of them all.'[54]

At the same time, however, pursuing empirical research doggedly, Morris's work has documented more Israeli massacres of Palestinians and a dozen or so cases of rape by Israeli soldiers (Morris 2004). In an interview in *Haaretz* of 9 January 2004 ('Survival of the Fittest'), he even acknowledges a pattern of atrocities in the Galilee:

> In some cases four or five people were executed, in others the numbers were 70, 80, 100. There was also a great deal of arbitrary killing. Two old men are spotted walking in a field – they are shot. A woman is found in an abandoned village – she is shot. There are cases such as the village of Dawayima [in the Hebron region], in which a column entered the village with all guns blazing and killed anything that moved. The worst cases were Saliha (70-80 killed), Deir Yassin (100-110), Lod [Lydda] (250), Dawayima (hundreds) and perhaps Abu Shusha (70). There is no unequivocal proof of a large-scale massacre at Tantura, but war crimes were perpetrated there. At Jaffa there was a massacre about which nothing had been known until now. The same at Arab al Muwassi, in the north. About half of the acts of massacre were part of Operation

---

54. Guy Erlich in *Ha'ir*, 6 May 1992.

Hiram [in the north, in October 1948]: at Safsaf, Saliha, Jish, Eilaboun, Arab al Muwasi, Deir al Asad, Majdal Krum, Sasa. In Operation Hiram there was an unusually high concentration of executions of people against a wall or next to a well in an orderly fashion.

Morris adds:

That can't be chance. It's a pattern. Apparently, various officers who took part in the operation understood that the expulsion order they received permitted them to do these deeds in order to encourage the population to take to the roads. The fact is that no one was punished for these acts of murder. Ben-Gurion silenced the matter. He covered up for the officers who did the massacres.[55]

Both Israeli 'new history' (Chapter 5) and Palestinian oral testimonies (Chapter 6) confirm that in almost every Palestinian village occupied by the Haganah and other Jewish militias during 1948-49, war atrocities – murders, execution of prisoners and rape – were committed (Finkelstein 1995: 110-12; Prior 1999: 208-9). In *The Ethnic Cleansing of Palestine*, Ilan Pappé, commenting on the massacres carried out by Jewish forces during the Nakba, writes:

Palestinian sources, combining Israeli military archives with oral histories, list thirty-one confirmed massacres – beginning with the massacre in Tirat Haifa on 11 December 1947 and ending with Khirbat Illin in the Hebron area on 19 January 1949 – and there may have been at least another six. We still do not have a systematic Nakba memorial archive that would allow one to trace the names of all those who died in the massacres. (Pappé 2006: 258)

Dayr Yasin, 9 April 1948

The most striking outcome of the combined evidence coming from the 'new history' of Israel and oral testimonies of the Palestinian refugees is the shifting of the discourse away from the traditional Zionist interpretation of the Dayr Yasin massacre as 'exceptional'. The focus of study is no longer so much on the terrorism carried out by the Irgun Tzvai Leumi (National Military Organisation,

55. Shavit, 'Survival of the Fittest? An Interview with Benny Morris'.

or Irgun), the military arm of Betar Zionism, and Lehi irregular forces before and during the 1948 war, but on the conduct of the mainstream Haganah/Palmah and Israeli Defence Force (IDF). At issue are the roles and involvement of the Haganah and the Israeli army in the numerous atrocities of 1948. Palestinian scholars Saleh Abdel aJawad and Sharif Kanaana (of Birzeit University) have documented through eyewitness oral testimonies a pattern of massacres in 1948. Abdel Jawad comments:

> When the pattern of massacres is considered in its entirely, I argue that it is enough to demonstrate a centralised Zionist/Israeli policy of ethnic cleansing, even without "smoking gun" documents attesting to such a centralised policy. (Abdel Jawad: 2007: 61-2)

Kanaana places the massacre of Dayr Yasin and the evacuation of Arab West Jerusalem in 1948 within the framework of what he terms the Zionists' 'maxi-massacre pattern' in their conquest of large Palestinian cities: Jewish attacks produced demoralisation and exodus; a nearby massacre would result in panic and further flight, greatly facilitating the occupation of the Arab city and its surrounding towns and villages (Kanaana 1992: 108).

Although not the bloodiest massacre of the war, Dayr Yasin was the site of the most notorious mass murder of Palestinian civilians in 1948 – an event which became the single most important contributory factor to the 1948 exodus, a powerful marker of the violence at the foundation of the State of Israel. On 9 April, between 120 and 254 unarmed villagers were murdered, including women, the elderly and children.[56] There were also instances of rape and mutilation. Most Israeli writers today have no difficulty in acknowledging the occurrence of the Dayr Yasin massacre and its effect, if not its intention, of precipitating the exodus. However, most of these writers take refuge in the fact that the wholesale killing was committed by 'dissidents' of the Irgun, then commanded by Menahem Begin[57] (later prime minister of Israel), and Lehi, then

---

56. The number of those massacred at Dayr Yasin is subject to dispute. The widely accepted death toll has been that reported in the *New York Times* of 13 April 1948: 254 persons.

57. Begin sent a congratulatory note to the Irgun fighters who had carried out the

co-commanded by Yitzhak Shamir (who would also later become prime minister of Israel), thus exonerating Ben-Gurion's Haganah, the mainstream Zionist military force. Recently published Hebrew material, however, shows that: (a) in January 1948, the mukhtar of Dayr Yasin and other village notables had reached a non-aggression agreement with the Haganah and the neighbouring Jewish settlements of Giva't Shaul and Montefiori; (b) the Irgun's assault on the village on 9 April had the full backing of the Haganah commander of Jerusalem, David Shaltiel, who not only chose to break his agreement with the villagers, but also provided rifles and ammunition for the Irgunists; (c) the Haganah contributed to the assault on the village by providing artillery cover; (d) a Haganah intelligence officer in Jerusalem, Meir Pa'il, was dispatched to Dayr Yasin to assess the effectiveness and performance of the Irgun forces (Masalha 1988: 122-3; Morris 1987: 113-15).

Although the actual murders of the non-combatant villagers were carried out by Lehi and the Irgun, the Haganah must share responsibility for the atrocity (Masalha 1988: 122-3). The massacre was roundly condemned by liberal Jewish intellectuals, most prominent of which was Martin Buber, who wrote repeatedly to prime minister and defence minister Ben-Gurion about Dayr Yasin. In one of his letters, Buber, together with three Jewish scholars, asked Ben-Gurion to leave Dayr Yasin uninhabited. Ben-Gurion chose not to respond to this proposal. Eventually his secretary replied that the prime minister had been too busy to read the letter (Ellis 1999: 32). Ben-Gurion was, at the same time, explicitly sanctioning the expulsions of the Palestinians.

Also, crucially, the recently published Israeli material shows that Dayr Yasin was only one of many massacres carried out by Jewish forces (mainly the Haganah and the IDF) in 1948. Recent research proves that the Palestinians were less prone to evacuate their towns and villages in the second half of the war. Hence the numerous massacres committed from June 1948 onwards, all of which were aimed at forcing mass evacuation.

Dayr Yasin massacre: 'Accept congratulations on this splendid act of conquest. Tell the soldiers you have made history in Israel'; quoted in Ellis 1999: 31.

Rape and Sexual Assault by Jewish Forces in 1948

The use of rape and other forms of sexual violence by Jewish forces in 1948 as weapons of war and instruments of ethnic cleansing has yet to be studied. In 1948 the rape of Arab women and girls was not a rare or isolated act committed by individual forces, but rather was used deliberately as an instrument to terrorise the civilian population and push people into fleeing their homes. In Arab society sexual violence is often associated with shame and family dishonour, and in 1948 rape and fear of rape had a devastating impact on Palestinian society. But precisely because of the shame and humiliation attached to this issue, it has remained under-reported and under-investigated.

Some of the survivors from the Dayr Yasin massacre were driven by the Irgun in a triumphal procession around Jewish Jerusalem and then shot. Surviving women gave harrowing descriptions of their experiences to investigating Red Cross and British Mandate officials. One British investigator, Richard Catling, described how difficult it was to persuade terrified women to describe their ordeal and that of other women who did not survive:

> I interviewed many of the womenfolk in order to glean some information on any atrocities committed in Deir Yasseen but the majority of those women are very shy and reluctant to relate their experiences especially in matters concerning sexual assault and they need great coaxing before they will divulge any information. The recording of statements is hampered also by the hysterical state of the women who often break down ... while the statement is being recorded. There is, however, no doubt that many sexual atrocities were committed by the attacking Jews. Many young schoolgirls were raped and later slaughtered. Old women were also molested. One story is current concerning a case in which a young girl was literally torn into two. Many infants were also butchered and killed. (quoted in Sayigh 1979: 76)

Benny Morris explains that the dozen cases of Israeli rape reported in 1948 were only the 'tip of the iceberg':

> In Acre four soldiers raped a girl and murdered her and her father. In Jaffa, soldiers of the Kiryati Brigade raped one girl and tried to rape several more. At Hunin, which is in the Galilee, two girls were raped

and then murdered. There were one or two cases of rape at Tantura, south of Haifa. There was one case of rape at Qula, in the centre of the country. At the village of Abu Shusha, near Kibbutz Gezer [in the Ramle area] there were four female prisoners, one of whom was raped a number of times. And there were other cases. Usually more than one soldier was involved. Usually there were one or two Palestinian girls. In a large proportion of the cases the event ended with murder. Because neither the victims nor the rapists liked to report these events, we have to assume that the dozen cases of rape that were reported, which I found, are not the whole story. They are just the tip of the iceberg.[58]

In 1948, al-Dawayma, situated in the western Hebron hills, was a very large village, with a population of some 3,500 people. Like Dayr Yasin, al-Dawayma was unarmed. It was captured on 29 October 1948 without a fight. The massacre of between eighty and one hundred villagers was carried out at the end of October 1948, not in the heat of the battle but after the Israeli army had clearly emerged victorious in the war. The testimony of Israeli soldiers present during the atrocities establishes that IDF troops under Moshe Dayan entered the village and liquidated civilians, throwing their victims into pits. 'The children they killed by breaking their heads with sticks. There was not a house without dead.' The remaining Arabs were then shut up in houses 'without food and water' as the village was systematically razed. 'One commander ordered a sapper to put two old women in a certain house ... and blow up the house ... One soldier boasted that he had raped a woman and then shot her. One woman, with a newborn baby in her arms, was employed to clear the courtyard where the soldiers ate. She worked a day or two. In the end they shot her and her baby' (Morris 1987: 222-3). Evidence from several sources indicates that the atrocities were committed in and around the village, including at the mosque and in a nearby cave, that houses with old people locked inside were blown up, and that there were several cases of the rape and shooting of women (Masalha 1988: 127-30; Morris 1987: 222-3; Khalidi 1999).

---

58. Shavit, 'Survival of the Fittest? An Interview with Benny Morris'.

The Galilee Atrocities

The evidence surrounding the Galilee expulsions shows clearly the existence of a pattern of actions characterised by a large number of massacres deigned to intimidate the population into flight. On 29-31 October 1948, the Israeli army, in a large military campaign named Operation Hiram, conquered the last significant Arab-held pocket of the Galilee. According to new Israeli archival material, commanding officers issued expulsion directives: 'there was a central directive by Northern Front [command] to clear the conquered pocket of its Arab inhabitants' (Morris 1999: 70). The operation was characterised by murder and a range of brutalities carried out against the Palestinian civilian population (Morris 1995: 44-62, 1999: 68-76). On 6 November 1948, Yosef Nahmani, director of the Jewish National Fund office in the eastern Galilee between 1935 and 1965 and one of the most prolific Zionist diarists, toured the newly conquered areas. He was accompanied by Immanuel Fried of Israel's Minority Affairs Ministry, who briefed him on 'the cruel acts of our soldiers', which Nahmani recorded in his diary:

> In Safsaf, after ... the inhabitants had raised a white flag, the [soldiers] collected and separated the men and women, tied the hands of fifty–sixty *fellahin* [peasants] and shot and killed them and buried them in a pit. Also, they raped several women ... At Eilaboun and Farradiya the soldiers had been greeted with white flags and rich food, and afterwards had ordered the villagers to leave, with their women and children. When the [villagers] had begun to argue ... [the soldiers] had opened fire and after some thirty people were killed had begun to lead the rest [towards Lebanon].... In Saliha, where a white flag had been raised... they had killed about sixty–seventy men and women. Where did they come by such a measure of cruelty, like Nazis? ... Is there no more humane way of expelling the inhabitants than such methods? (Morris 1999: 55)

The Galilee atrocities in 1948 included: Safsaf, Jish, Sa'sa', Saliha, 'Eilabun, Majd al-Kurum, Dayr al-Asad, al-Bi'ene, Nasr al-Din, 'Ayn Zaytun and Kabri. The list below is only a partial inventory of other massacres committed in the Galilee and in other parts of the country, based on Palestinian oral history and Israeli and British archival documents.

- Balad al-Shaykh, 11 December 1947 and 31 December–1 January 1948: 14 civilians, of whom 10 were women and children were killed in the second attack by the Haganah.
- Jaffa Municipality and Welfare Centre, 4 January 1947: 17 Arab civilians were killed by attack by Lehi.
- Semiramis Hotel, Jerusalem, 5 January 1948: the Haganah blew up the hotel; 12 Arab civilians were killed, among them 4 women and 5 children.
- Nasr al-Din, 12 April 1948: a widely documented massacre by the Haganah.
- Ramle, 20 February 1948: an attack by the Irgun, killing 6 Arab civilians and wounding 31. Among the killed were 4 children.
- Qisarya (Caesarea), February 1948: the 4th Battalion of the Palmah forces, under the command of Yosef Tabenkin, conquered Qisarya. According to historian Uri Milstein, all those who did not escape from the village were murdered.
- Al-Husayniyya, 12 March and 16–17 March 1948: the Palmah 3rd Battalion twice attacked the village in upper Galilee. In the first attack, 15 Arabs were killed, including 10 women and children and 20 seriously wounded. In the second raid more than 30 Arab civilians were killed.
- Safad, 4 May 1948: a few days before the conquest of Safad, some 37 young men were among the 70 Arab detainees massacred by two Palmah 3rd Battalion soldiers.
- Abu Shusha, 14 May 1948: evidence of a large-scale massacre.
- Acre, 18 May 1948: according to a United Nations Observer from France, Lieutenant Petite, at least 100 Palestinians were murdered (Palumbo 1987: 119).
- Kabri, 20 May 1948: the Carmeli Brigade conquered the village of Kabri. One of the Israeli soldiers, Yehuda Rashef, got hold of a few youngsters, ordered them to fill up some ditches and then lined them up and fired at them with a machine gun. A few died but some of the wounded managed to escape.
- Al-Tantura, 22–23 May 1948: between 70 and 200 Palestinian civilians were killed (Fearn 2006: 424), in a large-scale, well-planned massacre; the atrocities were perpetrated by the 33rd Battalion of the Alexandroni Brigade of the IDF.

- Lydda, 11-12 July 1948: one of the bloodiest atrocities of 1948. According to Israeli historian Yoav Gelber, Dayr Yasin 'was not the worst of the war's atrocities ... the massacre of approximately 250 Arabs in Lydda ... took place following capitulation and not in the midst of combat' (Gelber 2001: 116, 162). Dozens of unarmed civilians who were detained in the Dahmash Mosque and church premises of the town were gunned down and murdered. One official Israeli source put the casualty figures at 250 dead and many injured. It is likely, however, that somewhere between 250 and 400 Arabs were killed in this IDF massacre; and an estimated 350 more died in the subsequent expulsion and forced march of the townspeople. On 6 May 1992, *Hebrew* daily published new revelations about the atrocities committed by the Palmah soldiers at Lydda. After Lydda gave up the fight, a group of stubborn Arab fighters barricaded themselves in the small mosque; the Israeli army gave an order to fire a number of shells at the mosque. The soldiers who forced their way into the mosque were surprised to find no resistance. Under the destroyed walls of the mosque they found the remains of the Arab fighters. A group of between twenty and fifty Arab civilians was brought to clean up the mosque and bury the remains. After they had finished their work, they were shot into the graves they had dug.
- Asdud, end August 1948: the Israeli army murdered 10 Arab fellahin in cold blood.
- Suqrir, 29 August 1948: 10 Arabs were killed by the Giva Brigade of the IDF (Morris 2004: 215).
- Safsaf, 29 October 1948: 50-70 were killed by the IDF.
- Al-Dawayma, 29 October 1948: 80-100 were killed by the IDF.
- Saliha, 30 October 1948: 70-80 were killed by the IDF.
- Majd El-Krum, 30 October 1948: 9 people, including 2 women, were murdered by the IDF (Palumbo 1987: 171).
- 'Eilabun, 30 October 1948: 13 were murdered by the Golani Brigade of the IDF (Palumbo 1987: 164; also Morris 1987: 229).
- Hula, October 1948: 35-58 were killed by the Cameli Brigade of the IDF.
- 'Arab al-Mawasi (eastern Galilee), 2 November 1948: 14 bedouin tribesmen were massacred by the IDF (Morris 2001: 57).

Dayr Yasin and other atrocities committed by the Israeli army in the Galilee prompted Israel's first minister of agriculture, Aharon Zisling (of the Mapam party), to say this at a cabinet meeting on 17 November 1948: 'I often disagree when the term Nazi was applied to the British ... even though the British committed Nazi crimes. But now Jews too have behaved like Nazis and my entire being has been shaken' (Segev 1986: 26). He held Ben-Gurion responsible for the destruction of Palestinian villages. His internal criticism was followed by the publication of a letter to the *New York Times* of 4 December 1948 by a group of Jewish intellectuals, including Albert Einstein, condemning the 'fascist' methods of the Irgun and Stern gangs that 'inaugurated a reign of terror in the Palestine Jewish community'.

Sixty-two years later, in July 2010, the daily *Haaretz* reported that Prime Minister Binyamin Netanyahu had extended the period for which material contained in government and state archives would remain classified by another twenty years. The new regulations mean that archived material scheduled to become available to researchers and the public after fifty years would now remain classified for seventy years. Many of these documents relate to the first two decades of the State of Israel. Apparently the Israeli internal security services (Shin Bet) – whose chief answers directly to the prime minister – and other security services exerted considerable pressure on the government to prevent the archives' opening. Yehoshua Freundlich, of the Israel State Archive authorities, told the daily *Haaretz* that some of the material was selected to remain classified because 'it has implications over [Israel's] adherence to international law'.[59] Israeli historian Tom Segev pointed out in a book review in *Haaretz* of 9 July 2010 that official Israeli documents on the war crimes carried out by Jewish forces in 1948, including in the notorious massacre Dayr Yasin, are still being kept secret by the Israeli state; this refusal to declassify the documents is backed by the Israeli Supreme Court.[60]

---

59. Barak David, 'State archives to stay classified for 20 more years, PM instructs', *Haaretz*, 29 July 2010, www.haaretz.com/print-edition/news/state-archives-to-stay-classified-for-20-more-years-pm-instructs-1.304449.

60. Tom Segev, *Haaretz*, 9 July 2010, www.haaretz.co.il/hasite/spages/1177968.html.

2

The Memoricide of the Nakba: Zionist-Hebrew Toponymy and the De-Arabisation of Palestine

Silencing the Palestinian Past

The Palestinians share common experiences with other indigenous peoples who have had their narrative denied, their material culture destroyed and their histories erased or reinvented by European white settlers and colonisers. In *The Invasion of America* (1976), Francis Jennings highlights the hegemonic narratives of the European white settlers by pointing out that for generations historians wrote about the indigenous peoples of America from an attitude of cultural superiority that erased or distorted the actual history of the indigenous peoples and their relations with the European settlers. In *Decolonizing Methodologies: Research and Indigenous Peoples*, Maori scholar Linda Tuhiwai Smith (1999) argues that the impact of European colonialism is continuing to hurt and destroy indigenous peoples; that the negation of indigenous views of history played a crucial role in asserting colonial ideology, partly because such perspectives were regarded as incorrect or primitive, but primarily because 'they challenged and resisted the mission of colonisation' (1999: 29). As Smith states:

> Under colonialism indigenous peoples have struggled against a Western view of history and yet been complicit with the view. We have often allowed our 'histories' to be told and have then become outsiders as

we heard them being retold ... Maps of the world reinforced our place on the periphery of the world, although we were still considered part of the Empire. This included having to learn new names for our lands. Other symbols of our loyalty, such as the flag, were also an integral part of the imperial curriculum. Our orientation to the world was already being redefined as we were being excluded systematically from the writing of the history of our own lands. (1999: 33)

In *The Ethnic Cleansing of Palestine* (2006) the concept of cultural memoricide is deployed by historian Ilan Pappé, who highlights the systematic scholarly, political and military attempt in post-1948 Israel to de-Arabise the Palestinian terrain; its names, ecology and religious sites; its village, town and cityscapes; and its cemeteries, fields, and olive and orange groves. Pappé conceives of a metaphorical palimpsest at work here, the erasure of the history of one people in order to write that of another people over it; the reduction of many layers to a single layer (2006: 225–34).

Zionist methods have not only dispossessed the Palestinians of their own land; they have also attempted to deprive Palestinians of their voice and their knowledge of their own history. Despite its distinct features and nationalist ideology, Zionist colonisation in Palestine followed the general trajectory of European colonialist projects in Asia, Africa and Latin America: taking another people's land, while seeking to remove or subjugate the indigenous inhabitants (Masalha 2007: 16). The founding myths of Israel have dictated the conceptual removal of Palestinians before, during and after their physical removal in 1948; the invention of euphemisms such as 'transfer' and 'present absentees' have been discussed elsewhere.[1] The de-Arabisation of Palestine, the erasure of Palestinian history and elimination of the Palestinians' collective memory by the Israeli state are no less violent than the ethnic cleansing of the Palestinians in 1948 and the destruction of historic Palestine: this elimination is central to the construction of a hegemonic collective Israeli-Zionist-Jewish identity in the State of Israel (Pappé 2005: 287).

---

1. See Masalha 1992, 1997, 2000, 2005a; Gabriel Piterberg, 'Erasure', *New Left Review* 10, July–August 2001, www.newleftreview.net/NLR24402.shtml#_edn23; accessed 16 September 2004.

Palestinian responses to the forced depopulation, dispossession
and ethnic cleansing of their villages and towns are 'discursively
rich, complex and protean'.[2] In recent decades novels, poems, films,
plays, ethnographic and photographic documentation, maps, oral
history archives, online websites, and a wide range of activities in
exiled and internally displaced communities have been and are
being produced, many with the aim of countering Israeli denial and
correcting distortions of omission and commission that eradicate
the Palestinian presence in the land. Also, a large number of books
have been produced, both inside Israel and at Birzeit University,
dedicated to villages depopulated and destroyed by Israel. These
form part of a large historical and imaginative literature in which
the destroyed Palestinian villages are 'revitalised and their existence celebrated'.[3]

Palestinian commemoration of the fiftieth anniversary of the
Nakba and protest against the dismemberment of Palestine, in
Jerusalem in 1998, was reported by the *New York Times*, under
the headline 'Mideast Turmoil: In Jerusalem Israeli Police in a
Clash with Arabs'. The newspaper quoted an anniversary message broadcast over the Ramallah-based Palestinian Radio by
Mahmoud Darwish, the Palestinian national poet and the single
most influential Palestinian narrator of recent decades, saying 'We
have triumphed over the plan to expel us from history.'[4] On the
same fiftieth anniversary, Palestinian author Dr Salman Abu-Sitta
produced and distributed a map showing that Palestinian refugees
departed from 531 villages in what was Mandatory Palestine. *All
That Remains* details the destruction and depopulation of hundreds of villages in 1948 and gives the circumstances of each
village's occupation. Of the 418 depopulated villages documented
by Khalidi, 293 (70 per cent) were totally destroyed and 90 (22
per cent) were largely destroyed. Seven survived, including 'Ayn

2. Susan Slyomovics, 'The Gender of Transposed Space', *Palestine–Israel Journal of Politics, Economics and Culture* 9, no. 4, 2002, www.pij.org/details.php?id=114.
3. Ibid.
4. Joel Greenberg, 'Mideast in Turmoil: In Jerusalem Israeli Police in a Clash with Arabs', 15 May 1998, *New York Times*, http://query.nytimes.com/gst/fullpage.html?res=9806EEDB1330F936A25756C0A96E958260&scp=24&sq=Mahmoud%20Darwish&st=cse.

Karim (west of Jerusalem), but were taken over by Israeli settlers. A few of the quaint Arab villages and neighbourhoods have actually been meticulously preserved. But they are empty of Palestinians – some of the former residents are internal refugees inside Israel (Masalha 2005) – and are designated as Jewish 'artistic colonies' (Benvenisti 1986: 25). While an observant traveller can still see some evidence of the destroyed Palestinian villages, in the main all that is left is a scattering of stones and rubble.

The Importance of Toponymy and the Politics of Renaming

The importance of toponymy, geographical renaming, mapping and remapping was recognised by the European colonial powers. In Palestine the Zionist-Hebrew toponymy project, which was critical to the ethno-racialisation of Jews and nationalisation of the Hebrew Bible, followed closely and faithfully British and American archaeological and geographical 'explorations' of the second half of the nineteenth century and first half of the twentieth. In line with the reinventions of European ethno-romantic nationalisms, Zionist ideological archaeology and geography claimed to 'own' exclusive 'national' inheritance in Palestine; the 'land of Israel' was treated as a matter of exclusive ownership. This process of ethno-nationalisation and reinvention of 'land of the Bible' intensified after the establishment of the Israeli state in 1948 as part of the general attempt to ethno-nationalise both Jews and the Hebrew Bible (Rabkin 2010: 130).

In Palestine of the nineteenth century geographical renaming of Palestinian Arab place names became a powerful tool in the hands of the competing European powers. The British were the first to recognise and exploit the power of typonymy and to link geographical renaming with biblical archaeology and colonial penetration of Palestine. The British Palestine Exploration Fund (PEF), which was founded in 1865 by a group of academics and clergymen, most notably the Dean of Westminster Abbey, Arthur P. Stanley, also worked closely with the British military establishment. With offices in central London, the Palestine Exploration

92   The Palestine Nakba

Fund today is an active organisation which publishes an academic journal, the *Palestine Exploration Quarterly*. In addition, the PEF presents public lectures and funds research projects in the Near East. According to its website, 'Between 1867 and 1870 Captain Warren carried out the explorations in Palestine which form the basis for our knowledge of the topography of ancient Jerusalem and the archaeology of the Temple Mount/Haram al-Sherif'; 'In addition to his explorations on, under, and around the Temple Mount/al-Haram al-Sharif, Warren surveyed the Plain of Philistia and carried out a very important [military] reconnaissance of central Jordan'.[5] Captain (later General Sir) Charles Warren (1840–1927), of the British Royal Engineers and one of the key officers of the PEF, who was sent to map the biblical topography of Jerusalem and investigate 'the site of the temple', noted: '[British] King Consul [James Finn] rules supreme, not over the natives of the city, but over strangers; but yet these strangers for the most part are the rightful owners, the natives, for the most part, are usurpers' (Shepherd 1987: 127–8).

Warren and the long-serving and famous British consul, Finn – both Christian Zionists involved with the Mission to the Jews (Shepherd 1987: 110) – apparently 'literally burrowed' beneath the Muslim shrines in Jerusalem to chart the 'original dimensions' of the 'Temple Mount'. The biblical archaeology, mapping, topography and toponymy of Warren and the Royal Engineers have remained basic data for many Israeli archaeologists, geographers and strategic planners of today (Shepherd 1987: 195; Benvenisti 2002: 11–27).

Following in the footsteps of the PEF, the British Mandatory authorities in Palestine set out to gather toponymic and 'biblical' information from the local Palestinian population. The British drive to present European colonialism as a continuation of an ancient Jewish ownership of the land meant that place names in Palestine became a site of fierce contest between the European Zionist settler-coloniser and the colonised Palestinians. Palestinian Arab names were (and continued to be) 'unnamed' and Hebrewised by the Zionists using a colonising strategy based on

5. www.pef.org.uk/Pages/Warren.htm.

Hebrew ('biblical') names. Indigenous Palestinian place names are considered 'redeemed' when they are rendered from Arabic into Hebrew (Slyomovics 1998, 2002). The genealogy of British colonial name commissions and the Zionist-Hebrew toponymy project, which began in the nineteenth century, continued under the British colonial system in Palestine[6] and was accelerated dramatically after the 1948 Nakba and the expansion of biblical and archaeological departments at Israeli universities.

Renaming as Self-reinvention: The Hebrewisation of Names after 1948

Although Eastern European Jewish colonisers claimed to represent an indigenous people returning to its homeland after 2,000 years of absence, in fact Russian nationals formed the hard core of Zionist activism. This reindigenisation required a great deal of effort to create the mythological New Hebrew Sabra Man and construct a new Jewish identity. No wonder, for the early Zionist settlers were intent not only on 'inventing a Land, and inventing a Nation' (Rabkin 2010: 130), but also on self-reinvention. In accordance with this new, Hebrew-imagined biblical identity, the post-1948 period saw top Zionist leaders, army commanders, biblical archaeologists and authors changing their names from Russian, Polish and German to 'authentic' Hebrew-sounding (biblical) names. Examples include the following:

- Moshe Sharett was born Moshe Shertok in Russia in 1894; he became Israel's foreign minister in 1948; he chose to Hebrewise his last name in 1949, following the creation of the State of Israel.
- Golda Meir was born Golda Mabovitch in Kiev in 1898; later Golda Meyerson; she Hebrewised her last name, interestingly, only after she became foreign minister in 1956; she was prime minister 1969–74.

---

6. Abdul-Rahim Al-Shaikh, 'Last Year in Jerusalem', *This Week in Palestine*, no. 141, January 2010, www.thisweekinpalestine.com/details.php?id=2969&ed=177&edid=177.

- Yitzhak Shamir was born Icchak Jeziernicky in eastern Poland in 1915; he was foreign minister 1981-82 and prime minister 1983-84 and 1988-92.
- Ariel Sharon was born Ariel Scheinermann in colonial Palestine in 1928 (to Shmuel and Vera, later Hebrewised to Dvora, immigrants to Palestine from Russia); he was prime minister 2001-06.
- David Green became David Ben-Gurion during the Mandatory period; in 1948 he became the first prime minister and defence minister of Israel.
- Yitzhak Ben-Tzvi was born Yitzhak Shimshelevitz in the Ukraine in 1884; he was the second president of Israel.
- Levi Eshkol was born in the Ukraine in 1895 as Levi Školnik; he was Israel's third prime minister, 1963-69.
- David Remez was born David Drabkin in Belarus in 1886; he was Israel's first minister of transportation.
- Pinhas Rutenberg (1879-1942), a prominent Zionist leader and the founder of Palestine Electric Company, which became the Israel Electric Corporation, was born in the Ukraine as Pyotr Moiseyevich Rutenberg.
- Avraham Granot (1890-1962), director general of the Jewish National Fund and later chairman of its board, was born in today's Moldova as Abraham Granovsky; he changed his name after 1948.
- Shimon Peres was born in Poland in 1923 as Szymon Perski; he was Israel's eighth prime minister and in 2007 was elected as its ninth president.
- Right-wing Russian Zionist leader Zeev Jabotinsky (1880-1940) changed his name from Vladimir Yevgenyevich Zhabotinsky during the Mandatory period.
- Prominent Labour leader Haim Arlozoroff (1899-1933) was born Vitaly Arlozoroff.
- Professor Yigael Yadin (1917-1984), the army's second chief of staff and a founding father of Israeli biblical archaeology, was born Yigal Sukenik.
- Professor Benyamin Mazar, co-founder of Israeli biblical archaeology, was born Benyamin Maisler in Poland; educated

in Germany, he emigrated to colonial Palestine in 1929 and Hebrewised his name.

- Yitzhak Sadeh (1890-1952), the commander of the Haganah's strike force, the Palmah, and one of the key army commanders in 1948, was born in Russia as Isaac Landsberg.
- Yitzhak Rabin, the first native-born Israeli prime minister, 1974-77 and 1992-95, was born in Jerusalem to a Zionist settler from the Ukraine, Nehemiah Rubitzov. Rubitzov became Rabin.
- Tzvi Tzur (1923-2004), the Israeli army's sixth chief of staff, was born in the Zaslav in the Soviet Union as Czera Czertenko.
- Moshe Ya'alon, former army chief of staff, was born in Israel in 1950 as Moshe Smilansky.
- Prominent Israeli author and journalist Amos Elon (1926-2009) was born in Vienna as Amos Sternbach.
- Israel's leading novelist Amoz Oz was born in Mandatory Palestine in 1939 as Amos Klausner.
- Israel's greatest poet, Yehuda Amichai (1924-2000), was born in Germany as Ludwig Pfeuffer; he emigrated to colonial Palestine in 1935 and subsequently joined the Palmah and the Haganah; in 1947 he was still known as Yehuda Pfeuffer.

Evidently many of these changes of name took place around or shortly after 1948. During the Mandatory (colonial) period, it was still advantageous for individuals to have their original European names.

The Zionist Superimposing of Hebrew Toponymy

In present-day Israel the claim is repeatedly made that the Bible is materially realised thanks to biblical archaeology, giving Jewish history flesh and bones, recovering the ancient past, putting it in 'dynastic order' and 'returning to the archival site of Jewish identity' (Said 2004: 46; see also Silberman 1982, 1989, 1993, 1997: 62-81; Silberman and Small 1997; Elon 1997: 35-47). Biblical archaeology was always central to the construction of Israeli-Jewish identity and the perceived legitimacy of the Israeli state. The debate about 'ancient Israel', biblical scholarship and biblical archaeology is also a debate about the modern State of Israel, most crucially because in the eyes of many people in the West the legitimacy of the Zionist project and Jewish 'restorationism' depends on the credibility of the biblical portrait. One facet of that debate is the argument in the public domain over the use of the term 'Israel' to denote the land west of the River Jordan, both in ancient and in modern times. The inevitable outcome of the obsession with the Hebrew Bible in Western biblical scholarship – its calling the land 'biblical' and its exclusive interest in a small section of the history of the land – has resulted in a focus on the Israelite identity of a land that has actually been non-Jewish in terms of its indigenous population for the larger part of its recorded history (Whitelam 1996). This state of affairs would not occur in any other part of the world. It is due to the Hebrew Bible and its influence in the West, where an inherited Christian culture supported the notion that Palestine has always been somehow essentially 'the land of Israel'.

In *Facts on the Ground: Archaeological Practice and Territorial Self-fashioning in Israeli Society* (2001), Nadia Abu El-Haj shows that in the post-1967 period the colonial practices of Israeli biblical archaeology went hand in hand with the use of bulldozers to clear ancient Palestinian sites and medieval Islamic architecture – in line with the efforts to make Jerusalem more of a Jewish-national site and eliminate the multiplicity of other histories in the city (Abu El-Haj 2001; Bowersock 1984: 130–41, 1988: 181–91; Glock 1999: 324–42). Biblical archaeology, geography and scholarship have been essentially 'Zionist' and have participated in the elimination of Palestinian identity and the Islamic heritage in Palestine, as if over 1,400 years of Muslim occupation of this land has meant nothing. This focus on a short period of history a long time ago participates in a kind of retrospective colonising of the past. It tends to regard modern Palestinians as trespassers or 'resident aliens' on someone else's territory.

Biblical archaeology, in particular, has played a key role in secular Zionist-Jewish nation-building as well as in the formation of Zionist Jewish collective identity before and after 1948. To root European Jewish identity in the land, after the establishment of Israel the science of archaeology was summoned to the task of constructing and consolidating that identity in secular time; both rabbis and university scholars specialising in 'biblical archaeology' were given sacred history as their domain (Said 2004: 45). Abu El-Haj's seminal work, *Facts on the Ground*, explores the centrality of selective biblical archaeology in the construction of Zionist Jewish collective identity before and after 1948. The work looks at colonial archaeological exploration in Palestine, dating back to British work in the mid-nineteenth century. Abu El-Haj focuses on the period after the establishment of Israel in 1948, linking the academic practice of archaeology with Zionist colonisation and with plans for the Judaisation and repossession of the land through the renaming of Palestinian geographical sites. Much of this de-Arabisation of Palestine if given archaeological justification; the existence of Arab names is written over by newly coined Hebrew names. This 'epistemological strategy' is designed around the construction of an Israeli Jewish identity based on assembling archaeological fragments and traces of the ancient past – scattered remnants of masonry, bits of ceramics, bones, fragments of scrolls, tombs – an identity which would function as a sort of special biography of the European Yishuv in Palestine (Abu El-Haj: 2001: 74; Said 2004: 47-8; Bowersock 1988: 181-91).

A large number of Israeli experts on and practioners of biblical archaeology – from General Yigael Yadin and General Moshe Dayan to General Ariel Sharon – have referred to it as the 'privileged Israeli science *par excellence*' (Said 2004: 45-6; Kletter 2003). Magen Broshi, a leading Israeli archaeologist, and a member of the Government Names Committee (see below), has noted:

> The Israeli phenomenon, a nation returning to its old-new land [echoing Herzl's German novel *Altneuland*] is without parallel. It is a nation in the process of renewing its acquaintance with its own lands and here archeology plays an important role. In this process archeology is part of a larger system known as *yedi'at haAretz,* knowledge of the land (the Hebrew term is derived most probably from the German *Landeskunde*). ... The European immigrants found a country to which they felt, paradoxically, both kinship and strangeness. Archeology in Israel, a *sui generis* state, served as a means to dispel the alienation of its new citizens. (quoted in Said 2004: 46)

In Jewish Zionism the 'selective reconstruction of Antiquity was part of the historical mission of reviving the ancient national roots and spirit. [Selective] Antiquity became both a source of legitimacy and an object of admiration' (Zerubavel 1995: 25). For the deeply secular founding fathers of political Zionism, in particular, the biblical narrative and ideology functioned essentially as the objective historical account of the Jewish 'title to the land' – a claim not necessarily borne out by archaeological findings. The passionate interest in biblical archaeology held by deeply secular military leaders and politicians such as David Ben-Gurion, Moshe Dayan and Yigael Yadin (the latter two army chiefs of staff), and the significance given to the 'last stand' at the biblical fortress of Masada, were designed to forge emotional bonds between the new Israeli army, European settlers and the land. The role of colonial archaeology in justifying South African apartheid has been described elsewhere (Hall 1988: 62-4, 1984: 455-67). In contrast, however, although a great deal has been written about the role of Israeli ethnocentric biblical archaeology in confirming the legitimacy of the Zionist claim, little attention has been paid to the role of the biblical paradigm of 'promised land, chosen people' and biblical archaeology in providing the ideological justification for the expulsion and dispossession of the Palestinians.

The Israeli historian and archaeologist Meron Benvenisti argues in *Sacred Landscape: The Buried History of the Holy Land since 1948* (2002) that Zionists have invented and constructed a history and chronology of Palestine

> so as to emphasize the Jewish connection to the land, adding designations such as the biblical, Hasmonean, Mishnaic, and Talmudic periods. From the 'early Muslim' period onward, however, they adopted the nomenclature of the 'conquerers' chronology,' since in this way it was possible to divide the approximately 1,400 years of Muslim-Arab rule into units that were shorter than the period of Jewish rule over the Eretz Israel/Palestine (which lasted at most for 600 years), and especially to portray the history of the country as a long period of rule by a series of foreign powers who had robbed it from the Jews – a period that ended in 1948 with the reestablishment of Jewish sovereignty in Palestine. It was thus possible to obscure the fact that the indigenous Muslim Arab population was part and parcel of the ruling Muslim peoples and

instead to depict the history of the local population – its internal wars, its provincial rulers, its contribution to the landscape – as matters lacking in importance, events associated with one or another dynasty of 'foreign occupiers'. (Benvenisti 2002: 300)

While the colonial attitudes of European and North American historians and social scientists towards former colonies of the West have been critiqued since the 1960s, Israeli social scientists and biblical scholars have chosen to maintain the colonial tradition. In Israel there has always been an obsession with 'biblical memory', and the convergence between biblical archaeology and Jewish settler-colonialism has always loomed large, becoming most pronounced after the post-1967 conquests. Furthermore, Israeli biblical archaeology has remained central to secular Zionism – most Orthodox Jews in Israel were and still are indifferent to its findings (Elon 1997: 38). Benvenisti observes that

British, American, and other academics engaged in the study of the archaeology and history of their former overseas colonies have begun to revaluate the attitudes that prevailed during the colonial period. They have admitted grave distortions that were introduced into the history of the colonies as an outcome of Eurocentric attitudes, ignoring or erasing remaining traces of the natives' past and their material culture. In the wake of this evaluation, Amerindian, Aborigine, and native African sites were studied and restored, and a new history was written, focusing on the organic chronicles of those regions, which had been a mere footnote in the history of the European peoples. The Israelis, by contrast, chose to maintain the colonial tradition with only minor changes ... The [Israeli] Antiquities Administration is aware of only two sites in Old Jaffa: the 'Biuim House' (the first home of this group of early Zionist pioneers in the country, in 1882) and the first building of the first [Zionist] Hebrew High School ('Gimnasiya Herzeliyya'), which have been declared 'antiquities' in accordance with Article 2 [of the Israeli Antiquities Law of 1978]. Of course no structure 'of historical value' to the Palestinians has been declared as a protected antiquity under Israeli law. (Benvenisti 2002: 304-5)

The Zionist Yishuv's toponymy project was established in the 1920s to 'restore' biblical Hebrew and to create new Hebrew-sounding names of symbolic meaning to the Zionist colonising of Palestine

(Ra'ad 2010a: 189). In the 1920s a JNF Naming Committee was set up to name the newly established Jewish colonies in Palestine to compete with the overwhelmingly Arabic map of Palestine; its renaming efforts were appreciated by the British Mandatory authorities and were incorporated into the Palestine government's official gazette (Benvenisti 2002: 26). An important part of the 'New Hebrew' identity was the Zionist-Hebrew toponymy, which gradually replaced the Palestinian Arabic toponymy (Cohen and Kliot 1981: 227–34). Under the heading 'Reclaiming by Naming', the American-Israeli academic Selwyn Ilan Troen (Brandeis University and Ben-Gurion University of the Negev), while rehashing standard Zionist myths, remarks on the continuity of European Zionist colonisation of Palestine and nineteenth-century Western biblical archeology:

> Zionism also set out to 're-imagine' and 're-constitute' the country's landscape. The process actually began with Christian explorers, and archaeologists and Bible scholars from Europe and the United States who visited Palestine from the mid-nineteenth century when the country was under Turkish rule. Contemporary Arab names were but adaptations or corruptions of ancient designations found in sacred texts or other historical sources. Zionist settlers continued the process, although for them it was not merely to recapture the Holy Land of Scriptures. Rather it was a deeply personal attempt to re-imagine themselves in the land of their ancestors. As a consequence, in renaming the land they consciously ignored or set aside many of the physical markers as well as the social and cultural ones of both Europe and the Arab neighbours ... Zionists celebrated the return to history of Biblical Rehovoth[7] and Ashkelon [one of the famous five cities of the Philistines] ... In addition, thousands of names were given to streets, public squares and the landscape, with signs in Hebrew everywhere. The total effect invited observers to appreciate that the settlements were the concrete manifestation of national revival by a people who could legitimately claim to be returning natives. (Troen 2008: 197)

This Zionist 'reclaiming by renaming' project was a pivotal factor in the colonisation of the land of Palestine and in creating an 'authentic' collective Zionist-Hebrew identity rooted in the land of

---

7. Founded in 1890, the new Zionist settlement/city of Rehovot was named after a biblical town of a similar name, Rehoboth, which stood at a completely different location in the Negev Desert.

the Bible. Referring candidly to the gradual replacement of Arabic place names (and of Palestinian villages) by Hebrew place names (and Jewish settlements) during the Mandatory period, Israeli defence minister Moshe Dayan – and the author of *Living with the Hebrew Bible* (1978) – had this to say in an address in April 1969 to students at the Technion, Israel's prestigious Institute of Technology in Haifa:

> Jewish villages were built in the place of Arab villages. You do not even know the names of these villages, and I do not blame you because geography books no longer exist. Not only do the books not exist, the Arab villages are not there either. Nahlal arose in the place of Mahlul; Kibbutz Gvat in the place of Jibta; Kibbutz Sarid in the place of Hunefis, and Kefar Yehushua in the place of Tal al-Shuman. There is not a single place built in this country that didn't have a former Arab population.[8]

Dayan, who spoke Arabic, knew that the name of his own settlement (*moshav*), Nahlal, founded in 1921, was in fact a Hebrew rendering of the name of the Arabic village it had replaced, Mahloul; however, to give it a 'biblical authenticity', the Hebrew sounding Nahlal was linked by the Zionists to the biblical site mentioned in Joshua (19:15). Also Kibbutz Gvat, set up in 1926, was a Hebrew rendering of the Arabic place name it had replaced, the Palestinian village Jibta, but Gvat also echoes the Aramaic name Gvata (meaning hill) and a biblical site in the Galilee. In the 1920s the Palestinian lands of Wadi al-Hawarith[9] in the coastal region were purchased ('redeemed') by the Jewish National Fund from Arab absentee landlords, subsequently leading to the eviction of many Arab farmers. The Jewish settlement of Kefar Haro'e was established in 1934 on these lands. The Arabic name was rendered into the Hebrew-sounding Emek Hefer (Hefer Valley). In some cases the Zionist-Hebrew colonising toponymy simply translated Arabic names into Hebrew.

Other Hebrew place names did not preserve the Arabic names: for instance, the first Zionist settlement in Palestine, Petah Tikva,

---

8. Reported in *Haaretz*, 4 April 1969.
9. Also the name of a Palestinian village depopulated in 1948.

was originally set up by Jewish settlers in 1878 (abandoned and re-established in 1882), on the lands of, and eventually replacing, the destroyed Palestinian Arab village of Mlabbis. Petah Tikva is known in Zionist historiography as *Im Hamoshavot* – the 'Mother of the Colonies'. The Zionist religious founders asserted that the name of Petah Tikva came from the biblical prophecy of Hosea (2:17). The land of Petah Tikva was bought from two Arab absentee landlords based in Jaffa, Salim al-Kassar and Anton al-Tayyan. Six decades after the Nakba, Palestinian citizens of Israel still call the Jewish city of Petah Tikva 'Mlabbis'.

The destruction of Palestinian villages during and after the Nakba and the conceptual deletion of Palestinians from history and cartography after 1948 meant that the names of depopulated Palestinian villages and towns were removed from the map. The physical disappearance of Palestine in 1948, the deletion of the demographic and political realities of historic Palestine and the erasure of Palestinians from history centred on key issues, the most important of which is the contest between a 'denial' and an 'affirmation' (Said 1980; Abu-Lughod et al. 1991). The deletion of historic Palestine from maps and cartography was designed not only to strengthen the newly created state but also to consolidate the myth of the 'unbroken link' between the days of the biblical Israelites and the modern Israeli state.

The historic Arabic names of geographical sites were replaced by newly coined Hebrew names, some of which resembled biblical names. The deletion of Arabic place names and the renaming of Palestinian sites follows roughly the guidelines suggested by Edward Robinson (1794-1863), the father of 'biblical geography' and biblical archaeology, who had argued a hundred years earlier, in *Biblical Researches in Palestine, Mount Sinai and Arabia Petraea* (1841), that hundreds of place names of Arab villages and sites in Palestine, seemingly Arab, were in fact Arabic renderings or translations of ancient Hebrew names, biblical or Talmudic. From its beginnings in the nineteenth century and throughout the first half of the twentieth, biblical archaeology-cum-biblical geography became one of the most successful of all European colonial enterprises, re-creating the land of the Bible, reinventing the Jewish people, silencing Palestinian history and de-Arabising Palestinian typonomy (Masalha 2007; Whitelam 1996; Long 1997, 2003). Israel's biblical industry, with its Hebrew renaming projects, was embedded in this richly endowed and massively financed colonial tradition. In *A History of Modern Palestine*, Israeli historian Ilan Pappé remarks:

> [W]hen winter was over and the spring of 1949 warmed a particularly frozen Palestine, the land as we have described ... – reconstructing a period stretching over 250 years – had changed beyond recognition. The countryside, the rural heart of Palestine, with its colourful and picturesque villages, was ruined. Half the villages had been destroyed, flattened by Israeli bulldozers which had been at work since August 1948 when the government had decided to either turn them into cultivated land or to build new Jewish settlements on their remains. A naming committee granted the new settlements Hebraized versions of the original Arab names: Lubya became Lavi, and Safuria [Saffuriya] Zipori [Tzipori] ... David Ben-Gurion explained that this was done as part of an attempt to prevent future claim to the villages. It was also supported by the Israeli archaeologists, who had authorized the names as returning the map to something resembling 'ancient Israel'. (2004a: 138–9)

The post-1948 project concentrated on the biblicisation/ Hebrewisation of Palestinian Arab geography and the practice of naming events, actions, places in line with biblical terminology. The Hebrewisation project deployed renaming to construct new places and new geographic identities related to supposed biblical places. The new Hebrew names embodied an ideological drive and political attributes that could be consciously mobilised by the Zionist hegemonic project (Peteet 2005: 153–72).

The official project began with the establishment of the Governmental Names Committee (*Va'adat Hashemot Hamimshaltit*) by Prime Minister Ben-Gurion in July 1949. Ben-Gurion had visited the Naqab (Negev) in June and had been struck by the fact that no Hebrew names existed for geographical sites in the region. The 11 June 1949 entry for his War Diary reads: 'Eilat ... we drove through the open spaces of the Arava ... from 'Ayn Husb ... to 'Ayn Wahba ... We must give Hebrew names to these places – ancient names, if there are, and if not, new ones!' (Ben-Gurion 1982, vol. 3: 989).

Biblical Myths, Old and New:
The Complicity of the Israeli Academy

In a modern settler-colonial (and science-based) society like Israel scholarly knowledge follows closely the Foucauldian paradigm of knowledge/intelligence gathering/data collection/record-keeping and state power (Foucault 1980). Already during the Zionist Yishuv period many Zionist leaders, settlement executives, Haganah commanders and intelligence officers (David Ben-Gurion, Yosef Weitz, Yosef Nahmani and Ezra Danin included) were also prolific diarists and record-keepers. In the 1930s and 1940s the various departments of the Jewish Agency, Haganah and Jewish National Fund instituted a massive intelligence-gathering operation relating to Palestinian society. In 1938 the British Mandatory authorities allowed the Jewish Agency to copy hundreds of thousands of official documents and practically all the official material and records existing on land registration and in tax offices relating to hundreds of Palestinian villages (Masalha 1992: 99). Moreover, from the late 1939s onwards the various agencies of the Yishuv amassed a huge amount of data and detailed information on the Palestinian villages: the 'Village Files' (Pappé 2006: 17-22).

After 1948 the Israeli internal security service, Shin-Bet, and other state agencies began compiling massive files on the Palestinian citizens of Israel (Cohen 2010). Israeli academic institutions have continued the colonialist tradition of intelligence-gathering and data collection. The Israeli military and Israeli biblical academy, in particular, have always been close partners in nation-building. Nationalist mobilisation through the mobilisation of the Bible and myth-making involving spurious scholarly activity engages a large number of Israeli academics and social scientists, in particular archaeologists, political geographers and orientalists. The Governmental Names Committee, which has operated since the early 1950s from the Prime Minister's Office, is perhaps the best example of the production of academic knowledge through myth-making.

Israeli biblical archaeologists and geographers have played a major role on behalf of the Committee in its efforts to manufacture new Hebrew names and a new hegemonic Israeli memory. In 2010, the Prime Minister's Office website listed the large number of academics who are members of the Committee, including: Avraham Biran, Committee chairman, archaeologist; architect Avinoam Avnon of the Ministry of Transportation; Azariah Alon of the Society for the Protection of Nature; Yehoshua Ben-Arieh, a geographer at the Hebrew University; Moshe Brawer, a geographer at Tel Aviv University; Magen Broshi of the Israel Museum; Esther Goldberg of the Academy for the Hebrew Language; Amiram Gonen, a geographer at the Hebrew University; Avinoam Danin, a botanist at the Hebrew University; Yehuda Ziv, chairman of the Sub-committee for Settlement Names, an IDF representative; Moshe Kochavi, an archaeologist at Tel Aviv University; Avi Goren, a representative of the JNF; Zeev Mashal, an archaeologist at Tel Aviv University; Dov Nir, a geographer at the Hebrew University; Zeev Safray, of the Israel Studies Department at Bar-Ilan University; Yoram Tzafrir, chairman of the Sub-committee for Historical Names, an archaeologist at the Hebrew University; Naftali Qadmon, chairman of the Sub-committee for Geographical Names, at the Hebrew University; Zachariah Kali, archaeologist at the Hebrew University; Richav Rubin, a geographer at the Hebrew University; Benyamin Ricardo, a representative of the Ministry of the Interior; Baruch Partzman, a geographer at the Centre for the Survey of Israel; Moshe Sharon, an orientalist at the Hebrew University; Hannah Bitan, a geographer and the scientific coordinator of the committee.[10] Today there is still no sign that the Governmental Names Committee has any intention of producing maps which mention the original Arabic place names or destroyed villages.[11]

In the immediate post-Nakba period Israeli archaeologists and members of the Israeli Exploration Society on the Government

10. www.pmo.gov.il/PMOEng/PM+Office/Departments/depgovnames.htm.

11. In 2007 Yehuda Ziv, chairman of the Sub-committee for Settlement Names, was reported as saying: 'I support the mention of the Arab names of various sites, including villages, streams and other places, and I think that they should not have been erased from the map. One reason is that these names often teach us about the country's Jewish past. There is an additional reason, and that is the fact that these names teach us the history of the country and its landscape. I claimed that original Arab names of existing communities should be added as part of a first map of Israel in Arabic being prepared by the Israel Mapping Center, but I was told that there is no room for that. However, regarding destroyed villages, I think that we should make do simply with a mention of the name of the village.'

Names Committee concentrated their initial efforts on the creation
of a new map for the newly occupied 'Negev' (Abu El-Haj 2001:
91–4). Throughout the documentation produced by the Committee,
commissioned to create Hebrew names for the newly occupied
Palestinian landscape, were references to 'foreign names'. The
Israeli public was called upon 'to uproot the foreign and existing
names' and in their place 'to master' the new Hebrew names. Most
existing names were Arabic names. The Committee duly assigned
Hebrew names to 561 different geographical features in the Negev
– mountains, valleys, springs and waterholes – using the Bible as
a resource. Despite the obliteration of many ancient Arabic names
from the Negev landscape, some were transformed into similar-
sounding Hebrew names: for example, 'Seil 'Imran' became 'Nahal
'Amram', apparently recalling the father of Moses and Aaron;
the Arabic Jabal Haruf (Mount Haruf) became Har Harif (Sharp
Mountain); Jabal Dibba (Hump Hill) became Har Dla'at (Mount
Pumpkin). After rejecting the name Har Geshur, after the people
to whom King David's third wife belonged, as a Hebrew appellation
for the Arabic Jabal Ideid (Sprawling Mountain), the Committee
decided to call it Har Karkom (Mount Crocus), because crocuses
grow in the Negev.[12] However, the sound of the Arabic name Ideid
was retained in the nearby springs, which are now called Beerot
Oded (the Wells of Oded), possibly after the biblical prophet of the
same name.[13] The Committee report of March 1956 stated:

> In the summarized period 145 names were adopted for antiquities sites,
> ruins and tells: eight names were determined on the basis of historical
> identification, 16 according to geographical names in the area, eight
> according to the meaning of the Arabic words, and the decisive majority
> of the names (113) were determined by mimicking the sounds of the
> Arabic words, a partial or complete mimicking, in order to give the
> new name a Hebrew character, following the [accepted] grammatical
> and voweling rules. (quoted in Abu El-Haj 2001: 95)[14]

---

12. Don C. Benjamin, 'Stories and Stones: Archaeology and the Bible, an Introduction
with CD Rom', 2006, www.doncbenjamin.com/Archaeology_&_the_Bible.pdf, p. 254,
note 78.
13. Yadin Roman, www.eretz.com/archive/jan3000.htm.
14. Approximately one-quarter of all geographical names were derived from the Arabic
names on the basis of the similarity of sound. Abu El-Haj 2001: 95.

In *Hidden Histories* (2010a) Palestinian scholar Basem Ra'ad, citing a 1988 study, *Toponymie Palestinienne: Plaine de St. Jean d'Acre et corridor de Jerusalem*, by Thomas L. Thompson, F.J. Goncalves and J.M. van Cangh, shows that the Israeli toponymy committees went far beyond their original mandates:

> There was simply not enough [biblical] tradition to go by, so [the project] could only continue by picking out biblical or Jewish associations at random. It had to Hebraize Arabic names, or in other cases translate Arabic to Hebrew to give the location an ideologically consistent identity. For example, some locations were rendered from Arabic into the Hebrew phonetic system: Minet el-Muserifa became Horvat Mishrafot Yam and Khirbet el Musherifa was changed to Horvat Masref. Sometimes, in this artificial process, the committees forgot about certain genuine Jewish traditions, as in the case of the total cancelling of the Arabic name Khirbet Hanuta, not recognizing that it probably rendered the Talmudic Khanotah. This forced exercise of re-naming often even went against biblical tradition, most notably in erasing the Arabic names Yalu and 'Imwas [after 1967]. Yalo became Ayallon, while 'Imwas, Western Emmaus, associated with the Christ story, was one of the three villages, along with Beit Nuba, razed in 1967. The old stones from the villages were sold to Jewish contractors to lend local tradition and age to new buildings elsewhere, and the whole area was turned into the tragic Canada Park, made possible by millions from a Canadian donor. (Ra'ad 2010a: 188–9; Thomas et al. 1988)

Of the nearly 500 destroyed and depopulated villages in 1948, several have survived until today, but were taken over by Israeli settlers. In *The Birth of the Palestinian Refugee Problem, 1947–1949* (1987), Benny Morris gives the misleading impression that the hundreds of Palestinians villages were depopulated and destroyed in the heat of the battle in 1948 or shortly after in the period 1948–49; in effect he argues that, with the near-total physical destruction of the villages, refugee 'return' had became practically impossible by the end of 1949.

In fact dozens of deserted Palestinian villages survived intact well into the mid-1960s when the official programme of village destruction was renewed by the Israeli authorities; many villages that survived 1948 were gradually and methodically razed in the 1950s and 1960s. When in 1953 the Israeli High Court ruled that the state must honour its 1948 promise and allow the internal refugees from Bir'im to return, the army pre-empted the ruling by bombing the village from the air; today the only surviving building in Bir'im is the Maronite church. During the course of his research in Israeli official archives, historian Aharon Shai of Tel Aviv University discovered that in 1965 the Israeli government had recruited the staff of the Jewish National Fund and prominent archaeologists to an official project to 'clean' the land of these deserted Palestinian villages. In the first two decades of Israel there was still a general anxiety among Israeli leaders that, should the empty villages remain standing, the Palestinian refugees might lobby the international community successfully for their repatriation to their homes inside Israel (Pappé 2006: 188; Cook 2008: 30). According to Israeli revisionist historian Tom Segev, the arguments put forward in the mid-1960s for renewing the destruction programme included the observation that

> The deserted villages spoiled the beauty of the landscape and constituted a neglected nuisance. There were pits filled with water which endangered the well-being of visitors, particularly children, as well as many snakes and scorpions. The Ministry of Foreign Affairs was concerned about the 'unnecessary questions' which tourists would present regarding deserted villages.[15]

Renewal of the destruction and further cleansing of Palestinian sites was a joint project organised by the army, the Jewish National Fund, the Israel Lands Authority and the Association of Archaeological Survey. The last issued permits needed by the government to make the continued programme of destruction 'lawful', while a body called the Society for Landscape Improvement lobbied to preserve any architecturally important buildings. Historic or scenic mosques were left intact: one in Caesarea became a restaurant and bar, for example, while another in Az-Zeeb, a village located 13.5 kilometres north of Acre on the Mediterranean coast, was incorporated into the new Jewish site's beach-front resort, to house the village's old olive presses (Cook 2008: 31).

---

15. Tom Segev, 'We Are All These Villages, Where Are They?', *Between the Lines*, October 2002, translated from the original Hebrew article in *Haaretz*, 6 September 2002, quoted in Cook 2008: 31 and 256 n73).

The destruction of a Palestinian site and the negation of its Islamic history by the heritage-style values of an exclusively biblical archaeology are evident in az-Zeeb. The village, with a population of 2,000 in 1948, was mentioned by Arab geographers in the early Middle Ages. After 1948 the Arab village was razed and Kibbutz Gesher HaZiv (Bridge of Splendour) and Kibutz Sa'ar (Storm) were established on its land. Sa'ar was set up by members of the social-ist-Zionist youth movement Hashomer Hatza'ir (which founded the Mapam party). The Akhziv National Park was also established on its land. Az-Zeeb has been renamed Achziv, supposedly after a site (Achzib) mentioned in the Book of Joshua (15:44); Achziv is mentioned in the Bible as one of the cities that the 'tribe of Asher' did not inherit. The archaeological excavations that have been conducted from the 1940s to the present (and, more recently, on behalf of the Institute of Archaeology of the Hebrew University of Jerusalem) on the site have uncovered four cemeteries associ-ated with a large Phoenician settlement.[16] Today the domed stone mosque has been restored and serves as a tourist site; the house of the last mukhtar (village head), Husayn Ataya, is now a museum (Khalidi 1992a: 36). In *Disappearing Palestine*, Jonathan Cook writes:

> Maps were changed too: over the course of several years [after 1948] a Jewish National Fund committee replaced Arab place names with Hebrew ones, often claiming as justification to have 'discovered' bibli-cal sites. The committee hoped to invent an ancient, largely mythical landscape all the better to root Israeli Jews in their homeland. The real landscape of hundreds of destroyed Palestinian villages was entirely missing from the new maps. Cleared of Palestinian traces, the 'empty' lands were handed over to Jewish agricultural communities, the kib-butzim and moshavim, for exclusive Jewish use. (Cook 2008: 30)

The large and beautiful Palestinian village of 'Ayn Karim (Karim's Spring), in the Jerusalem district, was depopulated in July 1948. In 1945, of the estimated 3,180 people who lived in 'Ayn Karim, 2,510 were Palestinian Muslims and 670 Palestin-ian Christians (Khalidi 1992a: 272). After its depopulation and

---

16. http://archaeology.huji.ac.il/depart/BIBLICAL/EILATM/achziv.asp.

de-Arabisation the name was changed to the Hebrew/biblical
sounding Ein Kerem (Vineyard's Spring), and the village became
a Jewish suburb of Israeli West Jerusalem. Archaeological evidence
indicates that the village site was occupied as early as the second
millennium BCE. According to Christian tradition, this was the site
where John the Baptist was born and that Christ and the Virgin
Mary visited. According to Muslim tradition, the third caliph,
Umar ibn al-Khattab, passed by the village and held prayers in it
during the Islamic conquest of Jerusalem (Khalidi 1992a: 271-2).
During the British Mandatory period Christian churches and
monasteries proliferated in the village, which became a popular
destination for Christian pilgrims. According to Walid Khalidi,

> 'Ayn Karim was one of the few villages to survive its depopulation
> with its buildings intact. The others were Tarbikha (Acre District);
> 'Ayn Hawd, Balad al-Shaykh, and al-Tira (Haifa District); al-Safiriyya
> (Jaffa District); and Dayr Yasin and al-Maliha (Jerusalem District). The
> village houses are inhabited by Jewish families. One Christian Arab
> family, exiled from the village of Iqrit (Acre District) in 1949, lives
> in the village, in an old school building attached to the Franciscan
> monastery. Some of the larger houses are beautiful lime-stone buildings
> two or three storeys high with arched windows and doors recessed
> into a larger arched facade. Some doors open onto balconies with
> metal railings. There are seven Christian churches and monasteries
> in the village. There is also a Christian cemetery beside the Russian
> monastery; a Muslim cemetery in the center of the village, covered with
> refuse and dirt, contains a prominent tomb with a large structure. The
> village mosque, in a state of disrepair, still stands with its minaret.
> The spring of 'Ayn Maryam [Mary's Spring] flows out of the mosque
> courtyard. An Israeli hospital, Haddasa, has been built on the village
> site. Israeli tourist facilities with hotels and swimming pools have been
> built northeast of the village. (Khalidi 1992a: 273)

Also hundreds of agricultural structures that once served the
magnificent network of irrigation of 'Ayn Karim can still be found
around the village.[17]

17. Zafrir Rinat, 'Out of Sight Maybe, But Not Out of Mind', *Haaretz*, 13 June 2007,
www.haaretz.com/print-edition/features/out-of-sight-maybe-but-not-out-of-mind-
1.222986.

European Artists' Colonies
as Places of Amnesia and Erasure

The Zionist-Hebrew place names of the Jewish 'artistic colonies' were superimposed on the Palestinian Arab toponomy. The story of the Palestinian village of 'Ayn Hawd and the Israeli artistic colony of Ein Hod, one site with two identities in the Carmel Mountains south of the city of Haifa, recounts Palestinian Arab memory covered over by Zionist-Jewish memory, just as Maurice Halbwachs showed how medieval Christian memory superimposed itself on Jewish memory. Founded in 1953, the Jewish artists' colony of Ein Hod has come to replace an agriculture-based Palestinian village of traditional stone houses that traces its establishment to the twelfth century (Slyomovics 1998, 2002). Many of the inhabitants of 'Ayn Hawd were driven out in 1948 and ended up in the Jenin refugee camp (in the West Bank). Those internally displaced inhabitants of 'Ayn Hawd who managed to survive the Nakba were not allowed to return to their houses; they established a new village nearby, 'Ayn Hawd al-Jadidah' (New 'Ayn Hawd). According to Walid Khalidi:

> The village was not destroyed; it has been an artists' colony since 1954, and is designated as a tourist site. The village mosque has been turned into a restaurant/bar, the 'Bonanza' ... The lands around the site are cultivated and surrounding forests are used as parks. Those few villagers who did not leave the country as refugees stayed nearby and built a new village, also called Ayn Hawd, which was not legally recognised by the Israeli government and hence was denied all municipal services (including water, electricity, and roads). In the 1970s the Israeli government erected a fence around this new village in order to prevent them from expanding ... The 130 inhabitants of the new 'Ayn Hawd have built a new mosque to replace the old one. Muhammad Abu al-Hayja, the son of a leader of the old village, represents the new village in its struggle to win municipal status. (1992a: 151)

This new Palestinian village, rebuilt in Israel and named by Palestinians dispossessed of their former village, is the architectural statement of a tenacious indigenous Palestinian presence in the land.[18] It was recognised by the Israeli state only in 1992.

18. Susan Slyomovics, 'The Gender of Transposed Space', *Palestine–Israel Journal of*

The European artists' colony of Ein Hod came to symbolise not only the displacement of the Palestinian village but also the contested nationalist narratives of Palestinians and Israelis as well as the selective memory of one man, the artist Marcel Janco (1895–1984), a Romanian-born Israeli painter and architect and one of the founders of the Dada movement. Arriving in Palestine in 1948, Janco proclaimed Ein Hod a 'new' utopian social movement (Slyomovics 1998, 2002). Established in 1953 by Janco and his followers on the ruins of 'Ayn Hawd, Ein Hod (*hod* is Hebrew for 'glory') now houses the Janco–Dada Museum (opened in 1983), which features Janco's work and explores the history of the Dada movement.[19] Paradoxically the erasure of Palestinian landscape and presence was carried out through the manipulation of a selective Jewish memory and the mobilisation of the rhetoric of a European pacifist movement established by a group of exiled poets, painters and philosophers in Zurich, who were opposed to war, racism and oppression in Europe.

To the north of 'Ayn Hawd, the depopulated Arab village of Balad al-Shaykh, near Haifa, which houses the grave of the legendary guerrilla leader Sheikh 'Izz ad-Din al-Qassam (1882–1935), became the Jewish town of Nesher (Vulture). Many of the Palestinian houses and shops are still standing and are occupied by the Jewish inhabitants of Nesher; today Balad al-Shaykh's cemetery is in an advanced state of neglect (Khalidi 1992a: 152–3).

The Reconsecration of Muslim Shrines as Jewish Shrines

The Israeli toponymy project has deployed a range of means to ensure the effectiveness of the de-Arabisation of Palestine. One of these centres on official Israeli road signs, which are often in Hebrew, Arabic and English. Significantly both Arabic and English are *transliterations* of the new Hebrew place names – rather than reflecting the use of the original Palestinian Arabic name. Of

Politics, Economics and Culture 9, no.4, 2002, www.pij.org/details.php?id=114.
19. www.jancodada.co.il/he/index.php.

course the overwhelming majority of Israelis cannot read Arabic; so this functions partly to remind the indigenous Palestinians inside Israel of the need to internalise the new Hebrew toponymy or perhaps seek the express approval of the vanishing Palestinian Arab (Shohat 2010: 264) and also to make Arabic complicit in the de-Arabisation of Palestine.

Another tool of the Israeli colonisation project has been the reconsecration of Muslim shrines – shrines which had never been part of the Jewish tradition – as Jewish shrines. Throughout the country the Hebrewisation project included renaming Muslim holy men's graves and holy sites as Jewish and biblical-sounding ones. In *Sacred Landscape: The Buried History of the Holy Land Since 1948* (2002), Meron Benvenisti observes:

> In the fifties and sixties the location and 'redemption' of holy men's graves was in the hands of the religious establishment – especially the Ministry of Religions – and of Ashkenazi Haredi groups ... According to an official list, issued by a group known as the Foundation of the World and appended to a book published by the Ministry of Defense [Michelson et al., *Jewish Holy Places in the Land of Israel*, 1996], there are more than 500 Jewish holy places and sacred graves in Palestine (including the Occupied Territories). Many of these, albeit not the majority, are former Muslim sites. (2002: 282)

In the centre of the country, south of Jaffa, the large Arab village of al-ʿAbbasiyya was depopulated in 1948; many of its residents ended up as refugees in Jordan. Until the 1930s the Palestinian village was known as 'al-Yahudiyya'. According to Palestinian oral-history sources, the Arabic name had originated from the Muslim shrine in the village: 'Maqam al-Nabi Huda' (Arabic for the 'Shrine of Prophet Huda').[20] According to Benvenisti, although the Arabic name derived from its biblical-Hebrew origin, Yahud, the name of a biblical town (Book of Joshua 19:45), the Muslim shrine in the village was not part of the Jewish tradition (Benvenisti 2002: 276). During the Mandatory period, the Zionists claimed that the name 'al-Yahudiyya' was an Arabic rendering of

---

20. See, for instance, 'Palestine Nakba Oral History: Interview with Hasan al-Kanash', Part 1, www.PalestineRemembered.com/Jaffa/al-ʾAbbasiyya/Story1595.html.

the Hebrew word 'the Jewish'. In 1939, under the impact of the intense Palestinian–Zionist struggle, the residents of the village decided to change its name to al-'Abbasiyya. According to Israeli sources, this was 'primarily in memory of Sheikh al-'Abbas, who was buried there, but also an allusion to the Abbasid Muslim empire' (Benvenisti 2002: 276, 348 n6). The British Mandatory authorities, however, refused to recognise the new name.[21]

Al-'Abbasiyya was occupied on 10 July 1948 and depopulated; in the autumn of that year it was repopulated by the first wave of Jewish settlers and immigrants. In 1953 the settlement of 'Yehud' (Hebrew, literally 'Judaisation') was established on the site of the Arab village. The new Jewish town was populated by Ladino-speaking Jews of Turkish origin and subsequently also by Jews from Poland. In total five Jewish settlements, including Savyon, populated by Israeli millionaires, were built on the lands of the Arab village. A number of Arab houses remain, but they have been occupied by Jewish residents. The main mosque and the Muslim shrine (Maqam al-Nabi Huda) still stand. In the early 1950s, this Muslim shrine, which had never been part of the Jewish tradition, was consecrated as a Jewish holy place and as the burial place of 'Yehuda ben-Ya'acov' (Hebrew, Judah son of Jacob). It was reinvented as a biblical site and a place of Jewish 'pilgrimage, prayer, and for miracles and healing the sick' (Benvenisti 2002: 276).

Among the many Judaised Muslim shrines and holy places were two sites, Nabi Yamin and Nabi Sama'an, located one kilometre east of the Jewish town of Kfar Sava – a Jewish settlement itself named after a Palestinian village destroyed in 1948 (Kafr Saba). Until 1948, Benvensiti writes, these two sites were

> sacred to Muslims alone, and the Jews ascribed no holiness to them. Today they are operated by ultraorthodox Jewish bodies, and members of the religion from which they were taken do not set foot there, despite the fact there is a large Muslim population in the area. (Benvenisti 2002: 276-7)

Muslim tombs and shrines were renamed as Jewish holy places. The tomb of Nabi Yamin was renamed the grave of Benjamin,

21. Ibid.

representing Jacob's youngest son, and Nabi Sama'an became the grave of Simeon. Jewish women seeking to bear offspring pray at the grave of Benjamin:

> The dedication inscriptions from the [Muslim] Mamluk period remain engraved in the stone walls of the tomb, and beside them hang tin signs placed there by the National Center for the Development of the Holy Places. The cloths embroidered with verses from the Qur'an, with which the gravestones were draped, have been replaced by draperies bearing verses from the Hebrew Bible. (Benvenisti 2002: 277)

From Al-Majdal to Biblical Ashkelon, 1948–56

In 1948 the towns and villages of southern Palestine, including the cities of Beer Sheba and al-Majdal, were completely depopulated. Al-Majdal was established in the sixteenth century near the medieval Muslim city of Asqalan, a city which had a long history and a multilayered identity dating back to the ancient Canaanites and Philistines. Its medieval Arab name, Asqalan, preserved its ancient Philestine/Palestinian name, Ashkelon. (Al-Majdal is its modern Arabic name). With the oldest and largest seaport in Canaan, it was one of the five cities of the Philistines (Gaza, Gath, Ashkelon, Ashdod, Ekron). Al-Majdal, on the eve of the 1948 war, had 10,000 (Muslim and Christian) inhabitants, and in October 1948 thousands more refugees from nearby villages joined them. Al-Majdal was conquered by the Israeli army on 4 November 1948, whereupon many of its residents and refugees fled, leaving some 2,700 inhabitants, mostly women and the elderly, *in situ*. Orders in Hebrew and Yiddish were posted in the streets of the town, warning the soldiers to be aware of 'undesirable' behaviour on the part of the town's residents. 'As was customary in such instances', the Israeli intelligence officer wrote, 'the behaviour of the population was obsequious and adulatory'.[22] In December 1948,

---

22. Gideon Levy, 'Exposing Israel's Original Sins', *Haaretz*, book review, 11 March 2000, www3.haaretz.co.il/eng/scripts/article.asp?mador=8&datee=11/03/00&id=99286. Levy was reviewing Benny Morris's (Hebrew) book, *Correcting a Mistake: Jews and Arabs in the Land of Israel 1936-1956* (2000b).

Israeli soldiers 'swept through' the town and deported some 500 of its remaining inhabitants. In 1949 the commanding officer of the Southern Command, in the south, Yigal Allon, 'demanded ... that the town be emptied of its Arabs' (Masalha 1997: 9). This was followed by an inter-ministerial committee's decision to thin out the Palestinian population; another ministerial committee – 'on abandoned property' – decided to settle al-Majdal with Jews; the town was duly Judaised, and, with 2,500 Jewish residents, named Migdal-Ad. In December 1949, more Palestinians were deported to vacate more houses for Jewish settlers – this time for discharged Israeli soldiers. In the meantime the Israeli army made the life of those Palestinians who remained a misery, hoping they would leave. The new commanding officer of the Southern Command, Moshe Dayan, returned to the idea of Yigal Allon: 'I hope that perhaps in the coming years, there will be another opportunity to transfer these [170,000 Israeli] Arabs out of the Land of Israel', he declared at a meeting of the ruling Mapai party on 18 June 1950. Dayan also submitted a detailed proposal for 'the evacuation of the Arab inhabitants of the town of Majdal'. The army chief of staff agreed and Prime Minister Ben-Gurion authorised the plan on 19 June 1950 (Masalha 1997: 9).

In the summer of 1950, almost two years after the 1948 war, the inhabitants of al-Majdal received expulsion orders and were transported to the borders of Gaza over a period of a few weeks. They were loaded onto trucks and dropped off at the border. The last delivery of 229 people left for Gaza on 21 October 1950. Israeli officials distributed the 'abandoned' houses among new Jewish settlers. To this day the Palestinian former inhabitants of al-Majdal live in the shacks and shanties of the refugee camps in Gaza. In 1956, Migdal-Ad changed its official name to a biblicised/Israelised version of the name of the ancient Philistines' city. Since then it has been kept as a purely Jewish city.[23]

---

23. Ibid.

Appropriating Palestinian Place Names

Jewish settlements were established on the land of destroyed and depopulated Palestinian villages. In many cases these settlements took the names of the original Palestinian villages and distorted them into Hebrew-sounding names. This massive appropriation of Palestinian heritage provided the European Jewish colonisers with support for their claim to represent an indigenous people returning to its homeland after two thousand years of exile. For instance, the Jewish settlement that replaced the large and wealthy village of Bayt Dajan (with 5,000 inhabitants in 1948) was named Beit Dagon, founded in 1948; Kibbutz Sa'sa' was built on Sa'sa' village; the cooperative moshav settlement of 'Amka on the land of 'Amqa village; moshav Elanit ('tree' in Hebrew) on the land of al-Shajara ('tree' in Arabic) village (Wakim 2001b; Boqa'i 2005: 73). Al-Kabri in the Galilee was renamed Kabri; al-Bassa village Batzat; al-Mujaydil village (near Nazareth) Migdal Haemek (Tower of the Valley). In the region of Tiberias alone there were 27 Arab villages in the pre-1948 period; 25 of them – including Dalhamiya, Abu Shusha, Hittin, Kafr Sabt, Lubya, al-Shajara, al-Majdal and Hittin – were destroyed by Israel. The name Hittin – where Saladin famously defeated the Crusaders in 1187, leading to a siege and their defeat and loss of control over Jerusalem – was changed to the Hebrew-sounding Kfar Hittim (Village of Wheat). In 2008 the Israel Land Authority, which controls the Palestinian refugee property, gave some of the village's land to a new development project: a $150 million private golf resort. Nearby the road to Tiberias was named 'Menahem Begin Boulevard'; meanwhile heavy iron bars were placed over the entrance to Hittin's ruined mosque and the staircase leading to its minaret was blocked.[24]

Kibbutz Ein Dor (Dor Spring) was founded in 1948 by members of the socialist-Zionist Hashomer Hatza'ir (Mapam) youth movement and settlers from Hungary and the United States. It was founded on the land of the depopulated and destroyed village of Endur, located 10 kilometres south-east of Nazareth. Whether or

---

24. Gideon Levy, 'Twilight Zone/Social Studies Lesson', *Haaretz*, 31 March 2004, www.haaretz.com/hasen/spages/410906.html.

not the Arabic name preserved the ancient Endur, a Canaanite city, is not clear. After 1948 many of the inhabitants became internal refugees in Israel ('present absentees' according to Israeli law) and acquired Israeli citizenship – but were not allowed to return to Endur. In accordance with the common Zionist practice of bestowing biblical-sounding names on modern sites and communities, the militantly atheist colonists of Hashomer Hatza'ir appropriated the Arabic name, claiming that Ein Dor was named after a village mentioned in Samuel (28:3-19). However, it is by no means certain that the kibbutz's location is anywhere near to where the biblical village supposedly stood. An archaeological museum at the kibbutz contains pre-historical findings from the area.

In the centre of the country the once thriving ancient Palestinian town of Bayt Jibrin (or Bayt Jubrin), 20 kilometres north-west of the city of al-Khalil, was destroyed by the Israeli army in 1948. The city's Aramaic name was Beth Gabra, which translates as the 'house of [strong] men'; in Arabic Bayt Jibrin also means 'house of the powerful', possibly reflecting its original Aramaic name; the Hebrew-sounding kibbutz of Beit Guvrin (House of Men), named after a Talmudic tradition, was established on Bayt Jibrin's lands in 1949, by solders who had left the Palmah and the Israeli army. Today Byzantine and Crusader remains survive and are protected as an archaeological site under the Hebrew name of Beit Guvrin; the Arabo-Islamic heritage of the site is completely ignored. Thus we have the erasure of the history of one people at Bayt Jibrin in order to superimpose that of another people over it; the reduction of many layers of history to a single (Jewish) layer.

Fifty-six years after the Nakba, in March 2004, Israeli journalist Gideon Levy published an important article in *Haaretz* entitled 'Twilight Zone/Social Studies Lesson'.[25] The article describes an excursion to the hidden side of the Galilee – the ruins of depopulated Palestinian villages in eastern Galilee and the Tiberias region. The guided tour was organised in commemoration of the 'Land Day' of 1976, organised by three NGOs: the Haifa-based Emile Toma

---

25. An earlier version of this article appeared in *Haaretz*, 31 March 2004, www.haaretz.com/hasen/spages/410906.html.

Centre, the Association for the Defence of the Rights of the Internally Displaced in Israel (ADRID) and Zochrot (Remembering). Zochrot is a small group of Israeli citizens working to raise awareness of the Nakba, marking the location of Palestinian communities that were destroyed in 1948 as part of an effort to make Israelis recognise their responsibility for the Nakba and the right of refugees to return to their villages.

> The Zionist collective memory exists in both our cultural and physical landscape, yet the heavy price paid by the Palestinians – in lives, in the destruction of hundreds of villages, and in the continuing plight of the Palestinian refugees – receives little public recognition. Zochrot works to make the history of the Nakba accessible to the Israeli public so as to engage Jews and Palestinians in an open recounting of our painful common history. We hope that by bringing the Nakba into Hebrew, the language spoken by the Jewish majority in Israel, we can make a qualitative change in the political discourse of this region. Acknowledging the past is the first step in taking responsibility for its consequences. This must include equal rights for all the peoples of this land, including the right of Palestinians to return to their homes.[26]

The March 2004 tour was led by Palestinian guides from the Galilee. Gideon Levy writes:

> Look at this prickly pear plant. It's covering a mound of stones. This mound of stones was once a house, or a shed, or a sheep pen, or a school, or a stone fence. Once – until 56 years ago, a generation and a half ago – not that long ago. The cactus [*sabr*] separated the houses and one lot from another, a living fence that is now also the only monument to the life that once was here. Take a look at the grove of pines around the prickly pear as well. Beneath it there was once a village. All of its 405 houses were destroyed in one day in 1948 and its 2,350 inhabitants scattered all over. No one ever told us about this. The pines were planted right afterward by the Jewish National Fund (JNF), to which we contributed in our childhood, every Friday, in order to cover the ruins, to cover the possibility of return and maybe also a little of the shame and the guilt.[27]

26. www.nakbainhebrew.org/index.php?lang=english.
27. *Haaretz*, 31 March 2004, www.haaretz.com/hasen/spages/410906.html.

3

Fashioning a European Landscape, Erasure and Amnesia: The Jewish National Fund, Afforestation and Green-washing the Nakba

> When I look out my window today and see a tree standing there, that tree gives me a greater sense of beauty and personal delight than all the vast forests I have seen in Switzerland or Scandinavia. Because every tree here was planted by us.
>
> David Ben-Gurion, *Memoirs*[1]

Forests as a Space of Amnesia and Erasure

In the post-Nakba period the Jewish National Fund planted hundreds of thousands of European trees, intended to conceal newly destroyed Palestinian villages, such as al-Tira in the Haifa region, and help to establish the Carmel National Park. An area on the southern slopes of Mount Carmel, closely resembling the landscape of the Swiss Alps, was nicknamed 'Little Switzerland'.[2]

The JNF's forests, such as the Carmel National Park, became an icon of Zionist national revival in Israel and in Israeli Hebrew literature, symbolising the success of the European Zionist project in 'striking roots' in the ancient homeland. Children were often named after trees, and children's Hebrew literature described

---

1. Cited in Max Blumenthal, 'The Carmel wildfire is burning all illusions in Israel', *The Electronic Intifada*, 6 December 2010, http://electronicintifada.net/v2/article11661.shtml.
2. Ibid.

young trees as children (Zerubavel 1996: 60-99). Personal names such as Ilan ('tree'), Oren ('pine tree'), Tomer and Tamar (male and female respectively, 'palm tree'), Amir ('tree top'), Elon or Allon ('oak tree') are very common in Israel. Israeli historian and journalist Amos Elon, who was born in Vienna as 'Amos Sternbach', was renamed 'Amos Oak'. Elon emigrated to Palestine in 1933. In 2004 he moved to Italy, citing disillusionment with developments in Israel since 1967. In *The Israelis: Founders and Sons* Elon writes: 'Few things are as evocatively symbolic of the Zionist dream and rationale as a Jewish National Fund Forest' (1983: 200). Israel's reforestation policies enjoy international support. Planting a tree confirms the undeniable ethical value of Israel (and by extension the West's project in the East). Afforestation is also linked, materially and symbolically, to the Holocaust, and thousand of trees have been planted in memory of the lost communities and individual victims (Elon 1983: 200). For Palestinians, however, few things encapsulate better the most notorious role of the JNF since the Nakba.[3] Interestingly, however, the evacuated Palestinian lands were forested by non-indigenous conifers, pine trees (native to the northern hemisphere) and cypress trees, after the uprooting of indigenous trees and destruction of the terraced landscape and the ethnic cleansing of over 500 villages in the areas that are now supposedly 'forested'. This has been an ecologically very destructive policy pursued largely for political purposes to wipe out the ancient landscape and render the newly acquired areas Jewish European.

The JNF has always been and continues to be instrumental in the colonisation of Palestine and the expropriation of Palestinian land. Central to the construction of the Israeli-Zionist collective memory is the persistent claim that the European Jewish pioneers and settlers on the land purchased by the JNF from Arab landlords transformed the desolate and neglected Asiatic desert of Palestine into a blooming green European terrain of forest (Massad 2004: 61). After 1948 afforestation and signposting were key tools used by the Israeli State and the JNF to de-Arabise Palestine and erase

---

3. Hazem Jamjoum, 'Challenging the Jewish National Fund', *The Electronic Intifada*, 21 July 2010, http://electronicintifada.net/v2/article11406.shtml.

traces of the destroyed Palestinian villages. All signs of the Palestinian presence have been systematically levelled and disguised by the JNF. A recent study by Noga Kadman found that eighty-six destroyed Palestinian villages were inside the JNF forests.[4]

The Birya Forest is the largest JNF forest in the Galilee, covering a total of 20,000 dunums.[5] It conceals the lands of six Palestinian villages destroyed in 1948: Biriyya, 'Alma, Dishon, Qaddita, 'Amqa and 'Ayn Zaytun. Today the Jewish *moshav* of Birya, built in 1971, is situated in the location of and takes its name from the Palestinian village of Biriyya. Located in the Safad region, the Birya Forest was created partly through the joint efforts of the JNF and the Israel Antiquities Authority. Analysing the information that the JNF provides on the Birya Forest, Ilan Pappé observes that none of the destroyed villages is mentioned; all disappear behind the website's descriptions of the forest's wonderful charms, its Jewish heritage and the archaeological attractions of the region:

> No wonder that in such a huge forest one can find a plethora of interesting and intriguing sites: woods, bustans [Arabic for 'garden'], springs and an old synagogue. (cited in Pappé 2006: 230)

'In many of the JNF sites', Pappé (who analyses several sites mentioned in the JNF website, including the Jerusalem Forest) – observes,

> bustans – the fruit gardens Palestinian farmers would plant around their farm houses – appear as one of many mysteries the JNF promises the adventurous visitor. These clearly visible remnants of Palestinian villages are referred to as an inherent part of nature and her wonderful secrets. At one of the sites, it actually refers to the terraces you can find almost everywhere there as the proud creation of the JNF. Some of these were in fact rebuilt over the original ones, and go back centuries before the Zionist takeover. Thus, Palestinian bustans are attributed to nature and Palestine's history transported back to a biblical and Talmudic past. Such is the fate of one of the best known villages, Ayn

---

4. Cited in Zafrir Rinat, 'Out of Sight Maybe, but Not Out of Mind', *Haaretz*, 13 June 2007, www.haaretz.com/print-edition/features/out-of-sight-maybe-but-not-out-of-mind-1.222986.

5. 4 dunums = 1 acre.

al-Zeitun, which was emptied in May 1948, during which many of its inhabitants were massacred. (2006: 230)

Described as a Jewish settlement, the destroyed village of 'Ayn Zaytun is described as follows:

> Ein Zeitun has become one of the most attractive spots within the recreational ground as it harbors large picnic tables and ample parking for the disabled. It is located where once stood the settlement of Ein Zeitun, where Jews used to live ever since the medieval times and until the 18th century. There were four abortive [Jewish] settlement attempts. The parking lot has biological toilets and playgrounds. Next to the parking lot, a memorial stands in memory of the soldiers who fell in the Six Day War. (Pappé 2006: 230-31)

Pappé also points out that the JNF publishes information about unique sites in the Jerusalem Forest and Sataf that testify to the extensive agricultural activity in the region. The information emphasises the presence of terraces, describing them as ancient, biblical or Talmudic history, even if they were built and maintained by the Palestinian villages destroyed in 1948 (2006: 231-2).

In 1948 'Ayn Zaytun was an entirely Muslim farming community of 1,000 inhabitants, cultivating olives, grain and fruit, especially grapes; the name is Arabic for 'Spring of Olives'. Walid Khalidi has described the site as follows:

> The rubble of destroyed stone houses is scattered throughout the site, which is otherwise overgrown with olive trees and cactuses. A few deserted houses remain, some with round arched entrances and tall windows with various arched designs. In one of the remaining houses, the smooth stone above the entrance arch is inscribed with Arabic calligraphy, a fixture of Palestinian architecture. The well and the village spring also remain. (1992a: 437)

Today the old stone mosque, parts of which are still standing, is not mentioned by the JNF website. In 2004 the mosque was turned into a milk farm; the Jewish owner removed the stone that indicated the founding date of the mosque and covered the walls with Hebrew graffiti (Pappé 2006: 217). Other mosques belonging to destroyed villages were turned into restaurants, in the case of

al-Majdal and Qisarya; a shop, in the case of Beersheba; part of
a tourist resort, in the case of az-Zeeb; a bar/restaurant (called
'Bonanza') and a tourist site, in the case of 'Ayn Hawd (Pappé
2006: 217; Khalidi 1992a: 151).

In eastern Galilee, near Tiberias, Lavi (Lion) is a kibbutz
founded in 1949 on the fertile lands of the Palestinian village
of Lubya, which was depopulated during 1948 by the Haganah
forces. Anyone can tell that the source of the Hebrewised name
Lavi is the Palestinian village Lubya; the Zionists, however, have
claimed that the name Lavi comes from the ancient Jewish village
that existed in the days of the Mishana and Talmud. At Lubya the
JNF put up a sign: 'South Africa Forest. Parking. In Memory of
Hans Riesenfeld, Rhodesia, Zimbabwe'. The 'South Africa Forest'
and the 'Rhodesia parking area' were created atop the ruins of
Lubya, of whose existence not a trace was left. Here was a large
village whose sons and daughters are now scattered throughout
the world and who continue to carry their memories with them.[6]
Dr Mahmoud 'Issa, a son of Lubya and a Danish citizen, who accompanied Gideon Levy on the above excursion, made a film in
Danish (with English subtitles) about his village. Dr 'Issa, an oral
historian, also published a book based on interviews with refugees
from Lubya (Issa 2005: 178–96). Levy writes:

> Deep in the grove, one can find a single wall that survived from the
> village, as well as a stone archway that covered a cavern used to store
> crops. The dozens of wells that belonged to the village ('Issa says there
> were more than 400) are surrounded by barbed wire. They are wrecked
> and full of garbage left behind by hikers in the South Africa Forest who
> must have thought that the JNF had dug big trash cans in the ground.
> How were they to know that these were freshwater wells?[7]

The history of the JNF before and after the Nakba, and its
politics of afforestation and planting, are well documented (Lehn
with Davis 1988; Cohen 1993; Pappé 2006; Nathan 2005: 129–54;
Tal 2002). In 1948 the JNF was instrumental in the ethnic cleansing

---

6. Gideon Levy, 'Twilight Zone/Social Studies Lesson', *Haaretz*, 31 March 2004,
www.haaretz.com/hasen/spages/410906.html.
7. Ibid.

of Palestine. Today it continues to play a central role in maintaining Israel's land regime. Founded in 1901 and registered as an English company in 1907, the JNF was created to acquire land and property rights in Palestine for exclusive Jewish settlement, while the indigenous inhabitants of the land were barred from leasing or working on formerly Arab-owned land. Its Memorandum of Association defines its 'primary objective' as 'to purchase, take on lease or in exchange, or otherwise acquire any lands, forests, rights of possession and others rights, easements and other immovable property in the prescribed region [Palestine, Syria and the surrounding areas] ... for the purpose of settling Jews on such lands'. The JNF was expressly prohibited from selling any land, to ensure that it would control these lands in the name of the Jewish people in perpetuity (quoted in Lehn with Davis 1988: 31-2).

During the British Mandatory period the leaders and executives of the JNF, including Menahem Ushishkin (1863-1941; the Russian chairman of the JNF, 1923-41) and Yosef Weitz (1890-1972), director of its Land Settlement Department and Afforestation Department, were perhaps the most consistent, extreme and relentless advocates of the ethnic cleansing of the Palestinians. Weitz was a Polish Jew who arrived in Palestine in 1908 and later became head of the Israeli government's official 'Transfer Committee' of 1948. He was at the centre of Zionist land-purchasing activities for decades. His youngest son, Yehiam, was killed in a Palmah attack on 16 June 1946 (Tal 2002: 82). Weitz's intimate knowledge of and involvement in land purchase made him sharply aware of its limitations. As late as 1947, after half a century of tireless efforts, the collective holdings of the JNF – which constituted about half of the Yishuv total – amounted to a mere 3.5 per cent of the land area of Palestine. A summary of Weitz's political beliefs is provided by his diary entry for 20 December 1940:

> Amongst ourselves it must be clear that there is no room for both peoples in this country ... After the Arabs are transferred, the country will be wide open for us; with the Arabs staying the country will remain narrow and restricted ... There is no room for compromise on this point ... land purchasing ... will not bring about the state ... The only way is to transfer the Arabs from here to neighbouring countries, all of them,

except perhaps Bethlehem, Nazareth, and Old Jerusalem. Not a single village or a single tribe must be left. And the transfer must be done through their absorption in Iraq and Syria and even in Transjordan. For that goal, money will be found – even a lot of money. And only then will the country be able to absorb millions of Jews ... there is no other solution. (Weitz 1940: 1090-91)

A countryside tour in the summer of 1941 took Weitz to a region in central Palestine. He recorded in his diary seeing

large [Arab] villages crowded in population and surrounded by cultivated land growing olives, grapes, figs, sesame, and maize fields ... Would we be able to maintain scattered [Jewish] settlements among these existing [Arab] villages that will always be larger than ours? And is there any possibility of buying their [land]? ... and once again I hear that voice inside me call: *evacuate this country*. (Weitz 1941: 1204; emphasis in the original).

Earlier, in March 1941, Weitz wrote after touring Jewish settlements in the Esdraelon Valley (Marj Ibn 'Amer):

The complete evacuation of the country from its [Arab] inhabitants and handing it to the Jewish people is the answer. (Weitz 1941: 1127)

In April 1948 he recorded in his diary:

I made a summary of a list of the Arab villages which in my opinion must be cleared out in order to complete Jewish regions. I also made a summary of the places that have land disputes and must be settled by military means. (Weitz 1948: 2358)

After 1948 the JNF was repackaged as an environmentalist organisation carrying out afforestation and developmental activities. Today the JNF and its affiliate organisations enjoy charitable status in over fifty countries as environmental bodies; in Europe these are entitled to tax-exempt status.[8] In 1953 the Jewish National Fund Law was passed by the Knesset for the purpose of defining the special legal status and role of the JNF in Israel's land and 'development' policies. On 28 November 1961 a joint covenant with

---

8. Alternative Information Centre, www.alternativenews.org/english/index.php/topics/news/2646-stop-the-jnfstop-greenwashing-apartheid-call-for-endorsements.

the Israeli government (following a series of Knesset laws) consolidated the position of the JNF; one of the covenant's principles was the 'State's pronouncement that the Land of Israel was owned by the Jewish people and must not be sold in perpetuity' (Tal 2002: 89-90). In 1966 the JNF planted the 'Yatir Forest' in the northern Naqab (Negev), named after the biblical town of Yatir.

While early Zionist farmers followed in the footsteps of Palestinian fellahin, planting vineyards, almond orchards and citrus groves, after the Nakba the JNF concentrated on ecological colonialism, the reshaping of the physical environment, transforming the Arab landscape, planting forests and demarcating the 'Israeli space' (Tal 2002). In *The Other Side of Israel* (2005), Susan Nathan, an Israeli author of English origin, shows how after 1948 the JNF planted many forests on the sites of the destroyed Palestinian villages; olive, fig, pomegranate and carob trees and *sabr* plants (particularly the fruit-bearing type of cactus that flourishes in Palestine), which were cultivated for generations and upon whose fruits and oil Palestinian villagers had traditionally relied, were cut down and replaced by predominantly pine and cypress trees (Nathan 2005: 129-30; Tal 2002). The JNF afforestation policy was aimed at erasing traces of the Arab presence prior to 1948 and covering up the destroyed villages and towns (Nathan 2005: 151-2).

Until 1948 the JNF owned some 600,000 dunums of land. By 2007 it controlled directly 13 per cent of the total land in Israel, about 3.5 million dunums.[9] It appoints six out of thirteen members of the governing board of the Israel Lands Authority, which manages much of the 'public' land in Israel. Today the JNF controls directly and indirectly vast properties belonging to millions of Palestinian refugees and internally displaced Palestinians; its current projects of afforestation, displacement and Judaisation centre on Arab localities in the Galilee and the Naqab – areas inhabited by Palestinian citizens of Israel.

In *Pollution in a Promised Land: An Environmental History of Israel*, Alon Tal observes that the control 'of such controversial lands [belong to Palestinian refugees] remains an enormous source

9. Alaa Mahajneh, 'Situating the JNF in Israel's Land Laws', *Badil*, www.badil. org/en/al-majdal/item/1404-mahajneh-jnf-and-israeli-law.

of bitterness and outrage for Arab-Israelis and Palestinians, who still see the JNF as representing the most imperialist aspects of Zionism' (Tal 2002: 57). The JNF's activities were not limited to the part of Mandate Palestine that became Israel in 1948. The JNF's Canada Park in the Latrun region, for example, covers the remains of the Palestinian villages 'Imwas, Yalu and Bayt Nuba, which were depopulated and razed in the course of the 1967 war. Today visitors to Canada Park, one of the most popular hiking and picnic sites on the way to Jerusalem, would have no idea that the park was built on the ruins of three Palestinian villages whose inhabitants were forcibly evicted in 1967.

Operating through its subsidiary, Hemnuta, the JNF has also illegally acquired lands and houses in the occupied West Bank, and particularly in 1967-occupied Arab Jerusalem.[10] Inside the Green Line the JNF continues to operate as a state-chartered discriminatory organisation and enforces a colonial system of land tenure. And as Palestine solidarity organisations from around the world have begun to challenge this colonial land regime operated by the JNF, the 'Lord Sacks Forest', 'South Africa Forest', 'Carmel Forest Spa Resort', 'Yatir Forest', Canada Park and other forests and historical and archaeological theme parks built on the lands and ruins of hundreds of destroyed Palestinian villages have continued to veil from public view the continuing official Israeli policy to erase traces of the ethnic cleansing of Palestine. According to Zochrot, the Israeli remembrance organisation, eighty-six JNF parks have been established on the sites of depopulated and destroyed Palestinian villages (Cook 2008: 40). The JNF has been fundamentally complicit in the denial of displaced Palestinians' right to return, restitution and compensation, and in green-washing Israel's regime of colonisation and occupation.[11]

The JNF historical and archaeological theme parks and forests are particularly popular with Israeli revellers and for picnicking on Independence Day. For Palestinian citizens of Israel, especially

---

10. Alternative Information Centre, www.alternativenews.org/english/index.php/topics/news/2646-stop-the-jnfstop-greenwashing-apartheid-call-for-endorsements.

11. Alternative Information Centre, 3 June 2010, www.alternativenews.org/english/index.php/topics/news/2646-stop-the-jnfstop-greenwashing-apartheid-call-for-endorsements.

the internal refugees, they are a poignant reminder of the Nakba. In *The Other Side of Israel*, Susan Nathan writes critically:

> In April 2004, during the national celebrations for Independence Day, when Israeli Jews enjoy a day of rejoicing over the founding of their state, I joined a family from Nazareth who quietly commemorated the Palestinians' mirror event, Nakba Day, which marks the Palestinians' loss of their homeland. We visited a Jewish moshav called Tzipori, close to Nazareth, which has been built over the ruins of their parents' village, Saffuriya ... the site of the Arab village is now hidden behind barbed wire and covered by the thick growth of yet another forest planted by the JNF. The only visible clues that Palestinians once lived there are the great mounds of cacti that Arab communities traditionally used as the boundaries to separate properties. Despite the best efforts of the JNF to poison and burn these indigenous Middle Eastern plants, the cacti have refused to die or disappear. (2005: 131)

Located 6 kilometres north-northwest of Nazareth, Saffuriya in many ways encapsulates the multilayered Palestinian identity and heritage deeply rooted in the land. In 1948 Saffuriya was the largest Palestinian village in the Galilee, in terms of both its land size and its population. It thrived agriculturally on olives, figs, pomegranates and wheat. After the eviction of the inhabitants (on 16 July), most of the inhabitants were driven to Lebanon, many ending up in the refugee camps of 'Ayn al-Hilwa, Sabra and Shatila. The remainder became internal refugees (or 'present absentees' in Israeli terminology) in Nazareth, Israel. In the 1950s some families accepted compensation from the Israeli state, while others refused (Humphries 2009: 132-3). The land of the village was distributed between Kibbutz Sde Nahum, Kibbutz Hefziba and Kibbutz Ha-Solelim. The olive, fig and pomegranate trees were replaced with crops for cattle fodder (Benvenisti 2002: 216). With the destruction of the village, Israel sought to eliminate the diverse cultural heritage of the area. The Hebrew-sounding Jewish *moshav* Tzipori (established in 1949) was named after the Hellenised town of Sepphoris of the Roman period. Archaeology has shown that the site holds a rich and diverse historical and architectural legacy that includes Assyrian, Hellenistic, Jewish, Babylonian, Roman, Islamic, Crusader, Palestinian Arab and Ottoman influences. The remains of structures at the site include a Roman theatre, a Roman villa, two early Christian churches, a sixth-century synagogue, more than forty different mosaics, and a Crusader fortress that was restored and rebuilt by Palestinian leader Daher El-Omar in the eighteenth century (Shahin 2005). The upper part of this still-standing fortress was used as an Arab school from the early 1900s until 1948 (Petersen 2002: 270). Since 1992 the former Arab village has been designated a modern 'national park', run by the Israeli National Park Authority. In *Marketing Heritage: Archaeology and the Consumption of the Past* (2004), Yorke Rowan and Uzi Baram show the selective appropriation of the past and collective amnesia promoted by the Israeli heritage industry and the way the history of the site of Saffuriya is presented by the National Park Authority: it covers the 'Jewish heritage' and the periods up to Roman and Byzantine rule, with a brief mention of the Crusades; the fourteen centuries of Arab and Muslim rule and the rest of the modern history of the site are not mentioned at all (Rowan and Baram 2004: 222; also Baram 2007: 299-325).

Ironically some of the lands of the destroyed Palestinian villages which have been taken over by the JNF are dedicated to revolutionary South American heroes of liberation and struggle for independence. (The JNF itself maintains offices in the capitals of Bolivia and Venezuela, where they raise funds to entrench further the Israeli apartheid system and erase the traces of the Nakba.) An example is the Eshtaol Forest, which covers the lands of the former villages Islin and Ishwa, and parts of the lands of Bayt Mahsir and Bayt Susin. The Forest has three courts. The first is dedicated to the memory of Simón Bolivar, the revered nineteenth-century liberator of Latin America from European Spanish colonialism; it stands on the land of the village Ishwa. The other two are dedicated to another leader of Latin America liberation, General José de San Martín; they stand on the land of Bayt Mahsir. Moshav Eshtaol, built on the ruins of Ishwa, is a settlement of Jewish immigrants from the Yemen, who were transferred by the Zionist movement to Palestine shortly after 1948.[12]

---

12. Rahela Mizrahi, 'JNF presence in S. America perpetuates Palestine injustice', *The*

Fashioning a European-biblical Landscape?

On 16 June 2010 at a ceremony near Jerusalem the JNF celebrated the planting of 'Lord Sacks Forest', named after the British chief rabbi, Lord Jonathan Sacks. The celebration and fund-raising project, which was attended by Lord and Lady Sacks, were in 'recognition of his [Sacks's] personal contribution to the spiritual and intellectual life of the country [Israel] and an honour for the whole Jewish community ... [and] ... a lasting contribution to the beauty and environment of Israel and Jerusalem in particular'. In response the chief rabbi declared that of 'all the honours that Elaine and I have received, the planting of a forest in our name by JNF counts amongst the greatest of them all'.[13]

Is the British chief rabbi a refugee from the reality of the millions of Palestinian refugees? Isn't he contributing to the Israeli settler-colonial policies and efforts to construct a sterile English 'biblical' landscape completely divorced from reality and morality? Surely he must be fully aware of the role of the JNF in camouflaging the traces of the destroyed villages and its activities aimed at green-washing the Palestinian Nakba.

Around Jerusalem thousands of acres of pine forest are designed to fashion a new pastoral biblical landscape and create a new collective memory and give the impression of an 'authentic' timeless biblical landscape in which trees have been standing forever. But this 'natural landscape' is a carefully constructed scene to camouflage the systematically expropriated land of Palestinian villages, the destruction of cultivated olive groves and the ethnic cleansing of the Nakba. The underlying intention is to obscure the locations of the Palestinian villages and prevent any cultivation of the land by non-Jews. The Israeli architects Rafi Segal and Eyal Weizman, commenting on Israeli settlement activities in occupied East Jerusalem and the West Bank and their underlying Zionist ideology, write:

Electronic Intifada, 13 August 2009, http://electronicintifada.net/v2/article10708.shtml.

13. www.jnf.co.uk/trees_lord_sacks.html.

In the ideal image of the pastoral landscape, integral to the perspective of colonial traditions, the admiration of the rustic panorama is always viewed through the window frames of modernity. The impulse to retreat from the city to the country reasserts the virtue of a simpler life close to nature ... the re-creation of the picturesque scenes of Biblical landscape becomes a testimony to an ancient claim on the land. The admiration of the landscape thus functions as a cultural practice, by which social and cultural identities are formed. Within this panorama, however, lies a cruel paradox: the very thing that renders the landscape 'Biblical' or 'pastoral', its traditional inhabitants and cultivation in terraces, olive orchards, stone buildings and the presence of livestock, is produced by the Palestinians, who the Jewish settlers came to replace. And yet, the very people who came to cultivate the 'green olive orchards' and render the landscape Biblical are themselves excluded from the panorama. The Palestinians are there to produce the scenery and then disappear ... The gaze that sees a 'pastoral Biblical landscape' does not register what it does not want to see, it is a visual exclusion that seeks a physical exclusion. Like a theatrical set, the panorama can be seen as an edited landscape put together by invisible stage hands ... What for the state is a supervision mechanism that seeks to observe the Palestinians is for the settlers a window on a pastoral landscape that seeks to erase them. The Jewish settlements superimpose another datum of latitudinal geography upon an existing landscape. Settlers can thus see only other settlements, avoid those of the Palestinian towns and villages, and feel that they have truly arrived 'as the people without land to the land without people'. (Segal and Weizman 2003: 92)

The Liberal Coloniser Facing the European Forests

Israeli historical revisionism and the 'new history' of the 1980s (see Chapter 5) is deeply rooted in the liberal Zionist narratives of the 1950s and 1960s. In the first two decades of the state Israelis had a deep anxiety about the discovery of the truth about 1948 and the 'nightmarish' prospect of Palestinian refugees retuning to their towns and villages in Israel. *Facing the Forests* (*Mul Ha-Ye'arot*), one of A.B. Yehoshua's early fictional works, was published in 1968. The short story was an attempt by the novelist to bring the truths of the Nakba repressed within the Israeli psyche back to the surface. It also shows that fourteen years after the publication of Yizhar's *Khirbet Khiz'ah* (1949; see Chapter 5), the events surrounding the destruction of Palestine in 1948 had been effectively suppressed in the Israeli collective memory.

Facing the Forests tells of a mute Palestinian forest watchman who burns down a JNF forest to reveal the hidden ruins of his former village, destroyed in 1948. The story opens with the destruction of the village during the Nakba and the planting of the forest. It recounts the story of an Israeli student who is preoccupied with the history of the Latin Crusaders. Looking for a break and solitude, he finds a job as a forest ranger. When he arrives in the watch house in the forest he finds an Arab man whose tongue had been cut out and the man's daughter. Shortly after his arrival the student begins to suffer from nightmares; he is constantly anticipating a catastrophe. As the summer continues the student begins to desire the man's daughter. The tension between the two men escalates and suddenly the man sets fire to the forest, which burns to the ground. At dawn the student 'turns his gaze to the smoking hills and frowns: there, out of the smoke and haze, the ruined village appears before his eyes; born anew, in its basic outlines as an abstract drawing, as all things past and buried'. While the student fails to see the truth unearthed by his research on the Crusades, the fire reveals it (Yehoshua 1968; also quoted in Gover 1986: 37–8).

Designed to cover up the truth, the JNF website tells us that the organisation is 'the caretaker of the land of Israel', on behalf of its owners – Jewish people everywhere, including the British chief rabbi and other Jewish supporters of an apartheid system of land tenure.

The Destruction of al-Araqib, July 2010

In a recent example of ethnic cleansing in the Naqab/Negev, on 27 July 2010 the Israeli police razed an entire Palestinian Bedouin village, al-Araqib, to the ground to make way for a JNF forest. The destruction of al-Araqib (situated to the north of Beersheba) was carried out by a 1,300-strong contingent of security forces, police and civilian guard equipped with guns, stun grenades and bulldozers. Also Jewish high-school students, members of the civilian guard (which has a programme designed to incorporate Israeli children into the state's military apparatus), participated in the levelling of the village. It was part of a larger project designed to reinforce Israeli apartheid and force the indigenous Bedouin communities of the Naqab away from their ancestral lands and into Indian-reservation-style shanty towns constructed for them by the Israeli government. The land of the Bedouins will then be open to Jewish settlers. During a three-hour raid forty homes were demolished and 300 residents were evicted, including 200 children, whilst fruit orchards and olive and carob trees were uprooted. The demolitions were facilitated by the Israeli government to make way for another forest sponsored by the JNF. Today there are 155,000 Palestinian Bedouins in the Naqab, many of whom have been repeatedly displaced since 1948 (Abu-Sa'ad 2005: 113–41); 83,000 of them live in 'unrecognised villages', without electricity or running water and with no access to municipal or government assistance.

Dr Neve Gordon, of Ben-Gurion University of the Negev, who witnessed the destruction of al-Araqib, wrote that the flattening of the village lent legitimacy to the expulsion of Israel's Bedouin citizens from the Negev in order to Judaise it.

> This time the impact of the destruction sank in immediately. Perhaps because the 300 people who resided in al-Arakib, including their children, were sitting in the rubble when I arrived, and their anguish was evident; or perhaps because the village is located only 10 minutes from my home in Be'er Sheva and I drive past it every time I go to Tel Aviv or Jerusalem; or perhaps because the Bedouins are Israeli citizens, and I suddenly understood how far the state is ready to go to accomplish its objective of Judaising the Negev region; what I witnessed was, after all, an act of ethnic cleansing.[14]

---

14. Neve Gordon, 'Ethnic Cleansing in the Israeli Negev', *Guardian*, 28 July 2010, www.guardian.co.uk/commentisfree/2010/jul/28/ethnic-cleansing-israeli-negev.

4

Appropriating History:
Looting of Palestinian Records, Archives
and Library Collections, 1948-2011

It is widely recognised by historians and archaeologists that Palestine had a remarkably stable population from the end of the Neolithic period, some 6,000 years ago, when the Mediterranean economy was first established in the region (Thompson 1992: 171-352, 1999: 103-227). Long before the creation of the Jewish State in 1948, Palestine had a diverse and multicultural population and a multilayered identity deeply rooted in the ancient past. The appropriation of the ancient history of Palestine, the historicisation of biblical legends and the narrative of the New Hebrew Society have all given the Zionist narrative its force. Appropriation of the Palestinian heritage and its voices has been central to Zionist colonial practice before and since the Nakba. In 1948 the Israeli state appropriated for itself immovable Palestinian assets and personal possessions, including schools, libraries, books, pictures, private papers, historical documents and manuscripts, furniture, churches, mosques, urban residential quarters, transport infrastructure, police stations, prisons and railways (Khalidi 1992a).

After the 1967 conquests, the Israeli state, constructed as it was on the basis of biblical mythologies, was bound to base its conception of Jerusalem upon a mythologised entity, 'Jerusalem of Gold', and to claim historical and ideological rights over the newly acquired territories, as well as resting its claim on territorial

expansion and domination. The same process of appropriation of
Palestinian heritage and the superimposition of Zionist Hebrew
colonising toponymy on Palestinian sites continued after 1967.
Almost immediately after the conquest of East Jerusalem the Palestine Archaeological Museum, which represented the multilayered
identity and heritage of Palestine, was renamed the Rockefeller
Museum. Some items were taken to the Shrine of the Book (Heikhal
Hasefer), a wing of the Israel Museum in West Jerusalem, which
houses parts of the Dead Sea Scrolls discovered in 1947–56 in the
Qumran caves. The Palestine Archaeological Museum had been
located on Karm al-Shakyh (Vineyard of the Shaykh), a hill just
outside the north-eastern corner of the Old City. The museum had
been conceived and established during the Mandatory period, with
financial support from the Rockefeller family. It was opened to
the public in January 1938. The museum housed a large collection
of artefacts unearthed in the excavations conducted in Palestine
between 1890 and 1948. Also among the museum's possessions
were eighth-century wooden panels from the al-Aqsa Mosque and
twelfth-century (Crusader period) marble lintels from the Church
of the Holy Sepulchre.

The museum was run by an international board of trustees until
1966, when it was taken over by the Jordanian state. Since 1967
the museum has been jointly managed by the Israel Museum and
the Israel Department of Antiquities and Museums, subsequently
renamed the Israel Antiquities Authority. The site is now the
headquarters of the Authority. While the Palestine Archaeological
Museum of the Mandatory period still represented the positive
diversity of religions and ethnicities that characterised Jerusalem
and Palestine for many centuries, the Israel Museum and Shrine of
the Book represent that single-minded determination by the Israeli
Antiquities Authority and Israel's heritage industry to Judaise and
colonise both the ancient and the modern history of Palestine.

The systematic destruction of Palestinian infrastructure in 1948
and the appropriation of the records, documentation and cultural
heritage of the Palestinians by the Israeli state made it possible for
Benny Morris – who cannot read Arabic and whose main emphasis
is on official (Israeli and Western) documents rather than on the

people or voices behind those documents – to appropriate and thereby silence Palestinian voices and assert that Palestinians produced no '"state" papers' and that there is

> no Arab *documentation* [on 1948] of the sort historians must rely on
> ... [in contrast with the 'profusion of first rate, illuminating Israeli,
> Western and UN documentation'] What exists in Arabic or translated
> from Arabic into Hebrew or English are some Arab political and mili-
> tary memoirs, newspaper clippings, chronicles, and histories... Much
> of this material ... is slight, unreliable, tendentious, imaginative and
> occasionally fantastical. (Morris 1994: 42-3)

Other Israeli historians have also emphasised the availability of copious Israeli literary and archival materials and contrasted this with the paucity of comparable Palestinian documentation. Nothing is said about the asymmetrical power relationship between Israel and the Palestinians and the reinforcement of this asymmetry by (among others things) the repeated cycles of Israeli looting of Palestinian historical documents, archives and library collections in and since 1948.

Following the Nakba the Palestinians found themselves physi-cally dispersed, stateless and marginalised at a time when most of the Arab people had achieved statehood. Palestinian statelessness has remained a key feature of Palestinian national life since 1948. Today exile, physical dispersal and fragmentation are at the centre of Palestinian social and political life. A major difficulty of dispersal and statelessness is the near impossibility of establishing and main-taining 'public archives', museums and documentation centres, either in exile or under Israeli occupation. Furthermore, as we shall see below, what Palestinian research institutions and archival and documentation centres there are have been regularly raided and their documents confiscated by Israeli forces. This has been widely documented in the two cases of the Palestinian Research Centre in Beirut in 1982 and the Arab Studies Society archive at Orient House in East Jerusalem in 2001. Both had served as a depository of Palestine's historical, political and cultural heritage.

The long history of Israel's 'creating facts on the ground', de-stroying the physical reality of historical Palestine, plundering

and destroying Palestinian documents goes all the way back to the
Nakba. Already in 1948, several private collections of manuscripts
and tens of thousands of Palestinian books were looted by the
Haganah and never returned (Rose 1993). Parts of these private
collections, including the diary and private papers of Khalil al-
Sakakini (1878–1953), ended up in the library of the Hebrew University of Jerusalem.[1] Al-Sakakini was one of the country's leading
Palestinian educators, linguists and authors. He kept a now-famous
diary (from 1907 to 1952), which is widely considered to be among
the most important Palestinian records of the time. Ironically
Benny Morris's *The Birth of the Palestinian Refugee Problem,
1947–1949* (1987) uses extracts in Hebrew from al-Sakakini's 1948
diary without mentioning the fact that it was in fact looted by
Israel in 1948. The Sakakinis were forced to leave their home in
the Qatamon neighbourhood, which was occupied and depopulated
by Israel; the Judaised Palestinian neighbourhood was officially
given a Hebrew name, Gonen.

A footnote to this story is that in the Israeli reoccupation of
Palestinian cities and towns in the West Bank in the spring of
2002, Israeli soldiers vandalised the Khalil Sakakini Cultural
Centre in Ramallah,[2] which was set up to preserve Palestinians'
cultural heritage.[3]

More recently an Israeli doctoral student, at Ben-Gurion University of the Negev, discovered, through research in Israeli archives,
that Israel had plundered and destroyed tens of thousands of Palestinian books in the early years after the state's establishment. In an
interview with Al Jazeera (published on its website), the researcher

1. 'The Looted Archives of the Orient House', *Jerusalem Quarterly* 13, Summer 2001, www.jerusalemquarterly.org/ViewArticle.aspx?id=184.
2. Ewen MacAskill, 'Human Rights Abuses and Horror Stories', *Guardian*, 20 April 2002.
3. A report compiled by Tom Twiss, Government Information Librarian, University of Pittsburgh, dated 2 August 2002 (and revised 16 January 2003), gives a long list of the damage caused by the Israeli army in the spring of 2002 to Palestinian institutions across the West Bank, including public libraries and public archives, records, files, confiscation of computers and theft of equipment, books and journals. Educational and research facilities, cultural organisations and media outlets, as well as Palestinian Authority ministries were also targeted. In Ramallah and Bethlehem, public archives were gutted and property records destroyed; many years of research and valuable bibliographical information and databases were lost.

revealed the destruction of the Palestinian books the Israeli army had collected in 1948 in Jerusalem, Jaffa, Haifa, Safad, and other Palestinian towns. In 1958, a decade after the Nakba, the Israeli authorities destroyed 27,000 books, most of them Palestinian textbooks from the pre-1948 period, claiming that they were either useless or threatened the state. The authorities sold the books to a paper plant. 'This was a cultural massacre undertaken in a manner that was worse than European colonialism, which safeguarded the items it stole in libraries and museums', the researcher told Al Jazeera.[4]

The 1948 defeat and Nakba resulted in the destruction of the network of public figures and urban notables, the end of the old social, political, cultural and national elites of Palestine; ethnic cleansing effectively emptied the urban hinterlands of this sector of the population. The Palestinian leadership, led by the Arab Higher Committee, their main political organ in Mandatory Palestine, and headed by the reactionary leader Haj Amin al-Husseini, the Mufti of Jerusalem, were totally discredited in the post-Nakba period (Achcar 2010). As Palestinian scholar Yezid Sayigh shows,

> The establishment of the State of Israel over most of mandate Palestine in 1948 deprived its Arab inhabitants of the national base in which territory, economy and society met. *Al-nakba* decisively ended any hope for the emergence of a Palestinian national base along the lines of the entities that had already taken root and gained independence in surrounding Arab countries since the end of direct European rule. The loss of land and other means of production undermined the sense of identity in what was a predominantly agrarian society, and removed its sources of autonomous wealth and economic reproduction. The impact was compounded by the physical dispersal of the population and its subjection to separate, often rival, Arab authorities in its various places of refuge.
>
> As serious for Palestinian society, the destruction of the old elite of large landowners, merchants, and officeholders in 1948 was accompanied by the precipitate flights of a large part of the urban-based middle class. The exodus of civil servants, professionals, businessmen, and

---

4. 'Israel Committed Cultural Massacre, Destroyed Palestinian Books', 29 January 2010, http://aljazeera.com/news/articles/34/Israel-Committed-Cultural-Massacre-Destroyed-Pale.html.

other educated Palestinians removed the social strata that were already on the rise and that would normally have provided an alternative focus of national leadership and organisation. Instead, the middle class was fragmented and marginalized at a critical juncture. Palestinians of peasant or working-class background gathered in destitute refugee camps in impoverished rural areas or in the peripheries of Arab cities, while those of middle-class background used their moveable capital, skills, and family connections to find residence and employment in the cities or further abroad. The equalizing impact of the *al-nakba* had not so much destratified Palestinian society as disarticulated it. (Sayigh 1997: 665)

As Palestinian sociologist Jamil Hilal has pointed out, from the Nakba until the mid-1960s there was no Palestinian national elite. This vacuum was filled largely by local leaders, mukhtars or tribal leaders (Hilal 2002: 29-32). Despite this fragmentation and dispersal, in the decade after 1948 Palestinian 'marginality' (to use bell hooks's term[5]) became 'a site of resistance' (1990: 241-3). From 'below', popular and refugee-led resistance and 'Palestinianism [were] a natural response to *al-nakba*, but it was the experience of social and political marginality that effectively transformed it from "a popular grass-roots patriotism" into a proto-nationalism in the decade after 1948' (Sayigh 1997: 46).

Until the establishment of the PLO in the 1960s Palestinians were in effect without formal political or social representation; there was no single territorially based cultural elite.

The Beirut Archives of the Palestinian Research Centre, 1965–82

For many years stateless and exiled Palestinians had to rely on the Beirut-based Palestinian Research Centre and the Institute for Palestine Studies (also in Beirut) to preserve their national heritage. The staff of the two institutions collected and archived a large quantity of historical documents and worked tirelessly to preserve the historical heritage of the land.

---

5. bell hooks is the pen name of Gloria Jean Watkins, an American scholar and feminist activist. She has published many books and articles under the lower-case moniker.

The establishment of the two institutions in the mid-1960s coincided with the founding of the Palestine Liberation Organisation (PLO), which for decades would stand as the embodiment of Palestinian nationalism and the symbol of Palestinian collective empowerment in exile, before suffering a decline in support in the 1980s and almost total marginalisation after the Oslo Accords of 1993 and the establishment of the Ramallah-based Palestinian Authority.

The PLO had always represented the uneasy relationship between Palestinian nationalism and liberation, the two goals for an indigenous people engaged against ongoing Zionist/Western colonialism. In the late 1960s and 1970s, under the leadership of Yasser Arafat (1929–2004), the PLO pursued a combined strategy of armed struggle and building social and cultural institutions. In 1970 the PLO was forced to move its headquarters from Amman to Beirut. It was during this Beirut period (which lasted until the massacres of Sabra and Shatila in 1982 and the PLO's departure to Tunisia) that a single territorially based cultural elite was created by the Palestinian guerrilla movement. The PLO espoused liberationist politics as a means of decolonising Palestine. Its anti-colonial struggle was inspired by the Algerian and Vietnamese experiences and other struggles of indigenous peoples. The Palestine Research Centre (Markez al-Abhath), the only PLO institution officially recognised by the Lebanese government, had been established in Beirut in 1965. It employed academics, researchers, journalists, editors, film-makers, artists, poets and novelists. Palestinian cultural institutions in Beirut, in particular, promoted the poster as a means of popularising a nationalist narrative and symbols, historical landmarks and commemorative rituals. Important uprisings and battles were immortalised in such posters and in annual commemoration. Zionist massacres were documented and martyrs remembered.[6] The PLO even entertained the ambition of setting up a Palestinian museum in Beirut.

The initiative for the founding of the Palestinian Research Centre came from independent Palestinian intellectual and author Dr Fayez Sayigh (1922–1984), who, inspired by the pluralism in

---

6. www.thetownhousegallery.com/isp/readings/1/Outline.doc.

Beirut's cultural and political life, took the initiative to the founder and first chairman of the PLO Ahmad Shuqueri. In 1947 Sayigh had departed for the United States to complete his doctoral studies at Georgetown University in Washington DC. Shortly after, his family was driven out of Tiberias during the Nakba. In the 1950s and 1960s he lectured in politics at several American universities, including Yale and Stanford, and worked for the Arab States delegation to the UN in New York. In 1965 he duly founded and became the director general of the Palestine Research Centre in Beirut. Sayigh's encyclopaedic knowledge and towering intellectual legacy are evident in his 500 written works, several hundred tape recordings and films of speeches and interviews, and personal library of some 5,000 volumes, including collections on politics, Israeli affairs, theology, international law, US foreign policy, world history and philosophy.[7] The massive collection of Fayez Sayigh (covering the period 1901–1984), which consists of correspondence, pamphlets, news clippings, journal publications, essays, books and personal files, was entrusted by his widow to the J. Willard Marriott Library, University of Utah.[8] Fayez Sayigh was succeeded by his brother, Dr Anis Sayigh (1931–2009), as director general of the Research Centre. Born in Tiberias and a former lecturer at Cambridge University, Anis Sayigh was one of the main driving forces behind the *Palestinian Encyclopedia* (*al-Mausua al-Filastiniyya*, Damascus, 1984). In 1972 he was the target of an Israeli assassination attempt, receiving a letter bomb which resulted in the partial loss of his eyesight and the loss of several fingers.

Throughout its seventeen years in Beirut, the Palestinian Research Centre published history books, organised cultural events and art exhibitions, and produced films and posters.[9] Together with the Beirut-based independent Institute for Palestine Studies, the Centre distinguished itself as a major Palestinian intellectual-cultural institution and played an important role in the field of

---

7. Andrew I. Killgore, '25 Years After His Death, Dr. Fayez Sayegh's Towering Legacy Lives On', *Washington Report on Middle East Affairs* December 2005, pp. 22-3, www.wrmea.com/archives/December_2005/0512022.html.
8. http://content.lib.utah.edu/cdm4/item_viewer.php?CISOROOT=/UU_EAD&CISOPTR=3229.
9. www.thetownhousegallery.com/isp/readings/1/Outline.doc.

historical research on Palestine and Palestinian affairs. The Centre published the annual *Al-Wathaiq al-Filastiniyyah* (Palestinian Documentation) and from 1971 produced a monthly journal *Shuun Filastiniyya* (Palestinian Affairs). The Centre established vast archival collections and its holdings included the private papers of a number of leading Palestinian and Arab figures politically active in the first half of the twentieth century, such as 'Awni 'Abd al-Hadi, Muhib al-Din al-Khatib, Fawzi al-Qawuqji and 'Izzat Darwaza (Khalidi 2006: 222–3 n39).

> The Centre worked extensively to gather, preserve and classify all documents and books related to these [Palestinian] matters. The library accumulated approximately 25,000 bound volumes, and its documents collection was one of the most extensive in this field anywhere in the world. Through the years, the Centre devoted itself to offering free services to researchers, as well as students and institutions and universities, whether Arab or foreign, concerned with matters pertaining to the Arab–Israeli conflict. The Centre published more than 400 books and various other publications, serving as important reference, works in the fields they covered. (Rubenberg 1983: 61)

Although the PLO provided the bulk of funding for the Research Centre and its main organ, *Shuun Filastiniyya*, virtually all its heads and editors of the journal, including the fiercely independent Anis Sayigh, Mahmoud Darwish and Elias Khoury, strongly opposed the repeated interference of the authoritarian Yasser Arafat and fought hard to preserve their autonomy.

The resourcefulness and popular success of the Palestinian Research Centre were resented by the Israeli state and Israeli academia. The Centre established and amassed Palestinian archives, disseminated historical and scholarly research on Palestine and preserved Palestinian popular culture and heritage. Before the Israeli invasion of Beirut in September 1982, two attempts were made by Israel, in July and August, to destroy the Centre completely (Rubenberg 1983: 61–2).

In 1982, as the PLO evacuated Beirut during the Israeli invasion, Palestinian institutions in the city were destroyed. In mid-September, the Israeli army raided the Palestinian Research Centre along with other Palestinian and Lebanese institutions.

Nearly all Palestinian cultural institutions in Beirut were pillaged, including the Palestine Cinema Institute, the Samed Workshop and the Palestinian Red Crescent clinic. The contents of the Research Centre were systematically looted; its historical archives and a 25,000-volume library and microfilm collection were looted and carted away by the Israeli army (Khalidi 2006: xxxvii; Chomsky 1999: 422). During the week that Israeli forces stayed in the area of Ras Beirut, the neighbourhood where the Centre was situated, an Israeli military unit stole its priceless collections. They filled huge military trucks and carried off most of the Centre's contents in daily convoys directly to Israel. Some materials were destroyed inside the building itself.

The Israeli invaders took from the library all the books in Arabic, Hebrew, English and French, including hundreds of rare volumes, important reference works and precious manuscripts. They also stole the files and microfilms from the archives and all the apparatus used by the Centre (including microfilm-making devices, classifying and recording machines, tape-recorders, radios, televisions, printing and photocopy machines), along with precious documents, dating back centuries, that the Centre had purchased in Europe and restored to the cultural custody of the Palestinians. Not satisfied with this degree of plunder, Israeli forces also carried back to Israel all furniture and fittings that were in good condition, including telephones and telex machines, electrical appliances, ashtrays, chairs, rugs and personal effects of Centre employees (Rubenberg 1983: 62-3).

On 5 February 1983 the Research Centre was destroyed by a bomb that killed twenty people, including the wife of its director Sabri Jirys (Chomsky 1999: 422). By then all the historical archives had been largely looted or destroyed by the Israelis – whatever has survived was stored in private or personal collections. Some of the archival collections of the Research Centre, however, were returned to the PLO by Israel as part of a prisoner exchange in 1984 – minus the film collection.[10] Apparently these returned collections were initially transferred to Algeria, but in 2006 their

---

10. 'The Looted Archives of the Orient House', *Jerusalem Quarterly* 13, Summer 2001, www.jerusalemquarterly.org/ViewArticle.aspx?id=184.

whereabouts were unknown (Khalidi 2006: 223 n40). The staff of the Centre subsequently moved to Cyprus.

The Jerusalem Archives of the Arab Studies Society/Orient House, 1979–2001

In 2001 the Israeli government closed the Orient House (Bayt al-Sharq) in East Jerusalem and confiscated its archive and the collections of the Arab Studies Society housed in it. These archives included the private papers of the prominent Palestinian leader Musa al-'Alami (1897–1984) and the Arab Information Office that he headed during the Nakba (Khalidi 2006: 222–3 n39). Unlike the looting of the archives of the Research Centre in Beirut, the seizure of the Orient House archives occurred despite a signed agreement between Israel and the PLO.

The Arab Studies Society Library and the archives of the Orient House were a piece of living history and a monument to the long and continuing Palestinian struggle for survival in Jerusalem. The Orient House mansion itself had been built by the al-Husseini family in 1897, which has owned it since. The archives of the Arab Studies Society were set up by Faisal al-Husseini (1940–2001), a leading Palestinian figure in Jerusalem and the son of 'Abd al-Qader al-Husseini, the legendary commander of local Arab forces in the Jerusalem area during 1948, who was killed in the Qastal battle with the Haganah. Faisal Husseini later served as head of the Palestinian delegation to the Madrid Middle East Peace Conference of 1991. In 1979 he founded the Arab Studies Society in East Jerusalem and a year later established its library:

> a specialized library focused on Palestinian history, politics, and society; the Arab World; and the Arab–Israeli conflict. In 1983 the Arab Studies Society moved to its current headquarters in the grand premises of the Orient House at number 8 Abu Abeida St. in the Sheikh Jarrah neighborhood of East Jerusalem. Then in 1988 the center was ordered shut by the Israeli government and remained closed for four years. The process of collecting books, however, continued at other locations. Beginning with only 200 volumes in 1980, the collection currently includes approximately 17,000 books in both English and Arabic, and 70 periodicals. These holdings include the private library of Musa

al-Alami, the chairman of the Arab Office in Jerusalem from 1947-49. In addition to the library there is a Document Center with a document archive, a photograph archive, a press archive, and a section of documents on important contemporary and historical personalities. The aim of the Document Center is to preserve and protect the intellectual and physical records of Palestine from deterioration. The collection contains 200,000 hard copies of documents and 300,000 copies on microfilm and microfiche. 60 percent of the papers are original documents. The collection covers Palestinian history chiefly from the last period of the Ottoman Empire through to the present and is divided according to subjects such as political parties, economy, education, land sales, Palestinian women, Jewish immigration to Palestine, and Jewish political organizations. The most important documents are those acquired from the Arab Office of Jerusalem, established in 1945 by the Arab League. The Arab Office of Jerusalem was one of 7 Arab Offices set up around the world, the others being in London, France, Lebanon, Iraq, Washington, and Rio de Janeiro. The Jerusalem office, under the direction of Musa al-Alami, served to give voice abroad to the opinions and ideas of Arabs and Palestinians concerning events in Palestine. There are also papers of the Arab Higher Committee, of the Palestinian army, *al-Jihad al-Muqaddas*, and many others collected from families and private institutions.

The photograph section contains a large collection of original photographs from the Ottoman period to the present. They include glass negatives that go back to the Ottoman period and a fine collection of family photographs from the Mandate period. The collection also contains a photographic survey of Palestine that was conducted by the Arab Studies Society from 1980 to 1984. The library is currently in the process of organizing and developing the archive and digitizing the collection for viewing on CD-ROM. In addition to the personalities section and the press archive section already mentioned, there is a small Oral History collection consisting of 100 cassettes devoted chiefly to interviews with Palestinians who lived through the Arab Revolt of 1936-1939.[11]

Until 2001 the Orient House constituted the only representation of Palestinian political institutions in the city. In this capacity, it was recognised by all the international powers involved in the peace negotiations since the Madrid Peace Conference in 1991. Moreover, 'the Israeli government had underwritten this

11. *Jerusalem Quarterly* 6, Autumn 1999, www.jerusalemquarterly.org/ViewArticle.aspx?id=250.

legitimacy in the letter of assurances sent by then Israeli Foreign Minister Shimon Peres to his Norwegian counterpart, the late Johan Jurgen Holst, on October 11th, 1993.'[12] In this exchange of letters preceding the 1993 Oslo Accords Israel promised that it would not violate the right of the House to continue to operate freely.[13] On 10 August 2001, shortly after Husseini's death, the Israeli police raided the Orient House and closed its offices, along with nine other Palestinian institutions in East Jerusalem. Items confiscated by the Israeli government under the pretext of 'security' included personal belongings, a large number of documents relating to the Jerusalem issue and the 1991 Madrid Conference and the Arab Studies Society photography collection. Also the personal books and documents of the late Faisal al-Husseini were summarily impounded.[14] The significance of the looting lies in the Arab Studies Society photography collection located in the Orient House building:

> This collection – also pillaged from the Orient House – represents a unique record of Jerusalem's ethno-graphic relations among its 19th and 20th century population. Although its theft is unlikely to arouse anger as long as people remain unaware of its significance or even of its existence, it is an irreplaceable and invaluable archive.[15]

Since the loss of Beirut as the most important Palestinian intellectual, cultural and documentation centre and the confiscation of the collections of the Orient House in Jerusalem, other Palestinian documentation and resource centres have emerged, including Birzeit University's Centre for Research and Documentation, Shaml-Palestinian Diaspora and Refugee Centre in Ramallah, the Palestinian Return Centre in London and the Palestine Center in Washington DC, which was founded by Palestinian intellectual and Georgetown University academic Hisham Sharabi in 1991. However, nothing can compensate for the loss of the unique archival and photographic collections stolen by Israel from Beirut and the Orient House.

---

12. 'The Looted Archives of the Orient House'.
13. Ibid.
14. Ibid.
15. Ibid.

5

Post-Zionism, the Liberal Coloniser and Hegemonic Narratives: A Critique of the Israeli 'New Historians'

The Myths of Zionism

Ben-Gurion was right ... Without the uprooting of the Palestinians, a Jewish state would not have arisen here ... There are circumstances in history that justify ethnic cleansing. I know that this term is completely negative in the discourse of the 21st century, but when the choice is between ethnic cleansing and genocide ... I prefer ethnic cleansing.

Benny Morris, 'Survival of the Fittest? Interview with Ari
Shavit', *Haaretz*, magazine, 9 January 2004

Ever since the Nakba, a bitter controversy has raged over its causes and circumstances. The Palestinians have always maintained that the refugees were either directly expelled or terrorised into flight. Mainstream Israeli historians and pro-Zionist authors and publicists in the West, on the other hand, still claim that the refugees either left of their own accord or were advised or ordered to do so by their own leaders. The Israeli narrative has been a classic case of mendacity and denial: denial of any wrong-doing, denial of the ethnic cleansing of Palestine, denial of the refugees' 'right to return' (in accordance with UN Resolution 194), denial of any moral responsibility or culpability for the creation of the refugees, and denial of restitution of property or reparations (Masalha 2003).

Since 1948 Israel has denied any responsibility for the Palestinian Nakba. This was challenged in the late 1980s and early 1990s by a group of Israeli revisionist historians. However, for over six decades Israel's land and demographic policies have been designed to foster a new collective and public memory based on the founding myths of Zionism: 'making the desert bloom', establishing settlements on 'swamp lands' and 'empty hills', 'exile and return' to 'a land without a people for a people without a land' (Masalha 1997), and the 'triumph of the few against the many'. Furthermore, since 1948 Palestinian attempts to constitute a coherent narrative of their past have often been challenged and silenced by Israelis and pro-Zionist lobbies in the West. In fact until recently the Nakba has been completely excluded from Western discourses on Israel–Palestine.

A New Regime of Knowledge?

No need to hear your voice when I can talk about you better than you can speak about yourself. No need to hear your voice. Only tell me about your pain. I want to know your story. And then I will tell it back to you in a new way. Tell it back to you in such a way that it has become mine, my own. Re-writing you I write myself anew. I am still author, authority. I am still colonizer the speaking subject and you are now at the center of my talk.

bell hooks (1990: 241-3)

Since the late 1980s a great deal of the rewriting of the history of 1948 has been undertaken by a small group of Israeli 'new historians'. Ironically, although the Nakba is central to the Palestinian collective memory and society of today, only a relatively small number of Palestinian historians and researchers – including Walid Khalidi (1959: 21-4, 1959b: 22-32, 1961: 22-8, 1992, 1997: 5-21); Elias Shoufani (1972: 108-21, 2001: 5-19); Nafiz Nazzal (1974a, 1974b, 1978); Nur Masalha (1992, 1997, 2003, 2005a, 2008: 123-56); Elias Sanbar (1984); Rashid Khalidi (2001: 12-36); Sami Hadawi (1967); Sharif Kanaana (1992); Abdel Jawad (2007: 59-127); Sa'di and Abu-Lughod (2007) – have investigated its actual roots and causes. This is rather ironic since the debate over the causes and circumstances of the 1948 Nakba-cum-refugee exodus are reflected in the array of proposed solutions to the 'refugee problem'.

Central to this revisionist historiography are debates on the 1948 Palestinian refugee exodus (expulsion versus flight), the impact of the British Mandate on Palestinian Arab and Jewish societies, the regional balance of power in 1948, the questionable nature of Zionist acceptance of the 1947 UN Partition Plan, and the revelations about early secret peace negotiations between Israeli and Arab leaders. The picture that emerges from the 1948 war, for example, as historian Avi Shlaim has shown, is not the fictional one (still repeated by Israeli spokespersons) of Israel standing alone against the combined might of the Arab world. It is rather one of convergence between the interests of Israel and those of Hashemite Transjordan and the 'tacit alliance' between the Zionists and Hashemites (backed by the British) against other members of the divided Arab 'war coalition' (Shlaim 2001: 79-103) and especially against the creation of an independent state for the Palestinians, within the UN Partition Plan.

In settler-colonial societies, Frantz Fanon writes, it is the coloniser who makes history and is conscious of making it (1963: 51). This power/record/history writing nexus, with its 'regimes of truth/knowledge', was famously dissected by Michel Foucault in *The Archaeology of Knowledge* (1972) and *Power/Knowledge* (1980). Foucault also argued for a non-linear approach to history and an appreciation of the importance of discontinuities and accidents in history. In his recent work, *The Israel–Palestine Conflict: Contested Histories* (2010), the Canadian liberal Jewish historian Neil Caplan, who is sensitive to the asymmetrical power relationship between Israel and the Palestinians, comments extensively and enthusiastically on the works of the Israeli 'new historians' and laments the lack of an equivalent Palestinian 'new history' capable of recognising the legitimacy of Zionism and the Jewish 'national' yearning for the 'ancient homeland'. For Caplan (as for Benny Morris) the answer lies in a variety of reasons, top of which is the Western (and, by implication, Israeli) scholarly and democratic tradition of open debates and the opening of Israeli state archives and access to public archives:

Primary sources in the form of diplomatic correspondence and memoranda are plentiful and more easily accessible on the Israeli side. The Western [and Israeli] tradition of open public archives is not generally replicated in the Arab world. The Palestinian community, stateless and dispersed, lacked the structures and resources needed to facilitate and promote the accumulation of authoritative documentation on Palestinian history on the same scale as the rival Central Zionist Archives and Israel State Archives. For years, exiled Palestinians relied on the Beirut-based PLO Research Center and the Institute for Palestine Studies to collect and preserve these parts of their national heritage; but much of the task of preservation of documents was left to individuals and families. The limitations of the written testimony are being partially counteracted by a new generation of collectors of oral history. (Caplan 2010: 241)

In Israel there is a great deal of 'patriotic' self-censorship on the part of mainstream historians. Also the way in which record-keepers and archivists determine access to sensitive records and archival material is based on their assessment of the political leaning of the researcher. In an article entitled 'Sifting People, Sorting Papers: Academic Practice and the Notion of State Security in Israel', Tania Forte shows that the whole notion of free access to the archives is totally alien to the country (2003: 215-23). In fact the revisions of mainstream historical accounts were partly, although not primarily, due to the release of previously unavailable Israeli archival data on the early state period. Caplan is conscious of the relationship between knowledge, power and history writing, multi-vocal historical experiences and the problematisation method of historical writing, as well as the ethical implications of rewriting history on the Israel–Palestine struggle (Caplan 2010: 241). But has the emergence of Israeli 'new history' narrative reduced or reinforced the asymmetrical power relationship between Israel and the Palestinians? For Caplan (as for Benny Morris, Zeev Sternhell and most Israeli 'new historians'), Zionism is not a brutal settler-colonial movement; on the contrary, it is a 'national liberation movement' of the Jewish people; for him the 'new history' is largely the product of an 'open and democratic' Israeli tradition and a question of releasing and declassifying archives and discovering new documents. Of the nexus of power and knowledge

– the immense power asymmetry between coloniser and colonised; between a powerful state, armed to the teeth with nuclear and conventional weapons, and the occupied and exiled Palestinians (nearly 70 per cent of whom are refugees) – there is barely mention. Of the systematic appropriation of Palestinian cultural heritage by the Israeli state and the repeated destruction of Palestinian documentation centres and appropriation of Palestinian archives and collective memory, we learn little if anything. Such issues are either not discussed at all or, where they are, are considered of no import.

Amidst deep social and political crises, anniversaries often produce soul-searching and reflection on the past. Coinciding with the fortieth anniversary of the establishment of the State of Israel, Israeli revisionist historiography sought to tackle '1948' and the 'exodus' of the Palestinians. The 'new historians', who captured the attention of the Israeli media, were led by a loosely defined group of political journalists and academics – including Tom Segev (1986),[1] Simha Flapan (1987) (d. 1987), Amnon Kapeliouk (1987: 16–24) (d. 2009), Benny Morris (1986a, 1987, 2004), Avi Shlaim (1988; Rogan and Shlaim 2001), Ilan Pappé (1992, 1999, 2006, 2010) – in the period immediately following the 1982 Israeli invasion of Lebanon and the Sabra and Shatila massacres in Beirut. Four of those named above were high-profile journalists: Segev wrote for *Haaretz*, Flapan and Kapeliouk wrote for *'Al-Hamishmar*, and Morris was for twelve years a correspondent for the *Jerusalem Post*. As with all modern consumer products, branding was central to the success of the 'new history' project. The new narrative in the 'New Israel' was helped along by the rise to hegemony in Israel in the 1980s of neoliberalism (free-market economics) (D'ana 2006: 1–26; Shafir and Peled 2001) and the West[2] and the subsequent explosion of the new global media (the Internet, satellite television), which have given it maximum publicity.[3] It was largely skilful exposure of the phenomenon of 'new history' in the new media

---

1. The Hebrew edition of Segev's book, *1949: Hayisraelim Harishonim*, was published by Domino in 1984.

2. For further discussion of neoliberalism, see Harvey 2007.

3. As we shall see in Chapter 6, the new global media, and the Internet in particular, have also increased the role of Palestinian oral history and personal narratives of

and by sympathetic journalists in the West, such as Ian Black of the *Guardian* in Britain and the editors of *Le Monde diplomatique* in France, which ensured it gained maximum exposure.

Also a number of Israeli films of the period, such as Ram Levi's *Khirbet Khiz'ah* (1978) and Avi Mograbi's *Deportation* (1989), portrayed the brutal expulsion of Palestinians from their homeland. This sharp turn towards public criticism of the founding fathers of the Israeli state followed the significant socio-political shift in 1977 which saw the first election of the Likud Party. Stimulated partly by the ascendance of right-wing Zionism and the shattering of the Zionist consensus (D'ana 2006: 1–26), in fact the 'new history' narrative was a reflection of the deep crisis of Israeli society following the invasion of Lebanon in 1982. This journalism-driven historical revisionism was given an impetus by the opening up of Israeli archives for the years 1935–55 and the discovery of an astonishing number of Hebrew documents.[4]

In *Power/Knowledge* (1980), Michel Foucault argues that historical developments are not necessarily linked in an orderly linear procession of cumulative knowledge. Rather, periods of intellectual coherence that engender (academic and public) 'discourses' – systems of power and regimes of knowledge – can be products of various power/knowledge systems with their own particular historical discourses (Foucault 1980: 197). Nation-building, state power, the construction of public archives, and the selective release and deployment of official documents have always been closely connected with history writing and academic regimes of knowledge.

A Historiographic Revolution?

In 2007 journalist-turned-academic Benny Morris, in the volume *Making Israel*, an edited collection on the 'new Israeli historiography' featuring contributions from both Israeli 'revisionists' and 'traditionalists' (including Uri Ram, Avi Shlaim, Yoav Gelber,

---

the Nakba in shaping Palestinian historical consciousness and contemporary public debate.

4. For the first critical assessment by an Arab historian of the Israeli 'new historiography' and its scholarship, see Masalha 1988: 121–37, 1990: 71–97, 1991: 90–97).

Anita Shapira, Mordechai Bar-On and Yechiam Weitz) triumphantly proclaimed that Israel had undergone a 'historiographic revolution' (Morris 2007: 1). Two decades earlier Morris and fellow Israeli historians, using Israeli state papers, had set out to demonstrate that history belongs to the powerful and the victors.[5] History is mostly written and rewritten by those in power – in possession of records and state papers – that is, by the conquerors and colonisers. The Israeli state is the dominant party in the conflict and the Israelis are the (European) colonisers of Palestine. It is hardly surprising therefore that, given the political stakes, the 'new historiographic revolution' was accompanied by much fanfare, triumphalism and media hype, designed to reinforce Israeli superior power/knowledge and 'scientific' historiography and to stress the inferior skills and the subordination of the Palestinians.

The term 'new historians' (*haHistorionim haHadashim*) was cleverly coined by Benny Morris and widely trumpeted by fellow revisionists. The term first appeared in the autumn of 1988 in the American liberal Jewish magazine *Tikkun* in an article by Morris entitled 'The New Historiography: Israel Confronts its Past' (1988: 19-23, 99-102). Here Morris describes himself and three other authors (academics Avi Shlaim and Ilan Pappé, and political journalist Simha Flapan) as the 'new historians', arguing that they had together undertaken to expose the skeletons in Zionism's closet and offer a challenge to its official historical narrative. Conceived by Morris, the 'new history' narrative was assiduously promoted by his two close colleagues at the time, Avi Shlaim, of the Middle East Centre at St Antony's College (Oxford University), and Ilan Pappé, then at Haifa University (Pappé 2010a) in publications and on joint platforms, often speaking at the same academic conferences in Israel and the West. In the late 1980s and early 1990s Morris, Pappé and Shlaim were also close friends; however, Pappé and Morris (both of whom had carried out doctoral and post-doctoral research at St Antony's College) were later to fall out publicly and spectacularly, while Shlaim stayed on good terms with both (see below). Many years later, in 2011, Pappé fondly recalled the three

---

5. Tom Segev, *Haaretz*, 9 July 2010, www.haaretz.co.il/hasite/spages/1177968.html.

colleagues travelling to a conference at the liberal Zionist Van Leer Institute in Jerusalem in 1992:

> When, in 1992, we were invited to a conference in Jerusalem after participating at one in Tel Aviv, we decided to go by car. Knowing the doubtful driving abilities of my colleagues I insisted on being the driver, fearing that otherwise an accident would kill the new history 'all together'. (2010a: 19)

Almost from the beginning, however, the 'new history' project was presented – in psychological, sociological and epistemological terms – by Morris and others as a project of renewal, rejuvenation and catharsis. It was cast as a project closely associated with dynamism and the younger generation of Israelis – in Pappé's words 'a group of young (idealist) scholars' (Pappé 1995: 70) – in contrast to the 'old guard' of traditionalist court historians and decaying orthodox narratives. However, the Israeli 'new historians' – in sharp contrast with the gender-sensitive Palestinian oral and narrative historians – were exclusively middle class and male, and, with the exception of Avi Shlaim (who emigrated from Baghdad to Israel),[6] of European (Ashkenazi) origins.

One of these establishment/state historians was Benny Morris's own father, Yaakov Morris, Zionist socialist pioneer, Israeli diplomat, published historian and later ambassador to New Zealand. The Morris family had left Belfast in Northern Ireland in 1946 and arrived in colonial Palestine in 1947. Benny was born a year later, in 1948. As an infant he lived on Kibbutz Yasur, which had been established in 1949 on the ruins of the destroyed Palestinian village of Al-Birwa. In 1953 Yaakov published his book *Pioneers from the West: History of Colonization in Israel by Settlers from the English-speaking Countries*. His *Masters of the Desert* (1961) contained an introduction by Prime Minister David Ben-Gurion.

---

6. Shlaim wrote in 2010: 'I was five years old in 1950 when my family reluctantly moved from Baghdad to Ramat Gan. We were Arab Jews, we spoke Arabic, our roots went back to the Babylonian exile two and a half millennia ago and my parents did not have the slightest sympathy with Zionism. We were not persecuted but opted to leave because we felt insecure. So, unlike the Palestinians who were driven out of their homes, we were not refugees in the proper sense of the word. But we were truly victims of the Arab-Israeli conflict.' Shlaim, review of Martin Gilbert, *In Ishmael's House*, in *Financial Times*, 30 August 2010, www.ft.com/cms/s/2/8ae6559c-b169-11df-b899-00144feabdco. html#axzz1cSyYb2g6.

Exercising a degree of self-censorship, in 2007, two decades after the publication of *The Birth of the Palestinian Refugee Problem, 1947–1949* (1987), Benny Morris chose to reveal, for the first time, to a *Washington Post* journalist that in the early 1980s, while sifting through declassified Israeli official files and archival documents, he had discovered a Foreign Ministry document, written by an Israeli diplomat, Morris's own father, Yaakov Morris, dismissing reports that Jewish militiamen had murdered more than 100 Palestinian men, women and children in Dayr Yasin in April 1948. His father's memo was a series of talking points distributed to Jewish 'diplomatic missions' in the West on how to deny what became one of the 1948 War's most notorious events.[7]

The key themes of the 'Zionist Revolution' followed closely the European tradition of the grand historical narrative and identity invention/construction of the nineteenth century. With its sweeping interpretation of Jewish history from antiquity to the present, its invention of the mythological New Hebrew (*sabra*) Man (Zerubavel 2002: 115–44), and its obsession with the invention of a new Jewish collective memory and identity based on grand narratives such as Jewish 'Return to History', the Zionist Revolution's claim that Jews were carriers of European Enlightenment and (universal) civilisation ('a light unto the nations') to a backward, empty and underdeveloped land (Massad 2004: 61) has always permeated Israeli discourse on history and historiography. In many ways the 'new historiographic revolution' chimes in well with age-old Zionist claims of renewal and revivalism. The 'new/young' versus 'old' theme is at the heart of the 'Zionist Revolution'; Zionist new thinking is deeply embedded in Israeli rhetoric and is central to the construction of Israeli national identity based on the so-called return to history and the construction of a New Judea and New Jerusalem. The 'New Hebrew Man' theme is derived from the early European Zionist lexicon which sought to reinvent not only Judaism but also a 'New Hebrew' language and a 'New Hebrew

7. Scott Wilson, 'Israel Revisited: Benny Morris, Veteran "New Historian" of the Modern Jewish State's Founding, Finds Himself Ideologically Back Where It All Began', *Washington Post*, 11 March 2007, www.washingtonpost.com/wp-dyn/content/article/2007/03/10/AR2007031001496.html.

Man', as the antithesis of the Diaspora Jew. Political Zionism had constructed a whole edifice of rhetoric based on the 'New Yishuv' versus the 'Old Yishuv' – a pre-1882 space inhabited by non-Zionist religious Jews living in the mixed Arab-Jewish cities of Jerusalem, Tiberias, Safad and al-Khalil (Hebron). The new European society was made of modern, scientific-minded, rational and civilised people. This 'new history' discourse of the late 1980s and early 1990s found a contemporary spin in Shimon Peres's book *The New Middle East* (1993). Peres's rhetoric was itself a take on an earlier Zionist Orientalist discourse on *ha-Mizrah ha-Hadash* (The New East) – which effectively meant the legitimisation and normalisation of the reality of a (new, young) Zionist Jewish state in the Middle East.

On the face of it, Morris's 'understanding of historiography as a cumulative process in which each historian and each generation of historians add new layers of knowledge and interpretation to those already built by previous historians' (Morris 1999: 75) sounds rather old-fashioned – traditionalist, simplistic, detached and morally and politically neutral; but in essence it reflects his framing of the 'new history' narrative as a renewalist project, one designed to revitalise Israeli Zionist historiography by adding a fresh and more sophisticated layer. However, as we shall see below, it is this essential claim about the moral neutrality and disinterestedness of his methodology which reveals itself in his illiberal conclusions and subsequent support for the racist, murderous ethnic cleansing of Palestine.

Also, crucially, most of the 'new historians' – unlike Israeli civil rights activists and public intellectuals, such as Israel Shahak (1933–2001) or Moshe Machover – were decidedly not 'anti-Zionist'. However, despite proclaiming themselves liberal Zionists, the 'new historians' faced a campaign of mud-slinging and vilification from mainstream and 'old historians'. But they benefited from and exploited the tensions in Zionism in the post-1982 (Lebanon invasion) period and, especially, during the first Palestinian popular uprising, the 'Intifada of the Stones', in the late 1980s. But precisely because of the predominantly Zionist character of this historiography, the phenomenon was bound to be undermined by the emergence of a new 'Jewish consensus' in the post-Second Intifada period. In fact the much-needed euphoria and catharsis generated by the 'new history' within Zionist liberal circles in the late 1980s and 1990s helped the Israeli settler state to move to the next stage of colonisation and suppression of the Palestinians. Recognising the nexus between power and history writing, early European Zionist historians developed an obsession with Jewish history writing and the rewriting and reinvention of a new Jewish tradition – what Shlomo Sand has described as the 'Invention of the Jewish People' (2009). This 'new' Zionist tradition of historical writing and its obsession with the rewriting of the history of the 'Jewish people' were further developed by Israeli historians and authors dedicated to 'writing the homeland' through what Laor has dubbed *Narratives With No Natives* (1995).

Crucially, being predominantly liberal Zionists wedded to elite narratives, the 'new historians', with the exception of Ilan Pappé, have failed to engage with key writings of the post-colonial discourse of Subaltern Studies, to produce a counter-hegemonic decolonising narrative in Israel or to challenge many of the enduring themes of Zionist colonisation of Palestine – mega-narratives which contain several intertwined foundational myths that underlie contemporary Israeli culture. These include the 'negation of exile' (*Shlilat ha-Galut*), the 'return to history' (*ha-Shiva la-Historia*) and the 'return to the land of Israel' (*ha-Shiva le-Eretz Yisrael*) (Raz-Krakotzkin 1993/4: 23–56, 113–32; Piterberg 2001: 31–46).[8] The 'negation of exile', in particular, allows Zionism to establish a mythical line of unbroken continuity between the stories and legends of the Hebrew Bible and a present that 'renews' them in the colonisation and resettlement of Palestine (Piterberg 2001: 31).

'New History' and the Liberal Coloniser: *Khirbet Khiz'ah* and Zionist Narratives

In May 1949 the Hebrew novella *Khirbet Khiz'ah* was published by S. Yizhar (real name Yizhar Smilansky, 1916–2006), an army officer

---

8. Piterberg explains that his discussion of the foundational myths of Zionism was informed by Evron (1995), Myers (1995) and Raz-Krakotzkin (1993: 23–56, 1994: 113–32).

during the 1948 war.⁹ *Khirbet Khiz'ah* came out around the same time Arab historian Constantine Zurayk published in Arabic *Ma'na al-Nakba* (*The Meaning of the Nakba*) (1949, 1956). *Khirbet Khiz'ah* was never translated into Arabic and *Ma'na al-Nakba* was never published in Hebrew. Four decades later, in the late 1980s when the 'new historians' began writing about 1948, Yizhar declared himself 'the man who had [in 1949] laid bare the original sin of the State of Israel (Shapira 2000: 1–62, 2007: 81–123).

In May 1949, in contrast to the almost total obliviousness and forgetfulness of today (see Noga Kadman's study *Erased from Space and Consciousness* [2008], discussed below), few 'new Israelis' were unaware that hundreds of Palestinian villages had been forcibly depopulated and destroyed by their army. Israeli historian Anita Shapira has shown that the veracity of the story of *Khirbet Khiz'ah*, widely discussed in Hebrew in the early 1950s, was never internally questioned or challenged at the time. The 'new historians', when they began to publish findings from research in previously clas- sified archives, also sought to remind Israelis of what they had forgotten from the mid-1950s onwards. Although Zionist atrocities in 1948 were widely known in Israel in the early 1950s, they were subsequently suppressed and rendered unknowable for the vast majority of Israeli Jews. Writing in 2006, 'new historian' Ilan Pappé observed:

> educators, historians, novelists, and cultural producers in general have all been involved in a campaign of denial and concealment. The horrors of 1948 were hidden from the public eye and from generations to come by those who committed them. Only at the end of 2000 did Gideon Levy,¹⁰ a voice in the wilderness, cry out in an article in *Haaretz*: How could you have lied to us for so many years? Very few ask this question now, and even fewer are willing to answer it. (2006: 287–8)

Khirbet Khiz'ah describes the expulsion of Palestinians from their village by the Israeli army, putting onto trucks those who did not evacuate their village, including the old and the sick who were unable to flee before the arrival of Israeli troops. Written in the

---

9. Ibis Editions, Jerusalem, 1949, 2008.
10. *Haaretz*, 1 November 2000.

immediate aftermath of the 1948 war, *Khirbet Khiz'ah* is a poignant account, fictionalised but recognisably partly autobiographical, of the ethnic cleansing of a fictional Palestinian village of that name. In 1949–51 the book generated a degree of public debate in Israel (Shapira 2007: 88–96). In Arabic the word *khirbeh* means literally 'ruins', but in the local Palestinian dialect, notwithstanding Israeli and Hebrew usage, it means simply a relatively new small village established by several families that move out of a large mother village.[11] However, according to Ronit Lentin, the Hebrew novella was not named *Khirbet Khiz'ah* (The Ruins of Khiz'ah) incidentally: '[T]he story is replete with love for the landscape and contempt for its Palestinian inhabitants' (Lentin 2010: 58). Indeed Yizhar's longing for an imagined biblical land and his contempt for the indigenous inhabitants (Lentin 2010: 57–60) are deeply rooted in Zionist colonialist myth-making; in Zionist Hebrew literature the word *khirbeh* often implies that the 'land of the Bible' was semi-deserted or neglected by the local Arabs before the advent of the European Zionist colonists, who made it productive.

S. Yizhar was born in the Zionist settlement of Rehovot, to a family of Zionist settlers who had arrived from the Ukraine. Rehovot was established in 1890,[12] by middle-class Jewish businessmen and merchants on 10,000 dunums of land bought from the indigenous Palestinian Arabs of Khirbet Duran. Regardless of the motivation for the novella's title, in the early years of Israel the self-criticism of *Khibet Khiz'ah*, especially in internal circles, and the catharsis produced by the work, were used by the ruling Labour Zionist establishment to rationalise Zionist ethics, the seizure and Judaisation of Palestinian land and the reinforcement of Israeli domination: first they took the land, then they constructed the ethics. Yizhar Smilansky was in some ways (to borrow an expression from Albert Memmi's *The Colonizer and*

---

11. For example, the names of several villages adjacent to the town of Umm Al-Fahem (Al-Bayada, Mosmos, Musherfa) begin with 'Khirbeh'. Information supplied by Dr Ahmad Sa'di.

12. Rehovot was named after a biblical site of the same name (transliterated Rehoboth in the Bible), which stood at a completely different location in the Naqab/Negev desert.

the Colonized (1957[13]), a typical example of the self-critical 'left-wing coloniser'. This phenomenon of self-criticism by a minority of the Zionist colonists has accompanied the Zionist project from its outset. It has also contributed to shielding it, at least in the West, from the reality of colonialism in Palestine. Earlier patterns of settler self-criticism were produced by dissident settlers such as Yitzhak Epstein, who warned of the moral implications of Zionist colonisation methods.

Yizhar's famous uncle, Moshe Smilansky (1874–1953), described the attitudes prevalent among the majority of Zionist colonists concerning the indigenous Palestinian population, which ranged from indifference and disregard to patronising colonial superiority. Smilansky was a prominent Zionist writer, Labour leader and one of the founders of the Jewish farmers' association. In 1911 he published a series of stories about the life of the Palestinian Arabs entitled simply *The Arabs* (*Bnei 'Arav*). Smilansky had emigrated from the Ukraine to Palestine in 1890 and settled as a farmer and landowner in the colony of Rehovot:

> Let us not be too familiar with the Arab fellahin lest our children adopt their ways and learn from their ugly deeds. Let all those who are loyal to the Torah avoid ugliness and that which resembles it and keep their distance from the fellahin and their base attributes. (quoted in Gorny 1987: 50; see also 62)

Moshe Smilansky even showed how deeply rooted the concept of the ethnic cleansing of Palestine was in the narrative of early Zionist colonists. He recounted a dialogue that took place in 1891 between two pioneers of Hovevei Tzion (Lovers of Zion), who had settled in Rehovot:

> 'We should go east, into Transjordan. That would be a test of our movement.'
> 'Nonsense ... isn't there enough land in Judea and Galilee?'
> 'The land in Judea and Galilee is occupied by the Arabs'.
> 'Well, we'll take it from them'.
> 'How?' (silence)

---

13. First published in French under the title *Portrait du colonisé, précédé par Portrait du colonisateur.*

'A revolutionary doesn't ask naive questions'.
'Well then 'revolutionary', tell us how'.
'It is very simple. We'll harass them until they get out ... Let them go to Transjordan'.
'And are we going to abandon all of Transjordan?' asks an anxious voice.
'As soon as we have a big settlement here we'll seize the land, we'll become strong, and then we'll take care of the Left Bank [of the Jordan River]. We'll expel them from there; too, Let them go back to the Arab countries'.[14]

In 2008, six decades after the Nakba, *Khirbet Khiz'ah* was finally translated from Hebrew and published in English by a small, non-profit Israeli publisher based in Jerusalem, Ibis Editions, under the title *Khirbet Khiz'ah*.[15] According to the publisher, this is 'a recognised classic in Israel, part of the canon of Hebrew literature'. If this is the case, why wait six decades to make it available to an English-speaking readership? Clearly for this tiny liberal Zionist publisher the issue is less to do with the need to remember the 1948 Palestinian Nakba and more to do with currently liberal Zionism's moral ambiguities regarding the ongoing ethnic cleansing of Palestinians.

Yizhar's language in the novella is saturated with references to the biblical landscape and the Bible. This perhaps explains why it was a best-seller in its first years and discussed widely in Hebrew newspapers and magazines. The story contains the following:

'They're just like animals', Yehuda explained to us, but we did not reply. The women were gathered onto another truck, and they began to scream and weep. We felt a mood of beggary, pus, and leprosy, and all that was lacking was the sound of dirges and charity saveth from death. 'Ugh, revolting!' said Shlomo.
'Better they should die!' said Yehuda.

Yizhar's narrator has an epiphany:

14. M. Smilansky, 'In the Steppe', *Works*, Vol. 1: *1891–1893*, Tel Aviv: n.d., p. 206, quoted in El Kodsy and Lobel 1970: 120.
15. Translated from Hebrew by Nicholas de Lange and Yaacob Dweck, with a Foreword by David Shulman of the Hebrew University of Jerusalem.

Something struck me like lightning. All at once everything seemed to mean something different, more precisely: exile. This was exile. This was what exile was like. This was what exile looked like ... I had never been in the Diaspora – I said to myself – I had never known what it was like ... but people had spoken to me, told me, taught me, and repeatedly recited to me, from every direction, in books and newspapers, everywhere: exile. They had played on all my nerves. Our nation's protest to the world: exile! It had entered me, apparently, with my mother's milk. What in fact had we perpetrated here today? ... We'd open a cooperative store, establish a school, maybe even a synagogue. There would be political parties here. They'd debate all sorts of things. They would plough fields, and sow, and reap, and do great things. Long live Hebrew Khiz'ah! Who, then, would ever have imagined that once there had been some Khirbet Khiz'ah that we emptied out and took for ourselves? ... My guts cried out. Colonizers, they shouted. Lies, my guts shouted. Khirbet Khiz'ah is not ours. The Spandau gun never gave us any rights. Oh, my guts screamed. What hadn't they told us about refugees. Everything, everything was for the refugees, their welfare, their rescue – our refugees, naturally. Those we were driving out – that was a totally different matter. Wait. Two thousand years of exile. The whole story. Jews being killed. Europe. We were masters now. (Yizhar 2008).

In discussion at an Israeli cabinet meeting on 17 November 1948, Israel's (Mapam's) Minister of Agriculture, Aharon Zisling, drew a parallel between the behaviour of Jewish and Israeli troops in 1948 and the Nazis in Europe: 'now Jews too have behaved like Nazis and my entire being has been shaken' (Segev 1986: 26). In *Khirbet Khiz'ah* Yizhar makes similar comparisons: Israeli officers had ordered atrocities and had carried them out. The guns Israeli Jews aimed at Palestinians were German Spandaus and the transport onto which Jews loaded Palestinians were called 'boxcars'. Yizhar showed that Israelis carried out war crimes against innocent Palestinian civilians in 1948.

The debate and public controversy surrounding Yizhar's *Khirbet Khiz'ah* in 1949-51 was limited to Hebrew readers and Israeli politicians (Shapira 2007: 96). As Gabriel Piterberg points out, this cannot be compared to the situation now, shaped as it is by an Israeli public relations machine that has continued to perpetrate deliberate deception about what happened in the Nakba of 1948.

He has shown that, following the book's publication, within the 'safe and generally hidden confines' of their own Hebrew language some Israelis were grappling with how to deal with the true story of the mass ethnic cleansings of 1948 (Piterberg 2009: 31-3).

> *Khirbet Khiz'ah* became a set book in Israeli secondary schools in 1964 ... The story, which deals with the cleansing of rural Arab Palestine as Yizhar experienced it, goes to the heart of the Zionist–Palestinian conflict and has given rise to great unease, even evasiveness, among liberal commentators in Israel ...
> ... Yizhar [is] perhaps the greatest poet of Palestinian landscape in modern Hebrew. He is also a historian of destruction and expulsion. In the closing pages of the story, watching the humiliated Palestinians [who have previously been described as 'most of them elderly or women or children'] huddling in Israeli lorries.

Piterberg (2009: 31-3) cites an interview Yizhar gave to *Haaretz* in 2005, shortly before his death. In it, the interviewer asked, 'Why were you the only member of your generation who saw the catastrophe that befell the Arabs?' Yizhar replied:

> The others were attentive only to relationships with other people, among themselves. I looked at the landscape, the landscape was a central part of my personality, and that's why I saw the Arabs. The landscape was the paper, on which everything was written, and afterwards it gets torn and nobody looks at the paper.

Yizhar, himself a so-called *sabra*, sought to 'nativise' the New Israeli and endow him/her with a new Israeli narrative. In his largely autobiographical novel, *Preliminaries*, completed only in 1991, when he was 75, Yizhar recounts many details of his youth growing up in Rehovot, and into adulthood. He seems to have had a great fondness for the landscape of rural Palestine and an understanding, as Piterberg notes, that what had made it look so appealing was precisely the labour expended there over generations by its Palestinian Arab landowners and farmers:

> The people who had planted and tended all those 'Biblical' accoutrements of the landscape like olive-trees and grape-vines; who tended the sheep, made the wine and olive oil, and did all those other 'Biblical' things that made the land so attractive for the Zionist settlers.

Piterberg writes that at the end of *Preliminaries*,

> Yizhar delivers his final verdict on the Zionist project. The child is
> haunted less by the possibility that Zionism in the shape of a powerful,
> durable settler nation-state might not succeed than by the certainty that
> its realisation would erase the landscape of pre-1948 rural Palestine.
> In the final scene the boy is sent to collect baskets of grapes from a
> nearby vineyard and realises that 'soon ... none of this will remain,
> neither this vineyard nor this sandy path ...' He thinks of the extinction
> of the villages and the fate of their inhabitants: 'These Arabs will not
> remain ... Zarnuga will not remain and Qubeibeh will not remain and
> Yibneh will not remain, they will go away and start to live in Gaza.'
> (2009: 31-3)

Other Israeli writers have offered a different interpretation of
the novella. This maintains that Yizhar wanted to demonstrate only
that Israelis had carried out war crimes in 1948; furthermore, he
wanted to show that the liberal coloniser was not afraid to admit
these crimes – at least within the generally hidden confines of
their own Hebrew language. Thus the aim of the novella was not
to tell how the Israelis had brutally carried out the ethnic cleansing
of Palestine, but to show that they were capable of self-criticism
and did not lack a conscience.[16] One reviewer of *Khirbet Khiz'ah*
even observed that the novella was included in the optional list of
standard literature texts in Israeli secondary schools. Notably, in
the Foreword to the English edition Professor David Shulman of the
Hebrew University writes: 'it's not at all clear that young Israelis
who read this tale of what is, for them, a very distant past are likely
to connect it in any meaningful way to their lives today.'[17]

There are no indigenous Palestinian voices in Yizhar's novella;
the story reflects the Israeli-Jewish 'elegiac yet triumphalist postwar
mood' (Lentin 2010: 59). Like Yizhar, the liberal Zionist settler-
coloniser cannot possibly produce a counter-hegemonic narrative
or reflect indigenous voices. Yizhar himself was the most important
writer of the Palmah generation – those who, in the elite shock
troops of the Haganah, spearheaded the expulsions and massacres
of the Nakba. In 1959 he was awarded the prestigious Israel Prize

---

16. Noah Efron, 'The Price of Return', *Haaretz*, 23 November 2008.
17. Ibid.

(Shapira 2007: 97, 108). Yizhar's writings produced a much-needed catharsis and ultimately reinforced the Zionist settler-colonial narrative; they helped the settler state to justify taking over Palestinian land and provide the ethical justification, and in the process proceed to the next stage of colonisation. Yizhar's own personal politics are another case in point: he served in the first Israeli Knesset in 1949, remaining an uncritical MK for the ruling Mapai party until the mid-1960s (Shapira 2007: 81–123). In 1965 he even joined the hard-line Rafi party founded by Ben-Gurion, a breakaway of eight MKs from Mapai; Rafi supported the continuation of the military administration imposed on, and systematic discrimination against, the Palestinian citizens of Israel.

Twenty-seven years after the publication of *Khirbet Khiz'ah*, in early 1977, Israeli film-maker Ram Levi attempted to bring the truths of the Nakba, hitherto entirely repressed within the Israeli psyche, back to the surface. Levi managed to persuade the Israel Broadcasting Authority to sponsor a television film dramatisation of Yizhar's novella. Levi had first proposed the project in 1972, but it was then rejected by the Authority. On 17 May 1977, at which time the drama was being filmed in the West Bank, Menahem Begin's Likud party came to power. In January 1978, when the film *Khirbet Khiz'ah* (1978) was ready to be aired on Israeli television, to coincide with Israel's thirtieth 'Independence Day', the education minister, Zevulun Hammer, intervened and cancelled the broadcast. In support of the ban was leading Israeli journalist Tommy Lapid, who a quarter of century later would become justice minister.

> even if the Fatah Information Bureau were headed by a genius, he couldn't have come up with a better one than this. And even if Goebbels were directing Arab propaganda efforts, they couldn't have had greater success. And even if a fifth column were operating in our television studios, they couldn't have performed a better service to aid the enemies of our state.[18]

Eventually the film was aired on 13 February 1978, but immediately after was shelved. It was not shown again until 1993.

---

18. Ibid.

Although Yizhar and Levi earned a reputation as iconoclasts in liberal Zionist circles – both were recipients of the Israel Prize – this form of 'narrativisation' of moral Zionism, via a cycle of self-criticism and catharsis, has been repeated over and over again: other instances are philosopher Martin Buber in the 1940s, A.B. Yehoshua's *Facing the Forest* in the late 1960s, the 'new history' in the late 1980s and early 1990s. Yet six decades after the publication of *Khirbet Khiz'ah* and two decades after the emergence of the new Israeli historiography, the hundreds of Khirbet Khiz'ahs that had been wiped from the map have remained completely absent from Israeli collective memory and consciousness. Noga Kadman's *Erased from Space and Consciousness* (2008) shows how the destroyed villages remain entirely absent from Israeli national discourse. Kadman, who travelled to 250 sites of destroyed villages, documents this total obliviousness of Israelis today to the Palestinians ethnically cleansed in 1948. The book examines the non-existence and marginalisation of these villages in information given to visitors in tourist and recreation sites in Israel. For the liberal coloniser the hundreds of Khirbet Khiz'ahs were dictated by necessity.

Yizhar in fact had no intention of painting a picture of systematic Zionist injustice in Palestine. In a 1978 essay in the daily *Yedi'ot Ahronot*, he rejected the treatment of his novella as an archetype:

> There's no duty or necessity whatsoever for a story about some specific events to have to symbolise something more general … And what you find in a given tale is not necessarily a model for everything that happened in the history of a people or a country at a particular time.[19]

While Foucault powerfully argued that we should be able to appreciate non-linearity, accidents, interruptions and discontinuities in historical writing, this should not exclude the possibility of recurring patterns (to use Ibn Khaldun's terminology) in history. Such a pattern is evident in Israeli 'new history', which shows the embedding of Zionist patterns and narratives that reaffirm

---

19. Cited in Efron, 'The Price of Return'.

the domination of Israeli liberal discourse, silence the unpleasant events in Zionism's history, while producing, from time to time, self-critical and cathartic Israeli narratives; meanwhile the Israeli settler society of today remains totally oblivious to the vanished indigenous Palestinian communities.

The New Myths of Liberal Zionism: 1967

Liberal Zionists locate the 'original sin' – the Israeli colonial project – in 1967. Most 'new historians' go back to 1948. For my part, *Expulsion of the Palestinians: The Concept of 'Transfer' in Zionist Political Thought, 1882–1948* (1992), on the basis of Hebrew documents in the Israeli archives and research going back to the late nineteenth century, shows that the ethnic cleansing of Palestine and the Nakba were in fact the culmination of over half a century of efforts, plans and, finally, brute force.

The Jewish colonial project in Palestine began in 1967 beyond the Green Line – so states the newly invented liberal Zionist myth. The failure of the new historians – with the exception of Ilan Pappé – to dissect many of the enduring themes and myths of Zionism was coupled with the invention of new post-1967 myths. This is best encapsulated in the reinvention of post-1967 left-wing Zionism, with its myth that Zionist colonisation in Palestine began with the occupation of the West Bank and Gaza. A good illustration of this 'colonisation perspective' is the massive collection of papers, edited by Israeli philosopher Adi Ophir et al., entitled *The Power of Inclusive Exclusion: Anatomy of Israeli Rule in the Occupied Palestinian Territories* (2009).

The June war of 1967 simply marked another stage, albeit a turning point, in the long history of the Zionist colonisation of Palestine, particularly with regard to the occupied West Bank and East Jerusalem. The overwhelming Israeli victory, the seizure of the remainder of historic Palestine with its sizable Palestinian population, the resultant outburst, and later upsurge, of right-wing neo-Zionism and growing Israeli confidence all contributed to the prompt and inevitable revival of the project of territorial expansionism. But, as we have already seen, the Zionist colonisation of Palestine did not begin in 1967, as supporters of the Israeli peace camp claim. In 2005, shortly before leaving Haifa University, Pappé reflected on the invention of the 'post-1967 myth of colonisation' by liberal Zionists:

> Historians and educators are the main villains ... they helped to construct and preserve a national narrative that eliminates the collective Palestinian memory. This elimination is no less violent than expulsion and destruction: it is the main constitutive element in the construction of collective Jewish identity [in Israel] ... It is manifested in the tales told by child minders on Independence Day and Passover, in the curriculum and textbooks in elementary and high schools, in the ceremonies of freshmen and the graduation of officers in the army. It is broadcast in the printed and electronic media as well as in the speeches and discourse of the politicians, in the way artists, novelists, and poets subject their work to the national narrative, and in the research produced by academics in the universities about the Israeli reality in the past and the present.
>
> This act of symbolic violence and thought control intensified after October 2000. It is particularly evident now in the educational system and the media, but mostly in Israeli academia ... that supports oppression, occupation, and discrimination.
>
> This self-control keeps even peacemakers in Israel from opening the Pandora's box of 1948 and the whole question of victimhood. This can be seen in the posture adopted by the Peace Now movement... For its members, peace and reconciliation are translated into the need for mutual recognition between the two national narratives... to make divisible everything that is visible: land, resources, blame, and history into a pre-1967 mind-set when 'we the Jews were right and just' and a post-1967 mind-set 'when you the Palestinians were right and just'... The same righteous approach ... applies to the early ... chapter in the history of the conflict ... in which the Jews were the victims ... This periodisation is very important, since the earlier period is considered to be more crucial; thus, being just then, in the formative period of the conflict, justifies the existence of Zionism and the whole Jewish project in Palestine. At the same time, it casts doubt on the wisdom and morality of Palestinian actions in that period. It obliterates from any discussion the ethnic cleansing carried out by the Jews in 1948. (Pappé 2006: 287–8)

Struggling to reconcile the nationalist ('liberationist') and settler-colonial narratives of Zionism, Shlaim conceives of the conflict
as having originated in a 'clash of two legitimate nationalisms',
which has evolved in the post-1967 period into a clash of the
'colonial' with the indigenous. This liberal Zionist conception
of the Israel–Palestine struggle echoes, for instance, Amos Oz's
idea of 'the clash of two justices' (Laor 2009) – hence Shlaim's
emphasis on the need for mutual recognition between two national
liberation movements and two legitimate national narratives. This
also explains Shlaim's rejection of the Palestinian refugees' 'right
of return' to their homes and villages in Israel. In point of fact
Pappé is the only 'new historian' who supports the refugees' 'right
of return' unequivocally. He also – in contrast to Shlaim – under-
stands the Palestine conflict within a straightforward paradigm of
settler-colonialism.

Shared Responsibility for the Catastrophe?

most Israelis have yet to internalize their share of the responsibility
for the creation of the Palestinian tragedy and until they do so,
there's no chance for peace.

Tom Segev, 'A History Lesson'[20]

Benny Morris is central to the rise and decline of the Israeli 'new
history' project. Since the publication of *The Birth of the Palestinian Refugee Problem, 1947–1949* (1987), Morris, in particular, has
been treated in the West as the ultimate authority on the 1948
war and the creation of the Palestinian refugee problem. Morris
began his scholarly career by arguing for 'shared responsibility'
for the Palestinians over their catastrophe; he ended up with the
claim that the Palestinians had brought the Nakba on themselves.[21]
He became the symbol of a 'new history' in collusion with ethnic
cleansing, neo-colonialism and war crimes in Palestine, past,
present and future.

---

20. *Haaretz*, 29 June 2001.
21. See, for instance, interview with Morris by Ari Shavit, in 'Survival of the Fittest',
Haaretz, 9 January 2004.

Indeed Morris's work has contributed to demolishing some of the long-held myths (at least in the West) and misconceptions surrounding Israel's birth. His subsequent collection of essays, *1948 and After: Israel and the Palestinians* (1990), revisited the ground covered in *The Birth*, bringing to light new material he discovered himself or which became available only after the completion of the first book.

Critics of Morris, including this author, took issue with his conclusion that 'The Palestinian refugee problem was born of war, not by design, Jewish or Arab. It was largely a by-product of Arab and Jewish fears and of the protracted, bitter fighting that characterised the first Israeli–Arab war; in smaller part, it was the deliberate creation of Jewish and Arab military commanders and politicians' (Morris 1987: 286; see also Masalha 1991: 90–97, 2003: 49–66; Finkelstein 1991: 66–89; Kanaana 1992). Morris's central thesis is summed up in the following passage from *1948 and After* (1990):

what occurred in 1948 lies somewhere in between the Jewish 'robber state' [i.e. a state which had forcibly expelled the Palestinians] and the 'Arab orders' explanations. While from the mid-1930s most of the Yishuv's leaders, including Ben-Gurion, wanted to establish a Jewish state without an Arab minority, or with as small an Arab minority as possible, and supported a 'transfer solution' to this minority problem, the Yishuv did not enter the 1948 war with a master plan for expelling the Arabs, nor did its political and military leaders ever adopt such a master plan. What happened was largely haphazard and a result of the war. There were Haganah/IDF expulsions of Arab communities, some of them at the initiative or with the *post facto* approval of the cabinet or the defense minister, and most with General Staff sanction – such as the expulsions from Miska and Ad Dumeira in April; from Zarnuqa and Al Qubeiba, and Huj in May; from Lydda and Ramle in July; from the Lebanese border area (Kafr Bir'im, Iqrit, Al Mansura, Tarbikha, Suruh, and Nabi Rubin) in early November. But there was no grand design, no blanket policy of expulsion. (Morris 1990: 17)

In other words, only in 'smaller part' were Haganah/IDF expulsions carried out and these were impromptu, ad hoc measures dictated by military circumstance.

Under pressure from a wide range of critics (see, e.g., Masalha 1991: 90-97)[22] and mountains of Israeli archival evidence (see Masalha 1992) – Morris ultimately conceded that the 'transfer' had been more fully premeditated than he had at first suggested. In the substantially expanded 2004 edition of his 1987 book, entitled *The Birth of the Palestinian Refugee Problem Revisited*, Morris revises his original conclusion and acknowledges that 'pre-1948 "Transfer" thinking had a greater effect on what happened in 1948 than [he] had allowed for ... the evidence for the pre-1948 Zionist support for "Transfer" really is unambiguous' (Morris 2004: 5-6).

Already in 2001 Morris had written:

> Without doubt, the crystallization of the consensus in support of transfer among the Zionist leaders helped paved the way for the precipitation of the Palestinian refugee exodus of 1948. Similarly, far more of that exodus was triggered by explicit acts and orders of expulsion by Jewish/Israeli troops than is indicated in *The Birth*. (Morris 2001: 56)

By the late 1990s, under pressure from critics (Masalha 1992; Achcar 2010: 178; Morris 2000a: ch. 4 nn, 678 nn, 116, 124-5, 128-30, 138; Morris 2000b: 15-16, 211 n112, 2001: 37-56, 2004), Morris had begun to argue that, although he still could find no document ordering a blanket expulsion of the Palestinians in 1948, the concept of Zionist 'transfer' developed in the period 1937-48 from a haphazard idea to a near consensus. This major shift is conceded in the essay 'Revisiting the Palestinian Exodus of 1948' (Rogan and Shlaim 2001), where Morris writes that the Zionist political and military leaders arrived at 1948

> with a mindset which was open to the idea and implementation of transfer and expulsion. And the transfer that occurred [in 1948] – which encountered almost no serious opposition from any part of the Yishuv

---

22. Finkelstein writes: 'Morris has substituted a new myth, one of the 'happy medium' for the old. ... [T]he evidence that Morris adduces does not support his temperate conclusions. ... [S]pecifically, Morris's central thesis that the Arab refugee problem was "born of war, not by design" is belied by his own evidence which shows that Palestine's Arabs were expelled systematically and with premeditation' (1991: 66-89); Benny Morris, 'Response to Finkelstein and Masalha', *Journal of Palestine Studies* 21, no. 1, Autumn: 98-114.

– transpired smoothly in large measure because of this pre-conditioning ... all or almost all came to understand ... that transfer was what the Jewish state's survival and well-being demanded ... Much more work needs to be done on the Yishuv's attitude to transfer ... Of particular interest might be the papers from 1937-47 of the majors and colonels and generals of 1948 who actually carried out the transfer, such as Yigal Allon and Yitzhak Sadeh and Moshe Carmel. (2001: 48)

In the subsequent *The Birth of the Palestinian Refugee Problem Revisited*, Morris writes that 'from the inception of the movement [the transfer idea was toyed with to solve the problem] of a large Arab minority that was opposed to the existence of a Jewish state or to living in it', and that 'each major bout of Arab violence triggered renewed Zionist interest in a transfer solution' (2004: 59, 44).

Fellow revisionist historian Tom Segev came to the same conclusion:

The notion of population transfer is deeply rooted in Zionist ideology, a logical outgrowth of the [Zionist] principle of segregation between Jews and Arabs and a reflection of the [Zionist] desire to ground the Jewish state in European, rather than Eastern, culture. (Segev 2000: 407)

While mainstream Israeli historians have refused to admit Zionist responsibility for the Palestinian Nakba, the 'new historians' (in particular Shlaim, Morris and Segev) opted for the happy medium. They seized upon Morris's conclusion which allowed for a formula of 'shared responsibility' on the part of the Palestinians for their catastrophe (Shlaim 1994: 26-7, 2010: 55-61; Segev 2001). Shlaim, in particular, took up Morris's 'multi-cause' explanation of the 1948 Palestinian refugee exodus to promote the idea of the Palestinians' 'shared responsibility' with the Zionist Jewish leadership for the dismantlement of Palestine in 1948 and the catastrophe.[23] Shlaim was notably highly critical of my conclusions with regard to the historical roots of the Nakba. This approach is much evident in his recent book *Israel and Palestine: Reappraisals, Revisions, and Refutations* (2009).

---

23. *Financial Times*, 30 August 2010, www.ft.com/cms/s/2/8ae6559c-b169-11df-b899-00144feabdco.html#axzz1cSyYb2g6.

When the UN voted in favour of the partition of Palestine on 29 November 1947, Ben-Gurion and his colleagues in the Jewish Agency accepted the plan despite deep misgivings about the prospect of a substantial Arab minority, a fifth column as they saw it, in their midst. The Palestinians, on the other hand, rejected partition, some vehemently and violently. By resorting to force to frustrate the UN plan, they presented Ben-Gurion with an opportunity, which he was not slow to exploit, to extend the borders of the proposed Jewish state and to reduce the number of Arabs inside it. By 7 November 1949, when the guns finally fell silent, 730,000 persons had become refugees.

For Masalha this mass exodus was not an accidental byproduct of the war but the inevitable accompaniment of the birth of Israel: 'the result of painstaking planning and an unswerving vision ... stated and restated with almost tedious repetitiveness for almost fifty years'. Chaim Weizmann, who became Israel's first president, hailed the Arab evacuation as 'a miraculous clearing of the land: the miraculous simplification of Israel's task'. For Masalha it was 'less of a miracle than it was the result of over half a century of sustained effort and brute force'. The main strength of his book derives from the new material he has unearthed about Zionist attitudes to transfer during the pre-1948 period.

But he spoils a good case by over-stating it. In the first place, he focuses very narrowly on one aspect of Zionist thinking and neglects the broader political context in which this thinking crystallized. Secondly, he portrays the Zionist movement as monolithic and single-minded in its support for transfer, ignoring the reservations, the doubts, the internal debates and the opposition. Thirdly, he presents transfer as the cornerstone of Zionist strategy, when it was in fact only one of the alternatives under consideration at various junctures in the conflict over Palestine. Fourthly, while sharply critical of the Zionist design and of the means by which it was achieved, he completely ignores the part played by the Palestinians themselves in the disaster that eventually overwhelmed them, or the part played by their leader, Haj Amin al-Husseini, who had about as much political sense as the Good Soldier Schweik. (Shlaim 2009: 56–9, 1994: 26–7)

In other words, the Palestinians should share the blame for their own Nakba. Of course Shlaim is right to point out the strategically disastrous leadership of the Mufti, Haj Amin al-Husseini.[24] The very idea that Germans and Jews might have a shared responsibility for

24. For a critical discussion of the role and leadership of the Mufti, see Achcar 2010; Pappé 2010b.

the Jewish Holocaust would rightly be considered deeply offensive. Yet when it comes to the destruction of Palestine and the ethnic cleansing of the (predominantly Muslim) Palestinians, entirely different ethical standards are applied. For such a comparison is wholly incompatible with the logic of Zionist colonisation of Palestine and the objective of establishing an exclusive Jewish state in a country overwhelmingly inhabited by another population (Rouhana 2005: 267). More crucially, while claims that there was no 'transfer' design and premeditation or systematic ethnic cleansing policy in 1948 cannot be sustained by the mountains of archival evidence, in effect the conclusion of both Shlaim and Morris deflects serious responsibility for the Palestinian catastrophe away from the Zionist leadership. While I acknowledge the major contribution Morris has made to our knowledge surrounding the events of 1948, in denying any overall responsibility for the ethnic cleansing of Palestine his narrative remains firmly attached to its Zionist roots, supporting the wider context for Israeli hegemonic discourses and Israel's politics of denial (Masalha 2003: 62).

A Post-colonial History?

Almost inevitably, since the late 1980s the Israeli 'new historians' in general and Benny Morris in particular have come to be seen in the West as the 'ultimate authority' on 1948, the birth of the Palestinian refugee problem and the Nakba. The 'new historians' fitted the bill. They were all Western-educated (with connections to Oxford and Cambridge universities), male, white, young, Ashkenazi descendants of the ancient Hebrews, highly professional and scientifically minded and authoritative; their work is grounded in official documents and state archives, and so they could now represent everyone, especially those indigenous Palestinians located at the bottom of the pile. Exaggerating the impact of 'new history', and trumpeting their newly found fame, the 'new historians' even sought to patronise the 'annoyed' and 'jealous' Palestinian historians. As Pappé writes in *The Israel/Palestine Question: Rewriting Histories* (prefacing my 'A Critique of Benny Morris'): 'there was something disturbing and annoying in these claims becoming valid only after Israeli Jews made them, as if Palestinian historians were suspect of non-professionalism (1999: 211).

In Gramscian and Foucauldian terms of hegemonic discourses, the Ashkenazi-led 'new history' project appeared to be structured epistemologically as a sort of hierarchy of spaces dominated by the European, or the 'New Hebrew Man', in European Zionist terms, with new social sciences and new historiography sitting at its centre on top of everyone, especially the Mizrahi Jews and Palestinian Arabs. So, paradoxically – and for some of the 'new historians' inadvertently – the 'new history' may even have contributed to reinforcing Israeli and pro-Israeli domination of discourses in the history and historiography of the Palestine question. Overstating the impact of the 'new historians' on the Israeli academy and Israeli society, Pappé – who thought the 'new historians' could bridge the 'narrative gap' and gender divide in Palestine-Israel – wrote in 1995 that the 'new history', Israeli scholarship and academia in general could now include as well as represent dispossessed Palestinian refugees, marginalised Mizrahi Jews and even silenced Palestinian women:

> The Israeli academia is an integral part of the global academic system and thus it is not surprising that historians and sociologists in it adopted the same interdisciplinary, skeptical and subjective view towards their own history. Such a methodology will naturally reflect their wish to represent the Palestinians, the *Sephardis* and the women's side of the story... Important chapters in the Palestinian historical narrative about the origins of the [1948] war, its course and consequences are thus accepted by Israel historians. (Pappé 1995: 72, 76)

Contrast this with Pappé's highly critical view of the deeply entrenched colonial attitudes of the Israeli academy ten years later (see below). He is also fully aware that speaking in favour of the oppressed and subaltern is different from the oppressed and subaltern speaking for themselves.

Pappé, inspired by academic developments in historiography and post-colonial theories in the West, advanced a view that ascribed the emergence of the 'new history' project to methodological innovations globally as well as to the 'rise' of post-colonial stud-

ies in Israel (D'ana 2006: 1–26). But as Palestinian scholar Seif
D'ana points out, the claim that the 'new history' as a whole is
a product of a dialogue with *la nouvelle histoire* in the West is
completely unfounded and largely ahistorical (D'ana: 2006: 1–26).
The same criticism was voiced by Ella Shohat, who pointed out
that, in contrast to the post-colonial discourses in the West, Israeli
liberal intellectuals did not engage with the key anti-colonial
writings of Césaire, Memmi and Fanon (Shohat 2010: 321–2). In
the US academy the anti-colonial discourse appeared after Black
History Studies, Latin American Studies, Indigenous American
Studies, (Shohat 2010: 323). By contrast, in Israel Islamic and
Middle Eastern Studies are predominantly Orientalist in perspective and heavily influenced by the requirements of the Israeli
security/intelligence-gathering establishment. In her brilliant
critique of Israeli 'post-Zionism' and the ideological context of
the new 'history project', Shohat remarks:

> In the Anglo-American academy, postcolonial theory emerged out
> of the anti-colonialist movement and Third Worldest perspective;
> that is, at least partly, what makes it 'post.' Post-Zionist-postcolonial
> writing in Israel, in contrast, comes out of an academic context often
> untouched by the history of anti-colonialist debates. Thus [in Israel] we
> find the 'post' without the past ... in Israel, it was not the anti-Zionist
> discourse that gave way to post-Zionist discourse, but rather Zionist
> discourse that gave way to post-Zionist discourse. To argue for moving
> beyond 'the colonial,' as suggested by post-colonial theory, within a
> nation-state and within an academic space hardly touched, historically,
> by Third Worldist perspective requires that we ask the question of the
> (anti)colonial with even more vigor. (Shohat 2010: 323)

Furthermore, as we will see below, neither Pappé nor Shlaim
shared Morris's passionate Zionism or his nationalist methodologies. While Pappé and Shlaim have sought to advance an inclusive
approach to rewriting histories in Palestine–Israel, Morris, by
contrast, has always been contemptuous of Palestinian voices,
Palestinian oral history and even Palestinian suffering;[25] in this
regard he has closely followed in the footsteps of the Israeli old

---

25. See, for instance, Morris's interview with Ari Shavit, 'Survival of the Fittest?'
Haaretz, Friday magazine, 9 January 2004.

guard and their Zionist colonising methodologies, including the Hebrewisation of Palestinian geography and the de-Arabisation of Palestinian toponymy. In his perceptive critique of Morris, American Jewish historian Joel Beinin, of Stanford University, comments on Morris's old-fashioned methodology and positivist-linearist approach to history:

> Morris's empiricist and positivist historical method excludes Palestinian Arab voices from his narratives to nearly the same extent as the old historians and the political leadership with which they were organically connected. Explaining that he was brought up believing in the value of documents, Morris claims to distrust [Palestinian refugee] oral evidence. Moreover, he asserts that there is simply no Arab documentation of the sort historians must rely on. What exists in Arabic or translated from Arabic into Hebrew or English are some Arab political and military memoirs, newspaper clippings, chronicles and histories. Much of this material is slight, unreliable, tendentious, imaginative and occasionally fantastical.
>
> Despite this contempt for the existing Arabic sources, Morris's position has a respectable professional pedigree derived from the work of Leopold von Ranke. Like many positivist historians, Morris does not consider the intellectual or political implications of his choice of historical method. Indeed, like most traditional Israeli historians he rejects the view that proper scholarly practices have political implications. Despite the sympathy it might arouse for their plight, Morris's historical method contributes to the historical and political marginalization of the Palestinians. Moreover, his positivist and literalist approach to reading archival evidence results in a historical incoherence which renders the experiences of the Palestinians and other Arabs obscure if not incomprehensible.[26]

The nineteenth-century German historian Leopold von Ranke was the father of modern historical positivist, empiricist methodology.[27] Like Ranke and his empiricist followers, Morris's literalism places the emphasis on official documents, state archives, state history, high politics narratives, a top-down approach to national and

---

26. Joel Beinin, 'No More Tears: Benny Morris and the Road Back from Liberal Zionism', *Middle East Report*, no. 230, Spring 2004, www.merip. org/mer/mer230/230_beinin. html.

27. For a discussion of Ranke's philosophy of history, see Tholfsen 1967: 157-86.

international politics, military campaigns and war histories – but without a critical approach to the power relations that underpin this official documentary history.

Morris also displays a complete disregard for Palestinian voices and the people behind the official documents. His contempt for the victims of the Nakba is much in evidence in his writings; for instance, he rarely describes the suffering of the Palestinian refugees. In fact in the Hebrew edition of *1948: A History of the First Arab Israeli War* (2008, 2010) he even implies that the Palestinian inhabitants of Lydda and Ramle – who had to endure ethnic cleansing, mass deportation and a 'death march' in July 1948 – should be grateful for their mass expulsion. He also argues that 'most' of the Palestinian refugees are, in fact, not refugees at all – since they were expelled to what became known as the West Bank and Gaza.[28]

The Impact of the 'New Historians'/Post-Zionists

> Why do ruling classes fear history? Because, beyond their crimes, and beyond the tragedies and ironies which are so demanding of hope and spirit, they see and they know – as did their forerunners – that history has been, and remains, a process of struggle for freedom and for justice – and increasingly, at least since the late eighteen century, it has been, as the late Raymond Williams once put it, a 'Long Revolution', at the political heart of which is the fight for liberty, equality and democracy.
>
> Harvey Kaye, 'Why Do Ruling Classes Fear History?'
> (1995: 96)

How influential were the 'new historians'/post-Zionists and what was their overall impact? Was 1990–2000 a 'post-Zionist decade'? Is it possible to frame the conflict in post-colonial theory, while Zionist settler-colonialism in Palestine is expanding, with no sign of decolonisation in or liberation for Palestine?

First, benefiting from hitherto secret documents, the 'new historians' helped debunk many official Israeli myths. The rise of

28. Tom Segev, *Haaretz*, 9 July 2010, www.haaretz.co.il/hasite/spages/1177968.html.

what was seen at the time as an influential, though controversial, revisionist historiography was a significant development in the public understanding of the Palestine–Israel conflict. Second, the 'new historians' made a huge impression on fellow academics and historians in the West. Their influence on academic and scholarly discourses on Israel in the West cannot be overstated. One example of their 'spectacular' impact on the Israeli public debate, often cited by Ilan Pappé (2002: 27, 2010: 35), is *Tekuma*, Israel Television's 1998 documentary aired on the occasion of the Israeli state's jubilee celebrations in 1998. According to Pappé, *Tekuma*'s 'twenty-two parts tried to recognize the narratives of all those who were victims of the Zionist projects of Israeli policies in the past ... It was a fitting jewel in the crown of the post-Zionist television of the decade 1990–2000' (2002: 27).

Interestingly, however, the documentary was given the ideologically nationalist and emotionally charged Zionist Hebrew salvationist title *Tekuma*. In Hebrew Zionist terminology, the word generally means Jewish national 'revival', 'resurrection', resistance and recovery, and 're-establishment' in the 'land of Israel'. The discourse of *Tekuma* fuses the establishment of Israel in 1948 with the language of Theodor Herzl, especially in his 1902 novel *Altneuland* ('Old-New Land'). In his 'Old versus New' discourse, Herzl argues for a Jewish 'return to history', the creation of a 'New Society' and a 'New Hebrew Man', and insists on a European Jewish civilising mission in the Middle East.

Although most of the important revisionist works appeared in the mid-1980s and early 1990s, the phenomenon still attracts the keen interest of Western academia, especially in the USA, Canada, Britain and France. On the whole the terms of the debate in the West on the early history of the Israeli state and the 'birth of the Palestinian refugee question' have been partly transformed under the impact of this scholarly phenomenon. Containing remarkable discoveries based on Hebrew and archival material, these works closely scrutinised the conduct of the (Labour Zionist) founding fathers of the Israeli state, thus contributing to the demolition of many of the long-held myths surrounding Israel's birth. Several powerful myths surrounding 1948 have been examined and discarded as part of an Israeli *hasbara*[29]/public relations campaign.

Third, in contrast to their influence on Western academia, the impact of the new historians in Israel was limited. For a short while the development caught the public's attention, but the great debate about 'new history' was largely confined to the late 1980s and early 1990s. During that period the debate was repeatedly aired in the mainstream media, divided generations and drove the Zionist 'old guard' to a bitter defence of their turf against the encroachment of the 'new historians' (Kimmerling 1995: 47-52). It also soon became apparent that the revisionist historiography was part of a much wider development of new critical discourses in Israel. This process encompassed several academic disciplines within the social sciences (especially sociology[30]), and included contributions from a long list of authors, many of them holding teaching positions in Israeli universities. At the same time the older generation of Israeli academics, many of them responsible for the founding myths of Zionism, accused the 'new historians' of shaking the foundations of the Israeli state and threatening its legitimacy. A leading Israeli novelist and supporter of Labour Zionism, Aharon Megged,[31] accused them of rewriting the history of Zionism in the image of its enemies: of dedicating themselves to the destruction of Zionism by sapping its legitimacy. He detected a 'suicidal instinct' in Israeli society, and expressed amazement at its propensity to hasten its own demise (Kimmerling 1995: 48).

Illustrating how limited was the impact of the 'new history', *Tekuma* or post-Zionism on the Israeli educational system, in 2008, two decades after the emergence of the 'new history', Professor

29. Wikipedia has an entry for the term Israeli term *hasbara*, 'public diplomacy'. A literal translation of the Hebrew is 'explanation'. Hence it centres on 'explaining' Israeli government policies – in effect a euphemism for official propaganda, in the same way that the Hebrew term *ha'avara*, or 'transfer', served in the pre-1948 period as a euphemism for ethnic cleansing of the Palestinians. See http://en.wikipedia.org/wiki/Hasbara; accessed 15 May 2010.

30. The critical sociologists included Gershon Shafir (1989, 1996a), Baruch Kimmerling (1983) and Uri Ram (1995); among the revisionist historians was Bar-Joseph (1987).

31. Megged was born in Poland and emigrated to Palestine in 1926; he served as the cultural attaché to the Israeli embassy in London from 1968 to 1971.

Ismaʻel Abu-Saʻad of Ben-Gurion University of the Negev could write:

> The [Israeli] education system is essential to making the displacement of indigenous history and presence 'official', through texts such as that quoted from the 6th grade geography curriculum in Israeli schools, which teaches Palestinian children that the history of the coastal plain began only a hundred years ago, with the advent of European Jewish settlement and their transformation of this previously 'abandoned area'. In the text, modern (Jewish) Tel Aviv overrides any mention of Arab Jaffa; modern (Jewish) Ashdod of (Arab) Isdud; modern (Jewish) Ashkelon of (Arab) Al-Majdal. Modern Jewish Rishon Litzion and Herzliya and numerous other new towns are superimposed upon an unacknowledged landscape of Palestinian villages emptied and demolished in 1948. The indigenous landscape is erased *from* the curriculum, while it is simultaneously being erased *by* the curriculum, because of its absence from the official historical and geographical materials being taught about the region. (2008: 24–5)

Fourth, it should be noted that almost from the beginning it was evident that, both academically and ideologically, these Israeli authors were neither a monolithic group nor representative of a coherent intellectual current. For instance, from the outset Morris and Pappé offered two completely contradictory interpretations of the political objectives of Plan Dalet, adopted by the Haganah militia in early March and implemented in early April 1948. Although they were predominantly liberal Zionists with a positivist/empiricist approach to history and historiography, politically, however, these authors ranged from liberal Zionist coloniser to left-wing Zionist (Simha Flapan and Tom Segev respectively) to 'post-Zionist' (Pappé).

Recent developments have demonstrated that the 'new historians' were in fact divided from the beginning. While some conceive of the phenomenon as a form of Zionist catharsis, a 'cleansing' of the soul, 'renewing' Zionism and reinforcing Israeli domination, others used it to develop a fundamental critique of Zionism. Early on Benny Morris announced that he was passionately Zionist; that 1948 was a 'heroic Jewish struggle for survival'; that he was intellectually and empirically impartial; and that the only reliable sources for the reconstruction of the 'birth of the Palestinian refugee problem' are Israeli official 'documents' and the archives of the Israeli army.

The Historian's Methodology and Bridging the Narrative Gap

Morris did acknowledge that the Zionists had carried out a planned expulsion of Palestinians in 1948.[32] Morris's uncritical use of Israeli official documents led him to characterise the objectives of Plan Dalet as follows: 'the Plan called for the securing of the future country's border areas (to close off the expected invasion routes) and of its internal lines of communication (to guard against the threat of fifth column activity by the country's Arab minority) while the Haganah was engaged along the borders' (Morris 1991: 98-114).

From the beginning the works of Benny Morris, which were a landmark contribution to Israeli revisionist scholarship, were deeply anchored in both traditional Zionist moorings and the writings of the Israeli academic colonisers. I have argued that Morris had treated the Palestinian Nakba as 'a debate amongst Zionists which has little to do with the Palestinians themselves', and of ignoring the long history that the idea of 'transfer' (ethnic cleansing) had among mainstream Zionist leaders (Masalha 1991: 90-97), and that the Israeli revisionist historians' excessive or even exclusive reliance on Israeli archives had limited their narrative and conclusions.

The debate about historical methodology was one of the key themes of a conference held in Paris in May 1998, at the height of the Oslo euphoria, in which Benny Morris, Edward Said, Ilan Pappé, Zeev Sternhell,[33] Itamar Rabinovich (Israeli Ambassador to the USA from 1993 to 1996 and later president of Tel Aviv

---

32. Responding to my critique of *The Birth of the Palestinian Refugee Problem*, in a well-known debate, which also involved Norman Finkelstein, in the *Journal of Palestine Studies* of Autumn 1991; I was highly critical of Morris's conclusions on 1948.
33. Sternhell's *The Founding Myths of Zionism* (1999), which benefited from the emergence of the revisionist historiography, was first published in Hebrew in 1995.

University), Elias Sanbar and I, among others, took part.[34] While
Rabinovich had always been an establishment historian rooted in
the Arabist-Orientalist tradition of Zionist academia, the other
Israeli participants reflected three distinct ideological currents
within the 'new history': the 'passionate Zionist' (Morris); the
liberal Zionist (Sternhell); the post-Zionist critic (Pappé). In Paris,
the tensions were palpable.

Benny Morris began his scholarly career as in many ways a typical Israeli (Ashkenazi-European) observer and liberal coloniser:
empiricist, 'detached', 'objective' 'dispassionate', 'disinterested',
'rational', 'non-partisan'; his insistence was on a 'neutral' scholarship more concerned with 'historical findings' than with their
political and moral implications.[35] At the Paris conference Pappé
found himself on the side of the Palestinian participants, and was
criticised by Sternhell for promoting Palestinian nationalist myths
and for applying the same positivist-empiricist approach to history
and methodology in his work as other Israeli 'new historians'.
Pappé, on the other hand, criticised the 'detachment' claims by
Morris and Rabinovich, arguing for 'engaged' and 'involved' historiography, and against the Israeli historians at the conference who
extolled the virtue of detached scholarship (Kabha 2007: 299–319).
Edward Said described Pappé as an involved 'anti-Zionist socialist
historian'.[36] At the conference Said expressed the view that it was
not possible to 'bridge the narrative gap' between the Zionist
colonisers and the colonised indigenous inhabitants of the land.

Sternhell – like other liberal Zionist intellectuals and authors,
Martin Buber, Amos Oz, Amos Elon, S. Yizhar and A.B. Yehoshua
included – embodies the liberal coloniser who promotes the myth of
'the clash of two rights and two justices', of (Buber's idea) the 'land
of two people',[37] and of the fallacy of balance and false symmetry
between the colonised and the coloniser, between the indigenous

34. Subsequently Edward Said published an article on the conference entitled 'New
History, Old Ideas', *Al-Ahram Weekly* online, 21–27 May 1998, http://weekly.ahram.
org.eg/1998/378/pal2.htm.
35. Gideon Levy, 'Exposing Israel's Original sins', *Haaretz*, book review, 11 March 2000,
www3.haaretz.co.il/eng/scripts/article.asp?mador=8&datee=11/03/00&id=99286.
36. Said, 'New History, Old Ideas'.
37. See, in particular, Mendes-Flohr 1983.

and the European settler, between the ethnically cleansed and the ethnic cleanser. The conscientious liberal Zionist, represented in S. Yizhar's *Khirbet Khiz'ah* (1949) and A.B. Yehoshua's 'Facing the Forests' (1968) and *Between Right and Right (Bein Zechut Le-Zechut)* (1980, 1981) – whose narrative found strong echoes in the enthusiastic reception accorded in the West to the 'heroic new historians' – is always torn by the demands of Zionist patriotism and the need for human decency. At the Paris conference, expressing a view which is typical of the Israeli liberal narrative, Sternhell acknowledged the colonising aspects of Zionism and recognised the great injustice done to Palestinians. But he insisted that, in view of the European Jewish catastrophe, the Zionist military conquest of Palestine and the expulsion of the Palestinians was dictated by necessity.

Said describes the 'profound contradiction bordering on schizophrenia' that lies at the heart of Israeli historical revisionism and the works of Morris, Sternhell and Shlaim; while acknowledging what happened in 1948 the new historians (with the exception of Pappé) end up justifying it in the name of Zionism and, at the same time, denying the Palestinian refugees the 'right of return' which is enshrined in UN resolutions and international law.

One very powerful impression I had was that whereas the Israeli participants – who were by no means of the same political persuasion – often spoke of the need for detachment, critical distance, and reflective calm as important for historical study, the Palestinian side was much more urgent, more severe and even emotional in its insistence on the need for new history. The reason is of course that Israel, and consequently most Israelis, are the dominant party in the conflict: they hold all the territory, have all the military power, and can therefore take the time, and have the luxury to sit back and let the debate unfold calmly. Only Ilan Pappé, an avowed socialist and anti-Zionist historian at Haifa University, was open in his espousal of the Palestinian point of view, and, in my opinion, provided the most iconoclastic and brilliant of the Israeli interventions. For the others in varying degree, Zionism was seen as a necessity for Jews...
One of the most remarkable things about the Israelis, again except for Pappé, is the profound contradiction, bordering on schizophrenia that informs their work. Benni [*sic*] Morris, for example, ten years ago

wrote the most important Israeli work on the birth of the Palestinian refugee problem. Using Haganah and Zionist archives he established beyond any reasonable doubt that there had been a forced exodus of Palestinians as a result of a specific policy of 'transfer' which had been adopted and approved by Ben-Gurion. Morris's meticulous work showed that in district after district commanders had been ordered to drive out Palestinians, burn villages, systematically take over their homes and property. Yet strangely enough, by the end of the book Morris seems reluctant to draw the inevitable conclusions from his own evidence. Instead of saying outright that the Palestinians were, in fact, driven out he says that they were partially driven out by Zionist forces, and partially 'left' as a result of war. It is as if he was still enough of a Zionist to believe the ideological version – that Palestinians left on their own without Israeli eviction – rather than completely to accept his own evidence, which is that Zionist policy dictated Palestinian exodus.[38]

Historians and authors in the West continue to display a bias in favour of Israeli archival sources and documentation. The overall bias towards Israeli 'archives' and the lack of sufficient attention given to Palestinian oral history have contributed to silencing the Palestinian past. Although breaking boundaries within Israeli historiography by focusing on Israeli archival documents, Morris and other Israeli revisionist historians did not place Palestinians as subjects or agents in their own history (Humphries 2009: 79). Morris continues to dismiss Palestinian oral history and the testimonies of the refugees, In recent debates and publications both Pappé and I, by contrast, have highlighted the vitality of Palestinian oral testimony as an essential methodology in the reconstruction of the Palestinian past and understanding of the Nakba. As is the case with other subaltern groups, refugee oral testimony is a crucial source for recovering the voice of the victims of ethnic cleansing and for constructing a more comprehensible narrative of the *experience* of ordinary Palestinian refugees (Masalha 2005a, 2008: 123-56).

With hindsight a more productive judgement on the Israeli 'new history' discourse is now possible. First, any assessment of the impact of 'post-Zionism' on the settler state that is Israel must

---

38. Said, 'New History, Old Ideas'.

take into account the fact that the right-wing Likud and its allies have dominated Israeli politics for much of the past three decades, and continue to do so. Therefore it would be absurd to argue (as some commentators in the West do) that the 'new historians' and 'post-Zionists' dominated Israeli discourse in the 1990s, only to be betrayed by the Palestinians and undermined by the Second (al-Aqsa) Intifada in September 2000.

The Israeli 'post-Zionism' debate began in the mid- to late 1980s, in parallel with the 'new history'. In late 1985/early 1986, shortly after the Knesset reaffirmed the definition of Israel as 'the State of the Jewish people' – in contrast to its simultaneous and explicit rejection of a proposal to define Israel as 'a Jewish state and the country of all its citizens' – a heated public debate on the nature of Israeli identity erupted between Anton Shammas, an 'Israeli-Palestinian' writer, and the author A.B. Yehoshua, who is known for his 'liberal' views and was once described by the *New York Times* as 'a kind of Israeli Faulkner'. Shammas began to work for Israel Television in 1975. He also wrote extensively for Hebrew-language newspapers on the problem of Israeli–Palestinian identity in a Jewish state and published an anthology *No Man's Land* (1979). In 1986 Shammas wrote his now-famous novel *Arabesques* in Hebrew – the language of the coloniser – a highly original literary work which epitomises what is often referred to in post-colonial discourse as 'hybrid cultural identity'.

Promoting what later came to be recognised as a key post-Zionist theme, Shammas argued that Zionism had completed its mission in 1948 with the establishment of Israel; that the Israeli Law of Return, which confers on Jews a favoured status and exclusive rights and denies Palestinian aspirations, is blatantly discriminatory and should be replaced by Western-style immigration laws; that Israeli Jews should come to terms with the reality of a multicultural and bi-national Israeli society in which 'Israeli Palestinians' (who constitute one-fifth of the population) would be accepted as full, equal citizens; and that a single (liberal) civil identity common to all those living within the borders of the State of Israel should be promoted. Both Israelis and Palestinians, Shammas thought, should move away from an obsession with identity politics.

Palestinians inside Israel have attempted to construct an 'authentic' Palestinian identity for themselves inside the Green Line. This has often been met with denial and rejection by liberal Zionists, for whom the existence of a Palestinian identity and Palestinian culture inside Israel was a negation of Israel's Zionist identity. Yehoshua's response to Shammas was typical of the 'Zionist liberal' colonising discourse. Reflecting the fundamental Zionist-Jewish opinion that views the Law of Return as the legal embodiment of the Zionist-Jewish character of the state, and for which Israeli identity is essentially the consummate expression of 'Jewish identity', he rebuked those who did not repudiate Shammas's vision of 'a non-sectarian democratic state for all its citizens':

> The Law of Return is the moral basis of Zionism ... if you accept the morality of the whole Zionist process in this sense, then with a clear conscience you can come to Anton Shammas and say: You, the Israeli Arab, or the Palestinian with Israeli citizenship, you are a minority here ... If you want your full identity, if you want to live in a state with an independent Palestinian personality, with an authentic Palestinian culture, get up, take your belongings and move yourself one hundred metres to the east, to the Palestinian state which will be established alongside Israel.[39]

There were those liberal Israelis who understood Yehoshua's 'get up, take your belongings and move yourself one hundred metres to the east' as a call for the expulsion of the Palestinians from Israel; as the commentator for the daily *Haaretz* noted on 17 January 1986, '[Rabbi Meir] Kahane would not have formulated it better'.[40] Shammas responded sharply, lumping Yehoshua with 'his brothers, the members of the Jewish terror organisation'. He also wrote that if and when the Palestinian state is established, 'I do not wish to leave my country and my kindred and my father's house for the land he, in this case, A.B. Yehoshua, will show me' (cited in Grossman 1993: 251).

Two and a half decades later, the Palestinian state to which Yehoshua suggested Shammas should move does not exist and

39. *Politikah* 4 (December 1985), cited in Beinin 1994: 82, 90.
40. Ibid.; and Grossman 1993: 251.

senior Israeli ministers and officials (not only members of the far-right Yisrael Betenu) are openly threatening the Palestinians with expulsion. In late January 2011 hundreds of leaked confidential Palestinian documents (the 'Palestine Papers', released to the Al Jazeera television channel and Britain's *Guardian* newspaper) showed that the Israeli foreign minister Tzipi Livne, in secret negotiations with Palestinian Authority officials in 2007–08, repeatedly pressed for the 'transfer' of some of Israel's own Palestinian Arab citizens into a future Palestinian state.[41] Although it is not clear how many of Israel's 1.4 million Palestinian citizens would have been affected by this new 'transfer' wave, apparently Livne's adviser, Udi Dekel, listed several Palestinian villages inside Israel that would be transferred to a future Palestinian state, including Beit Safafa, Barta'a, Baqa al-Sharqiyeh and Baqa al-Gharbiyyeh.[42] Livne's proposal was made within the context of a land swap with a future Palestinian state, but it also echoes an open 'population transfer' long proposed by current Israeli foreign minister Avigdor Lieberman, the leader of Yisrael Betenu. Shammas himself now lives in voluntary exile in the USA and teaches modern Middle Eastern literature at the University of Michigan.

A number of works on the 'post-Zionism' debate have been published in the USA and Britain since the mid-1990s (Pappé 1997: 37-43, 1998: 99-105; Nimni 2003; Silberstein 1999, 2008; Segev 2002; Hilliard 2009), although the impact of the post-colonial discourse on Israeli settler-colonial society has been marginal. With their critical success mostly outside Israel, the 'new historians' have not substantially changed the terms of political debate inside Israel or challenged the fundamental nature of Zionist colonialism in Palestine. Not only is settler-colonialism still at

---

41. The example of villages located on the Green Line was given at a meeting at the Inpal Hotel (Larome), in Jerusalem, on 8 April 2008, which was attended, on the Palestinian side, by Ahmad Qurei (Abu Ala), Saeb Erekat, Samih Al-Abed, Salah Ilayan and Zeinah Salahi, and, on the Israeli side, by Tzipi Livni, Udi Dekel and Tal Becker. See minutes of the meeting at http://transparency.aljazeera.net/ar/node/2484. For further details of the string of concessions in the secret documents, which were shared exclusively with the *Guardian*, see Ian Black and Seumas Milne, *Guardian*, 23-27 January 2011; also Jonathan Cook, 'The Palestine Papers: Israel's peacemakers unmasked', 26 January 2011, www.redress.cc/palestine/jcook20110126.

42. 'Livni offered to transfer Israeli Arabs to Palestine', *Jerusalem Post*, 25 January 2011, www.jpost.com/Headlines/Article.aspx?id=205062.

the heart of Israeli society, and Israeli academia still structured around the colonisation of minds, in fact the post-Second Intifada period has witnessed a colonial resurgence in Israel. In a colonising country the vast majority of Israeli academics support the system that employs them and funds their research and publications. In the 1990s 'post-Zionism' (which was influenced by the rise of 'post-colonial' discourse in the West) and historical revisionism were largely academic phenomena – indeed were on the margins of Israeli academia. It did not reflect the emergence of a new grassroots or social movement. The phenomenon never grew into an all encompassing anti-Zionist cultural, political or ideological movement or decolonising methodology.

Crucially 'post-Zionism' failed to reverse or even slow down the Israeli colonisation of the West Bank; it never changed Israeli society in significant ways, be it public school curricula or the nature of Palestinian–Israeli relations. Throughout the 1990s the Israeli Ministry of Education and the academic establishment in Israel continued to promote an official version of Zionist history in which the facts were sacrificed to self-justifying myths. Furthermore, under the cover of the Oslo peace process in the 1990s Israel consolidated its colonies – by tripling its settler population in the West Bank and consolidating its Bantustans. In *The Myths of Liberal Zionism*, Israeli poet and novelist Yitzhak Laor, commenting on the 'return' of the colonial to Israel, shows how Zionist settler-colonial strategy

> preceded even the outbreak of the 2000 intifada. It ran throughout the Oslo [peace process] years, while the colonisation deepened, the number of settlers tripled, lands were expropriated, roads for Jews [only] were paved in the occupied territories, IDF assassination squads were killing Palestinian youths, and Arafat kept promising his people independence. (Laor 2009: 46)

The ongoing construction of a segregation/apartheid wall at the heart of colonised Palestine, with devastating consequences for the lives of many Palestinians, is strongly backed by the Zionist left and the likes of Benny Morris. Paradoxically the catharsis produced by the 'new history' was subsequently exploited by Morris and other supporters of Labour Zionism to propagate the myth of the 'generous offer' supposedly made by Ehud Barak to Yasser Arafat at Camp David (Laor 2009: 40–46).[43]

Racism, Justification of Ethnic Cleansing and the Resurgence of Neo-colonial Epistemology

Morris's 'new history' project began by challenging some of the Zionist myths surrounding 1948 and ended up by providing a neo-colonial moral rationale for the dispossession of the Palestinians.

Tom Segev observes in a review of the Hebrew edition of Morris's work, *1948: A History of the First Arab–Israeli War* (2008, 2010) that Morris has, in recent years, been rewriting his own 'new history' of 1948 along social Darwinist racist lines: enthusiastically accepting transfer and elimination, promoting 'a survival of the fittest' and a 'clash of civilisations' between Israel and the West, on the one hand, and Islam and the Palestinians, on the other.[44]

The failure of the *mission civilisatrice* of the West in the backward Orient and the 'return of Islam' brought about the resurgence of neo-colonial racist epistemology and neo-colonial lobbies. The neo-con academy in Europe (particularly in France) and the USA, armed with the 'clash of cultural identities'/'clash of civilisations' doctrine, is seeking to rewrite the history books and recast the Israeli–Palestinian conflict as driven by 'Islamic fundamentalism'.[45] Historically it was the French who coined the term *mission civilisatrice* as a rationale for 'benevolent' intervention or colonisation, proposing to contribute to the spread of French/European

---

43. For further discussion of the 'generous offer', see Seth Ackerman, 'The Myth of the Generous Offer: Distorting the Camp David Negotiations', *Fair*, July–August 2002, www.fair.org/index.php?page=1113.
44. Tom Segev, *Haaretz*, 9 July 2010, www.haaretz.co.il/hasite/spages/1177968.html.
45. See, for instance, Chris McGreal, 'Texas Schools Board Rewrites US History with Lessons Promoting God and Guns', *Guardian*, 16 May 2010. On 23 February 2005 the centre-right majority in the French National Assembly, Union pour un Mouvement Populaire, led by Nicolas Sarkozy, then a key contender in the 2007 presidential election, voted in favour of a law compelling history textbooks and teachers to 'acknowledge and recognise in particular the positive role of the French presence abroad, especially in North Africa'. At www.admi.net/jo/20050224/DEFX0300218L.html. French critics argued that the law was tantamount to denying that racism was inherent in French colonialism. President Jacques Chirac later had the law repealed.

enlightenment and civilisation among what they perceived as backward peoples and cultures. Its intellectual origins can be traced back to the Latin West and the fundamentalist Crusaders of the late Middle Ages, while the European Enlightenment and *mission civilisatrice* became the underlying principle of French colonial rule in the late nineteenth and twentieth centuries and was influential in the colonies of North Africa, West Africa and Indochina.

Dividing human beings into a hierarchy of races, ethnicities and cultures, the racist 'clash of civilisations' thesis reduced and dehumanised Arabs and Muslims. The term itself was first used by veteran British (and US-based) Jewish Orientalist Bernard Lewis in an article in the September 1990 issue of the *Atlantic Monthly* entitled 'The Roots of Muslim Rage'.[46] But it was Samuel Huntington (1927-2008) an American Jewish political scientist, who originally formulated it in a 1992 lecture at the Washington DC-based American Enterprise Institute for Public Policy Research,[47] a neo-con think-tank closely associated with the American pro-Israel lobby. Huntington then developed his thesis in a 1993 *Foreign Affairs* article titled 'The Clash of Civilizations?' Later, competing with rivals in the policymaking ranks, theorists such as Francis Fukuyama and his 'end of history' ideas,[48] Huntington expanded the thesis in a 1996 book *The Clash of Civilizations and the Remaking of World Order*. His thesis, which attracted a lot of media attention, proposed that 'cultural and religious identities' (not ideologies or economics) will be the primary source of conflict in the post-Cold War 'new political order'. Huntington, Lewis and other policy experts have contributed to the 'Israelisation' of American Middle East policy discourse.[49]

The Palestine-Israel conflict is not a 'clash of religions' or a 'clash of cultural identities'. Reframing the issue as an anti-

---

46. The Roots of Muslim Rage, *Atlantic Monthly*, www.cis.org.au/Policy/summer01-02/polsummo1-3.pdf.

47. www.aei.org/issue/29196.

48. Edward W. Said, 'The Clash of Ignorance', *The Nation*, 22 October 2001, www.thenation.com/article/clash-ignorance.

49. For further discussion of the Israelisation of American discourse, see Beinin 2003: 125-39.

apartheid and anti-colonial struggle is central to peace and re-conciliation in the Middle East. The Israeli academy has played a major part in Zionist settler-colonialism, through history writing, conceptual and linguistic conformity and ideological framing of the conflict, all in the service of a state-run *hasbara*/propaganda system. By and large the Israeli 'new historians' have been either unable or unwilling to step outside the liberal Zionist *hasbara* industry and process of self-construction. The problem lies both in the framing of the conflict and in methodology. Morris, Shlaim and Pappé adopt three completely different perspectives in rewriting the history of the Israel–Palestine conflict. With the exception of Pappé, all the 'new historians', Morris and Shlaim included, have failed to meet the challenge of applying decolonising methodologies to Palestine–Israel.

Since the Nakba of 1948, the 'right of return' has been at the heart of the Palestinian liberation struggle. Among the 'new historians', only Pappé has spoken courageously and openly in favour of this principle. In *The Ethnic Cleansing of Palestine* (2006) Pappé 'explore[s] both the mechanism of the 1948 ethnic cleansing [of Palestine] and the cognitive system that allowed the world to forget'. He 'want[s] to make the case for the paradigm of ethnic cleansing and use it to replace the paradigm of war as the basis for the scholarly research of, and the public debate about, 1948'.

Shlaim cemented his formidable reputation as a revisionist historian with *Collusion Across the Jordan: King Abdullah, the Zionist Movement, and the Partition of Palestine* (1988: 183–6). The dismantling of Palestine through the catastrophic collusion between the Zionists and Hashemites, and its erasure from the political lexicon, were rebranded positively two years later in *The Politics of Partition: King Abdullah, the Zionists, and Palestine 1921–1951* (1990), a work which harks back to the Zionist Jordanian option and, more crucially, completely ignores the mountains of Israeli archival sources that show how Zionist support for partition in the 1930s and 1940s was made conditional on 'transfer' and ethnic cleansing. Shlaim's pro-Hashemite sympathies[50] are also to

---

50. In particular, Shlaim is a great admirer of Prince Hassan of Jordan, a patron of the Middle East Centre at St Antony's College. Oxford.

be found in *Lion of Jordan: The Life of King Hussein in War and Peace* (2007), a conventional account of the Hashemite regime of King Hussein and a sophisticated take on the Israeli discourse on the shrewd and 'plucky little king' and Zionism's 'best enemy'. The lionisation of the Jordanian king sounds more like Niccolò Machiavelli's shrewd advice in *The Prince*. Shlaim must be fully aware of the Hashemite kingdom of fear – a police state allied with Zionist Israel – a regime that has much in common with the deeply corrupt and autocratic regimes of Hosni Mubarak in Egypt and Zain El-Abideen ben Ali in Tunisia overthrown by popular uprisings in 2011. As a leading expert on the Zionist–Hashemite alliance, Shlaim also knows that both Zionist and Hashemite regimes pursued de-Palestinisation strategies, with Jordan formally annexing the West Bank in 1950: both refused to recognise the existence of the Palestinian people or a separate Palestinian identity; both sought to fragment the Palestinians and eliminate their identity through Israelisation/Hebrewisation and Jordanisation/annexationist methods; both occupied and sought to colonise the two halves of Jerusalem after 1948; both imposed a tight system of control and surveillance on their respective Palestinian populations – and a neo-colonial system of patronage through which notables and villages mukhtars were co-opted and integrated into their colonial power structures; both used their internal security services (the Shin Bet in Israel and Mukhabarat in Jordan) to torture dissidents, silence independent Palestinian voices and impose their hegemonic narratives.

Furthermore, Shlaim, like most Israelis and in contrast to Pappé, is against the Palestinian 'right of return'. A shrewd political analyst, he has maintained a nuanced liberal Zionist (nationalist) version of the conflict. He is a sensitive expositor of the context within which the 1917 Balfour Declaration emerged, describing it as a 'colonial document' that supported the right of Jews to a state in Palestine despite the fact that they constituted less than 10 per cent of the population of Palestine at the time. He also accepts that the UN 1947 Partition Plan (General Assembly Resolution 181, which recommended a Jewish state on 55 per cent of historic Palestine) was 'unfair', but nonetheless claims that it was 'legal' and thus established a hugely expanded Israel as a 'legitimate state'[51] on the ruin of Palestine, on a territory encompassing 78 per cent of historic Palestine. Like other liberal Zionists, Shlaim locates the origin of the Zionist colonial project in 1967, not in 1948. In *Israel and Palestine: Reappraisals, Revisions, Refutations* (2009), Shlaim presents a collection of articles published over two decades on Israeli 'revisionist historiography'. Chapter 9 is entitled 'Benny Morris and the Betrayal of History'. Commenting on Morris's 'conversion', Shlaim has this to say:

> [Morris's] new version of the recent history of the conflict has more in common with propaganda than with genuine history ... It would appear that Benny can no longer tell the difference between genuine history, and fiction or fabrication along the lines of *The Protocols of the Elders of Zion*. At this rate Benny is in danger of becoming what Isaiah Berlin once described as 'a very rare thing – a genuine charlatan' ... His post-conversion interpretation of history is old history with a vengeance. It is indistinguishable from the propaganda of the victors. (2009: 361-3).

The collection is at its best when discussing political history. However, although Shlaim criticises the political history of Zionist movements and the actions of the Israeli state, 'Zionism itself goes blithely unscathed', as one perceptive reviewer in the Electronic Intifada puts it.[52] Like the liberal coloniser in Yizhar's *Khirbet Khiz'ah* (2008), Shlaim uses revisionist history as a means of redeeming the decaying Zionist project. Commenting critically on Shlaim's revisionist history and its failure to critique Israel as a settler state, Max Ajl, one of the key coordinators of the Gaza Freedom March,[53] writes:

> This evasion takes two forms. One is that Shlaim seems temperamentally unable to practice *ideologiekritik*, criticism of society and its governing ideology. He cannot lay bare the basic fact of Zionism – its core and

---

51. http://heathlander.wordpress.com/2010/03/03/avi-shlaim-rocks-cambridge/; accessed 15 May 2010..
52. Max Ajl, *The Electronic Intifada*, 26 January 2010, http://electronicintifada. net/v2/article11032.shtml.
53. An international non-violent political campaign to end the blockade of the Gaza Strip launched in 2009.

necessary subordination of the national rights of an indigenous people
to the ostensible national rights of a settler-colonial people, arriving
from Europe, some of them the desperate refugees from genocide.
Ostensible, but Shlaim thinks immanent, as he refers to the 'moral
case for a Jewish state' being 'unassailable.' But this moral case was not
tried before magistrates adjudicating the merits of various land masses,
finally setting on the Palestine Mandate, unpopulated, awaiting Jewish
settlement – a social fact of the Zionist imaginary. The moral right
granted by horrific Jewish suffering meant, in turn, the abrogation of
another set of rights – those of a people living on their land.

Max Ajl exposes the contradictions inherent in Shlaim's liberal
Zionist position, especially with regard to UN General Assembly
Resolution 181 of 1947:

> [Shlaim] says this affirms the 'legality' of the Israeli state. This is tenu-
> ous, if not outright disingenuous – the history of that vote is too well
> known: the diplomatic pressure by the United States and the Zionist
> movement's bartering and promises to sway votes. The United Nations
> General Assembly in those days was only barely grasping at legitimacy
> as an institution. Legitimacy differs from legality anyway, and legality
> differs from a legalism that's a mere veneer for power-dynamics shaped
> by wrenching collective guilt. Shlaim seems unable to step outside the
> Zionist self-construction of its own actions and sharply assess those
> actions and the context within which they occur. For example, when
> commenting on Israel's invasion of Gaza, Shlaim insists on the Israeli
> right to self-defense. But a blockade is an act of war, and it was Israel
> that broke the June 2008 ceasefire on 4 November 2008, not Hamas.
> It was Israel and not Hamas that had other options, such as ending the
> asphyxiating blockade or ending the occupation, the chief grievances
> behind violent resistance. Shlaim also seems unable to link the core
> tenets of Zionism with Israeli history ... Shlaim repeatedly criticizes
> the Israeli interpretation of security by claiming that it is one-sided or
> unaccommodating to the genuine security concerns of the Palestin-
> ians. Yet he won't reconcile it with the claim that this conception has
> nothing remotely to do with security and everything to do with ter-
> ritorial maximalism, which has been embedded in the Zionist political
> project from the outset, as a bit of time with the primary documents
> makes obvious. Shlaim is obviously aware of these documents and the
> voluminous secondary literature analyzing them, and that he ignores
> them is disappointing. This decision is, perhaps, due to Shlaim's own
> ideological predispositions. While he acknowledges the tragedy of

the Palestinian Nakba or forced dispossession in 1948 and Israel's responsibility for the destruction of Palestinian society and the creation of the Palestinian refugees, he sees the June 1967 War as the inflection point... [and] Zionism's transformation from a legitimate movement of national self-determination to an ideology tightly entwined with a colonial occupation. This legerdemain summons up a pre-1967 Israel brimming with innocence, and contrasts it with a post-1967 occupying power that is simple European settler-colonialism redux ... this one is contrived. The aspiration to the whole of the land was embedded in Zionism from the outset, as was a privileging of the rights of European Jews over the territory's native inhabitants. An excessive emphasis on the decay of the Zionist project [after 1967] distracts Shlaim from these core points ... It's time for the 1967 Zionists to move past this [nationalist] tribalism – or past time.[54]

The failure of the 'new history' brought Morris, once considered a liberal Zionist, back to old Zionist history. This radical shifting of ground has puzzled many observers. In 2008 the managing editor of *The Nation* in New York, Roane Carey, asked whether it is possible for someone like Morris, 'who supports crimes against humanity[,] to be a good historian?'[55] Carey (and Shlaim, see below) consider that Morris's character combines both 'Dr Jekyll and Mr Hyde'. Carey was commenting on an extraordinary January 2004 interview with Morris in the Israeli daily *Haaretz*. Not only does Morris refrain from morally condemning the ethnic cleansing of 1948, he openly and explicitly endorses it:

> That is what Zionism faced. A Jewish state would not have come into being without the uprooting of 700,000 Palestinians. Therefore it was necessary to uproot them. There was no choice but to expel that population. It was necessary to cleanse the hinterland and cleanse the border areas and cleanse the main roads. It was necessary to cleanse the villages from which our convoys and our settlements were fired on.[56]

Threatening the Palestinians with another Nakba, Morris now believes that Ben-Gurion failed to do 'a complete job' in 1948; 'this place would be quieter and know less suffering if the matter

---

54. Ajl, *The Electronic Intifada*.
55. Roane Carey, 'Dr. Benny and Mr. Morris', *Counterpunch*, 19-21 July 2008.
56. Shavit, 'Survival of the Fittest?'

had been resolved once and for all.' He makes this threat in the interview:

> The Israeli Arabs are a time bomb. Their slide into complete Palestini-
> sation has made them an emissary of the enemy that is among us. They
> are a potential fifth column. In both demographic and security terms
> they are liable to undermine the state. So that if Israel again finds itself
> in a situation of existential threat, as in 1948, it may be forced to act as
> it did then. If we are attacked by Egypt (after an Islamic revolution in
> Cairo) and by Syria, and chemical and biological missiles slam into our
> cities, and at the same time Israeli Palestinians attack us from behind,
> I can see an expulsion situation. It could happen. If the threat to Israel
> is existential, expulsion will be justified.[57]

Edward Said, in *Orientalism* (1978), made the powerful argument that Orientalist and new colonialist historians had practised
a kind of subjugation of eastern cultures and Islamic societies by
writing about them from a perspective that unconsciously assumed
their characteristics were inherent traits of inferiority compared to
the West. Promoting a typically hegemonic new-colonial narrative,
Benny Morris reproduces Theodor Herzl's Eurocentric observa-
tions made eleven decades earlier. He has asserted the inherent
'superiority' of Israel and the West: 'We are an outpost of the West,
as they see it and as we also see ourselves, in a largely Islamic,
backward and in some ways even barbaric area.'[58]

In the pre-1948 period, Zionist proponents of 'transfer' continuously asserted in private discussions that there was nothing
immoral or unethical about this racist solution. Today Morris
openly provides a 'moral justification' not only for the ethnic
cleansing of Palestine in 1948 – something he did not offer before
the eruption of the Second Intifada in October 2000 – but also
for a new Nakba, for expelling Palestinians from Israel and the
West Bank and Gaza.[59] According to Joel Beinin,

57. Ibid.
58. Scott Wilson, 'Israel Revisited: Benny Morris, Veteran "New Historian" of the
Modern Jewish State's Founding, Finds Himself Ideologically Back Where It All Began',
Washington Post, 11 March 2007, www.washingtonpost.com/wp-dyn/content/ar-
ticle/2007/03/10/AR2007031001496.html.
59. Beinin, 'No More Tears'.

The racism Morris has openly expressed during the second *intifada* is prefigured by his historical method, beginning with his earliest publications during the first intifada. All his work is characterized by the near total exclusion of Arab testimony.[60]

Morris's 'new empirical findings' also reflect the profound contradictions that inform much Israeli historical revisionism. Morris, of course, is fully aware that Israeli revisionist historiography has shown that in reality throughout the 1948 war the Jewish army not only outnumbered all the Arab forces operating in the Palestine theatre, but also outgunned them. However, as a reincarnated neocon, he clearly views the Israel–Palestine struggle in terms of a new-colonial 'clash of cultures'. Morris's thinking remains deeply wedded to old Zionist settler-colonialism and new 'separation/apartheid wall' policies. This is how Herzl put it in *The Jewish State*:[61] 'For Europe we would constitute part of the wall of defense against Asia: we could serve as an outpost against barbarism. As a neutral state we would remain in contact with all of Europe, which would have to guarantee our existence' (Herzl 1970: 52).

For Morris, Beinin writes, 'The entire historical project of demonstrating Israel's ethnic cleansing of the Palestinians in 1948 is emptied of its obvious current political implications and reduced to an antiquarian curiosity.'[62] In *The Returns of Zionism: Myths, Politics and Scholarship in Israel*, Gabriel Piterberg comments critically on Morris's embrace of the 'clash of civilisations' narrative:

> There is something irresistible about the brutal candour of Benny Morris. For two decades he has been a notable historian of the Arab-Israeli conflict. He meticulously and thoroughly documented the ethnic cleansing that was an integral part of the birth of the state of Israel in the 1948 war as well as other episodes in that conflict's history. The 2000 Camp David fiasco caused Morris to shed any lingering inhibitions: he pronounced that the ethnic cleansing of 1948 should be completed, and that Israel is the West's crusading outpost in its clash of civilisations with Islam. This combination of scholarly integrity and

---

60. Ibid.
61. *Der Judenstaat* (1896).
62. Beinin, 'No More Tears'.

authority on the one hand, and on the other unmasked social Darwin-
ism that would have made Max Nordau blush, prompted the editor of
the *New Left Review* to publish verbatim a striking interview Morris
gave to *Haaretz* ... [in 2004] entitled (aptly in both languages) 'Survival
of the Fittest' in the English edition and 'Awaiting the Barbarians' in
the Hebrew original. The *New Left Review*'s introduction justifiably
states that the interview is a 'document of unusual significance in
the modern history of Zionism ... To his shocked interlocutor, Morris
sets out two unpalatable truths: that the Zionist project could only be
realized by deliberate ethnic cleansing; and that, once it was embarked
upon, the only reasons for stopping short of the complete elimination
of the Arab population from Palestine were purely temporary and
tactical ones. (2008: 28–9)

Today Morris is a self-declared admirer of prime minister David
Ben-Gurion and his ethnic cleansing policies in 1948. Initially
unable to find an academic job in Israel, he was invited in 1996
by Israel's President 'Ezer Weizman (a nephew of Israel's first
president, Chaim Wiezmann) to his office, whereupon the latter
arranged a post for him at Ben-Gurion University of the Negev
in Beersheba,[63] where he lectures today and fulfils the role of an
establishment professor. Fellow revisionists, especially Pappé,
are scathing about Morris's openly Islamophobic and pro-ethnic-
cleansing, racist views.[64]

The Israeli Academy and the
Political–Military–Security Establishment

It is in the nature of imperialism that citizens of the imperial power
are always among the last to know – or care – about circumstances
in the colonies.

Bertrand Russell, at the International War Crimes
Tribunal on Vietnam, November 1967

In July 2010, Morris, echoing threats by the Israeli political-
military establishment, threatened Iran with mass murder – 'an

---

63. Wilson, 'Israel Revisited'.
64. Ilan Pappé, 'Response to Benny Morris' "Politics by other means" in the New
Republic', *The Electronic Intifada,* 30 March 2004, http://electronicintifada.net/v2/
article2555.shtml.

Iran turned into a nuclear wasteland',[65] a threat designed to keep
Israel a dominant colonial power and the only nuclear power in
the Middle East.

In a highly militarised settler state, Morris's academic and
journalistic skills and bellicose rhetoric are much appreciated by
the Israeli political and military–security establishments. In June
2010 the Israeli Knesset enacted a bill that provides one year of
free tuition to any discharged soldier (reservist) who studies at
an institution of higher learning in the areas targeted for Israeli
Judaisation: the Galilee, the Naqab (Negev), and the illegal Israeli colonies in the occupied West Bank. A month later, Jewish
high-school students participated in the levelling of a Palestinian
Bedouin village in the Naqab, al-Araqib. Jewish high-school students are encouraged to join the civilian guard, an army-sponsored
programme designed to incorporate Israeli children into the state's
military apparatus. Of course the use of the educational system
and higher education institutions to buttress Israeli colonisation of
the Palestinian land is anything but new. Since the establishment
of the Israeli state on the ruins of Palestinian society, this close
partnership between the Israeli academy and the military–security
establishment has been emblematic of the settler-colonial militarised country. This partnership is never cause for comment among
Israeli academics, historians, artists or novelists. Even members of
the Israeli 'peace camp' by and large do not criticise the militarisa-
tion of the Israeli academy.[66]

Of course historical revisionism has not disappeared completely
from the Israeli scene, as recently demonstrated by Shlomo Sand's
The Invention of the Jewish People (2009). However, unlike the
'new historians', who have tried to undermine some of the assump-
tions of Israeli historiography by focusing on 1948 or on the British
Mandatory/colonial period, Sand, in a radical departure from the
Israeli 'new history', has gone back hundreds of years. Sand has
demolished the Zionist nationalist myth of enforced exile under the

65. Benny Morris, 'Using Bombs to Stave Off War', *New York Times*, 18 July 2010,
www.nytimes.com/2008/07/18/opinion/18iht-edmorris.1.14607303.html.
66. 'The Militarization of the Israeli Academy', *BRICUP Newsletter*, 31 August
2010.

Romans by showing that the Jewish Diaspora was the consequence, not of the expulsion of the Hebrews from Jerusalem and Palestine, but of proselytising across Southern Europe and North Africa.[67] He showed that the Jewish people never existed as a 'nation-race' with a common ethnicity or origin, but rather as an extremely diverse mix of communities of faith and groups that at various stages in history converted to Judaism and adopted the Jewish religion. But clearly Sand, like Pappé, is a non-Zionist historian. As a young man he was in the Union of Israeli Communist Youth and, for a short period, even joined the more radical anti-Zionist Matzpen in 1968. He had this to say in an article entitled 'Shattering a "national mythology"', in *Haaretz*:

> We must begin to work hard to transform our place into an Israeli republic where ethnic origin, as well as faith, will not be relevant in the eyes of the law. Anyone who is acquainted with the young elites of the Israeli Arab community can see that they will not agree to live in a country that declares it is not theirs. If I were a Palestinian I would rebel against a state like that, but even as an Israeli I am rebelling against it.[68]

However, two decades after the emergence of the 'new history', those courageous Israeli academics who speak out against Israeli war crimes in the occupied territories are being threatened with expulsion from Israeli academia. The settler state of Israel still promotes itself as the state for all Jews. Commenting on this colonial resurgence in Israel, Yitzhak Laor had this to say in 2009:

> In today's Israel, it is not that easy to research the atrocities committed by Israeli soldiers in the war of 1948. People have lost their jobs in Israeli universities for less than that. It is not that easy to demonstrate against the war in Lebanon ... in any other place in the (white) world, a state of all its citizens would be a reasonable democratic and republican solution, a legitimate political idea – but this does not apply to Arabs ... This is the return of the colonial. (Laor 2009: 57)

67. See also Shlomo Sand, 'Zionist Nationalist Myth of Enforced Exile: Israel Deliberately Forgets Its History', *Le Monde diplomatique* 7 September 2008, http://mondediplo.com/2008/09/07israel.
68. Quoted in Ofri Ilani, 'Shattering a "National Mythology"', *Haaretz*, 21 March 2008, www.haaretz.com/general/shattering-a-national-mythology-1.242015.

It its first decade (from the late 1980s to the late 1990s) the 'new history' went through various positive developments, while throughout much of its second decade (especially since the Palestinian Second Intidafa) its protagonists have been at each other's throats. Morris began his 'new history' with the idea of the shared responsibility of the Palestinians for their 1948 catastrophe and ended up blaming the victims of the Nakba – for resisting the Zionist colonisation of Palestine – and threatening the Palestinians with another Nakba. Pappé, by contrast, went in the opposite direction.

He began his academic career in the 1980s as a positivist historian and 'liberal Zionist'; in the 1990s he promoted 'post-Zionism' and now is clearly 'anti-Zionist' and places a greater emphasis on Palestinian oral history approaches and popular memory narratives. Also significant is the current 'war of words'. Pappé denounces Morris as a Zionist fascist and 'a racist anti-Arab pundit' (2010a: 20). Shlaim, as we have seen, views Morris as both Jekyll and Hyde: the careful researcher and historian and the bigoted ideologue: 'There is the first-rate archival historian whose work is of utmost importance in understanding the Israeli–Arab conflict. And there is the third-rate political analyst who has little understanding of what is driving the modern conflict.'[69] Despite this criticism, Shlaim has remained a great admirer of Morris's scholarship and has continued to collaborate with him closely in 'new history' publications (Shlaim 2007a: 124-46, in Morris 2007).

Pappé and Morris, on the other hand, have been trading personal insults in public and exchanging accusations of falsifications of history and even outright fabrications of fact.[70] Today Morris, Shlaim and Pappé represent three distinct and even contradictory perspectives in Israeli historiography: the right-wing racist coloniser, the liberal coloniser and the anti-Zionist decoloniser. Pappé, in contrast to Morris, is a great believer in the idea of scholarship committed to historical truth, social justice, equality for all and human liberation. After serving for twenty-two years as a senior lecturer

69. Wilson, 'Israel Revisited'.
70. Benny Morris, 'Politics by Other Means', *The New Republic*, 22 March 2004; Ilan Pappé, 'Response to Benny Morris' "Politics by Other Means" in *The New Republic*', *The Electronic Intifada*, 30 March 2004, http://electronicintifada.net/v2/article2555.shtml, accessed 26 May 2010.

in the Department of Middle Eastern History and the Department of Political Science at Haifa University, he was effectively denied promotion, at which point he left for Exeter University in the UK, where he is now director of the newly established European Centre for Palestine Studies. His fascinating and courageous journey from Zionism to 'post-Zionism' and then 'anti-Zionism', and his being practically hounded out of Israel, are vividly described in *Out of the Frame: The Struggle for Academic Freedom in Israel* (2010).

6

Decolonising History and Narrating the Subaltern: Palestinian Oral History, Indigenous and Gendered Memories

I didn't grasp the true meaning of the word [Nakba] until I worked in Palestinian refugee camps in Lebanon. In the alleys and passages of the Shatila camp, I discovered the truth of the catastrophe. Villagers expelled from the Galilee had suddenly found themselves living in huts set up hastily to provide temporary shelter. But the temporary became permanent, and the people were forced to construct a nation for themselves out of words and memories. They gave the various sections of their camps the names of the villages they had fled, and they lived, as they said, 'waiting' in a suspended time. Even when the waiting went on too long and became 'exile,' they still refused to believe that no one would recognize and authenticate their tragedy.

Elias Khoury, 'For Israelis, an Anniversary.
For Palestinians, a Nakba' (2008)

The Nakba as Site of Palestinian Collective Memory

Collective memory and commemoration have played an important role in counter-hegemonic discourses, cultural resistance, decolonisation, liberation and nation-building processes and as a vehicle for victims of injustice and violence to articulate their experience of suffering. Narratives of memory and commemoration have also been part of grassroots initiatives to bring to life marginalised and counter-narratives that have been suppressed, either by hegemonic discourses or by unwillingness on the part of repressive regimes to acknowledge the past (Makdisi and Silverstein 2006). In the case of the indigenous inhabitants of Palestine the Nakba has been a key site of collective memory and history that 'connects all Palestinians to a specific point in time that has become for them an 'eternal present'' (Sa'di 2002: 177). While Palestinian national identity took root long before 1948, Palestinian memory and accounts of the post-Nakba period played a major role its reconstruction and the emergence of the PLO in the 1960s. In recent decades there has been a close relationship between the Nakba and the articulation of Palestinian national identity (Sanbar 2001a: 87–94; Sa'di and Abu-Lughod 2007: 4; Sa'di 2002: 175–98; Khalidi 1997; Fierke 2008: 34; Slyomovics 1998; Sayigh 2007a: 135).

In the post-1948 period Palestinians have maintained the multiple meaning of their Arabic names and the multilayered Palestinian identity (Doumani 1995) embedded in ancient names. Dr Hanan Mikhail Ashrawi, legislator, activist, scholar and formerly dean of the Faculty of Arts at Birzeit University, has reflected on the Palestinian naming tradition and memory in the post-Nakba period:

> My name means 'tenderness.' True to the Arab, and generally Semitic, tradition, we Palestinians attach a great deal of significance to names – their meaning and music, historical allusion and authenticity, identification and identity. More often than not our names are a form of indulgence in wishful thinking, rather than descriptive accuracy as in the case of rather homely daughters called Hilweh or Jamileh for 'pretty' or 'beautiful' ... But most important, our long series of names are proof of lineage, or roots for a people uprooted, of continuity for a history disrupted, and of legitimacy for an orphaned nation ... Hanan Daud Khalil Mikhail (Awwad)-Ashrawi is my personal and collective narrative. I am Tenderness, the daughter of David, who is the son of Khalil (Abraham) from the family of Michael (also the name of an ancestor), which is of the clan Awwad (the one who inevitably returns). (Ashrawi 1995: 132–4)

At the same time, however, in the post-1948 period new naming traditions and new resistance strategies emerged among the different communities of Palestinians, reflecting the various fates suffered by the indigenous population of Palestine. The depopulated and destroyed villages and towns were often kept alive by passing place names down through generations of Palestinian family members. Inside Israel, those internally displaced refugees regrouped in different localities to create new definitions of kinship structure. Post-Nakba conditions of displacement and dispersal gave rise to circumstances in which a person from the destroyed village of Ruways, for instance, would be given the surname Ruwaysi – someone from Ruways – instead of the customary clan eponymic (Slyomovics 2002). Village solidarity stood in place of the absent village and dispersed clan members. Also the name of the original village replaced the name of the *hamula* (clan), and the relationship among persons who belonged to the same original village became similar to hamula solidarity. The hamula did not disappear or weaken, but some of its basic functions were transferred to the wider kinship structure based on the original village (Al-Haj 1987: 72).

For those Palestinians forced into exile outside Palestine, 'another convention [was] to name children for the lost but not forgotten site', as Susan Slymovics observes:

Among Palestinian Arabs, the practice of naming a child after a lost or destroyed place seems to be reserved for daughters rather than sons. Muhammad Mubarak Abu al-Hayja' of Ein Houd al-Jadidah chose the name Sirin for his daughter to commemorate a destroyed Palestinian village, in the Baysan district, home to the greater Abu al-Hayja' clan before 1948. Afif Abdul Rahman Abu al-Hayaja', who lives in Irbid, Jordan, named his daughter Haifa after the town where he was born. ... Sirin cannot live in Sirin because it is destroyed, and Haifa, a Palestinian in Jordan, is barred from Haifa. Examples proliferate: Nazmi Jubeh, a professor at Birzeit University, has a daughter named Baysan, the appellation of an entire district now in Israel; one of the names given to the granddaughter of sociology professor Ibrahim Abu-Lughod is Jaffa, his former home town. Also pronounced Yafa, it is a popular post-1948 name for Palestinian girls. There are more: female children are named Safad to mark a town depopulated of its Arab inhabitants and Karmil for the mountains they cannot visit. After the 1967 war, a fresh list of girls' names came into existence to commemorate the latest group of threatened places in the Occupied West Bank. Wasif Abboushi, for example, who resides in the US, called his daughter Jenin, a name that passes easily into English as Janine.[1]

Today, with millions of Palestinians still living under Israeli settler-colonialism and occupation or in exile, the Nakba remains at the heart of Palestinian collective memory, national identity and the struggle for collective national rights. To begin with, there was always an intense relationship between the Nakba and the formation of Palestinian national identity, especially from the late 1950s onwards. Today the politicised collective memory of the Nakba plays a major role in Palestinian cultural resistance and the struggle for self-determination.

Today memory accounts of the traumatic events of 1948 are central to Palestinian society and its collective struggle. By Palestinian society I mean Palestinians inside Israel, those in the occupied territories, and the refugee and diaspora communities outside historic Palestine. The Nakba remains a key site of Palestinian collective consciousness and the single most important event that connects all Palestinians to a specific point in time. The collective memory of the Nakba unites the three constituencies deeply and emotionally – even though they are separated by geography and the politics of expediency; by historical fragmentation and the colonial boundaries imposed on the Palestinian people by the Israeli state; and by differences deriving from the legal and political conditions in Israel-Palestine and neighbouring countries.

In the absence of a Palestinian state, which might have been expected to devote material and cultural resources to commemorative events, memorialisation projects, archives and museums, Palestinian refugee communities in Lebanon and elsewhere in the Middle East have actively promoted Nakba commemoration and memorialisation as a form of cultural resistance (Khalili 2005: 30-45). Since 1948 Palestinian refugees from individual villages marked 'their' Nakba, or the anniversary of the date of the fall of their village. At the same time, however, for many years the topic

---

1. Susan Slyomovics, 'The Gender of Transposed Space', *Palestine-Israel Journal of Politics, Economics and Culture* 9, no.4, 2002, www.pij.org/details.php?id=114.

of the Nakba was hardly broached in Palestinian film-making – it was a memory too painful to evoke (Bresheeth 2007: 160–63). In *Nakba: Palestine, 1948, and the Claims of Memory* (2007) Ahmad H. Sa'di and Lila Abu-Lughod show how in the last decade this has changed dramatically, with Palestinian film-makers examining the history and the memories of this cataclysmic event. The book provides excellent accounts of memory of the Nakba in a number of recent Palestinian films. It also explores concepts of home and exile, identity and its relationship to memory, and exilic cinema and its characteristics, cinematic use of narrative devices and storytelling, and the struggle between two opposing narratives – the hegemonic (Zionist) narrative which tries to displace and suppress the narrative of the indigenous people of Palestine (Sa'di and Abu-Lughod 2007). Of course, as Palestinian film-maker Omar al-Qattan (2007: 191) points out, 'There is no single Palestinian memory' of the Nakba; 'rather, there are many tangled memories. A collective memory or experience is in its nature complex and elusive, constantly changing with time.'

Nakba: Palestine, 1948 and the Claims of Memory and *Catastrophe Remembered* (Masalha 2005) are two recent collections that explore the complex narratives of the Nakba. Drawing on the works of memory theorists such as Maurice Halbwachs (1980) and Pierre Nora (1996, 1997, 1998), Sa'di and Abu-Lughod show that authors dealing with Palestinian narratives of memory have not always been sensitive to the complex and multilayered relationships between collective memory, oral history, cultural resistance and historiography. As a result, studies of Palestinian collective memory have been largely divorced from the broader political context, national narratives and identities, elite discourses and the class structures which inform and shape them (Sa'di and Abu-Lughod 2007).

In 1998 there was a remarkable proliferation of Palestinian films, memoirs and archival websites – all created around the fiftieth anniversary of the Nakba, the exodus of the Palestinians and the dismemberment of Palestine. In conjunction, several films were released, including Edward Said's *In Search of Palestine*, Muhammad Bakri's *1948* and Simone Bitton's film about the poet Mahmoud Darwish, *Mahmoud Darwich: Et la terre, comme la langue* (Bresheeth 2007: 160–87). Further Nakba films were released in conjunction with the sixtieth anniversary, including Maryse Gargour's *La Terre parle arabe*.[2] In addition, since 1998 online archives have been created on oral history, refugee experiences and recollections of the Nakba.

Palestinian social history and refugee experiences – including stories from the past that appear in oral history collections, autobiographies, novels, poetry collections and memorial books – focus on both the symbolic and the emotional connections of individuals to their former homes and villages. This material is also the 'documentary evidence' that proves their existence and legal right to the land of their ancestors. Memory accounts of Palestine before 1948 reflect the beauty of the landscape, the richness of the land and the detail of village and city life. These affirmative narratives about the land testify to the intimate and intense experience of everyday life on the land: the names of the valleys and *wadis*, hills, tombs and shrines, streets, springs and wells, cultivated fields and vineyards; the importance of trees (olive, almond, grape) and other natural elements in memories of the past. Hand-drawn maps marking the places of importance to villagers, personal documents, individual memories and oral accounts all intertwine to create a larger picture and a collective narrative of life before the Nakba (Sa'di and Abu-Lughod 2007). Interestingly, however, Sa'di and Abu-Lughod show how until recently little research had been carried out into the underlying power claims within the context of what, following French sociologist Pierre Bourdieu, we can understand as the Palestinian 'symbolic marketplace' (Bourdieu 1977); a range of voices and multiple narratives of memory are the archaeology of a people criss-crossed with individual experiences – narratives of suffering and *sumud* (steadfastness), of courage and resistance, born out of anger and revolt against oppression (Sa'di and Abu-Lughod 2007).

2. This documentary film (with which I was personally involved) has won three international awards, including winner of the 13th International Award for Mediterranean Documentary and News.

Archiving Popular Memory and People's Voices: Palestinian Oral History and Subaltern Studies

Israeli positivist and revisionist historiography has long privileged state papers and official documents over the people's voices behind the documents. By contrast, in recent decades, oral history has attempted to redress the imbalance within modern historiography by developing methodologies for understanding the contexts and meanings of documents, facts and evidence, and generally for exploring the history and voices of the people behind state and other official papers. Oral history revolutionised historical methodology by bringing to light hidden, suppressed or marginalised narratives. Furthermore, it has brought together academics, archivists and librarians, oral historians, museum professionals and community-based arts practitioners. As a producer of meaning, oral history has become an important catalyst in creative practices and interpretations within history-related fields and in the construction of alternative histories and memories.

Oral history, like written documentation, is never free from factual error and has to be treated critically. Morris argues that written documents (and Israeli archives) are less liable to distort the record than interviews with Palestinian refugees (2004: 4). However, archival documentation is itself often based on memory; and can distort, misinform, omit or even fabricate evidence (Humphries 2009: 79–80). As Louis Starr notes, memory is 'fallible, ego distorts and contradictions sometimes go unresolved'; nevertheless

> Problems of evaluation are not markedly different from those inherent in the use of letters, diaries, and other primary sources ... the scholar must test the evidence in an oral history memoir for internal consistency and, whenever possible, by corroboration from other sources, often including the oral history memoirs of others on the same topic. (Starr 1984: 4–5)

From the 1970s on, oral history began to be considered in a more positive light by the academy, following work by scholars such as Luisa Passerini, who studied the history of the Turin working class under Italian Fascism (Humphries 2009: 78; Passerini 1998: 53–62).

There has since been a proliferation of oral history archiving memory projects in Britain and internationally, which promote the collection, preservation and use of recorded memories of the past and people's voices.[3] In the UK the BBC has developed an 'Archive of World War Two Memories', based on oral history and written by ordinary people,[4] and 'BBC Memoryshare', which is described as 'a living archive of memory from 1900 to the present day' – the majority of content on memoryshare is created by Memorishare contributors, who are members of the public'.[5] Ordinary people can contribute memories, research events and link to context material relating to any date back to 1 January 1900. As for the 'WW2 People's War Archive', the BBC asked the public to contribute their memories of World War II to a website between June 2003 and January 2006. This 'people's memory archive' contains 47,000 stories and 15,000 images – stories not just on air raids, military operations and the armed forces, but also on the concentration camps in Europe, on women's roles, on resistance and occupation, on civilian internment and conscientious objection.

Palestinian oral history, for its part, is a significant methodology not only for the construction of an alternative, counter-hegemonic history of the Nakba and memories of the lost historic Palestine but also for an ongoing indigenous life, living Palestinian practices and a sustained human ecology and liberation. In contrast with the hegemonic Israeli heritage-style industry of an exclusively biblical archaeology, with its obsessive assembling of archaeological fragments – scattered remnants of masonry, tables, bones, tombs – and officially approved historical and archaeological theme parks of dead monuments and artefacts in museums, in recent decades Palestinians have devoted much attention to the 'enormously rich sedimentations of village history and oral traditions' as a reminder of the continuity of native life and living practices (Said 2004: 49; Masalha 2008: 123-56).

---

3. For a list of organisations and resources in Britain and internationally, see www.oralhistory.org.uk/resources.php.
4. www.bbc.co.uk/ww2peopleswar/timeline.
5. www.bbc.co.uk/dna/memoryshare/lincolnshire/about.

In the context of rural and peasant Palestinian society, oral history is a particularly useful decolonising methodology. Throughout much of the twentieth century the majority of Palestinians lived in villages as fellahin (peasants); in 1944, 66 per cent of the population was agrarian with a literacy rate, when last officially estimated, of only 15 per cent (Esber 2003: 22). Their experiences in the fields, in their villages and in exile are largely absent from written history and from much recent historiography ('Issa 2005: 179–86). Moreover, the Nakba itself, and the political instability and repression faced by the dispersed Palestinian communities since 1948, have also impeded Palestinian research and study (Khalidi 1997: 89). In *Palestinian Identity*, Rashid Khalidi argues that modern Palestinian historiography has suffered from 'inherent historical biases' and that 'The views and exploits of those able to read and write are perhaps naturally more frequently recorded by historians, with their tendency to favour written records, than those of the illiterate' (Khalidi 1997: 98).

As has been observed, Palestinian oral accounts give voice to the subaltern: peasants, the urban poor, women, refugee camp dwellers and Bedouin tribes. An important feature of the Palestinian oral history initiative from its inception has been its popular basis, with the direct participation of the displaced community (Gluck 2008: 69). Since the mid-1980s this grassroots effort has shown an awareness of the importance of recording the events of the Nakba from the perspective of those previously marginalised in Palestinian elite and male-centred narratives. Although both female and male gender imagery and symbols have always been prevalent in Palestinian nationalist discourses (Khalili 2007: 22–3), the Palestinian National Charter of 1964 (revised in 1968) and the Palestinian Declaration of Independence of 1988 had both imagined the Palestinian nation as a male body and a masculinised political agency (Massad 1995: 467–83).

In 1949 Constantine Zurayk published *Ma'na al-Nakba* (*The Meaning of the Nakba*), which was translated into English in 1956. This was followed by Palestinian historian and native of Jerusalem 'Arif Al-'Arif, who published six volumes in Arabic in the period 1958–60, entitled *Al-Nakba: Nakbat Bayt al-Maqdis Wal-Firdaws al-Mafqud* (*The Catastrophe: The Catastrophe of Jerusalem and the Lost Paradise*). Also in the late 1950s and early 1960s, Walid Khalidi published three pioneering articles on the circumstances surrounding the Nakba (Khalidi 1959a: 21-4, 1959b: 22-32, 1961: 22-8). However, with the exception of these articles, which are based on written documentation, and an important article by Irish journalist Erskine Childers in 1961,[6] little was published in English about the Nakba during the first two decades following 1948. In 1972 Palestinian author Mustafa Dabbagh began publishing in Arabic his eleven-volume encyclopaedic work entitled *Our Country, Palestine*, describing all the villages of Palestine during the British Mandate (Dabbagh 1972-86). Nevertheless, with the exception of a few sympathetic books in English on the Palestinian question – which, tending to emphasise the loss of property in 1948, were largely legal, abstract and alienating, and recorded Palestinian elite voices but never those of the people[7] – there was almost total silence on the Palestinian Nakba, which was associated with defeat and shame. Consequently Palestinian people's voices went largely unheard until the 1970s.

Khalidi went on to co-found in December 1963 (since when he has served as secretary general) the Institute for Palestine Studies (IPS), established in Beirut as an independent research and publishing centre focusing on the Palestinian problem and the Israel-Palestine conflict. Under his guidance the IPS has produced a long list of publications in both Arabic and English and several important translations of Hebrew documents, texts and books into Arabic. In 1984 the IPS published *Before Their Diaspora: A Photographic History of the Palestinians, 1876-1948*, edited by Khalidi. However, Khalidi will always be known for his encyclopaedic work on the Palestinian villages occupied and depopulated by Israel in 1948, *All That Remains* (1992a). This monumental work of collective memory includes several hundred photographs and has clearly benefited from the contribution of Palestinian oral historians.

6. Erskine Childers, 'The Other Exodus', *Spectator*, 12 May 1961.
7. Rosemary Sayigh, interview by Toine van Teeffelen, *Jerusalem Times*, 10 October 1997, www.palestine-family.net/index.php?nav=3-83&cid=90&did=671.

Palestinian Oral History, Gendered
Memories and Liberating Experiences

It was not until the 1970s that published Palestinian oral history began to offer a picture of events from the perspective of the ordinary refugees who had experienced dispossession and dispersal. It should be noted, though, that this was before the opening of the Israeli governmental and institutional archives – in the late 1970s – and at least a decade before the emergence of the Israeli 'new historiography' in the mid- to late 1980s.

In the 1960s and early 1970s the collective nationalist resistance discourse, as articulated by the PLO, was dominant, effectively marginalising the personal narratives of refugees. Typically this 'heroic' nationalist discourse was designed to construct an ideal historical narrative and suppress the darker side of Palestinian history, including accounts of infighting and of Palestinian collaboration with Zionism. From the early 1970s, however, the *Journal of Palestine Studies*, *Shuun Filastiniyah*, the Centre for Palestine Studies, the Palestinian Research Centre (PLO) and *Arab Studies Quarterly* began publishing pioneering articles and books based on individual oral evidence, personal narrative and interviews with ordinary refugees to tell the history of Palestine before and during the Nakba. This included works by Elias Shoufani (1972: 108–21), Nafiz Nazzal (1974a: 58–76), Fawzi Qawuqji (1975), Rega-e Busailah (1981: 123–51), Elias Sanbar (1984), Walid Khalidi (1984) and 'Ajaj Nuwayhid (1993). In 1978 the Institute for Palestine Studies in Beirut published Nafiz Nazzal's *The Palestinian Exodus from Galilee 1948*, based on his doctoral dissertation (1974a), which brought to academic attention important oral accounts of Galilee dispossession as recalled by refugees exiled in Lebanon.

Ironically, Benny Morris, who claims to distrust Palestinian oral evidence on 1948 (Morris 1988: 2), cites Nazzal's work repeatedly and extensively (as well as Shoufani's) in *The Birth of the Palestinian Refugee Problem, 1947–1949* (1987). Notwithstanding his anti-Palestinian polemics, Morris found Nazzal's oral history research extremely useful in reconstructing several of the Israeli massacres of Palestinians in 1948.

The 1970s and 1980s were two of the most creative and inventive decades in Palestinian history and popular memory. In the 1970s Rosemary Sayigh, an anthropologist based in Lebanon, pioneered a whole new discipline of narrating the subaltern. She began to record and translate conversations with and individual testimonies of Palestinian refugees, writing them up into a number of articles in *Journal of Palestine Studies* (1977a, 1977b) and a book, *Palestinians: From Peasants to Revolutionaries* (1979). However, neither Sayigh – who pioneered working with women in the camps – nor Nazzal theorised oral history in their work; they simply recorded it. As Sayigh later recalled: 'In my approach to oral history I was simply doing it, using large chunks of what people told me. I didn't have any idea of what oral history was or about its potential for liberation struggles.'[8]

The seminal works of Sayigh and Nazzal encouraged further oral history projects at Birzeit University, initially proposed in 1979 by Sharif Kanaana and Kamal 'Abdel-Fattah. In 1985 the University Documentation Centre launched a series of monographs on the villages destroyed in 1948.[9] Since 1993 this work has been overseen by Saleh Abdel-Jawad (Gluck 2008: 69).

As time went on, Sayigh, while working with the General Union of Palestinian Women and women in the camps, became more theoretical in her approach. She later wrote her doctoral dissertation on the life stories of women in Shatila camp. She recalled:

> I was particularly interested to see how they would relate themselves to the national movement, how they would reflect through their own lives the nationalist discourse, and how this would interface with their gender identity. At this point I began to read about empowering methods in oral history.[10]

Subsequently there has been an explosion of popular history and subaltern studies of Palestine, including work by Sayigh, Dina Matar (2011), Humphries (2004: 213-31, 2009), Khalili (Humphries and Khalili 2007: 207-27), Gluck (1994, 2008: 68-80), Sa'di and

---

8. Sayigh, interview by Toine van Teeffelen.
9. See, for example, Sharif Kanaana and Nihad Zitawi, 'Dayr Yasin', Monograph No. 4, Destroyed Palestinian Villages Documentation Project, Birzeit University, 1987.
10. Sayigh, interview by Toine van Teeffelen.

Abu-Lughod (2007), Kassem (2011) and Masalha (2005a), much of it presenting original material relevant to the Palestinian women's movement, women's liberation struggle, narrative histories and gendered memory. Today Sayigh and other oral historians working with Palestinian refugees advocate a fresh examination of Palestinian history from an oral history perspective. They work in a field notable for dominant male and elite narratives which rely on official documentation and archival material. Their 'history from below' approach, with its emphasis on oral history and popular memory rather than high politics, political elites, decision-makers or top-down approaches, has both powerfully challenged and complemented the archival historiography of Palestine–Israel. In her book *What It Means to be Palestinian: Stories of Palestinian Peoplehood*, Dina Matar insists that her work on Palestinian popular memory 'aims to complement, rather than subvert, the top-down approaches prevalent in most modern histories of Palestine and adds to burgeoning oral history and popular memory research on the Palestinian people pioneered by the ethnographic work of Rosemary Sayigh and that of Nafiz Nazzal' (Matar 2011: 8). Sayigh's highly original contribution to the field of oral history has made it possible for the victims, the subaltern, the marginalised, especially women, to challenge Zionist hegemonic and Palestinian elite narratives. In 2002 the editors of a special oral history edition of the Beirut-based *Al-Jana: The Harvest*, published by the Arab Resource Centre for the Popular Arts, indicated that individual initiatives were being undertaken even before the 1980s, when more projects began to develop with institutional support, especially from NGOs.

Since the late 1980s, with the decline of the PLO, Palestinian historiography has further developed, fashioning a different discourse as part of a 'history from below' approach. This new direction upholds 'people's past as a source of authenticity'.[11] This was given a major boost in the 1990s with the publication of Ted Swedenburg's seminal work on the great Palestinian rebellion of 1936–39: *Memories of Revolt: The 1936–1939 Rebellion and the Palestinian*

---

11. Sayigh, interview by Toine van Teeffelen.

218   *The Palestine Nakba*

National Past (1995). Earlier, in 1990, Swedenburg commented on
the internal silencing of the Palestinian past and popular memory
by both the Palestinian traditional and PLO leaderships:

> Perhaps the sensitive nature of the subject of infighting during the
> [1936–39] revolt is one of the reasons why the PLO, which funded
> numerous projects in Lebanon during the seventies and early eight-
> ies, never supported a study of the [revolt] based on the testimony of
> the refugees living in Lebanon. Maybe the resistance movement was
> hesitant to allow any details about the internal struggle of the thirties
> to be brought to light because bad feelings persisted in the diaspora
> community. (1990: 152–3; also Swedenburg 1991: 152–79).

Al-Hakawati, the storyteller/narrator, is part of a long popular
and oral tradition in Palestinian and Arab societies and cultures.
In *Palestinian Women: Narrative Histories and Gendered Memory*,
Fatma Kassem shows that in Palestinian oral and verbal traditions
(as opposed to male-written official and religious traditions) the
storytellers are often women – women who are invisible in the
official version, and thus whose voices challenge and sometimes
undermine official and patriarchical narratives (Kassem 2011).
Popular storytelling and oral history were deployed in the post-
1948 period by the Palestinian refugee and internally displaced
communities as an 'emergency science' and a liberating experience.
Individual accounts of struggle and revolt (*thawra*), displacement
and exodus, survival and heroism served as a buffer against national
disappearance. Narrative histories, memory and oral history have
become a key genre of Palestinian historiography – a sub-discipline
whose function is to guard against the 'disappearance from history'
of the Palestinian people (Sanbar 2001a: 87–94; Yahya 1998).

Two distinct historiographical approaches concerning the birth
of the Palestinian refugee problem have evolved over the last three
decades. Debates about 1948 tell us something about the historian's
method and the meaning of the 'historical document' (Pappé
2004: 137). Methodologically, many historians have displayed a
bias towards archival sources; Israeli revisionist historians, in
particular, believe they are both ideologically and empirically
impartial (Masalha 2007: 286), and that the only reliable sources

for the reconstruction of the 1948 war are the IDF archives and official documents. This preference for high politics and 'archives' has contributed to silencing the Palestinian past. The silencing of the Nakba by Israeli historians follows the pattern given by Michel-Rolph Trouillot in *Silencing the Past: Power and the Production of History*:

> Silences enter the process of historical production at four crucial moments: the moment of fact creation (the making of sources); the moment of fact assembly (the making of archives); the moment of fact retrieval (the making of narratives); and the moment of retrospective significance (the making of history in the final instance). (1995: 26)

Nevertheless, historians (including the author) have not been able to resist the opportunity presented by the availability of mountains of Israeli and Hebrew archival sources on 1948 and the Mandatory period. Furthermore, in recent years historians have been paying increasing attention to the idea of 'social history from below' – or 'from the ground up', thereby giving more space to the voices and perspective of the refugees rather than those of 'policy-makers', and incorporating extensive refugee oral testimony and interviews. In that sense, the oral history of the Nakba is more than an intellectual project dictated by ideological commitments; for it can provide an understanding of the social history of the refugees 'from below' that Palestinian elite narratives and political history often obscure.

Of course the two methodologies can complement each other. In particular Israeli historians could benefit from the fact that in recent decades Palestinian researchers and film-makers have been producing a large volume of oral history and memories of the Nakba, While many authors in the West continue to rely on Morris and his publications as a key source for recovering and reconstructing the past, others influenced by the emergence of decolonising methodologies, post-colonial theory and post-modern studies are beginning to raise questions concerning the reliability and 'objectivity' of the IDF archives. Moreover, it is important to understand that a report by an Israeli officer from 1948 is as much an interpretation of the reality as any other human recollection of the same event: archival documents are never the reality itself (Masalha 2007: 286); the reality of 1948 Palestine can only be reconstructed using a range of sources. Even historians who rely extensively on written documents often resort to guesswork and imagination when reconstructing the past from official documents (Pappé 2004b: 189). Therefore the use of Palestinian 'oral history' methodologies in reconstruction of the past is vital to an understanding of the Nakba. The most horrific aspects of the Nakba – the dozens of massacres that accompanied the ethnic cleansing, as well as detailed description of the experience from the point of view of those 'ethnically cleansed' – can only be recovered when such a historiographical approach is applied (Pappé 2004a: 137).

With no independent government or state papers, and given the difficulties of establishing and maintaining public archives in exile or under Israeli occupation (see Chapter 3), the Palestinian elite and intellectuals produced and published a number of Nakba memoirs. However, in the absence of a rich source of contemporary Palestinian documentary records, oral history and interviews with (internal and external) refugees are an essential source for constructing a comprehensible narrative of the experience of ordinary Palestinian refugees and internally displaced Palestinians across the Green Line.

Taken as a whole, Palestinian oral history and refugee recollections give a good idea of the reality. However, in the case of the Palestinian Nakba, oral history is not merely a choice among methodologies. Rather, its use can represent a decision as to whether to record any history at all (Esber 2003). Indeed, oral history stands as the major means of reconstructing the history of the Palestinian refugees and internally displaced Palestinians as seen from the perspective of its primary subjects.

Oral History of the Holocaust, Yad va-Shem and Dayr Yasin

Oral history as a producer of meaning and testimony in the museum and gallery has been of great importance in the recollection and collective memorisation and memorialisation of the Holocaust.

The national memorial at Yad va-Shem, the 'Holocaust Martyrs' and Heroes' Remembrance' institution, is based predominantly on oral history and millions of pages of testimony. It was established in 1953 by a Knesset Act and located in West Jerusalem. According to its website, Yad va-Shem is a vast, sprawling complex of tree-studded walkways leading to museums, exhibits, archives, monuments, sculptures and memorials. It has been entrusted with documenting the history of the Jewish people during the Holocaust period, preserving the memory and story of each of the 6 million victims, and imparting the legacy of the Holocaust to generations to come through its archives, library, school, museums and recognition of the 'Righteous Among the Nations'. The archive collection of Yad va-Shem comprises 62 million pages of documents and nearly 267,500 photographs, along with thousands of films and videotaped testimonies of survivors. The Hall of Names is a 'tribute to the victims by remembering them not as anonymous numbers but as individual human beings'. The 'Pages of Testimony' are symbolic gravestones, which record the names and biographical data of millions, as submitted by family members and friends. To date Yad va-Shem has computerised 3.2 million names of Holocaust victims, compiled from some 2 million pages of testimony and lists. The collections of Yad va-Shem include tens of thousands of testimonies dictated, recorded and videotaped, in their own languages, by survivors of the Shoah in Israel and elsewhere. A second type of testimony consists of forms completed by survivors and relatives containing information about individuals, such as their names, place and date of birth, place of residence, vocation, place and circumstances of death, and so on.[12]

In contrast to the Israeli national memorial at Yad va-Shem and other Holocaust museums (including the Auschwitz-Birkenau Memorial and Museum in Oświęcim, Poland, and the US Holocaust Memorial Museum), there is no 'Nakba museum', no 'Nakba Hall of Names', no 'Central Database of Nakba Victims' Names', no tombstones or monuments to mark the hundreds of Palestinian villages ethnically cleansed and destroyed in 1948. This information has

12. The digitised pages of testimony are accessible to the public in the institution's central database, www.yad-vashem.org.il/about_yad/index_about_yad.html.

been suppressed; it has no place in Israeli popular consciousness. Especially chilling is the fact that the Dayr Yasin massacre of 9 April 1948 took place within sight of the place that became the Holocaust museum in Jerusalem; that is, only a mile from where Jewish martyrs are memorialised lie the Palestinian martyrs of Dayr Yasin, whose graves are unknown, unmarked (McGowan 1998: 6–7). In fact Yad va-Shem itself is situated on the lands of Dayr Yasin, as is the City of Jerusalem western (Jewish) cemetery (Davis 2003: 25). The irony is breathtaking: all Israelis and foreign visitors to Yad va-Shem go to Dayr Yasin, yet in dedication ceremonies at the Jewish memorial no one ever looks to the north and remembers the Palestinian dead (McGowan 1998: 6–7).

For Palestinians inside and outside Israel Dayr Yasin has remained a potent symbol of collective memory and cultural resistance. But in Israel the ghosts of Dayr Yasin, Lubya, Kafr Bir'im[13] and the hundreds of villages destroyed in 1948 are rendered completely invisible. Dr 'Azmi Bishara, a leading Palestinian intellectual from the Galilee, and a Member of the Israeli Knesset between June 1996 April 2007, wrote in October 1992:

The villages that no longer exist were forced out of [Israeli] public awareness, away from the signposts of memory. They received new names – of Jewish settlements – but traces [of their past] were left behind, like the sabr bushes [the Arabic name for a type of cactus which flourishes in Palestine] or the stones from fences or bricks from the demolished houses ... The Arab villages have no tombstones and there are no monuments to them. There will be no equality and there will be no democracy [in Israel], and there will be no historic compromise [between Israelis and Palestinians] – until they receive their tombstones. The Jewish site cast out utterly the other, the 'local' i.e., the other who was in that place. The response of the [Israel-Jewish] Left to the [Palestinian use of the] nomenclature of the collective memory was that this matter must be removed from the [Jewish-Arab national] compromise, [that] there is no room in the compromise of history. History itself will prove that it must be part of the compromise – in order for the victim to forgive, he must be recognised as a victim.[14]

13. On the story of Iqrit and Kafr Biri'm, see Ozacky-Lazar 1993.
14. 'Azmi Bishara, 'Between Place and Space' [Hebrew], *Studio* 37, October 1992, quoted in Benvenisti 2002: 267.

Recent developments have major implications for the study of Palestinian historical consciousness and Nakba memory. The rise of the new global media and the Internet, in particular, has strengthened the role of Palestinian oral history and personal narratives in shaping Palestinian historical consciousness. In the last decade the Internet has become one of the most important means of archiving Palestinian oral history and personal narratives. Moreover, since 2002 the Nakba Archive in Lebanon has recorded on digital video more than 500 interviews with first-generation Palestinian refugees living in the country about their recollections of 1948. This project was conceived as a collaborative grassroots initiative in which the refugees themselves were encouraged to participate in the process of representing this historical period. The project, which consists of some 1,000 hours of video testimony with refugees from 135 villages in pre-1948 Palestine, has centred its work on the twelve official UNRWA camps in Lebanon. But it has also conducted interviews within unregistered refugee 'gatherings', and with middle-class and elite Palestinians living in urban centres. Apparently six duplicate sets of the interviews have been produced, along with a detailed database and search engine; copies of the archive will be held at the Institute for Palestine Studies in Beirut, Birzeit University (Palestine), the American University of Cairo, and at Oxford and Harvard universities.[15] The project also forms part of the 'Remembrance Museum' which is being established by the Welfare Association in Palestine. According to its website this will be

> a national museum, to operate as an independent, non-profit organisation, for the purpose of recording and reflecting Palestinian history. A technical team of specialists in a variety of fields is engaged in planning the museum project. The museum is to be based in Jerusalem but satellite locations are being considered in Birzeit, Bethlehem and Abu Dis until a suitable Jerusalem location can be identified. The museum will concentrate on the last 300 years of Palestinian history and will contain permanent and multimedia exhibits, a library and research center, and an educational resource center.[16]

15. www.nakba-archive.org.
16. www.welfareassociation.org/english/special.htm.

The Limits of Israeli and Colonial
Records, Documents and Archives

The construction of both institutional and national archives in Israel was integral to Zionist nation-building and state formation. As we have seen in Chapter 5, the limitations of Israeli archival documents and 'new history' are very clear. Israeli archives can tell us little about the narrative of the Palestinian subaltern or about victims of the Nakba. Also those who have used Israeli archival sources know that many files of the Israeli army from 1948 remain closed and therefore not accessible to the historian or to the public.

What are the overall historiographical implications of the debate on 1948? The first point concerns the military historiography of 1948, which tends to dominate Israeli and Western accounts. The clashes that took place in Palestine during the late Mandatory period have been treated as part of an overall war between the Arab and Israeli armies. Such a perspective calls for the expertise of military historians (Pappé 2004b: 185-6). Military historians tend to concentrate on the balance of power and on military strategy and tactics. They see actions and people as part of the theatre of war, where events and actions are judged on a moral basis very different from that applicable in a non-combatant situation.

Therefore conventional writing of the historiography of 1948 is inherently biased and tends to favour military history and the victorious Israeli army. Ilan Pappé argues that the events of 1948 should be examined within the category of 'population transfer' and ethnic cleansing and not just as part of military history. Unlike the 1937 Peel partition proposal, the UN partition plan of November 1947 did envisage some form of bi-nationalism for Palestine–Israel; the UN certainly did not envisage an exclusive (ethnically cleansed) Jewish state. This means that the expulsion of Palestinians in 1948 by the Israeli army was an aspect of the *domestic* policies implemented by an Israeli regime vis-à-vis it own Palestinian citizens. The decisive factors in 1948 were ethnic ideology, colonial settlement policy and demographic strategy, rather than military plans or considerations (Pappé 2004b: 186). In *Expulsion of the Palestinians* (1992), I show that the concept of 'transfer' was from the start an integral part of Zionism and that much of the 'ethnic cleansing' of the Nakba was not related to the battles taking place between regular armies waging war.

Pappé makes a further important point, which centres on the difference between macro- and micro-histories. The Israeli 'new historiography' of 1948 has remained largely macro-historical. This is due partly to the nature of Israeli archival material. In general this gives us a skimpy picture of 1948. This means that a detailed description of what happened in the case of each Palestinian village and town remains largely elusive. Often a document produced in 1948 by an Israeli army officer refers briefly to the occupation of a Palestinian village, or to the 'purification' of another. Pappé points out that Palestinian oral history can produce historically accurate accounts of 1948, showing that the same events in 1948 appear in a detailed and graphic form in accounts of memory, often as a tale of expulsion, and sometimes even of massacre. Israeli historians who reject Palestinian oral history may conclude there was no massacre until precise documentary sources assure them otherwise. Avishai Margalit (2003), Alessandro Portelli (1994: 96-107, 1997) and others argue that 'Memory is *knowledge from the past*; it is not necessarily *knowledge of the past*' (quoted in Fierke 2008: 34); and that oral history tells less about events in history and much more about their significance. But written documents are also often the result of a processing of oral testimonies (Pappé 2004b: 186). Therefore refugee memory accounts could be as authentic as the documented ones. But it is also the case that narratives of individual villages and towns in Palestine can *only* be constructed with the help of Palestinian oral history. Consequently oral history is a crucial methodology for pursuing further research on the Nakba. Oral history can function as a substitute for archival material, especially where there is no documentary evidence and where the voices of victims are marginalised and silenced. Oral history can supply crucial material to fill gaps in historical evidence, and be cross-referenced with archival sources and documentary evidence.

Silencing Palestinian Women's Voices
within the Subaltern Story

For nearly three decades, as we have seen, Rosemary Sayigh has been working on oral history projects with Palestinian women in the refugee camps of Lebanon. In *Voices: Palestinian Women Narrate Displacement* (2005), a digital book, with an introduction by Sayigh, you can hear the voices of Palestinian women telling their stories of loss of home through displacement, refugeedom, deportation, imprisonment, Israeli shelling and the siege of refugee camps in Lebanon in 1982, and the total transformation of their environment.

The voices of Palestinian women and oral histories from survivors of destroyed villages in the Galilee provided the Lebanese novelist and narrator Elias Khoury (b. 1948) with material for his novel *Bab al Shams* (1998) (*Gate of the Sun*, 2006; filmed in 2004), an epic retelling of the life of Palestinian refugees in Lebanon since the Nakba, which subtly addresses the ideas of memory, truth and story-telling. Khoury was highly critical of the traditional male-dominated Palestinian leadership and its role in silencing the Nakba. In the late 1960s Khoury had joined Fatah, the largest resistance organisation within the PLO, and he subsequently worked as a researcher at the Palestine Research Centre in Beirut. Khoury had the initial idea of turning stories he heard in refugee camps in Beirut into a memorial narrative in the 1970s, when he worked for the Centre. He spent much of the 1980s gathering 'thousands of stories' before writing *Gate of the Sun*.[17]

The novel's story of love and survival is told by Khaleel, a doctor at a hospital in Shatila refugee camp in Beirut. It involves a dying Palestinian fighter called Yunis and his wife Naheeleh, an internal Palestinian refugee living in the Galilee, whose relationship forms during secret visits across the Lebanese–Israeli border to a cave renamed 'Bab al-Shams. The cave is 'a house, and a village, and a country', and 'the only bit of Palestinian territory that's been

---

17. Guy Mannes-Abbott, 'Elias Khoury: Myth and memory in the Middle East', *Independent*, 18 November 2005, www.independent.co.uk/arts-entertainment/books/features/elias-khoury-myth-and-memory-in-the-middle-east-515728.html.

liberated'. The relationship produces a 'secret nation': a family of seven children, who by the end of the book have borne four more Yunises. For Khoury,

> Yunis, of course, is a hero. He used to go to Galilee, he used to cross the borders ... but in the end we discover that he was nothing, that Naheeleh was this whole story; her relationship with the children, and how she actually defended life. In the refugee camps I met hundreds of women like Naheeleh. Then it's no more a metaphor. It's very realistic.[18]

Khoury was a close friend of Mahmoud Darwish, the Palestinian national poet, and had worked very closely with him in the PLO publication *Shuun Filastiniyya*. Both Darwish and Khoury were very critical of Palestinian elite and male-dominated narratives. In *Memory for Forgetfulness* (1987) and in other poems, Darwish attacked the record of the PLO leadership during the Lebanese period (1970–82) – including the construction of a 'state within a state' in Palestinian refugee camps in Lebanon – and that of Arab leaders during the Israeli invasion of Lebanon for their indifference to the Israeli shelling of Palestinian refugee camps and the sufferings of people in Beirut in August 1982. Remarking on Arab indifference and the silencing of the events surrounding the Nakba in Palestinian elite and male-dominated narratives, Khoury had this to say in 2005:

> a shame, a total defeat; it's a disaster, a real personal disaster. There are stories here about the woman who left her child, about a woman who killed her child. So it's not easy to talk about. The Palestinians did not realise, and if they realised they did not believe that this could happen, because actually this is something unbelievable.[19]

And again in 2008:

> I always considered the word 'catastrophe' [Nakba] inappropriate. It rendered the perpetrator anonymous, and it exempted the vanquished from bearing any responsibility for their defeat. Like many members of my generation, born around the time of the war, I tended to place the blame for our [1948] defeat on the traditional Palestinian leadership

---

18. Ibid.
19. Ibid.

under the sway of the mufti of Jerusalem, and the Arab regimes of the day.[20]

However, Palestinian women continue to be excluded, even within the subaltern narrative and the relatively more democratic new global media. Kassem (2011), Humphries (2009: 90-91), Humphries and Khalili (2007: 207-27) and Hammami (2003: 35-69) have all shown that gender narratives and women's voices and contribution to collective Nakba memory and Palestinian historical consciousness are doubly marginalised within the Palestinian refugee story. Often women's memories are silenced because they complicate Palestinian nationalist narratives, an issue that Palestinian subaltern studies have failed to address adequately (Humphries 2009: 90-91). Despite the interviews with women and the recording of women's voices, men are presented as the main protagonists in Michel Khleifi's *Ma'loul Celebrates Its Destruction* and Rachel Leah Jones's *500 Dunam on the Moon* (Humphries 2009: 90-91). Clearly more accounts of memory and further oral history research are needed to bring to light the events surrounding the Nakba and its traumatic aftermath as experienced and remembered by the whole non-elite majority of Palestinian society.[21]

---

20. Elias Khoury, 'For Israelis, an Anniversary. For Palestinians, a Nakba', *New York Times*, 18 May 2008, www.nytimes.com/2008/05/18/opinion/18khoury.html.

21. More recently Rochelle Davis (2007: 53-76) has examined the way Palestinian memorial books, written by ordinary people, recollect memories of village places in pre-1948 Palestine.

7

Resisting Memoricide, Reclaiming Memory: Nakba Commemoration among Palestinians in Israel

The Nakba led to the dispersal and fragmentation of the Palestinian people and produced a major division between the minority of Palestinians who remained inside Israel and the refugees forced outside its borders – today numbered in millions. Since 1967 Israel has fostered further Palestinian splits: between East Jerusalem and the West Bank; between the West Bank and Gaza; since the Oslo Accords of 1993 between the leadership of the Palestinian Authority and refugee and diaspora communities; and, more recently, between the main rival political movements, Fatah and Hamas. The shock and concessions of the Oslo Accords motivated Mahmoud Darwish, who was born and brought up in the Galilee, to draw painful parallels, in his poem sequence *Eleven Planets at the End of the Andalusian Scene*, between the loss of al-Andalus (Muslim Spain) in the sixteenth century and the ongoing dismemberment of historic Palestine. This chapter focuses on Nakba commemoration by Palestinians inside Israel in the last two decades. It situates memory and commemoration within the context of cultural resistance to the Zionist character of the Israeli State and the struggle for collective rights and Palestinian reunification.

In 1948 the Zionist concept of 'transfer' had not been applied universally, and the Israeli army's expulsion policy failed to rid the new Jewish state of a small Palestinian minority that remained *in situ.* However, having expelled 750,000 Palestinians from the greatly enlarged boundaries of the state and having reduced the Arab population from a large majority to a small minority, the pragmatic Labour leadership believed that it had largely, although not entirely, solved its land/settlement and political/'demographic' problems, and was prepared reluctantly to tolerate the presence of a small, politically subordinate and economically dependent Arab minority – some 160,000 Palestinians of the over 900,000 who used to reside in the areas that became the State of Israel in the aftermath of the 1948 war.

In search of international recognition for the newly proclaimed state, the Israeli Provisional State Council, the forerunner of the Knesset, included in its Independence Charter a promise that the Jewish state would 'uphold the full social and political equality of all its citizens, without distinction of religion, race, and sex'. What in fact took place was exactly the opposite. After its establishment, Israel treated the Palestinians remaining within its frontiers almost as foreigners. It swiftly imposed a military government in the areas inhabited by the Palestinian minority, expropriated over half of the lands of this 'non-Jewish' population, and pursued various policies of demographic containment, political control, exclusionary domination, and systematic discrimination in all spheres of life. The military government, imposed by prime minister and defence minister David Ben-Gurion, became closely associated with both his hostile attitude towards the Palestinian minority and his authoritarian style and almost unchallenged leadership of the ruling Labour Party.

Ben-Gurion's views on the Arab citizens echoed deep-seated sentiments within the Labour establishment, sentiments that found their crude embodiment in the establishment of military rule in the Arab areas. Generally speaking, the supporters of Ben-Gurion's militarist approach deemed that the 'security' aspect must take precedence over any other consideration in dealing with the Arab minority. Officially the purpose of imposing martial law and military government on Israel's Arab minority was security. However, its establishment, which lasted until 1966, was intended to serve a number of both stated and concealed objectives. The first was to prevent the return of Palestinian refugees – 'infiltrators' in Israeli terminology – to their homes. In the process, others who had not 'infiltrated' the country were sometimes driven out as well – the second objective. The third purpose of the military government was to maintain control and supervision over the Israeli Arabs, who were separated and isolated from the Jewish population.

The use of force and coercion formed an important element in Israel's policy towards its Arab citizens in the post-1948 period. The institution of the military government, together with the imposition of the Defence Emergency Regulations, promulgated by the British Mandatory authorities in 1945, empowered the military governors to close off the Arab localities and to restrict entry or exit only to those who had been issued permits by the military authorities. These regulations also enabled the Israeli authorities to evict and deport people from their villages and towns; to place individuals under administrative detention for indefinite periods without trial; and to impose fines and penalties without due process. The military governors also were authorised to close Arab areas in order to prevent internal Arab refugees (also referred to as 'present absentees', they were estimated at 30,000, or one-fifth of those remaining) from returning to their homes and lands that had been confiscated by the state and taken over by new and old Jewish settlements.

Although over the years Israeli Jews became more realistic in their attitude towards the existence of an 'Arab minority' in the country, Zionist premises and fundamental principles with regard to the Palestinian minority remaining under Israeli control have not altered. Today almost a quarter of all Palestinian citizens inside Israel are 'internal refugees' or 'present absentees' (*nifkadim nokhahim* in Hebrew). Inside Israel, after the Nakba, the key stipulation was (as it still is) that it was a state created for Jews; non-Jews, both present and 'present absentees', were treated as foreigners in their own homeland, despite being the indigenous inhabitants and formerly resident in the country. The 'present absentees' concept is a legal one, coined with Kafkaesque irony by Israel's legal bureaucracy in its 1950 Absentee's Property Law to describe those Palestinians who had been displaced from their homes and villages in 1948–49 and become 'internal refugees' within their own country. The 'internal refugees' originate primarily from forty-four destroyed villages located in northern Israel. A second and smaller group consists of those who have been displaced since 1948 due to internal 'transfer' and eviction, land expropriation and house demolition. This group consists largely of Palestinian Bedouins in the Naqab/Negev.

The Israeli population censuses carried out in the 1950s and 1960s did not include questions designed to distinguish between 'Israeli Arabs' who had become internally displaced and those who had not. This lack of attention to the 'internal refugees' was deliberate. It was also consistent with the general neglect suffered by the Palestinians inside Israel. Another reason for the lack of official Israeli statistics was the unwillingness on the part of the government to draw attention to the existence of the 'internal refugees' and their awkward situation by providing means of identifying them. To do so would serve as a reminder that the Palestinian refugee problem also existed within Israel. The internally displaced found themselves in a unique situation. Despite their historical, geographical, cultural and national ties with the Palestinian people, they were 'refugees' in their own homeland and their special situation was shared with the Palestinian national minority in Israel. Sharing common memories of their 'towns and villages of origin', they formed a distinct group (in a distinctly weak position) among the Palestinian citizens of Israel: 'a minority within the minority' – with the adverse consequences of 'double marginalisation'.

The displacement of the Palestinians did not end with the 1948 Nakba. The Israeli authorities continued to 'transfer' and dispossess Palestinians inside Israel during the 1950s. The Israeli state delegated the job of acquiring, settling and allocating land in the country to the Jewish National Fund (JNF), whose own mandate, as we have seen, was to build a homeland for the Jewish people only. Until 1966 Israel had a military government, and Palestinian villages wre declared 'closed military zones' to prevent the 'internal refugees' from returning. The Israeli army and the JNF became the two Zionist institutions responsible for ensuring that the internally displaced were unable to return to their lands, through their policy of the destruction of Palestinian villages and their transformation into Jewish settlements and national parks, planting forests in the depopulated villages to conceal Palestinian existence.

History Textbooks in Jewish and Arab Schools

In the first two decades after 1948 the Palestinian Arab minority inside Israel struggled for survival in a state defined as 'Jewish', established through Palestinian dispossession, and built on the ruins and erasure of Palestine. They were defined *a priori* as outsiders; the delegitimisation of their voices was expressed at the institutional level by the military government.

> Because of the destruction of the fabric of Arab society and the flight of most of the population in 1948, few intellectuals remained who could offer a coherent counter-narrative capable of contesting the Zionist narrative. Most efforts of those Palestinians who became citizens of the Israeli state to organize independent political and cultural institutions after 1948 were repressed. Mapam did criticize, even if for the most part ineffectually, the most extreme injustices of the Zionist project. But the activities of Arab party members were typically supervised by their Jewish comrades. Only the Communist Party offered Palestinian-Israelis a relatively free framework for cultural expression and political action.[1]

Since 1948 the Jewish and Arab school systems inside Israel have had separate curricula (each with its own instruction language: Hebrew and Arabic), but both systems are determined by the Ministry of Education. Arab students are required to learn Hebrew and English; Israeli students are required to learn English but not Arabic. The Israeli internal security service, Shin Bet, also plays a crucial role in maintaining state control over the Arab educational system. Today a quarter of all students inside Israel are Palestinian Arabs. The Israeli Ministry of Education maintains 'internal colonisation' processes through the formulation and provision of

---

1. Joel Beinin, 'No More Tears: Benny Morris and the Road Back from Liberal Zionism', *Middle East Report* 230, Spring 2004, www.merip.org/mer/mer230/230_beinin.html.

educational services to the 'Arab minorities' (in official parlance).
Hillel Cohen of the Hebrew University of Jerusalem notes in *Good Arabs: The Israeli Security Agencies and the Israeli Arabs, 1948–1967* (2010) how the Israeli state moved very quickly after the Nakba to 'de-Palestinize' the minority, who were officially recognised as 'minorities' (*me'utim*) or 'Israeli Arabs': it has tried to 'change the consciousness' of the Palestinian minority through the influence of schoolteachers, village mukhtars, collaborators and local sheikhs, with the aim of creating a 'new Israeli Arab identity' (Cohen 2010). Already in 1949 the Ministry of Education was working to 'emphasize and develop contradictions between the Druze, Christian and Muslim populations to diminish their Palestinian national identity' (Cook 2008: 31). Cohen also shows how Palestinian nationalists inside Israel resisted these efforts (Cohen 2010).

The Arab school curriculum in Israel, argues Isma'el Abu-Sa'ad, a Palestinian professor of education at Ben-Gurion University of the Negev,

> is designed to 'de-educate', or dispossess, indigenous Palestinian pupils of the knowledge of their own people and history. It gives them only carefully screened and censored exposure to their history, culture and identity; and suppresses any aspects that challenge or contradict the Zionist narrative and mission. Furthermore, the attempts of Palestinian educators to create a more balanced or inclusive curriculum have been largely excluded by the formal, state-approved curriculum. Yet, the Palestinian community [inside Israel] must play a crucial role in remembering, discussing and retelling its own history. (Abu-Sa'ad 2008: 17–43)

In 1953, the Israeli Law of State Education was enacted. It describes the Zionist discourse and general aims of the Israeli educational system:

> to base education on the values of Jewish culture and the achievements of science, on love of the homeland and loyalty to the state and the Jewish people, on practice in agricultural work and handicraft, on pioneer training and on striving for a society built on freedom, equality, tolerance, mutual assistance, and love of mankind. (quoted in Mari 1978: 50)

This law was amended in 2000. But it maintained the same educational objectives for state schools (both Arab and Jewish), emphasising 'Jewish values', 'Jewish history and culture', while ignoring or denying Palestinian history and cultural heritage (Abu-Sa'ad 2008: 19). In June 2001 the minister of education, Limor Livnat, announced that she would like to ensure that 'there is not a single child in Israel who doesn't learn the basics of Jewish and Zionist knowledge and values' (Abu-Sa'ad 2008: 19).

In Israel 'Zionist knowledge' and collective memory are promoted by schoolteachers, academics, educators, historians and novelists, and involve a campaign of Nakba denial and concealment. The horrors of the Nakba are completely hidden from Jewish schoolchildren, with teachers and educators helping to construct and preserve a national narrative that eliminates collective Palestinian memory. This elimination, Pappé observes,

is the main constitutive element in the construction of collective Jewish identity in the state of Israel. It is manifested in the tales told by child minders on Independence Day and Passover, in the curriculum and textbooks in elementary and high schools, in the ceremonies of freshmen and the graduation of officers in the army. It is broadcast in the printed and electronic media as well as in the speeches and discourse of the politicians, in the way artists, novelists, and poets subject their work to the national narrative, and in the research produced by academics in the universities about the Israeli reality in the past and the present. (2006: 287–8)

As we saw in Chapter 1, 'knowledge of the land of the Bible' (*yedi'at haaretz*) plays a big part in the state Jewish school curriculum. In the 1960s and 1970s Georges Tamarin, an Israeli educational psychologist and lecturer at Tel Aviv University, conducted research involving 1,000 Israeli school children 8–14 years old. The exercise involved reading to the children the biblical story of Joshua's sacking of Jericho. They were then asked the question, 'Do you think Joshua and the Israelites acted rightly or not? The outcome was that 66 per cent approved of Joshua's action; 26 per cent disapproved; the remainder (8 per cent) partially approved (Masalha 2000: 198).

Central to Zionist foundational myths is the theme that, until the arrival of European Zionist settlers, the land was barren, desolate and empty, waiting to be made fertile and populated by Israel; it was the rightful property of 'returning Jews' (Whitelam 1996: 40-45). The myth of an 'empty territory' runs through state education in Israel and finds strong expression in children's textbooks and literature. One such children's book contains the following story:

> Joseph and some of his men thus crossed the land [Palestine] on foot, until they reached Galilee. They climbed mountains, beautiful but empty mountains, where nobody lived ... Joseph said, 'We want to establish this Kibbutz and conquer this emptiness. We shall call this place Tel Hai [Living Hill] ... The land is empty; its children have deserted it [reference is, of course, to Jews]. They are dispersed and no longer tend it. No one protects or tends the land now.' (Gurvitz and Navon 1953: 128, 132, 134, quoted in El-Asmar 1986: 83)

In 1982 Israel's leading satirist, Dan Ben-Amotz, observed that 'the Arabs do not exist in our textbooks [for children]. This is apparently in accordance with the Jewish–Zionist–socialist principles we have received. "A-people-without-a-land-returns-to-a-land-without-people"' (Ben-Amotz 1982: 155). Six decades earlier the Anglo-Zionist-Jewish writer Israel Zangwill wrote:

> If Lord Shaftesbury was literally inexact in describing Palestine as a country without a people, he was essentially correct, for there is no Arab people living in intimate fusion with the country, utilising its resources and stamping it with a characteristic impress; there is at best an Arab encampment. (Zangwill 1920: 104)

This promotion by the Israeli educational system of the lie of an 'empty territory' ('underpopulated') is closely linked to the non-existence of the Palestinians as a nation and their non-attachment to the particular soil of Palestine. This propaganda of an 'empty territory' – empty not so much in the sense of the actual absence of its inhabitants, but more as a civilisational barrenness and a pastoral biblical landscape – helped in the construction of a mythical continuum of 'biblical' and modern Israel and justified Zionist colonisation, encouraging obliviousness to the fate of the

indigenous people of Palestine.[2] Moreover, this fabricated memory
of a mythical continuum between the ancient (theological, biblical)
and the modern (secular nationalist) means that this is a difficult
(untilled, 'desolate', 'ruined', 'inhospitable', 'silent', 'mournful')
land that resists agriculture and can only be 'redeemed' and made
to yield up its fertility by the extraordinary effort of Jewish immigrants and Zionist pioneers. It mattered little that in reality
most of Palestine, other than the Naqab desert, was not desert
but an intensely and successfully cultivated fertile land.[3] In 1999,
a decade after the emergence of Israeli new historiography, Israeli
school textbooks, especially children's storybooks, were surveyed
by Daniel Bar-Tal, a professor at Tel Aviv University. He studied 124
elementary, middle- and high-school books on Hebrew grammar
and literature, history, geography and citizenship. Bar-Tal found
the textbooks that portrayed Palestinians as 'murderers', 'rioters',
'robbers', 'bloodthirsty' and generally backward and unproductive.
Direct delegitimisation and negative stereotyping of Palestinians
and Arabs were the rule rather than the exception. By contrast,
the books presented Israelis as industrious, brave and determined
to 'improve the country in ways they believe the Arabs were inca-
pable of'. Hebrew-language geography textbooks from the 1950s
through the 1970s focused on the glory of the Jewish ancient past
and how the land was 'neglected and destroyed' by the Arabs until

---

2. The same myth of an empty country was invoked in 1914 by Chaim Weizmann, later
president of the World Zionist Congress and the first president of the State of Israel: 'In
its initial stage, Zionism was conceived by its pioneers as a movement wholly depending
on mechanical factors: there is a country which happens to be called Palestine, a country
without a people, and, on the other hand, there exists the Jewish people, and it has
no country. What else is necessary, then, than to fit the gem into the ring, to unite
this people with this country? The owners of the country [the Ottoman Turks?] must,
therefore, be persuaded and convinced that this marriage is advantageous, not only for
the [Jewish] people and for the country, but also for themselves' (Weizmann, 28 March
1914, cited in Litvinoff 1983: 115-16).
3. In the 1990s, Israeli leaders such as Prime Minister Binyamin Netanyahu propa-
gated the myth of an underpopulated land to justify Zionist colonisation (Netanyahu
1993: 39-40). In October 1991 Prime Minister Yitzhak Shamir, in his address to the
Madrid Peace Conference, resorted to quoting from *Innocents Abroad* by Mark Twain
(who visited Palestine in 1867 and whose description of its natives was either marked
by invective or humorously pejorative) to prove that Palestine was an empty territory,
a kind of civilisational barrenness that (in Shamir's words) 'no one wanted', 'A desolate
country which sits in sackcloth and ashes – a silent, mournful expanse which not even
imagination can grace with the pomp of life.'

the Zionist Jews 'returned from their forced exile and revived it'. Bar-Tal observes: 'This attitude served to justify the return of the Jews, implying that they care enough about the country to turn the swamps and deserts into blossoming farmland; this effectively delegitimises the Arab claim to the same land.' 'The message was that the Palestinians were primitive and neglected the country and did not cultivate the land.'[4]

At around the same time, another Israeli researcher, Adir Cohen, conducted an opinion survey among a group of 4th to 6th grade Jewish students at a school in Haifa, a mixed Arab–Jewish city. He found that 75 per cent of the children described the 'Arab' as a murderer, one who kidnaps children, a criminal and a terrorist; 80 per cent saw the Arab as someone dirty; 90 per cent stated they believed that Palestinians had no rights whatsoever to the 'land in Israel'. Cohen also researched 1,700 Israeli children's textbooks published after 1967. He found that 520 of the books contained humiliating, negative descriptions of Palestinians; of these 66 per cent referred to Arabs as violent, 52 per cent as evil, 37 per cent as liars, 31 per cent as greedy, 28 per cent as two-faced. Cohen observed that the authors of these children's books effectively instil hatred towards Palestinians by stripping them of their human nature. In a sampling of 86 books, Cohen counted the following descriptions used to dehumanise Arabs: the term 'murderer' was used 21 times, 'snake' 6 times, 'dirty' 9 times, 'vicious animal' 17 times, 'bloodthirsty' 21 times, 'warmonger' 17 times, 'killer' 13 times, 'believer in myths' 9 times, and 'a camel's hump' 2 times. Both Bar-Tal's and Cohen's studies revealed a culture of dehumanisation deeply rooted in Hebrew literature and Israeli history books. Cohen believes that Israeli authors and writers deliberately portray Arab characters in this stereotyping way, particularly to their younger readership, in order to influence their outlook early on so as to prepare them to 'deal with Arabs'.[5]

---

4. Maureen Meehan, 'Israeli Textbooks and Children's Literature Promote Racism and Hatred Toward Palestinians and Arabs', *Washington Report on Middle East Affairs*, September 1999, pp. 19–20, www.washington-report.org/backissues/0999/9909019. html.
5. Quoted in ibid.

Jamal Atamneh, coordinator of the Arab Education Committee in Support of Local Councils, a Haifa-based NGO, notes that
major historical events hardly get a mention either. 'When I was in
high school 12 years ago, the date "1948" barely appeared in any
textbooks except for a mention that there was a conflict. Palestinians refused to accept a UN solution and ran away instead. Today
the idea communicated to schoolchildren is basically the same.'
Atamneh explains that textbooks used by the nearly 1.4 million
Arab Israelis (one-fifth of Israel's population) are in Arabic but
are written and issued by the Israeli Ministry of Education, where
Palestinians have no influence or input. Professor Eli Podeh, of the
Hebrew University in Jerusalem, indicates that certain changes in
Israeli textbooks are slowly being implemented, but the discussion
of Palestinian national and civil identity is never touched upon.[6]

Today Israeli schoolteachers, academics, educators, broadcast-
ers, historians, biblical archaeologists, politicians, novelists and
tourist guides constantly speak of 'Judea and Samaria' as 'rightful'
parts of the Jewish state – claims made on the basis of the stories
and legends of the Hebrew Bible and without reference to the rights
of the land's indigenous inhabitants. This promotion by the Israeli
educational system of the foundational myth of continuity between
'biblical Israel' and modern Israel was hinted at in an article by
Israel's leading novelist Amos Oz shortly after 1967:

> When I was a child, some of my teachers taught me that after our Temple
> was destroyed and we were banished from our country, strangers came
> into what was our heritage and defiled it. The desert-born Arabs laid
> the land waste and let the terraces on the hillsides go to ruin. Their
> flocks destroyed the beautiful forests. When our first pioneers came
> to the land to rebuild it and to redeem it from desolation, they found
> an abandoned wasteland. True, a few backward, uncouth nomads wan-
> dered in it. ... It seems that the enchantment of 'renewing the days of
> old' is what gave Zionism its deep-seated inclination to see a country
> without inhabitants before it ... How fitting would it have been for the
> Return to Zion to have taken the land from the Roman legions or the
> nations of Canaan and Philistia. And to come to a completely empty
> country would have been even better. From there, it is only a short step

---

6. Both quoted in ibid.

to the kind of self-induced blindness that consists in disregarding the existence of the country's Arab population, or in discounting it and its importance on the dubious grounds that it 'has created no valuable cultural assets here', as if that would permit us to take no notice of its very existence. (In time, Naomi Shemer would express this state of mind in her song 'Jerusalem of Gold': ... the marketplace is empty / And no-one goes down to the Dead Sea / By way of Jericho'. Meaning, of course, that the marketplace is empty of Jews and that no Jew goes down to the Dead Sea by way of Jericho. A remarkable revelation of a remarkably characteristic way of thinking.) (Oz 1988)

Furthermore, in contrast to the construction and promotion of a national (Zionist-Jewish) identity in the curriculum developed for the Jewish schools, that developed by the Ministry of Education for Arab schools blurs rather than enhances the cultural identity of the indigenous Palestinian community. Palestinian cultural identity is treated as something non-existent, irrelevant or, at worst, completely antagonistic to the goals and aims of Zionist education in Israel (Abu-Sa'ad 2008: 20-21).

Professor Abu-Sa'ad, of the Department of Education, University of Ben-Gurion, using Israeli geography textbooks for both Jewish and Arab pupils in 2005-06, has shown what is present in the textbooks, alongside what is absent from, or left out of, the telling of the story. He illustrates how the Palestinian presence in the land is completely erased, making Palestinian Arab pupils in Israel into 'present-absentees' in their own homeland as they learn about the history of 'the land of Israel'. Produced nearly two decades after the appearance of the Israeli 'new history', the textbooks show that the state-sponsored curriculum for Arab elementary schools maintains an emphasis on Jewish settlement and Zionist colonisation of Palestine, while at the same time erasing Palestinian history and preventing Arab students learning about and identifying with the Palestinian people and their history (Abu-Sa'ad 2008: 21-4).

Educated within the framework of the 'Israeli Arab' education system, and subjected to a school curriculum dictated by an Ashkenazi Zionist elite (with its focus on the newly invented Hebrewised and Judaised 'Land of Israel'), the younger generation of Palestinians growing up inside Israel are often unfamiliar with many of the Arabic names and sites of historic Palestine. It seems imperative that a liberal Palestinian civil society, along with the NGOs inside Israel, make a greater effort to challenge this Zionist cultural hegemony and reinvention of history by educating the Palestinian youth in Israel about the material and cultural heritage of the indigenous inhabitants of Palestine.

In 2007, under intensive lobbying from Arab educationalists and Palestinian civil society organisations inside Israel, the Education Ministry, then headed by Yuli Tamir of the Labour Party, introduced a passage into a textbook taught in Arab schools in Israel, which describes the 1948 war as follows: 'The Arabs call the war the Nakba – a war of catastrophe, loss and humiliation – and the Jews call it the Independence War.' But the term 'Nakba' was never introduced into the curriculum in Jewish schools in Israel. Two years later (in July 2009), however, the Ministry of Education decided to remove the term 'Nakba' from the textbook in question, and indeed to ban any use of it in Arab schools. Prime Minister Binyamin Netanyahu had earlier stated that use of the term was tantamount to spreading propaganda against Israel. Palestinian human rights organisations in Israel reacted to the ban by calling the Ministry of Education's decision an attempt to distort the truth and seek confrontation with the Palestinians inside Israel.[7]

Crucially, today in the 'Jewish democracy' of Israel crude racism and an obsession with demography serve to vilify 20 per cent of the population: the Palestinian citizens of Israel who are labelled in Jewish children's textbooks a 'demographic threat'. The nearly 1.4 million Palestinian citizens of Israel are now being threatened with ethnic cleansing: removal to the Bantustans of the West Bank.

Nakba Day and the Struggle for Collective Rights inside Israel

Your celebration is our mourning.

Knesset Member 'Azmi Bishara, 30 April 2006

---

7. 'Israel Bans Use of Palestinian Term "Nakba" in Textbooks', *Haaretz*, 22 July 2009.

Because of the Nakba, your Independence Day is still an open bleed-
ing wound.

Knesset Member Jamal Zahalka, 30 April 2006[8]

Living inside the Jewish state, Palestinian citizens of Israel are
confronted with the Zionist dominance of the historical narrative
in multiple ways, from the shaping of their school curriculum to
the superimposition of Hebrew ('biblical') toponymy and physical
inscription over their own land (Humphries 2009: 96). Isabelle
Humphries (2009) shows the complexities and dilemmas facing
those trying to build a 'counter-hegemony' in the current political environment inside the Jewish state. It is hardly surprising,
therefore, that in the past two decades Palestinians in Israel – after
a long period of 'silence' and 'present absenteeism', encouraged by
the Israeli state – have begun to challenge the hegemonic Zionist
narrative and the officially imposed attempts to silence the Nakba.
Early efforts to resist the Israeli state's ban on commemorating
the 1956 massacre of Kafr Qasim (Cohen 2010: 144) shed new
light on the beginning of grassroots resistance to the suppression
of Palestinian memory inside the Jewish state (Robinson 2003:
393–416).

The new efforts at commemorating the Nakba, which have
brought a growth in confidence and encouraged politicisation,
have met with varying degrees of success. In 1998 the Israeli state's
jubilee served as a catalyst and focal point for intense feelings of
mourning and protest among the Palestinians inside Israel. Today
the Nakba Day on 15 May and the Land Day on 30 March are key
dates on the calendar of anniversaries not just for the Palestinians inside Israel but for those throughout historic Palestine.[9]
Interestingly in the past two decades the Nakba Day has been more
widely commemorated by this community than in the previous
four decades. The anniversary of the massacre of Kafr Qasim, 29

8. Dr Beshara, then a Palestinian member of the Israeli Knesset, told the Israeli
daily *Ma'ariv*: 'Independence Day is your holiday, not ours. We mark this as the day
of our Nakba, the catastrophe that befell the Palestinian nation in 1948'. Arik Bender,
'Hahag Shelachem hu Avel Shelanu' [Your celebration is our mourning'], *Ma'ariv*, 30
April 2006, www.nrg.co.il/online/1/ART1/079/396.html.
9. See, for instance, Qumsiyeh (2011: 133) on the 'Land Day' strikes and protests of
30 March 1987.

October, is a third key day of protests and demonstrations. The same community also discovered that a collective memory of the Nakba could be mobilised as a powerful tool of peaceful resistance and in the struggle for 'collective rights' inside Israel. The Nakba Day connects the previously isolated Palestinian community inside the Green Line with other Palestinian communities inside and outside historic Palestine. Collective memory helps to consolidate national bonds, mutual solidarity and shared history, memories and struggles.

Discrimination against the Palestinian citizens of Israel has remained blatant and institutionalised. Shimon Peres (president of Israel at the time of writing) stated in 1986 (then prime minister) that the per capita budget allocated for the Palestinians inside Israel was 30 per cent of that allocated for Jews (Beit-Hallahmi 1992: 90; Masalha 1997: 158–60). The same community is excluded from 90 per cent of the land within the Green Line.

Since 1948 the Palestinians inside Israel have experienced an improvement in living standards and in level of education. Many Palestinian villages now enjoy the modern services of running water, electricity, a high standard of housing, health care and schooling. Palestinian citizens of Israel have thus been transformed from a 'marginal group' (historically disparaged and marginalised by both Israel and the Palestinians outside the country) into a consolidated and politically aware community that 'recognises its own value and challenges the majority [Jewish] community by presenting documents demanding collective equality and the rights of an indigenous national minority', in the words of Meron Benvenisti.[10] Benvenisti is fully aware of the fact that the Zionist mindset could never accept Palestinians inside Israel as equal citizens. He also knows that these benefits for second-class citizens can easily be revoked – indeed, threats to revoke them are constantly made by Jewish politicians and public figures (Sa'di 2000: 25–37). In the last decade, public discussion of the 'transfer' of Israeli Palestinians into the West Bank has become common among mainstream Jewish politicians and even government ministers (Cook 2006:

---

10. Meron Benvenisti, 'Time to Stop Mourning', *Haaretz*, 23 December 2007, www. haaretz.com/print-edition/opinion/time-to-stop-mourning-1.235745.

116-22). It is the failure of decades of Israeli efforts to eliminate Palestinian identity within the Green Line – as evidenced by the recent reassertion of Palestinian identity and growing solidarity with Palestinians in the occupied territories – that has provoked the anger of the political and security establishment and the threats of another Nakba.

These developments and the threats of another Nakba also partly explain the growing mobilisation around the 'Nakba Day' by Palestinians inside Israel over the last two decades. 'Anyone examining the history of the Palestinian minority in Israel since the establishment of the state cannot but be surprised by its achievements', writes Meron Benvenisti, a former deputy mayor of Jerusalem (1971-78) and a well-known critic of Israel's collective discrimination and deeply institutionalised racism. Benvenisti is fully aware of the enormous 'subversive challenge' posed to Zionist hegemony by the alternative 'Nakba Day' marches, as Palestinians inside Israel gather on the ruins of Safuriyya and many of the hundreds of villages destroyed by Israel in 1948.[11] However, for him Nakba Day commemoration, which also focuses on Palestinian collective rights in Israel, is simply the outcome of a growing confidence and politicised consciousness:

> The Palestinian Israelis lived for many years under a repressive regime and they were mainly concerned with the difficulties of earning a living and the danger of their land being robbed. They had little confidence in themselves and the authorities worked to deepen this feeling. Under these conditions, one does not focus on collective rights, but rather on the daily struggle for improvement on a limited scope. Slowly, the economic, social and legal situation began to improve, and attention could then turn to the source of the deprivation: the collective discrimination and the ethnic labelling.

Expressions of protest such as the Nakba Day and the Land Day did not develop and become more acute because the deprivation became more severe. The opposite is true: the system became more flexible, the Arab minority grew fivefold and, despite the

---

11. For further discussion of the annual 'return marches' organised by ADRID, see Ben White, 'Israel's Alternative Independence Day', *New Statesman*, 9 May 2008, www. newstatesman.com/middle-east/2008/05/israel-palestinian-march-arab.

deprivation and discrimination in education and social services, many of its members recorded impressive achievements.[12]

Grassroots Activism and Palestinian
Civil Society inside Israel

Palestinian grassroots and civil society organisations inside Israel have been thrust into the forefront of the Palestinian national struggle in the last two decades. This is partly the outcome of the establishment of the Palestinian Authority in the 1967 occupied territories and the complete marginalisation of the PLO, whose sharp decline was accelerated by the Oslo peace process. With the Palestinian Authority choosing to collaborate with (rather than resist) Israeli settler activities in the West Bank and East Jerusalem, the rights of the refugees, especially the 'right of return', have been effectively removed as a 'central motivating factor' for the Palestinian leadership; throughout the Oslo process the Palestinian internal refugees inside Israel have been completely ignored by the Palestinian negotiating team (Jamal 2005: 133). Benvenisti observes that,

> while the PLO is changing from being the leader of a national liberation movement into a collection of beggars at international conferences, while Hamas bunkers itself in anachronistic positions that can only lead to tragedy, and while the Palestinian diaspora remains without leadership – the Palestinian-Israeli community becomes the standard bearer of Palestinian democratic nationalism, cognizant of the limitations of its power and intimately familiar with its Jewish-Zionist rival.[13]

Yet, in an article entitled 'Time to Stop Mourning', Benvenisti contradicts himself and bizarrely recommends that Palestinians inside Israel should 'extricate themselves from the sackcloth of the Nakba', and start 'celebrating their impressive accomplishments on the 60th anniversary of the state'.

Confronting the top-down, state-sponsored, entrenched Zionist hegemonic discourse – a discourse which has hardly been dented by the Israeli 'new history' of the last two decades – and the

---

12. Benvenisti, 'Time to Stop Mourning'.
13. Ibid.

erasure of Palestine, the struggles of the internal refugees inside Israel have, remarkably, taken place among the more educated second and third generations of Palestinians inside Israel. This struggle has been closely related to the growth of education and political consciousness within the community. Younger activists have made the village of origin a key project of collective memory and national identity, cultural resistance and struggle for collective rights inside Israel, and have expressed a stronger belief in future return than the older generation of internal refugees. The same younger generations have also learned from their parents' attempts to return without success in the past, taking into account the political developments that have taken place among Palestinians in Israel.

Younger generations of internal refugees began to recover the suppressed past and construct memory accounts of their village of origin. Until the 1980s the stories and memories of the older generation had existed largely in oral form, and within the social context of the host village. Since the early 1990s, however, there has been an effort to articulate a new narrative of return and memorialisation. In this regard, the internal refugees have been more fortunate than the Palestinian refugees in the diaspora, owing to the possibility of physical access, providing individuals and local groups with the opportunity to experience their origins. Visits to the villages, and preserving the holy sites, holding summer camps and organising marches within their boundaries, have become key components of the internal refugees' strategy in their attempt to articulate a new narrative. These activities aim to encourage displaced people to 'rediscover' themselves, and to empower their memory, sense of belonging and identity.

Storytelling and memory accounts have always been central to the struggle of internally displaced Palestinians inside Israel. Since 1948 the 'villages of origin' have been the centre of memory accounts and the important provider of 'legitimacy' for the internally displaced persons and for their struggle for return. Moreover, in recent years the local campaigns of internal refugees have reflected a strong relationship between memory accounts, identity and the desire to return to the place of origin. These three interconnected dimensions are closely linked to their current grassroots struggle. 'Socialisation' of the place of origin, promoted by many activists of the displaced communities, has aimed at creating a territorially based identity centred on the village. This, in turn, has helped to empower and renew the struggle for return. Such initiatives have taken place both within and beyond village boundaries. They extend to lobbying Arab parties and politicians, petitioning the Israeli courts, and generally articulating the new 'narrative' of the village of origin (Boqa'i 2005: 101; Masalha 2005b: 46-7).

The grassroots struggles of internal refugees residing in host villages in Galilee have to take into account everyday issues and living conditions.[14] Meanwhile, their political activism is directed against the Israeli government and its quasi-governmental arm the JNF. While becoming an important symbol for the provision of 'legitimacy' for the internal refugees, the village of origin also provides a collective identity within the host village. It shapes the perception of both past and future, and informs the collective memory and refugee identity, stimulating the desire to return. Social protests centring on the village of origin embody elements of indigenous resistance to both the Israeli authorities and the status quo in the host village. In this way internal refugees articulate a new and more assertive programme which can only be fulfilled through return to the place of origin (Boqa'i 2005: 101; Masalha 2005b: 43-51).

Younger activists have also learned from their fathers' attempts to return without success in the past. As Dawud Bader, a member of the second generation of internal refugees and one of the leaders of the Association for the Defense of the Rights of the Internally Displaced in Israel (ADRID) has put it:

> the internally displaced persons in Israel faced difficult experiences and bad conditions in the past. During the early years of military rule, displaced people could only find a shelter to live quietly and to try to advance themselves. Later, and gradually, the younger educated generation became more involved in political and national issues. The displaced persons became more advanced in many fields. They

---

14. On the adjustment patterns among Palestinian internal refugees inside Israel, see Al-Haj 1986: 651-73.

became more involved in confronting the Israeli authorities and their discriminatory policies. Israel doesn't distinguish in its policy between displaced persons and non-displaced persons in the fields of land confiscation and ethnic-national discrimination.[15]

As the secretary general of ADRID Wakim Wakim explains:

Our task is not only to confront the grandsons of Zionism on the issue of displacement, or to rewrite the Palestinian Nakba narrative, systematically and comprehensively; it is more than this. We aim to organise the displaced communities through the popular committees and relevant associations, and under the [umbrella] of the Displaced Committee [ADRID], as an organised national forum, and by encouraging the local committees to organise visits [to the villages of origin], by publishing bulletins to strengthen the belonging of the de-populated village as a microcosm of Palestine, by organising summer camps for displaced children, and by protecting the holy sites in the depopulated villages. (Wakim 2001b)

During the commemoration of the Nakba in 2000, ADRID organised, in coordination with local refugee committees, some twenty marches and trips to villages of origin (Badil 2002b).[16] In 2003 most of the Nakba commemoration activities were held in villages of origin (Sa'id. 1992, 1999; Boqa'i 2005: 103).[17]

Protection and preservation of the original villages' Muslim and Christian holy sites are carried out at both local and national levels. In March 2002 displaced people from al-Ghabisiyya organised public prayer in front of the closed village mosque. The participants had asked the Israeli authorities to reopen the mosque, which has been closed since 1997.[18] Some voluntary and semi-religious activities in villages of origin have been carried out by

15. Interview with Dawud Bader, 28 October 2002, Shaykh Dannun village, quoted in Boqa'i 2005: 102.
16. Most of the internally displaced persons' national activities in the commemoration of the *Nakba* were held under the slogan 'Their Independence. Our *Nakba*'. See ADRID press releases, 8 May 2000, 14 April 2001, 17 April 2001.
17. While the village of origin was the 'centre' of the 2003 Nakba commemoration activities of the internally displaced people inside Israel, Palestinian refugees have tried to focus on another 'symbol' of the Nakba: namely the refugee camp. Approximately half of the 2003 Nakba commemoration activities in the West Bank and Gaza Strip took place inside refugee camps. See Boqai' and Rempel 2003.
18. A*l-Ittihad*, 3 March 2002.

the Islamic-led Al-Aqsa Association, which has been looking after and maintaining the old mosques and cemeteries that remain. In 1994, for example, the Association oversaw the voluntary work of restoring the cemetery in the depopulated village of Husha. Similar activities were carried out in the old village of Balad al-Shaykh (Cohen 2000). It has continued to lobby the Israeli authorities for the reopening for prayer of all old mosques in villages of origin. This campaign has had some success, including the decision by the Israeli Ministry for Religious Affairs in the mid-1990s to spend some NIS300,000 (around $70,000) on repairing mosques (Sa'id 1999; Boqa'i 2005: 103).

Since 1987 displaced persons from Kafr Bir'im have organised annual summer camps on the site of this depopulated Arab village (Magate 2000). Working in coordination with various Arab NGOs, several village committees have organised summer camps in villages of origin. During these summer camps, individuals from the first generation of displacement are often invited to give talks about life in the village before the 1948 Nakba. Organisers of the Kafr Bir'im summer camps summed up the purpose of the events: 'it's not to talk about the village, but rather to live it 24 hours a day' (Sa'id 1999; Boqa'i 2005: 103-4).

In 1998 ADRID, in coordination with local committees of internal refugees and Palestinian NGOs inside Israel, began organising the 'Return March' as a major annual event. The 'Return March' is held on the same day as Israeli 'Independence Day' – which is marked according to the Hebrew calendar – with the participation of thousands of displaced people and Palestinians inside Israel. One of the key slogans of the 'return march' is 'Their Independence Day is our Nakba/catastrophe'. The route of the Return March included one of the host villages, ending with one of the villages of origin. In 1998, on the commemoration of the fiftieth anniversary of the Nakba, the March started from the town of Nazareth and ended in the pre-Nakba village of Saffuriya.[19] In 2000 the March began in the host village of Kabul and ended in al-Damun village of origin. In 2001 it began in the host village of Yafa and ended

19. *Haaretz*, 15 May 1998.

in the Ma'lul village of origin. In 2001 there was also a march to al-Birwa village of origin (Wakim 2001b; Badil 2001), and in 2003 to Umm al-Zinat village of origin.[20] Other national dates around which marches were held included Land Day, and the 1948 date of village occupation; for example, a march was held on 28 March 1998 from Shaykh Dannun host village to al-Ghabisiyya village of origin. These marches expressed a strong protest against the Israeli attitude towards the internal refugees; the 'return' each year to the village of origin on exactly the same day as Israel's 'independence' is symbolically powerful (Boqa'i 2005: 104).

Inevitably Palestinians inside Israel and Israeli Jews disagree fundamentally on the refugees' 'right of return' – a right that is at the heart of decolonising strategies in Palestine–Israel. Many Israeli Zionists rightly argue that the implementation of the 'right of return' would both undermine the Zionist project and transform Israel into a 'bi-national state'. For supporters of the 'ethnocratic' colonial regime of Israel (Yiftachel 2006), the victims, the ethnically cleansed indigenous inhabitants of the land, are a threat to Israel's demographic racism and 'Jewish character'. Indeed Zionist Israelis do not want the repatriation of the Palestinian refugees, who would question the colonial nature of Israeli society. Thus the decolonisation strategies of Palestinian citizens of Israel openly emphasise the already existing bi-national reality within the Green Line. Palestinians inside Israel would positively welcome and encourage the transformation of Israel into 'a state of all its citizens' and 'absentees' – that is, into a bi-national state. Clearly the refugees' 'right of return' is central to decolonisation in Palestine–Israel. It touches on the very nature of Israel as an exclusivist apartheid state and on the question as to whether it should become a multicultural democratic state – a state of all its citizens.

---

20. ADRID press release, 26 April 2003.

EPILOGUE

The Continuity of Trauma

For the millions of Palestinian refugees the past is still present and the sense of displacement remains heightened. The processes of ethnic cleansing and transfer in Palestine continue. As Juan Cole observes, 'the phrase "ethnic cleansing" conjures up a swift, comprehensive act of expulsion. But in reality, moving a large population off its land is the death of a thousand cuts, a slow, inexorable process of stealing property, harassment, forcing people into a condition of malnutrition.' The indigenous people of Palestine, like the native Americans or the Aborigines in Australia, 'were only sometimes forced off their land suddenly and en masse'.[1] Dina Matar shows in *What it Means to be Palestinian: Stories of Palestinian Peoplehood* (2011: 129-32) that the continuity of the trauma is not just the result of 1948 but an ongoing process, continuing into the present and linked to current Israeli settler policies and practices. Adi Ophir, of Tel Aviv University, in an article entitled 'Genocide Hides behind Expulsion', wrote in January 2004:

> under the conditions of Israeli control in the [occupied] territories today, transfer is being carried out slowly by the Ministry of Interior, by the civilian authority, at airports and border crossings, by sophisticated

---

1. Juan Cole, 'Israeli Taliban Torch Palestinian Girls' School, Destroy Olive Trees', 20 October 2010, www.juancole.com/2010/10/israeli-taliban-torch-palestinian-girls-school-destroy-olive-trees.html.

means such as forms, certificates, and denial of certificates, and by less
sophisticated means such as the destruction of thousands of homes,
and checkpoints and closures, and sieges, that are making the lives of
Palestinians intolerable and leading many of them to try to emigrate
in order to survive. (Ophir 2010: 162)

Contemporary Palestinian anxiety seems to be focusing on the
need to prevent the final Zionist ethnic cleansing of Palestine. In
particular, in the post-Second (al-Aqsa) Intifada period, marked
by increased Israeli repression, both the fear of another Nakba and
the yearning to return appear to be intensifying (Milshtein 2009:
64; Jamal 2005: 133–60). The threat of 'transfer' and continuing trauma are also apparent in the ongoing dehumanisation of
Palestinians inside Israel, which, as Elia Zureik noted in October
2010, 'takes its place in standard Israeli rhetoric among members
of the ruling establishment':

> Disregard for Palestinian life has characterized the attitudes of Israeli
> authorities towards its Arab citizens since the establishment of the
> state. The Palestinians constitute what the Italian philosopher Giorgio
> Agamben calls *homo sacer*, according to which the laws of humanity
> do not apply to them. For Israel, the Palestinians exist in conditions
> of 'bare life'. Their minimal existence is tolerated but not enhanced.
> Invariably, the law is suspended when it comes to rectifying Palestinian
> grievances. Israel is usually quick to cite 'national security' as justifica-
> tion for its lethal actions. Life for Palestinian citizens of the state is
> in a perpetual state of emergency where exception to the universal
> application of the law is the rule. As a colonial state, life in Israel is
> best viewed from a racialized prism where ethnicity and race govern
> the treatment of its citizens. As in all colonial regimes, territory and
> population are the two central elements which occupy the colonizer,
> and Israel is no exception. Both of these components provide the cor-
> nerstone of modern Zionism. Debates about demography, population,
> and settlements are the logical expressions of Zionism, and they will
> continue to be its cornerstone until Israel achieves its objectives of
> getting rid of as many of its Palestinian citizens as possible and bringing
> more land under its control.[2]

2. Elia Zureik, 'Israeli State Violence and the Value of Palestinian Life', *Jadal*
8 (Haifa) October 2010, http://jadal.mada-research.org/UserFiles/file/Jadal_PDF/
jadal8-eng/Elia-Zureik-final2-eng.pdf.

The Israelis continue to insist that Palestinians should accept Zionist colonisation of historic Palestine, while liberal Zionists believe in the existence of two distinct entities, one being the Israeli state (effectively an institutionalised apartheid state) and the other the fragmented and colonised areas (administered by the Palestinian Authority) that lie on the other side of the 1967 Green Line. No colonised people can be expected to give up their indigenous identity, accept the abrogation of their national rights, hand over most of their country, and then accept that this is right and just. As Israeli human rights activist Jeff Halper observes, only to the degree that Israel itself decolonises will true integration, acceptance, nornmalisation and reconciliation in historic Palestine be possible (Halper 2008: 221-2).

With responsibility for the 1948 Nakba, along with the history, rights and needs of the Palestinian refugees, excluded from recent Middle East peacemaking efforts, and with the failure of both the Israeli state and the international community to acknowledge the events of 1948, 'ethnic cleansing' continues to underpin the Palestine-Israel conflict. To write more truthfully about the Nakba is not just to practise a professional historiography; it is also a moral imperative of acknowledgement and redemption. Refugees' struggle to publicise the truth is a vital means of protecting their rights and keeping alive the hope for peace and justice. Peace will remain elusive as long as Israel's approach to Palestinian refugees is to erase them from history; as long as Palestinian property in the West Bank continues to be expropriated and developed for Israel; and as long as Palestinian families are uprooted and their homes demolished because they are not Jews.

Piecemeal solutions will not suffice. There is a need to address the questions of land and property, which have symbolic, religious, national, cultural and economic significance for the Palestinian refugee community. As long as the truth of the Nakba is denied, there can be no peace, no reconciliation in the Middle East.

We should not be enslaved – obsessed – by the past, but neither should we deny the potency of historical memory and its centrality to the continuing trauma. Remembering the Nakba is also vital because its most salient by-product was the Palestine refugee

254 *The Palestine Nakba*

problem, the greatest and the most enduring in the world. The last two decades have been witness to major contributions by Palestinian authors, many of whose accounts have been based on oral history of the refugees themselves, on 'social history from below'. Palestinian authors have also been producing data and memory accounts of the Nakba,[3] compiling and recording oral history and encouraging annual commemorations designed to preserve the memory of the catastrophe, while emphasising the link between refugee rights, collective identity and the challenge of return.

Remembrance seems to be about the past. While the Holocaust is an event in the past, the Nakba did not end in 1948. For Palestinians, mourning sixty-three years of al-Nakba is not just about remembering the 'ethnic cleansing' of 1948; it is also about marking the ongoing dispossession and dislocation. Today the trauma of the Nakba continues: the ongoing forced displacement of Palestinians caused by Israeli colonisation of the West Bank, land confiscation, continued closures and invasions, de facto annexation facilitated by Israel's 730-kilometre 'apartheid wall' in the occupied West Bank, and the ongoing horrific siege of Gaza. Palestinians in Gaza, the West Bank and East Jerusalem are denied access to land, water and other basic resources. Today the Nakba continues through the 'politics of denial'. There are millions of Palestinian refugees around the world, all of whom are denied their internationally recognised 'right of return' to their homes and land. The memory, history, rights and needs of Palestinian refugees have been excluded not only from recent Middle East peacemaking efforts but also from Palestinian top-down and elite approaches to the refugee issue (Boqai' and Rempel 2003).

The ongoing ethnic cleansing of Palestinians from Jerusalem, the West Bank and the Naqab, and the failure of both the Israeli state and the international community to acknowledge 1948 as such, continue to underpin the Palestine–Israel conflict (Masalha

---

3. Masalha 1992, 2005; Sanbar 1984, 1994, 1996 , 2001a, 2001b; Khalidi 1992; Abu Sitta 1998, 2004, 2010; Al-Azhari 1996; Sa'di and Abu-Lughod 2007; Sa'id 1992, 1999; Ashkar 2000; Cabaha and Brazilai 1996; Wakim 2001a, 2001b; Badil 2001, 2002a, 2002b, 2003a, 2003b; al-Qalqili 2004.

2005a: 4). A decade after the collapse of the Oslo process and the outbreak of the Second Palestinian Intifada, the current struggle in Palestine is increasingly marked by non-violent resistance to Israeli apartheid and ethnic cleansing policies.[4] Real change in Palestine is taking place 'from below' (Said 2002).

Mazin Qumsiyeh's recent work, *Popular Resistance in Palestine: A History of Hope and Empowerment* (2010), conceptualises a new frame for popular resistance in Palestine, a non-violent struggle to be combined with an anti-apartheid international campaign. This multi-track approach to resistance is intended to build on and deepen the 'changes from below' occurring in Palestine–Israel, end the paralysis in the Palestinian national arena, and address the enormous power asymmetry between Israel and the Palestinians.

Many Palestinian activists believe that the struggle to publicise the truth would be better served by the institutionalisation of Nakba commemoration. In Israel, Holocaust commemoration is heavily institutionalised; Holocaust remembrance is a state-funded

---

4. Timothy Crawley, a student working for Adalah, the Legal Centre for Arab Minority Rights in Israel, wrote in August 2009:

> Walk down what was formerly Al-Borj Street in Haifa, Israel, and you might catch sight of an old Jerusalem-stone building with arched doorways and windows cemented-over and a large Re/Max [an international real estate franchise] banner draped across the front. The house belongs to the Kanafani family, most of whom are living in exile in Lebanon but some of whom are now living as far away from home as San Francisco....
>
> For-sale signs have now appeared on dozens of these buildings across the state, and many have already been sold to private owners, frustrating the refugees' legal right to recover their homes. A grave breach of international law, Israel's sale of Palestinian homes is severing the refugees' connection to the land – the linchpin for negotiations in their right of return to their homeland....
>
> Nor is the continuing Nakba limited to those living in the occupied Palestinian territories or refugees in exile abroad unable to return home. Internally displaced Bedouin citizens of Israel living in the Negev Desert are building shacks from scrap metal adjacent to their previous homes that were demolished by Israeli bulldozers. Demolition orders have been issued by the state for entire villages to make room for new Jewish towns. The evacuation of the villages and the demolition of Bedouin homes represent the next step in the historical process of forcible displacement of Palestinian Arabs in favor of Jewish residents.
>
> The Kanafani family loses a home in Haifa; lands in the West Bank including East Jerusalem are further colonized; and Bedouin citizens of Israel are displaced yet again. The Nakba did not just happen in 1948. It is continuing for thousands of Palestinians who are systematically denied their basic rights to property, housing, employment – and their right to live at peace in their own homes.

Timothy Crawley, 'The Continuing Nakba', *San Francisco Chronicle*, 4 August 2009, p. A-9, www.sfgate.com/cgi-bin/article.cgi?f=/c/a/2009/08/03/EDPN193B7P.DTL.

industry. In 1959 the Knesset made Holocaust Remembrance Day (Yom Ha-Shoah) a 'nationalist' public holiday. In 1961 another law was passed that closed all public entertainment on that day; at ten in the morning a siren is sounded, at which point everything stops and people stand in remembrance. In the absence of a Palestinian state, the efforts to institutionalise Nakba commemoration in Palestine will remain patchy. But arguably the last thing the Palestinians need is a state-controlled Nakba industry, on the Jewish Holocaust model.

Of all the sectors and constituencies of the Palestinian people, the refugees – and the camp dwellers in particular – have a 'primordial interest' in reviving the PLO and making its institutions more representative of their rights and claims (Sayigh 2011: 61). However, that would not be sufficient. Across the board there is a need for grassroots-driven projects such as educational workshops on the Nakba, a Nakba museum and perhaps the institutionalisation of a People's Nakba Memorial Day as a *worldwide* event. Nakba remembrance at the grassroots level within and outside historic Palestine will serve to bind this generation directly to the older one, and bind the exiled to Palestine. It will also protect Nakba memory against its denial in Israel and around the world, and will force the Palestinian leadership to relocate the 'right of return' at the centre of peacemaking in the Middle East.

There is a clear need to articulate new counter-hegemonic narratives and devise fresh liberationist and decolonisation strategies. These must build on the recognition that the root cause of the Palestine conflict is the Nakba and on belief in the unity and territorial integrity of historic Palestine. The righting of the wrongs inflicted in 1948 and redressing the evils inflicted on the Palestinians ever since would allow both citizens and returnees to enjoy a normal and peaceful life on an equal basis in Palestine. But there can be no peace in the region until there is accountability, acknowledgement and acceptance of Israel's role in the continuing conflict. Public participation in peacemaking, the inclusion of international human rights principles, and recognition of refugees' rights are essential components in any peace agreement.

Remembrance should be an act of hope, liberation and decolonisation. Edward Said once argued that to write more truthfully
about what happened in 1948 is not merely to practise professional
historiography; it is also a profoundly moral act of redemption
and a struggle for justice and for a better world (Masalha 2007:
286). Remembering, as a work of mourning and commemorating,
with its regime of truth, opens up new possibilities for attending
to the rights of the victims of the Nakba (Sa'di and Abu-Lughod
2007). To remember is to put the wreckage of a painful past back
together in ways that help end suffering and facilitate the process
of healing (Grey 2007). Collective amnesia and contemporary forms
of silenced voices are not confined to the Palestinian refugees; they
are found among groups of migrant workers and asylum-seekers
in many countries. These silences are partly due to racism and
the lack of status granted to certain groups, people who fall into
the category of 'the despised Other'; they are often maintained
because they serve racist and colonial interests, or vested interests
(Grey 2007).

As long as injustice remains unaddressed in Palestine, violence
will continue to occur. How to break open the silence of injustice
and of multi-layered oppression, a key question faced in Palestine, is
a crucial dimension in building truth and effecting reconciliation.
As Archbishop Desmond Tutu remarked, 'it wasn't possible to move
forward in South Africa without listening to the painful stories of
victims of apartheid in the Truth and Reconciliation Commission.'
In 2002 Tutu reflected that Israel was practising apartheid in its
policies towards the Palestinians. He was 'very deeply distressed'
by a visit to the Holy Land, adding that 'it reminded me so much of
what happened to us black people in South Africa'.[5] In Guatemala,
also, there is the Recovery of Historical Memory Project (REMHI):
the truth-telling of memories of the killings to enable healing.
Truth-telling projects must be part of the solution in historic
Palestine. Acknowledging and remembering the Nakba will help
us to begin to tackle the Palestine refugee problem.

5. Cited by the BBC, 24 May 2004, http://news.bbc.co.uk/2/hi/africa/3743389.
stm.

References

Abdel Jawad, Saleh (2007) 'Zionist Massacres: The Creation of the Palestinian Refugee Problem in the 1948 War', in Eyal Benvenisti, Chaim Gans and Sari Hanafi (eds), *Israel and the Palestinian Refugees* (Berlin, Heidelberg and New York: Springer): 59–127.

Abu El-Haj, Nadia (2001) *Facts on the Ground: Archaeological Practice and Territorial Self-fashioning in Israeli Society* (Chicago: University of Chicago Press).

Abu-Lughod, Ibrahim, Roger Heacock and Khaled Nashef (eds) (1991) *The Landscape of Palestine: Equivocal Poetry* (Birzeit: Birzeit University Publications).

Abu-Lughod, Janet (1971) 'The Demographic Transformation of Palestine', in Ibrahim Abu-Lughod (ed.), *The Transformation of Palestine* (Evanston IL: Northwestern University Press): 139–63.

Abu-Rabia', 'Aref (1999) 'Bedouins in the Negev: Displacement, Forced Resettlement and the Natural Zones' [Arabic], *Nashrat al-Hijra al-Qasriyya* [Forced Migration Publication] 5: 31–3.

Abu-Sa'ad, Isma'el (2005) 'Forced Sedentarisation, Land Rights and Indigenous Resistance: The Palestinian Bedouin in the Negev', in Nur Masalha (ed.), *Catastrophe Remembered: Palestine, Israel and the Internal Refugees* (London: Zed Books): 113–41.

—— (2008) 'Present Absentees: The Arab School Curriculum in Israel as a Tool for De-educating Indigenous Palestinians', *Holy Land Studies: A Multidisciplinary Journal* 7, no. 1 (May): 17–43.

Abu Sitta, Salman (1998) *The Palestinian Nakba 1948: The Register of Depopulated Localities in Palestine* (London: Palestinian Return Centre).

—— (2004) *Atlas of Palestine 1948* (London: Saqi Books).

—— (2010) *The Atlas of Palestine 1917–1966* (London: Palestine Land Society).

Achcar, Gilbert (2010) *The Arabs and the Holocaust: The Arab–Israeli War of Narratives* (London: Saqi Books).

Adelman, Jonathan (2008) *The Rise of Israel: A History of a Revolutionary State* (London: Routledge).

Al-'Arif, Arif (1958–60) *Al-Nakba: Nakbat Bayt al-Maqdis Wal-Firdaws al-Mafqud, 1947–1952* [The Catastrophe: The Catastrophe of Jerusalem and the Lost Paradise, 1947–52], 6 vols (Beirut and Sidon, Lebanon: Al-Maktaba al-'Asriyya).

Al-Azhari, A. (1996) 'Memories of Saffuriyeh refugees with Israeli IDs', *Palestine–Israel: Journal of Politics, Economics and Culture* 3, no. 1 (Winter).

'Al Darchei Mediniyutenu: Mo'atzah 'Olamit Shel Ihud Po'alei Tzion (c.s.)-Din Vehesbon Male (1938) (21 July–7 August) [A Full Report on the World Convention of Ihud Po'alei Tzion, C.S.] (Tel Aviv: Central Office of Hitahdut Po'alei Tzion Press).

Al-Haj, Majid (1986) 'Adjustment Patterns of the Arab Internal Refugees in Israel', *International Migration* 24, no. 3: 651–73.

—— (1987) *Social Change and Family Processes: Arab Communities in Shefar-A'm* (Boulder CO: Westview Press).

Allen, Barbara, and William Lynwood Montell (1981) *From Memory to History: Using Oral Sources in Local Historical Research* (Nashville TN: American Association for State and Local History).

Al-Qalqili, 'Abd al-Fattah (2004) *Al-Ard fi Thakirat al-Filastiniyyun: I'timadan 'ala al-Tarikh al-Shafawi fi Mukhayyam Jenin* [The Land in Palestinian Memory: Based on Oral Histories in the Jenin Refugee Camp] (Ramallah, Palestine: Shaml-Palestinian Diaspora and Refugee Centre).

Al-Qattan, Omar (2007) 'The Secret Visitations of Memory', in Ahmad H. Sa'di and Lila Abu-Lughod (eds), *Nakba: Palestine, 1948, and the Claims of Memory* (New York: Columbia University Press): 191–206.

Anderson, Benedict (1991) *Imagined Communities: Reflections on the Origin and Spread of Nationalism* (London and New York: Verso).

Anderson, Kay (2000) 'Thinking "Postnationally": Dialogue across Multicultural, Indigenous, and Settler Spaces', *Annals of the Association of American Geographers* 90, no. 2: 381–91.

'Aqel, Mahmud (1992) *'Ayn Bayt 'Alma': Palestinian Refugee Camp, A Study in the Sociology of the Camps* [Arabic] (Jerusalem: Palestinian Academic Society for International Affairs).

Ashkar, Ahmad (2000) 'The Uprooted Palestinian Refugees Inside Israel', *Shaml Newsletter*, November (Ramallah, Palestine: Shaml-Palestinian Diaspora and Refugee Centre).

Ashrawi, Hanan Mikhail (1995) *This Side of Peace: A Personal Account* (New York: Simon & Schuster).

Ateek, Naim Stifan (1989) *Justice, and Only Justice: A Palestinian Theology of Liberation* (New York: Orbis).

Badil (2001) *First Annual Strategy Workshop* [Arabic], Ayia Napia, Cyprus (Bethlehem, Palestine: Badil Resource Centre for Palestinian Residency and Refugee Rights).

—— (2002a) *Internally Displaced Palestinians, International Protection and Durable Solution*, Badil Information and Discussion Briefs, no. 9 (Bethlehem, Palestine: Badil Resource Centre for Palestinian Residency and Refugee Rights).

—— (2002b) *Second Annual Workshop* [Arabic], Coalition for the Palestinian Right of Return, Brussels, (Bethlehem, Palestine: Badil Resource Centre for Palestinian Residency and Refugee Rights).

—— (2003a) *2002 Survey of Palestinian Refugees and Internally Displaced Persons* (Bethlehem, Palestine: Badil Resource Centre for Palestinian Residency and Refugee Rights).

—— (2003b) *Third Annual Strategy Workshop* [Arabic], Coalition for the Palestinian Right of Return, Copenhagen (Bethlehem, Palestine: Badil Resource Centre for Palestinian Residency and Refugee Rights).

Bar-Joseph, Uri (1987) *The Best of Enemies: Israel and Trans-Jordan in the War of 1948* (London: Frank Cass).

Bar-Tal, D., and Y. Teichman, (2005) *Stereotypes and Prejudice in Conflict: Representations of Arabs in Israeli Jewish Society* (Cambridge: Cambridge University Press).

Baram Uzi (2007) 'Appropriating the Past: Heritage, Tourism, and Archaeology in Israel', in P.L. Kohl, M. Kozelsky and N. Ben-Yehuda (eds), *Selective Remembrances: Archaeology in the Construction, Commemoration, and Consecration of National Pasts* (Chicago: University of Chicago Press): 299-325.

Beasley, Edward (2010) *The Victorian Reinvention of Race: New Racisms and the Problem of Grouping in the Human* Sciences (London and New York: Routledge).

Beinin, Joel (1988) 'Israel at Forty: The Political Economy/Political Culture of Constant Conflict', *Arab Studies Quarterly* 10, no. 3: 433-56.

—— (1992) 'New History, New Politics: A Revisionist Historical View', in Elizabeth W. Fernea and Mary E. Hocking (eds). *The Struggle for Peace: Israelis and Palestinians* (Austin: University of Texas Press): 80-86.

—— (1994) 'The Holocaust and the Politics of Memory', review essay, *Radical History Review* 60 (Fall): 217-23.

—— (2003) 'The Israelization of American Middle East Policy Discourse', *Social Text* 75, vol. 21, no. 2 (Summer): 125-39.

—— (2004) 'No More Tears: Benny Morris and the Road Back from Liberal Zionism', *Middle East Report* 230 (Spring), www.merip. org/mer/mer230/230_beinin.html.

—— (2005) 'Forgetfulness for Memory: The Limits of the New Israeli History', *Journal of Palestine Studies* 35, no. 2 (Winter): 6-23.

Beit-Hallahmi, Benjamin (1992) *Original Sins: Reflections on the History of Zionism and Israel* (London: Pluto Press).

Bell-Fialkoff, Andrew (1993) 'A Brief History of Ethnic Cleansing', *Foreign Affairs* 72, no. 3 (Summer): 110-21.

—— (1999) *Ethnic Cleansing* (London: Palgrave Macmillan).

Ben-Amotz, Dan (1974) *Kriah Tamah* [Reflections in Time] (Tel Aviv: Bitan).

—— (1982) *Seporei Abu-Nimr* [The Stories of Abu-Nimr] (Tel Aviv: Zmora-Bitan).

Ben-Gurion, David (1954) *The Rebirth and Destiny of Israel* (New York: Philosophical Library).

—— (1970) *Recollections*, ed. Thomas R. Bransten (London: MacDonald).

—— (1971-72) *Zichronot* [Memoirs], vols 3 and 4 (Tel Aviv: 'Am 'Oved).

—— (1972) *Ben-Gurion Looks at the Bible* (New York: Jonathan David).

—— (1982) *Yoman Hamilhamah* [War Diary], vols 1-3 (Tel Aviv: Misrad Habitahon).

Benvenisti, Meron (1986) *Conflicts and Contradictions* (New York: Villard).

—— (1987) *1987 Report: Demographic, Economic, Legal, Social and Political Development in the West Bank* (Jerusalem: West Bank Data Base Project).

—— (2002) *Sacred Landscape: The Buried History of the Holy Land Since 1948* (Berkeley: University of California Press).

References 261

Ben-Yehuda, Nachman (2002) *Sacrificing Truth: Archaeology and the Myth of Masada* (Amherst NY: Prometheus Books).

Benziman, 'Uzi (1973) *Yerushalayim: 'Ir Lelo Homah* [Jerusalem: A City without a Wall] (Tel Aviv: Schocken).

Benziman, 'Uzi, and 'Atallah Mansour (1992) *Subtenants: Israeli Arabs, Their Status and State Policy Towards Them* (Jerusalem: Keter).

Bersiach, Ernest (1994) *Historiography, Ancient, Medieval and Modern* (Chicago: University of Chicago Press).

Black, Ian (2010) 'Memories and Maps Keep Alive Palestinian Hopes of Return', *Guardian*, 26 November, www.guardian.co.uk/world/2010/nov/26/palestinian-refugees-middle-east-conflict.

Boqa'i, Nihad (2005) 'Patterns of Internal Displacement, Social Adjustment and the Challenge of Return', in Nur Masalha (ed.), *Catastrophe Remembered: Palestine–Israel and the Internal Refugee. Essays in Memory of Edward W. Said* (London: Zed Books): 73–112.

Boqai', Nihad, and Terry Rempel (2003) '"Our Right of Return is the Real Road Map to Peace", Elite vs. Popular Approaches to Resolving the Palestinian Refugee Issue', *Between the Lines* III, nos 23–24 (September), and no. 25 (December).

Bourdieu, Pierre (1977) *Outline of a Theory of Practice* (Cambridge: Cambridge University Press).

Bowersock, Glen W. (1984) 'Palestine: Ancient History and Modern Politics', *Grand Street*, Autumn: 130–41.

——(1988) 'Palestine: Ancient History and Modern Politics', in Edward W. Said and Christopher Hitchens (eds), *Blaming the Victims: Spurious Scholarship and the Palestinian Question* (London and New York: Verso): 181–91.

Bresheeth, Haim (1989) 'Self and Other in Zionism: Palestine and Israel in Recent Hebrew Literature', in *Palestine: Profile of an Occupation* (London: Zed Books): 120–52.

——(2007) 'The Continuity of Trauma and Struggle: Recent Cinematic Representations of the Nakba', in Ahmad H. Sa'di and Lila Abu-Lughod (eds), *Nakba: Palestine, 1948, and the Claims of Memory* (New York: Columbia University Press): 160–87.

Broshi, Magen (1987) 'Religion, Ideology and Politics and their Impact on Palestinian Archaeology', *Israel Museum Journal* 6: 17–32.

Busailah, Rega-e (1981) 'The Fall of Lydda, 1948: Impressions and Reminiscences', *Arab Studies Quarterly* 3, no. 2 (Spring): 123–51.

Cabaha, Mustafa, and Ronit Brazilai (1996) *Refugees in their Homeland: The Internal Refugees in State of Israel 1948–1996* [Hebrew], Skirot 'Al Ha'aravim BeYesrael, no. 2 (Giv'at Haviva: Institute for Peace Studies).

Caplan, Neil (2010) *The Israel–Palestine Conflict: Contested Histories* (Chichester: Wiley-Blackwell).

Césaire, Aimé (2001 [1955]) *Discourse on Colonialism* (London: Monthly Review Press).

Cheryl Rubenberg (1983) *The Palestine Liberation Organization: Its Institutional Infrastructure* (Belmont MA: Institute of Arab Studies).

Chomsky, Noam (1983) *The Fateful Triangle: The United States, Israel and the Palestinians* (London and Sydney: Pluto Press).

——(1999) *Fateful Triangle: The United States, Israel and the Palestinians*, updated edition (Cambridge MA: South End Press).

Cohen, Hillel (2000) *The Present Absentees: The Palestinian Refugees in Israel since 1948* [Hebrew] (Jerusalem: Centre for the Study of Arab Society in Israel, Van Leer Institute).

—— (2010) *Good Arabs: The Israeli Security Agencies and the Israeli Arabs, 1948–1967* (Berkeley CA and London: University of California Press).

Cohen, Saul B., and Nurit Kliot (1981) 'Israel's Place Names as Reflection of Continuity and Change in Nation Building', *Names* 29: 227–46.

Cohen, Shaul Ephraim (1993) *The Politics of Planting: Israeli–Palestinian Competition for Control of Land in the Jerusalem Periphery* (Chicago: University of Chicago).

Cook, Jonathan (2006) *Blood and Religion: The Unmasking of the Jewish and Democratic State* (London and Ann Arbor MI: Pluto Press).

—— (2008) *Disappearing Palestine: Israel's Experiments in Human Despair* (London and New York: Zed Books).

Curthoys, Ann, and John Docker (2005) *Is History Fiction?* (Sydney: UNSW Press).

—— (2008) 'Defining Genocide', in Dan Stone (ed.), *The Historiography of Genocide* (Basingstoke: Palgrave Macmillan): 9–41.

Curthoys, Ned (2007) 'The Refractory Legacy of Algerian Decolonisation: Revisiting Arendt on Violence', in Richard H. King and Dan Stone (eds), *Hannah Arendt and the Uses of History: Imperialism, Nation, Race, and Genocide* (New York: Berghahn): 109–29.

Dabashi, Hamid (2001) *Brown Skin, White Masks* (London and New York: Pluto Press).

Dabbagh, Mustafa Murad (1972–86) *Biladuna Filastin* [Our Country, Palestine] (Beirut and al-Khalil: Research Centre and Matbu'at Rabitat al-Jami'yyin fi-Muhafazat al-Khalil).

Dajani, Omar (2005) 'Surviving Opportunities: Palestinian Negotiating Pattern in Peace Talks with Israel', in Tamara Cofman Wittes (ed.), *How Israelis and Palestinians Negotiate: A Cross-cultural Analysis of the Oslo Peace Process* (Washington DC: United States Institute for Peace): 39–80.

D'ana, Seif (2006) 'Correcting Corrections: De-reifying the New Israeli Historiography', *Arab Studies Quarterly* 28, no. 2 (March): 1–26.

Darwish, Mahmoud (1987) *Memory for Forgetfulness* (Berkeley and Los Angeles: University of California Press).

Davies, Philip R. (1992) *In Search of Ancient Israel* (Sheffield: Sheffield Academic Press).

Davis, Rochelle (2007) 'Mapping the Past, Re-creating the Homeland: Memories of Village Places in pre-1948 Palestine', in Ahmad H. Sa'di and Lila Abu-Lughod (eds), *Nakba: Palestine, 1948, and the Claims of Memory* (New York: Columbia University Press): 53–76.

Davis, Uri (1987) *Israel: An Apartheid State* (London: Zed Books).

—— (2003) *Apartheid Israel: The Possibilities for Struggle Within* (London and New York: Zed Books).

Dayan, Moshe (1978) *Living with the Bible* (London: Weidenfeld & Nicolson).

Docker, John (2010) 'The Two-State Solution and Partition: World History Perspectives on Palestine and India', *Holy Land Studies: A Multidisciplinary Journal* 9, no. 2 (November): 147–68.

Doumani, Beshara (1995) *Rediscovering Palestine: Merchants and Peasants in Jabal Nablus, 1700–1900* (Berkeley: University of California Press).

El Kodsy, Ahmad, and Eli Lobel (1970) *The Arab World and Israel* (New York: Monthly Review Press).

References   263

El-Asmar, Fouzi (1986) 'The Portrayal of Arabs in Hebrew Children's Literature', *Journal of Palestine Studies* 16, no. 1 (Autumn): 81–94.

Ellis, Marc E. (1999) *Oh Jerusalem! The Contested Future of the Jewish Covenant* (Minneapolis: Fortress Press).

Elon, Amos (1983) *The Israelis: Founders and Sons* (London: Penguin).

—— (1996) *Jerusalem: City of Mirrors* (London: Flamingo).

—— (1997) 'Politics and Archaeology', in Neil Asher Silberman and David B. Small (eds), *The Archaeology of Israel: Constructing the Past, Interpreting the Present* (Sheffield: Sheffield Academic Press): 35–47.

Esber, Rosemarie (2003) 'War and Displacement in Mandate Palestine, 29 November 1947 to 15 May 1948', Ph.D. thesis, SOAS, University of London.

Evron, Boaz (1995) *Jewish State or Israeli Nation?* (Bloomington: Indiana University Press).

Falah, Ghazi (1996) 'The 1948 Israeli Palestinian War and its Aftermath: The Transformation and De-Signification of Palestine's Cultural Landscape', *Annals of the Association of American Geographers* 86: 256–85.

Fanon, Frantz (1952, 1967) *Black Skin, White Masks* (New York: Grove Press).

—— (1961) *Les Damnés de la Terre* (Paris: François Maspéro).

—— (1963) *The Wretched of the Earth* (New York: Grove Press).

Fearn, Robert W. (2006) *Amoral America: How the Rest of the World Learned to Hate America* (British Columbia), www.amoralamerica.info/AAmerica-Book9Jan07.pdf.

Fierke, K.M. (2008) 'Memory and Violence in Israel/Palestine', *Human Rights & Human Welfare* 8: 33–42.

Finkelstein, Israel, and Neil Asher Silberman (2001) *The Bible Unearthed: Archaeology's New Vision of Ancient Israel and the Origin of its Sacred Texts* (New York: Free Press).

Finkelstein, Norman (1991) 'Myths, Old and New', *Journal of Palestine Studies* 21, no. 1 (Autumn): 66–89.

—— (1995) *Image and Reality of the Israel Palestine Conflict* (London and New York: Verso).

Fischbach, Michael R. (2003) *Records of Dispossession: Palestinian Refugee Property and the Arab–Israeli Conflict* (New York: Columbia University Press).

Flapan, Simha (1979) *Zionism and the Palestinians* (London: Croom Helm).

—— (1987) *The Birth of Israel: Myths and Realities* (New York: Pantheon).

Forte, Tania (2003) 'Sifting People, Sorting Papers: Academic Practice and the Notion of State Security in Israel', *Comparative Studies of South Asia, Africa and the Middle East* 23, nos 1–2: 215–23.

Foucault, Michel (1972) *The Archaeology of Knowledge* (New York: Harper & Row).

—— (1980) *Power/Knowledge* (New York: Pantheon).

Fukuyama, Francis (1989) 'The End of History?' *The National Interest* 16.

—— (1992) *The End of History and the Last Man* (New York: Free Press).

Galbo, Joseph (2007) 'Albert Memmi's *Decolonisation and the Decolonized*: Review Essay', *Canadian Journal of Sociology Online*, March–April: 1–7, www.cjsonline.ca/reviews/decolonized.html.

Gelber, Yoav (2001) *Palestine 1948: War, Escape and the Emergence of the Palestinian Refugee Problem* (Brighton: Sussex Academic Press).

Gertz, Nurith (2000) *Myths in Israeli Culture: Captives of a Dream* (London:

Vallentine Mitchell).

Ghanem, As'ad, Nadim Rouhana and Oren Yiftachel (1998) 'Questioning "Ethnic Democracy": A Response to Sammy Smooha', *Israel Studies* 3, no. 2: 253–67.

Glock, Albert E. (1999) 'Cultural Bias in Archaeology', in Tomis Kapitan (ed.), *Archaeology, History and Culture in Palestine and the Near East: Essays in Memory of Albert E. Glock* (Atlanta GA: Scholars Press and American Schools of Oriental Research): 324–42.

Gluck, Sherna Berger (1994) *An American Feminist in Palestine: The Intifada Years* (Philadelphia PA: Temple University Press).

—— (2008) 'Oral History and *al-Nakbah*', *Oral History Review* 35, no. 1 (Winter/Spring): 68–80.

Gordon, Benjamin Lee (1919) *New Judea: Jewish Life in Modern Palestine and Egypt* (Philadelphia: J.H. Greenstone).

Gorny, Yosef (1987) *Zionism and the Arabs, 1882–1948* (Oxford: Clarendon Press).

Gover, Yerach (1986) 'Were You There, or Was It a Dream? Militaristic Aspects of Israeli Society in Modern Hebrew Literature', *Social Text* 13/14 (Winter–Spring): 24–48.

Grey, Mary (2007) *To Rwanda and Back: Liberation, Spirituality and Reconciliation* (London: Darton, Longman & Todd).

Grossman, David (1993) *Sleeping on a Wire: Conversations with Palestinians in Israel* (London: Jonathan Cape).

Guha, Ranajit (ed.) (1997) *A Subaltern Studies Reader, 1986–1995* (Minneapolis: University of Minnesota Press).

Guha, Ranajit, and Gayatri Chakravorty Spivak (eds) (1988) *Selected Subaltern Studies* (New York: Oxford University Press).

Gurvitz, Yehuda, and Shmuel Navon (eds) (1953) *What Story Will I Tell My Children?* (Tel Aviv: Amihah).

Hadawi, Sami (1967) *Bitter Harvest: Palestine between 1914–1967* (New York: New World Press).

Halbwachs, Maurice (1980) *Collective Memory* (New Your: Harper & Row).

Hall, Martin (1984) 'The Burden of Tribalism: The Social Context of South African Age Studies', *American Antiquity* 49, no. 3: 455–67.

—— (1988) 'Archaeology under Apartheid', *Archaeology* 41, no. 6: 62–4.

Halper, Jeff (2008) *An Israel in Palestine: Resisting Dispossession* (London and New York: Pluto Press).

Harvey, David (2007) *A Brief History of Neoliberalism* (Oxford: Oxford University Press).

Hammami, Rema (2003) 'Gender, *Nakbe* and Nation: Palestinian Women's Presence and Absence in the Narration of 1948 Memories', in Ron Robin and Bo Strath (eds), *Homelands: Poetic Power and the Politics of Space* (Brussels: P.I.E. Peter Land): 35–69.

Herzl, Theodor (1896) *Der Judenstaat: Versuch einer modernen Lösung der Judenfrage* (Leipzig and Vienna: M. Breitenstein's Verlags-Buchhandlung).

—— (1970) *The Jewish State*, trans. Harry Zohn (New York: Herzl Press).

—— (1972) *The Jewish State: An Attempt at a Modern Solution to the Jewish Problem* (London: H. Porders).

—— (2000 [1997]) *Old New Land* (Princeton NJ: Mirkus Wiener).

Hilal, Jamil (2002) *Takween al-Nukhba al-Filastiniyya Mundhu Nushu al-Haraka al-Wataniyya al-Filastiniyya ila ma ba'da Qiyam al-Sulta al-Wataniyya al-Filastiniyya* [The Making of the Palestinian Elite from the Eemergnce of the Palestinian National Movement until after the Establishment of the Palestinian National Authority] (Ramallah: Muwatin).

Hilliard, Constance B. (2009) *Does Israel Have a Future? The Case for a Post-Zionist State* (Dulles: Potomac Books).

Hobsbawm, Eric (1990) *Nations and Nationalism since 1780* (Cambridge: Cambridge University Press).

Hobsbawm, Eric, and Terence Ranger (1996) *The Invention of Tradition* (Cambridge: Cambridge University Press).

hooks, bell (1990) 'Marginality as a site of resistance', in Russell Ferguson et al. (eds), *Out There: Marginalisation and Contemporary Cultures* (Cambridge MA: MIT Press): 241-3.

Humphries, Isabelle (2004) 'Palestinian Internal Refugees in the Galilee: From the Struggle to Survive to the New Narrative of Return (1948-2005)', *Holy Land Studies: A Multidisciplinary Journal* 3, no. 2 (November): 213-31.

—— (2009), 'Displaced Voices: The Politics of Memory amongst Palestinian Internal Refugees in the Galilee (1991-2009)', doctoral dissertation, St Mary's University College and University of Surrey.

Humphries, Isabelle, and Laleh Khalili (2007) 'Gender of Nakba Memory', in Ahmad H. Sa'di and Lila Abu-Lughod (eds), *Nakba: Palestine, 1948, and the Claims of Memory* (New York: Columbia University Press): 207-27.

Huntington, P. Samuel (1993) 'The Clash of Civilizations?' *Foreign Affairs* 72, no. 3 (Summer): 22-49.

—— (1996) *The Clash of Civilizations and the Remaking of World Order* (London and New York: Simon & Schuster).

Isdud: District of Gaza (2006), www.palestineremembered.com/Gaza/Isdud/index.html; accessed 4 February 2006.

'Issa, Mahmoud (2005) 'The Nakba, Oral History and the Palestinian Peasantry: The Case of Lubya', in Nur Masalha (ed.), *Catastrophe Remembered* (London: Zed Books): 179-86.

'Jaffa', Wikipedia (2006), http://en.wikipedia.org/wiki/Jaffa; accessed 7 February 2006.

Jamal, Amal (2005) 'The Palestinian IDPs in Israel and the Predicament of Return: Between Imagining the Impossible and Enabling the Imaginative', in Ann M. Lesch and Ian S. Lustick (eds), *Exile and Return: Predicaments of Palestinians and Jews* (Philadelphia: University of Pennsylvania Press): 133-60.

Jamjoum, Hazem (2010) 'Challenging the Jewish National Fund', *The Electronic Intifada*, 21 July, http://electronicintifada.net/v2/article11406.shtml.

Jennings, Francis (1976) *The Invasion of America* (New York: W.W. Norton).

Jiryis, Sabri (1976) *The Arabs in Israel* (New York and London: Monthly Review Press).

Kabha, Mustafa (2007) 'A Palestinian Look at the New Historians and Post-Zionism in Israel', in Benny Morris (ed.), *Making of Israel* (Ann Arbor: University of Michigan Press): 299-319.

Kadman, Noga (2008) *Mehikat Melim: Shemot Derech Haim* [Erased from Space and Consciousness] (Jerusalem: November Books).

Kamen, Charles (1987) 'After the Catastrophe I: The Arabs in Israel 1948-1951', *Middle Eastern Studies* 23, no. 4: 453-95.

—— (1988) 'After the Catastrophe II: The Arabs in Israel 1948-1951', *Middle Eastern Studies* 24, no. 1 (January): 68-109.

Kanaana, Sharif (1992) *Still on Vacation: The Eviction of the Palestinians in 1948* (Jerusalem: Jerusalem International Centre for Palestinian Studies).

Kapeliouk, Amnon (1987) 'New Light on the Israeli-Arab Conflict and the Refugee Problem and Its Origins', *Journal of Palestine Studies* 16, no. 3. (Spring): 16-24.

Kapitan, Tomis (ed.) (1999) *Archaeology, History and Culture in Palestine and the Near East: Essays in Memory of Albert E. Glock* (Atlanta GA: Scholars Press and American Schools of Oriental Research).

Kassem, Fatma (2011) *Palestinian Women: Narrative Histories and Gendered Memory* (London and New York: Zed Books)

Kaye, Harvey J. (1995) 'Why Do Ruling Classes Fear History? *Index on Censorship* 24, no. 3: 85-98.

Kedourie, Elie (1960) *Nationalism* (London: Hutchinson).

Khalidi, Rashid (1992) 'The Future of Arab Jerusalem', *British Journal of Middle Eastern Studies* 19, no. 2: 139-40.

—(1997) *Palestinian Identity: The Construction of Modern National Consciousness* (New York: Columbia University Press).

— (2001) 'The Palestinians and 1948: The Underlying Causes of Failure', in Eugene Rogan and Avi Shlaim (eds), *The War for Palestine: Rewriting the History of 1948* (Cambridge: Cambridge University Press): 12-36.

—(2006) *The Iron Cage: The Story of the Palestinian Struggle for Nationhood* (Boston MA: Beacon Press).

Khalidi, Walid (1959a) 'Why Did the Palestinians Leave?' *Middle East Forum* 24 (July): 21-4. Reprinted as 'Why Did the Palestinians Leave Revisited', *Journal of Palestine Studies* 34, no. 2 (2005): 42-54.

— (1959b) 'The Fall of Haifa', *Middle East Forum* 35: 22-32.

— (1961) 'Plan Dalet: The Zionist Master Plan for the Conquest of Palestine', *Middle East Forum* 37, no. 9 (November): 22-8.

— (1984) *Before Their Diaspora: A Photographic History of the Palestinians, 1876-1948* (Beirut: Institute for Palestine Studies).

— (1988) 'Plan Dalet Revisited: Master Plan for the Conquest of Palestine', *Journal of Palestinian Studies* 18, no. 1 (Autumn): 3-37.

— (1991) 'The Palestine Problem: An Overview', *Journal of Palestine Studies* 21, no. 1 (Autumn): 5-16.

—(1992a) *All That Remains: The Palestinian Villages Occupied and Depopulated by Israel in 1948* (Washington DC: Institute for Palestine Studies).

—(1992b) *Palestine Reborn* (London: I.B. Tauris).

—(1997) 'Revisiting the UNGA Partition Resolution', *Journal of Palestine Studies* 27, no. 1. (Autumn): 5-21.

—(1999) *Dayr Yasin: Friday, 9 April 1948* (Beirut: Institute for Palestine Studies [Arabic]).

—(ed.) (2005) *From Heaven to Conquest: Reading in Zionism and the Palestine Problem Until 1948* (Washington DC: Institute for Palestine Studies).

Khalili, Laleh (2005) 'Places of Memory and Mourning: Palestinian Commemoration in the Refugee Camps of Lebanon', *Comparative Studies of South Asia, Africa and the Middle East* 25, no. 1: 30-45.

— (2007) *Heroes and Martyrs of Palestine: The Politics of National Commemoration* (Cambridge: Cambridge University Press).

Khoury, Elias (1998) *Bab al-Shams* (Beirut: Dar al-Adab).

—(2006) *Gate of the Sun* (Brooklyn NY: Archipelago Books).

— (2008) 'For Israelis, an Anniversary. For Palestinians, a Nakba', *New York*

Times, 18 May, www.nytimes.com/2008/05/18/opinion/18khoury.html.

Kimmerling, Baruch (1983) *Zionism and Territory: The Socio-Territorial Dimensions of Zionist Politics* (Berkeley: University of California Press).

—— (1995) 'Shaking the Foundations: Rewriting History', *Index on Censorship* 24, no. 3: 47-52.

—— (1999) 'Religion, Nationalism and Democracy in Israel', *Constellations* 6, no. 3: 339-63. Hebrew version in *Zmanim* 50, December 1994 (Tel Aviv: University School of History).

—— (2003) *Politicide: Ariel Sharon's War Against the Palestinians* (London and New York: Verso).

Kimmerling, Baruch, and Joel Migdal (1993) *The Palestinian People: A History* (Cambridge MA: Harvard University Press).

Kletter, Raz (2003) 'A Very General Archaeologist: Moshe Dayan and Israeli Archaeology', *Journal of Hebrew Scriptures* 4, www.arts.ualberta.ca/JHS/abstracts-articles.html#A27.

Korn, Alina (1991) *The Arab Minority in Israel during the Military Government 1948-1966* [Hebrew], Ph.D. dissertation, Hebrew University of Jerusalem.

Kretzmer, David (1987) *The Legal Status of the Arabs in Israel* (Tel Aviv: International Center for Peace in the Middle East).

Laor, Yitzhak (1995) *Anu Kotvim Otach Moledet* [Narratives with No Natives] (Tel-Aviv: Hakibutz Hameuhad Press).

—— (2009) *The Myths of Liberal Zionism* (London and New York: Verso).

Lehn, Walter, with Uri Davis (1988) *The Jewish National Fund* (London: Kegan Paul International).

Lemkin, Raphael (1944) *Axis Rule in Occupied Europe: Laws of Occupation – Analysis of Government – Proposals for Redress* (Washington DC: Carnegie Endowment for International Peace).

Lentin, Ronit (2000) *Israel and the Daughters of the Shoah: Reoccupying the Territories of Silence* (Oxford: Berghahn Books).

—— (2010) *Co-memory and Melancholia: Israelis Memorialising the Palestinian Nakba* (Manchester and New York: Manchester University Press).

Levy, Gideon (2000) 'Exposing Israel's Original Sins', book review, *Haaretz*, 11 March, www3.haaretz.co.il/eng/scripts/article.asp?mador=8&datee=11/03/00&id=99286.

Litvak, Meir (2009) 'Constructing a National Past: The Palestinian Case', in Meir Litvak (ed.), *Palestinian Collective Memory and National Identity* (Basingstoke: Palgrave Macmillan): 97-133.

Litvinoff, Barnet (ed.) (1983) *The Letters and Papers of Chaim Weizmann*, Vol. 1, Series B (Jerusalem: Israel University Press).

Long, Burke O. (1997) *Planting and Reaping Albright: Politics, Ideology, and Interpreting the Bible* (Pennsylvania: Penn State University Press).

—— (2003) *Imagining the Holy Land: Maps, Models and Fantasy Travels* (Bloomington IN: Indiana University Press).

Lustick, Ian (1982) *Arabs in the Jewish State: Israel's Control of a National Minority* (Austin: Texas University Press).

MacDonald, James G. (1951) *My Mission in Israel 1948-1951* (New York: Simon & Schuster).

Magate, Ilan (2000) *Birim*, Enlisted Memory Group, Skirot 'Al Ha'aravim BaYesrael, no. 26 (Giva't Haviva: Institute for Peace Studies).

Makdisi, Ussama, and Paul A. Silverstein (eds) (2006) *Memory and Violence from the Middle East and North Africa* (Bloomington: Indiana University Press).

Mannes-Abbott, Guy (2005) 'Elias Khoury: Myth and Memory in the Middle East', *Independent*, 18 November, www.independent.co.uk/arts-entertainment/books/features/elias-khoury-myth-and-memory-in-the-middle-east-515728.html.

Margalit, Avishai (2003) *The Ethics of Memory* (Cambridge MA: Harvard University Press).

Mari, Sami Khalil (1978) *Arab Education in Israel* (New York: Syracuse University Press).

Masalha, Nur (1988) 'On Recent Hebrew and Israeli Sources for the Palestinian Exodus, 1947-1949', *Journal of Palestine Studies* 18, no. 1 (Autumn): 121-37.

—— (1990) 'Israeli Revisionist Historiography of the Birth of Israel and its Palestinian Exodus', *Scandinavian Journal of Development Alternatives* 9, no. 1 (March): 71-97.

—— (1991) 'Debate on the 1948 Exodus: A Critique of Benny Morris', *Journal of Palestine Studies* 21, no. 1 (Autumn): 90-97.

—— (1992) *Expulsion of the Palestinians: The Concept of 'Transfer' in Zionist Political Thought, 1882-1948* (Washington DC: Institute for Palestine Studies).

—— (1997) *A Land Without a People* (London: Faber & Faber).

—— (2000) *Imperial Israel and the Palestinians* (London: Pluto Press).

—— (2003) *The Politics of Denial: Israel and the Palestinian Refugee Problem* (London: Pluto Press).

—— (ed.) (2005a) *Catastrophe Remembered: Palestine-Israel and the Internal Refugee. Essays in Memory of Edward W. Said* (London and New York: Zed Books).

—— (2005b) 'Present Absentees and Indigenous Resistance', in Masalha (ed.) *Catastrophe Remembered: Palestine-Israel and the Internal Refugee. Essays in Memory of Edward W. Said* (London and New York: Zed Books): 23-55.

—— (2007) *The Bible and Zionism: Invented Traditions, Archaeology and Post-Colonialism in Palestine-Israel* (London and New York: Zed Books).

—— (2008) 'Remembering the Palestinian Nakba: Commemoration, Oral History and Narratives of Memory', *Holy Land Studies: A Multidisciplinary Journal* 7, no. 2 (November): 123-56.

Massad, Joseph (1995) 'Conceiving the Masculine: Gender and Palestinian Nationalism', *Middle East Journal* 49, no. 3 (Summer): 467-83.

—— (2001) *Colonial Effects: The Making of National Identity in Jordan* (New York: Columbia University Press).

—— (2004) 'The Persistence of the Palestinian Question', in Begoña Aretxaga (ed.), *Empire and Terror: Nationalism/Postnationalism in the New Millennium* (Reno NV: University of Nevada Press and Reno Center for Basque Studies): 57-70.

—— (2008) 'Resisting the Nakba', *Al-Ahram Weekly Online*, no. 897, 15-21 May, http://weekly.ahram.org.eg/2008/897/op8.htm.

Matar, Dina (2011) *What It Means to be Palestinian: Stories of Palestinian Peoplehood* (London: I.B. Tauris).

McGowan, Daniel (1998) 'Deir Yassin Remembered', in Daniel McGowan and Marc H. Ellis (eds), *Remembering Deir Yassin: The Future of Israel and Palestine* (New York: Olive Branch Press): 3-9.

Memmi, Albert (1991 [1957]) *The Colonizer and the Colonized* (Boston MA: Beacon Press).

—— (2006) *Colonisation and the Colonized* (Minneapolis MN: University of Minnesota Press).

Mearsheimer, John J. (2010) 'Imperial by Design', *The National Interest*, 16 December, http://nationalinterest.org/article/imperial-by-design-4576.

Mendes-Flohr, Paul (ed.) (1983) *A Land of Two Peoples: Martin Buber on Jews and Arabs* (Oxford: Oxford University Press).

Michelson, Menachem, et al. (1996) *Jewish Holy Places in the Land of Israel* (Tel Aviv: Ministry of Defence).

Milshtein, Michael (2009) 'The Memory That Never Dies: The Nakba Memory and the Palestinian National Movement', in Meir Litvak (ed.), *Palestinian Collective Memory and National Identity* (Basingstoke: Palgrave Macmillan): 47-69.

Morris, Benny (1986a) 'Yosef Weitz and the Transfer Committees, 1948-49', *Middle Eastern Studies* 22, no. 4 (October): 549-50.

—— (1986b) 'Operation Dani and the Palestinian Exodus from Lydda and Ramle in 1948', *Middle East Journal* 40, no. 1 (Winter): 86-7.

—— (1986c) 'The Causes and Character of the Arab Exodus from Palestine: The Israel Defence Forces Intelligence Branch Analysis of June 1948', *Middle Eastern Studies* 22 (January): 5-19.

—— (1986d) 'Jewish Attacks Caused Most of Arab Exodus', *Jerusalem Post*, 2 March: 1.

—— (1987) *The Birth of the Palestinian Refugee Problem, 1947-1949* (Cambridge: Cambridge University Press).

—— (1988) 'The New Historiography: Israel Confronts its Past', *Tikkun* (November-December): 19-23, 99-102.

—— (1990) *1948 and After: Israel and the Palestinians* (Oxford: Clarendon Press).

—— (1991) 'Response to Finkelstein and Masalha', *Journal of Palestine Studies* 21, no. 1 (Autumn): 98-114.

—— (1994) *1948 and After: Israel and the Palestinians* (Oxford: Clarendon Press).

—— (1995) 'Falsifying the Record: A Fresh Look at Zionist Documentation of 1948', *Journal of Palestine Studies* 24, no. 3 (Spring): 44-62.

—— (1997) *Israel's Border Wars, 1949-1956: Arab Infiltration, Israeli Retaliation, and the Countdown to the Suez War*, 2nd edn (Oxford: Clarendon Press).

—— (1998) 'Looking Back: A Personal Assessment of the Zionist Experience', *Tikkun* 13, no. 1 (March-April), www.tikkun.org/9803/9803morris.html.

—— (1999) 'Operation Hiram Revisited: A Correction', *Journal of Palestine Studies* 28, no. 2 (Winter): 68-76.

—— (2000a) Righteous *Victims: A History of the Zionist-Arab Conflict, 1881-1999* (London: John Murray).

—— (2000b) *Tikkun Ta'ut: Yehudim ve-'Aravim be-Eretz Yisrael 1936-1956* [Correcting a Mistake: Jews and Arabs in the Land of Israel 1936-1956] (Tel Aviv: 'Am 'Oved).

—— (2001) 'Revisiting the Palestinian Exodus of 1948', in Eugene L. Rogan and Avi Shlaim (2001) (eds), *The War for Palestine: Rewriting the History of 1948* (Cambridge: Cambridge University Press): 37-59.

—— (2004) *The Birth of the Palestinian Refugee Problem Revisited* (Cambridge: Cambridge University Press).

—— (2007) 'Introduction', in Benny Morris (ed.), *Making Israel* (Ann Arbor: University of Michigan Press).

—— (2008) *1948: A History of the First Arab–Israeli War* (New Haven CT and London: Yale University Press).

—— (2010) *1948: Toldot Hamilhamah Ha'aravit-Hayisraelit Harishonah*, trans. Ya'acov Sharet (Tel Aviv: 'Am 'Oved).

Morris, Yaakov (1953) *Pioneers from the West: History of Colonization in Israel by Settlers from the English-speaking Countries* (London: Greenwood Press; Youth and Hechalutz Department, World Zionist Organisation, 1972).

—— (1961) *Masters of the Desert: 6000 Years in the Negev* (New York: G.P. Putnam).

Musa, Hasan (1988) 'Geographic Distribution of the Arab Refugees in their Homelands: The Galilee Area, 1948–1987' [Hebrew], M.A. thesis, Haifa University.

Myers, David N. (1995) *Reinventing the Jewish Past: European Jewish Intellectuals and the Zionist Return to History* (New York: Oxford University Press).

Nabulsi, Karma (2006) 'The Great Catastrophe', *Guardian*, 12 May: 16.

Nathan, Susan (2005) *The Other Side of Israel: My Journey Across the Jewish–Arab Divide* (New York: HarperCollins).

Nazzal, Nafiz (1974a) 'The Zionist occupation of Western Galilee, 1948', *Journal of Palestine Studies* 3, no. 3 (Spring): 58–76.

—— (1974b) 'The Flight of the Palestinian Arabs from the Galilee: A Historical Analysis', doctoral dissertation, Georgetown University, Washington DC.

—— (1978) *The Palestinian Exodus from Galilee 1948* (Beirut: Institute of Palestine Studies).

Netanyahu, Benjamin (1993) *A Place Among the Nations* (New York: Bantam).

Nimni, Ephraim (ed.) (2003) *The Challenge of Post-Zionism: Alternative to Israeli Fundamentalist Politics* (London and New York: Zed Books).

Nora, Pierre (1996) (ed.), *Realms of Memory: Conflicts and Divisions*, Vol. I (New York: Columbia University Press).

—— (ed.) (1997) *Realms of Memory: Traditions*, Vol. II (New York: Columbia University Press).

—— (ed.) (1998) *Realms of Memory: Symbols*, Vol. III (New York: Columbia University Press).

Nuwayhid, 'Ajaj (1993) *Mudhakkirat 'Ajaj Nuwayhid: Sittuna 'Aman ma' al-Qafila al-'Arabiyya* [The Memoirs of 'Ajaj Nuwayhid: Sixty Years with the Arab Caravan], ed. Bayan Nuwayhid al-Hout (Beirut: Dar al-Istiqlal lil-Dirasat wal-Nashr).

Ophir, Adi (2010) 'Genocide Hides behind Expulsion', in William A. Cook (ed.), *The Plight of the Palestinians: A History of Destruction* (New York: Palgrave Macmillan): 159–62.

Ophir, Adi, Michal Givoni and Sari Hanafi (eds) (2009), *The Power of Inclusive Exclusion: Anatomy of Israeli Rule in the Occupied Palestinian Territories* (New York: Zone Books).

Oz, Amos (1988) 'The Meaning of Homeland', *New Outlook* 31, no. 1 (January); originally published in the daily *Davar* in 1967.

Ozacky-Lazar, Sarah (1993) *Iqrit and Bir'im: The Full Story* [in Hebrew], Skirot al Ha'aravim BaYesrael, no. 10 (Giva't Haviva: Institute for Peace Studies).

Palumbo, Michael (1987) *The Palestinian Catastrophe: The Expulsion of a People from Their Homeland* (London: Faber & Faber).

Pappé, Ilan (1992) *The Making of the Arab–Israeli Conflict, 1947–1951* (London: I.B. Tauris).

—— (1995) 'The New History and Sociology of Israel', *Palestine–Israel Journal*

of Politics, Economics and Culture 2, no. 3: 70-76.
—— (1997) 'Post Zionist Critique on Israel and the Palestinians, Part 1: The Academic Debate', *Journal of Palestine Studies* 25, no. 3 (Winter): 37-43.
——(1998) 'Review Essay, Israeli Television's Fiftieth Anniversary Series: A Post-Zionist View?' *Journal of Palestine Studies* 27, no. 4 (Summer): 99-105.
—— (1999) (ed.) *The Israel/Palestine Question: Rewriting Histories* (London: Routledge).
——(2002) 'The Post-Zionist Discourse in Israel: 1990-2001', *Holy Land Studies: A Multidisciplinary Journal* 1, no. 1 (September 2002): 9-35.
—— (2004a) 'Palestine and Truth, Culture and Imperialism: The Legacy of Edward W. Said', *Holy Land Studies: A Multidisciplinary Journal* 2, no. 2 (March): 135-9.
——(2004b) 'Historical Truth, Modern Historiography and Ethical Obligations: The Challenge of the Tantura Case', *Holy Land Studies: A Multidisciplinary Journal* 3, no. 2 (November): 171-94.
——(2004c) *A History of Modern Palestine: One Land, Two Peoples* (Cambridge: Cambridge University Press).
——(2005) 'The Visible and Invisible in the Israeli-Palestinian Conflict', in Ann M. Lesch and Ian S. Lustick (2005) (eds), *Exile & Return: Predicaments of Palestinians & Jews* (Philadelphia: University of Pennsylvania Press).
—— (2006) *The Ethnic Cleansing of Palestine* (Oxford: Oneworld).
—— (2008) 'Zionism as Colonialism: A Comparative View of Diluted Colonialism in Asia and Africa', *South Atlantic Quarterly* 107, no. 4: 611-33.
—— (2010a) *Out of the Frame: The Struggle for Academic Freedom in Israel* (London and New York: Pluto Press).
——(2010b) *The Rise and Fall of a Palestinian Dynasty: The Husaynis 1700-1948* (London: Saqi Books).
Passerini, Luisa (1998) 'Work Ideology and Consensus under Italian Fascism', in Robert Perks and Alistair Thomsen (eds), *The Oral History Reader* (London: Routledge): 53-62.
Peres, Shimon (1993) *The New Middle East* (Shaftesbury: Element Books).
Peteet, Julie (2005) 'Words as Interventions: Naming in the Palestine-Israel Conflict', *Third World Quarterly* 26, no. 1 (March): 153-72.
Petersen, Andrew (2002) (ed.), *A Gazetteer of Buildings in Muslim Palestine*, Vol. I, British Academy Monographs in Archaeology (London: British Academy).
Petrovic, Drazen (1994) 'Ethnic Cleansing – An Attempted Methodology', *European Journal of International Law* 5, no. 3: 342-59.
Piterberg, Gabriel (2001) 'Erasures', *New Left Review* 10 (July-August): 31-46.
—— (2008) *The Returns of Zionism: Myths, Politics and Scholarship in Israel* (London and New York: Verso).
—— (2009) 'Cleanser to Cleansed', *London Review of Books* 31, no. 4 (26 February): 31-3.
Podeh, Elie (2002) *The Arab-Israeli Conflict in Israeli History Textbooks, 1948-2000* (Westport CT: Bergin & Garvey).
Polkehn, Klaus (1975) 'Zionism and Kaiser Wilhelm: Zionist Diplomacy with the Empire of Kaiser Wilhelm', *Journal for Palestine Studies* 4, no. 2 (Winter): 76-90.
Portelli, Alessandro (1994) 'The Peculiarities of Oral History', *History Workshop Journal* 12: 96-107.

272   *The Palestine Nakba*

—— (1997) *The Battle of Valle Giulia: Oral History and the Art of Dialogue* (Madison: University of Wisconsin Press).

Prakash, Gyan (1994) 'Subaltern Studies as Postcolonial Criticism', *American Historical Review* 99, no. 5 (December): 1475–90, 1476.

Prior, Michael (1997) *The Bible and Colonialism: A Moral Critique* (Sheffield: Sheffield Academic Press).

—— (1999) *Zionist and the State of Israel: A Moral Inquiry* (London and New York: Routledge).

——(2001) 'The Right to Expel: The Bible and Ethnic Cleansing', in Naseer Aruri (ed.), *Palestinian Refugees: The Right of Return* (London: Pluto Press).

——(2002) 'Ethnic Cleansing and the Bible: A Moral Critique', *Holy Land Studies: A Multidisciplinary Journal* 1, no. 1 (September): 44–5.

Qawuqji, Fawzi (1975) *Filastin fi mudhakirrat al-Qawuqji, 1936–1948* [Palestine in the Qawuqji Memoirs, 1936–1948], ed. Khayriyya Qasmiyya (Beirut: Markiz al-Abhath).

Qumsiyeh, Mazin B. (2011) *Popular Resistance in Palestine: A History of Hope and Empowerment* (London and New York: Pluto Press).

Ra'ad, L. Basem (2010a) *Hidden Histories: Palestine and the Eastern Mediterranean* (London: Pluto Press).

——(2010b) 'Cats of Jerusalem', *Jerusalem Quarterly* 41 (Spring), www.jerusalemquarterly.org/ViewArticle.aspx?id=340.

Rabkin, Yakov M. (2006) *A Threat from Within: A Century of Jewish Opposition to Zionism* (London and New York: Zed Books).

—— (2010) 'Language in Nationalism: Modern Hebrew in the Zionist Project', *Holy Land Studies: A Multidisciplinary Journal* 9, no. 2 (November): 129–45.

Ram, Uri (1993) 'The Colonization Perspective in Israeli Sociology', *Journal of Historical Sociology*, September: 327–50.

——(1995a) *Changing Agenda of Israeli Sociology: Theory, Ideology and Identity* (New York: State University of New York Press).

——(1995b) 'Zionist Historiography and the Invention of Modern Jewish Nationhood: The Case of Benzion Dinur', *History and Memory* 7, no. 1: 91–124.

—— (1999) 'The Colonization Perspective in Israeli Sociology', in Ilan Pappé (ed.), *The Israel–Palestine Question: Rewriting Histories* (London: Routledge): 55–80.

Raz-Krakotzkin, Amnon (1993/4) 'Galut Betoch Ribonut: Lebikoret Shlilat Hagalut Batarbut Hayisraelit' [Exile Within Sovereignty: Towards a Critique of the 'Negation of Exile' in Israeli Culture], in *Teurya Vi-Bikoret* [Theory and Criticism] 4: 23–56, and 5: 113–32.

Robinson, Edward (1841) *Biblical Researches in Palestine, Mount Sinai and Arabia Petraea: A Journal of Travels in the Year 1838* (London: J. Murray).

Riordon, Michael (2011) *Our Way to Fight: Israeli and Palestinian Activists for Peace* (London: Pluto Press).

Robinson, Shira (2003) 'Local Struggle, National Struggle: Palestinian Responses to the Kafr Qasim Massacre and its Aftermath, 1956–1966', *International Journal of Middle East Studies* 35, no. 3 (August): 393–416.

Rodinson, Maxime (1973a) *Israel: A Colonial-Settler State?* (New York: Monad Press).

—— (1973b) *Israel and the Arabs* (Hardmondsworth, Penguin).

—— (2001) *Cult, Ghetto, and State: The Persistence of the Jewish Question* (London: Saqi Books).

References

273

Rogan, Eugene, and Avi Shlaim (eds) (2001), *The War for Palestine: Rewriting the History of 1948* (Cambridge: Cambridge University Press).

Rose, John H. Melkon (1993) *Armenians of Jerusalem: Memories of Life in Palestine* (London: Radcliffe Press).

Rose, John (2004) *The Myths of Zionism* (London: Pluto Press).

Rouhana, Nadim (2005) 'Truth and Reconciliation: The Right of Return in the Context of Past Injustice', in Ann M. Lesch and Ian S. Lustick (eds), *Exile and Return: Predicaments of Palestinians and Jews* (Philadelphia: University of Pennsylvania Press): 261-78.

——(2006) '"Jewish and Democratic"? The Price of a National Self-Deception"', *Journal of Palestine Studies* 35, no. 2 (Winter): 64-74.

Rouhana, Nadim, and A. Ghanem (1993) 'The Democratization of a Traditional Minority in an Ethnic Democracy: The Palestinians in Israel', in Edy Kaufman, S. Abed and R. Rothstein (eds), *Democracy, Peace and the Israeli–Palestinian Conflict* (Boulder CO and London: Lynne Rienner): 163-88.

——(1999) 'The Democratization of a Traditional Minority in an Ethnic Democracy', in Ilan Pappé (ed.), *The Israel/Palestine Question* (London: Routledge): 223-46.

Rowan, Yorke M., and Uzi Baram (eds) (2004), *Marketing Heritage: Archaeology and the Consumption of the Past* (Walnut Creek CA: AltaMira Press).

Rubenberg, Cheryl A. (2003) *The Palestinians in Search of a Just Peace* (Boulder CO: Lynne Rienner).

Ruether, Rosemary Radford (1998) 'Christianity and the Future of Israeli–Palestinian Relations', in Daniel McGowan and Marc H. Ellis (eds), *Remembering Deir Yassin: The Future of Israel and Palestine* (New York: Olive Branch Press): 112-22.

Said, Edward W. (1978) *Orientalism* (London: Routledge & Kegan Paul).

——(1980) *The Question of Palestine* (London: Routledge & Kegan Paul).

——(1981) *Covering Islam* (New York: Vintage).

——(1994) *Culture and Imperialism* (New York: Random House).

——(1997) *Covering Islam: How the Media and the Experts Determine How We See the Rest of the World* (New York: Knopf).

——(1999) 'Palestine: Memory, Invention and Space', in Ibrahim Abu-Lughod, Roger Heacock and Khaled Nashef (eds), *The Landscape of Palestine: Equivocal Poetry* (Birzeit: Birzeit University Publications): 3-20.

——(2000) *Reflections on Exile and Other Literary and Cultural Essays* (London: Granta).

——(2002) 'Real Change Means People Must Change: Immediate Imperative', *CounterPunch*, 21 December.

——(2004) *Freud and the Non-European* (London and New York: Verso, in association with the Freud Museum).

Said, Edward W., and Christopher Hitchens (eds) (1988), *Blaming the Victims: Spurious Scholarship and the Palestinian Question* (London and New York: Verso).

Sa'di, Ahmad (2000) 'Israel as Ethnic Democracy: What Are the Implications for the Palestinian Minority?', *Arab Studies Quarterly* 22, no. 1 (Winter): 25-37.

——(2002) 'Catastrophe, Memory and Identity: Al-Nakbah as a Component of Palestinian Identity', *Israel Studies* 7, no. 2 (Summer): 175-98.

——(2005) 'The Politics of Collaboration: Israel's control of a National Minority and Indigenous Resistance', *Holy Land Studies* 4, no. 2 (November): 7-26.

Sa'di, Ahmad H., and Lila Abu-Lughod (2007) (eds) *Nakba: Palestine, 1948, and the Claims of Memory* (New York: Columbia University Press).

Sa'id, Mahmud (1992) 'The Internal Refugees' [Arabic], *Al-Aswar* 12 (Winter): 22-41.

—— (1999) *The Palestinian Refugees in Israel* [Arabic] (Ramallah, Palestine: Shaml, Palestinian Diaspora and Refugee Centre).

Sanbar, Elias (1984) *Palestine 1948: L'Expulsion* (Paris: Revue d'études palestiniennes).

—— (1994) *Les Palestiniens dans le siècle* (Paris: Gallimard).

—— (1996) *Palestine, le pays à venir* (Paris: L'Olivier).

—— (2001a) 'Out of Place, Out of Time', *Mediterranean Historical Review* 16, no. 1 (June): 87-94.

—— (2001b) *Le Bien des absents* (Paris: Actes Sud).

—— (2004) *Figures du Palestinien* (Paris: Gallimard).

Sand, Shlomo (2009) *The Invention of the Jewish People* (London and New York: Verso).

Sayigh, Rosemary (1977a) 'The Palestinian Identity among Camp Residents', *Journal of Palestinian Studies* 6, no. 3 (Spring): 3-22.

—— (1977b) 'Sources of Palestinian Nationalism: A Study of a Palestinian Camp in Lebanon', *Journal of Palestinian Studies* 6, no. 4 (Summer): 17-40.

—— (1979) *Palestinians: From Peasants to Revolutionaries* (London and New York: Zed Books).

—— (1994) *Too Many Enemies: The Palestinian Experience in Lebanon* (London and New York: Zed Books).

—— (2005) *Voices: Palestinian Women Narrate Displacement* (Al-Mashriq), recording and text, http://almashriq.hiof.no/palestine/300/301/voices/index.html.

—— (2007a) 'Women Nakba's Stories', in Ahmad H. Sa'di and Lila Abu-Lughod (eds), *Nakba: Palestine, 1948, and the Claims of Memory* (New York: Columbia University Press): 135-58.

—— (2007b) 'Product and Producer of Palestinian History: Stereotypes of 'Self' in Camp Women's Life Stories', *Journal of Middle East Women's Studies* 3, no. 1 (Winter) 86-105.

—— (2011) 'Palestinian Camp Refugee Identifications: A New Look at the "Local" and National', in Are Knudsen and Sari Hanafi (eds), *Palestinian Refugees: Identity, Space and Place in the Levant* (London and New York: Routledge): 50-64.

Sayigh, Yezid (1997) *Armed Struggle and the Search for State: The Palestinian National Movement, 1949-1993* (Oxford: Clarendon Press).

Schechtman, Joseph B. (1961) *Fighter and Prophet* (New York: Thomas Yoseloff).

Segal, Rafi, and Eyal Weizman (2003) 'The Mountain', in Rafi Segal and Eyal Weizman (eds), *A Civilian Occupation: The Politics of Israeli Architecture* (London and New York: Verso): 79-96.

Segev, Tom (1986) *1949: The First Israelis* (New York: Free Press).

—— (2000) *One Palestine Complete: Jews and Arabs under the British Mandate* (New York: Metropolitan).

—— (2001) 'A History Lesson', *Haaretz*, 29 June.

—— (2002) *Elvis in Jerusalem: Post-Zionism and the Americanization of Israel* (New York: Metropolitan Books/Henry Holt).

Shafir, Gershon (1996a) *Land, Labor and the Origins of the Israeli–Palestinian*

Conflict, 1882–1914 (Cambridge: Cambridge University Press).

—— (1996b) 'Zionism and Colonialism: A Comparative Approach', in M.N. Barnett (ed.), *Israel in Comparative Perspective: Challenging the Conventional Wisdom* (Albany: State University of New York Press): 227–44.

—— (1999) 'Zionism and Colonialism: A Comparative Approach', in Ilan Pappé (ed.), *The Israel/Palestine Question* (London: Routledge): 72–85.

Shafir, Gershon, and Yoav Peled (2001) *The New Israel Peacemaking and Liberalization* (Boulder CO: Westview Press).

Shahin, Mariam (2005) *Palestine: A Guide* (Northhampton MA: Interlink Books).

Shammas, Anton (1988) *Arabesques* (Toronto: HarperCollins).

Shapira, Anita (1992) *Land and Power: The Zionist Resort to Force* (New York: Oxford University Press).

—— (2000) 'Hirbet Hizah: Between Remembrance and Foregetting', *Jewish Social Studies* 7, no. 1 (Fall): 1–62.

—— (2007) 'Hirbet Hizah: Between Remembering and Forgetting', in Benny Morris (ed.), *Making of Israel* (Ann Arbor: University of Michigan Press): 81–123.

Shapira, Anita, and Derek J. Pensler (2003) (eds), *Israeli Historical Revision, From Left to Right* (London: Frank Cass).

Sharab, Muhammad Hassan (1987) *Mu'jam Buldan Falastin* [Encyclopaedia of Palestinian Towns] (Beirut: Dar Al-Mamoun Le-Turath).

Shavit, Ari (2004) 'Survival of the Fittest? An Interview with Benny Morris', *Haaretz*, 9 January.

Shepherd, Naomi (1987) *The Zealous Intruders: The Western Rediscovery of Palestine* (London: William Collins).

Shlaim, Avi (1988) *Collusion Across the Jordan: King Abdullah, the Zionist Movement and the Partition of Palestine* (Oxford: Clarendon Press).

—— (1994) 'It Can be Done', *London Review of Books* 16, no. 11 (9 June): 26–7, www.lrb.co.uk/v16/n11/avi-shlaim/it-can-be-done; accessed 28 May 2010.

—— (1998 [1990]) *The Politics of Partition: King Abdullah, the Zionists, and Palestine 1921–1951* (Oxford: Oxford University Press).

—— (1999) 'The Debate About 1948', in Ilan Pappé (ed.), *The Israel/Palestine Question* (London: Routledge): 171–92.

—— (2000) *The Iron Wall: Israel and the Arab World* (London: Penguin).

—— (2001) 'Israel and the Arab Coalition in 1948', in Eugene Rogan and Avi Shlaim (eds), *The War for Palestine: Rewriting the History of 1948* (Cambridge: Cambridge University Press): 79–103.

—— (2007a) *Lion of Jordan: The Life of King Hussein in War and Peace* (London: Allen Lane).

—— (2007b) 'The Debate About 1948', in Benny Morris (ed.), *Making of Israel* (Ann Arbor: University of Michigan Press): 124–46.

—— (2009) *Israel and Palestine: Reappraisals, Revisions, and Refutations* (London and New York: Verso).

Shohat, Ella (2010) *Israeli Cinema: East/West and the Politics of Representation* (London and New York: I.B. Tauris).

Shoufani, Elias (1972) 'The Fall of a Village', *Journal of Palestine Studies* 1, no. 4 (Summer): 108–21.

—— (2001) 'Testimonies from Tantura', *Journal of Palestine Studies* 30, no. 3 (Spring): 5–19.

Silberman, Neil Asher (1982) *Digging for God and Country* (New York: Alfred A. Knopf).

—— (1989) *Between Past and Present: Archaeology, Ideology and Nationalism in the Modern Middle East* (New York: Holt).

—— (1993) *Prophet Amongst You: The Life of Yigael Yadin* (Reading MA: Addison-Wesley).

—— (1997) 'Structuring the Past: Israelis, Palestinians and the Symbolic Authority of the Archaeological Monuments', in Neil Asher Silberman and David Small (eds), *The Archaeology of Israel: Constructing the Past, Interpreting the Present* (Sheffield: Sheffield Academic Press): 62–81.

Silberman, Neil Asher, and David B. Small (1997) *The Archaeology of Israel: Constructing the Past, Interpreting the Present* (Sheffield: Sheffield Academic Press).

Silberstein, Laurence J. (ed.) (1999) *The Postzionism Debates: Knowledge and Power in Israeli Culture* (London and New York: Routledge).

—— (2008) *Postzionism: A Reader* (Piscataway NJ: Rutgers University Press).

Slyomovics, Susan (1998) *The Objects of Memory: Arab and Jew Narrate the Palestinian Village* (Philadelphia: University of Pennsylvania Press).

—— (2002) 'The Gender of Transposed Space', *Palestine–Israel Journal of Politics, Economics and Culture* 9, no. 4, www.pij.org/details.php?id=114.

Smith, Anthony D. (1986) *The Ethnic Origin of Nations* (London: Blackwell).

—— (1989) 'The Origins of Nations', *Ethnic and Racial Studies* 12, no. 3 (July): 340–67.

Smith, Linda Tuhiwai (1999) *Decolonizing Methodologies: Research and Indigenous Peoples* (London and New York: Zed Books).

Smooha, Sammy (1997) 'Ethnic Democracy: Israel as an Archetype', *Israel Studies* 2, no. 2 (Fall): 198–224.

Sorek, T. (2004) 'The Orange and the "Cross in the Crescent": Imagining Palestine in 1929', *Nations and Nationalism* 10, no. 3: 269–91.

Spencer, Philip, and Howard Wollman (2002) *Nationalism: A Critical Introduction* (London: Sage).

Starr, Louis (1984) 'Oral History', in David K. Dunaway and Willa K. Baum (eds), *Oral History: An Interdisciplinary Anthology* (Nashville TN: American Association for State and Local History).

Stavans, Ilan (2008) *Resurrecting Hebrew* (Jerusalem: Schocken).

Sternhell, Zeev (1998) *The Founding Myths of Israel: Nationalism, Socialism, and the Making of the Jewish State* (Princeton NJ: Princeton University Press).

Stewart, Desmond (1977) *T.E. Lawrence* (London: Hamish Hamilton).

Sturgis, Matthew (2001) *It Ain't Necessarily So: Investigating the Truth of the Biblical Past* (London: Headline).

Swedenburg, Ted (1990) 'The Palestinian Peasant as National Signifier', *Anthropological Quarterly* 63, no. 1 (January): 18–30.

—— (1991) 'Popular Memory and the Palestinian National Past', in Jay O'Brien and William Roseberry (eds), *Golden Ages, Dark Ages: Imagining the Past in Anthropology and History* (Berkeley and Los Angeles: University of California Press): 152–79.

—— (1995) *Memories of Revolt: The 1936–1939 Rebellion and the Palestinian National Past* (Minneapolis: University of Minnesota Press).

Tal, Alon (2002) *Pollution in a Promised Land: An Environmental History of Israel* (Berkeley: University of California Press).

Tamarin, Georges (1973) *The Israeli Dilemma: Essays on a Welfare State* (Rotterdam: Rotterdam University Press).

Teveth, Shabtai (1985) *Ben-Gurion and the Palestinian Arabs* (Oxford: Oxford University Press).

Tholfsen, Trygve R. (1967) *Historical Thinking* (New York: Harper & Row).

Thompson, Thomas L. (1992) *The Early History of the Israelite People From the Written and Archaeological Sources* (Leiden: Brill).

—— (1999) *The Bible in History: How Writers Create a Past* (London: Jonathan Cape).

—— (2003a) 'Is the Bible Historical? The Challenge of "Minimalism" for Biblical Scholars and Historians', *Holy Land Studies: A Multidisciplinary Journal* 3, no. 1 (May): 1-27.

—— (ed.) (2003b) *Jerusalem in Ancient History and Tradition* (London and New York: T & T Clark/Continuum).

—— (2008) 'The Politics of Reading the Bible in Israel', *Holy Land Studies: A Multidisciplinary Journal* 7, no. 1 (May): 1-15.

—— (2009) 'Biblical Archaeology and the Politics of Nation-Building', *Holy Land Studies: A Multidisciplinary Journal* 8, no. 2 (November): 133-42.

—— (2011) 'The Bible, Zionism and the Heritage of an Empty Land: Review Article', *Holy Land Studies: A Multidisciplinary Journal* 10, no. 1 (May): 97-108.

Thompson, Thomas L., F.J. Goncalves and J.M. van Cangh (1988) *Toponymie Palestinienne: Plaine de St. Jean d'Acre et corridor de Jerusalem* (Louvain-la-Neuve: L'institut orientaliste de Louvain, Université catholique de Louvain).

Troen, Selwyn Ilan (2008) 'De-Judaizing the Homeland: Academic Politics in Rewriting the History of Palestine', in Philip Carl Salzman and Donna Robinson Divine (eds), *Postcolonial Theory and the Arab–Israel Conflict* (London: Routledge): 195-207.

Trouillot, Michel-Rolph (1995) *Silencing the Past: Power and the Production of History* (Boston MA: Beacon Press).

Van den Berghe, Pierre L. (1967) *Race and Racism: A Comparative Perspective* (New York and Sydney: Wiley).

—— (1978) 'Race and Ethnicity: A Sociobiological Perspective', *Ethnic and Racial Studies* 1, no. 4: 401-11.

—— (1981) *The Ethnic Phenomenon* (Westport CT: Praeger).

Wakim Wakim (2001a) *The Internally Displaced: Refugees in Their Homeland* [Arabic] (Cairo: Centre of Human Rights Studies).

—— (2001b) 'Internally Displaced in their Homeland and the Main Stations' [Arabic], *Al-Ittihad*, special supplement for Land Day, March.

Wasserstein, Bernard (2002) *Divided Jerusalem: The Struggle for the Holy City* (London: Profile Books)

Weinstock, Nathan (1989) *Zionism: False Messiah* (London: Pluto Press).

Weizmann, Chaim (1949) *Trial and Error: The Autobiography of Chaim Weizmann* (New York: Jewish Publication Society of America).

—— (1952) *Excerpts from His Statements, Writings and Addresses* (New York: Jewish Agency for Palestine).

Weitz Yosef (1940) *Diary*, A246/7 [Hebrew] (Jerusalem: Central Zionist Archives).

—— (1941) Diary, A246/7, entry dated 17 July 1941 [Hebrew] (Jerusalem: Central Zionist Archives).

—— (1948) Diary, A246/7, entry dated 18 April 1948 [Hebrew] (Jerusalem: Central Zionist Archives).

Wetherell, David Fielding (2005) 'The Use and Misuse of the Religious Language: Zionism and the Palestinians', *Holy Land Studies: A Multidisciplinary Journal* 4, no. 1 (May): 69–86.

Whitelam, Keith (1996) *The Invention of Ancient Israel: The Silencing of Palestinian History* (London and New York: Routledge).

Yahya, 'Adel (1998) *Palestinian Refugees 1948–1998: Oral History* [Arabic] (Ramallah, Palestine: Palestinian Institute for Cultural Exchange).

Yazbak, Mahmoud (1999) 'The Templars as Proto-Zionists? The German Colony in Late Ottoman Haifa', *Journal of Palestine Studies* 28, no. 4 (Summer): 40–54.

Yehoshua, A.B. (1968) 'Mul Ha-Ye'arot', in *Tisha'h Sippurim* ['Facing the Forests', in *Nine Stories*] (Tel Aviv: Hakibbutz Hameuhad Press).

—— (1980) *Bein Zechut Le-Zechut* [Between Right and Right] (Tel Aviv: Schocken).

—— (1981) *Between Right and Right: Israel, Problem or Solution* (Garden City NY: Doubleday).

Yiftachel, Oren (1992) 'The Ethnic Democracy Model and Its Applicability to the Case of Israel', *Ethnic and Racial Studies* 15, no. 1: 125–36.

—— (1993) 'The "Ethnic Democracy" Model and Jewish–Arab Relations in Israel: Geographical, Historical and Political Aspects' [Hebrew], *Ofakim Geografim* 37/38: 51–9).

—— (2006) *Ethnocracy: Land and Identity Politics in Israel/Palestine* (Philadelphia: University of Pennsylvania Press).

Yizhar, S. (2008 [1949]) *Khirbet Khiz'ah* (Jerusalem: Ibis Editions).

Young, Robert J.C. (2003) *Postcolonialism: A Very Short Introduction* (New York: Oxford University Press).

Zangwill, Israel (1920) *The Voice of Jerusalem* (London: Heinemann).

—— (1937) *Speeches, Articles and Letters* (London: Soncino Press).

Zerubavel, Yael (1995) *Recovered Roots: Collective Memory and the Making of Israeli National Tradition* (Chicago: University of Chicago Press).

—— (1996) 'The Forest as a National Icon: Literature, Politics, and the Archaeology of Memory', *Israel Studies* 1, no. 1 (Spring): 60–99.

—— (2002) 'The "Mythological Sabra" and Jewish Past: Trauma, Memory, and Contested Identities', *Israel Studies* 7, no. 2 (Summer): 115–44.

Zurayk, Constantine (1956 [1949]) *Ma'na al-Nakba* [The Meaning of the Nakba] (Beirut: Khayat).

Zureik, Elia T. (1979) *The Palestinians in Israel: A Study in Internal Colonialism* (London: Routledge & Kegan Paul).

Index

Index 285